CHRISTIANS
AMONG JEWS AND GENTILES

Essays in Honor of Krister Stendahl
on
His Sixty-fifth Birthday

Edited by
George W. E. Nickelsburg
with
George W. MacRae, S.J.

FORTRESS PRESS   PHILADELPHIA

Copyright © 1986
The President and Fellows of Harvard College

Library of Congress Cataloging-in-Publication Data

Christians among Jews and gentiles.

1. Bible. N.T.—Criticism, interpretation, etc.
2. Christianity and other religions—Judaism.
3. Judaism—Relations—Christianity. 4. Stendahl,
Krister. I. Stendahl, Krister. II. Nickelsburg,
George W. E., 1934–   . III. MacRae, George W.
BS2555.2.C495 1986   270.1   86-4694
ISBN 0-8006-1943-9

1420C86   Printed in the United States of America   1-1943

CONTENTS

PREFACE

This volume was planned as a tribute to a Harvard professor. It is dedicated to the Bishop of Stockholm. The change is not surprising and symbolizes the difficulty of devising a Festschrift for a man with many sides: professor, dean, historian of religion, theologian, churchman, pastor. Should one emphasize his work in New Testament studies and Christian origins; his special contributions to the interpretation of Matthew and Paul; his methodological insistence that historical exegesis be kept separate from theological interpretation; his concern with the factors that led to the schism between church and synagogue? What of his interest in the twentieth-century context of Christianity; the church's place in a pluralistic world; women's roles in the church; relationships and responsibilities between Christians and Jews?

In the end it was decided to focus on the professor and historian of early Christianity—but with a special emphasis. The Christian proclamation and the theologies, ethics, and institutions that it engendered were never purely Christian; the church arose as a constitutive part of a larger, Jewish and Gentile world. Within this framework, which shaped all of Krister's historical work, the contributors were asked to write on some aspect of the interaction between early Christianity and its Jewish and "pagan" environment.

In order to emphasize the rationale for the topic, it seemed appropriate to paraphrase the title of one of Krister's books. Following through on this association with Krister's work, quite a few contributors have taken as their point of departure topics of specific interest to Krister, articles by him, or even comments from his lectures. This underscores and enhances the tribute.

Among the contributors a number of people were invited who would extend the definition of "early Christianity" beyond the canonical first century into the later Roman and early Byzantine periods. Krister has emphasized the importance of *Nachgeschichte*—the ongoing history of early traditions—doubtless because he sees this as the bridge to the modern expression of these traditions. Although it was not possible systematically to solicit articles on this theological and ecclesiastical concern of Krister's, three contributors have written on matters of particular interest to him. Marc Saperstein discusses some little-studied medieval Jewish homiletical comments about Christians. W. D. Davies reflects on the canon of the Mormons, who understand themselves to be Christians genealogically connected with the Jews. Wayne A. Meeks suggests a hermeneutics that addresses some of the problems that arise from making the distinction between what a text *meant* in its original setting and what it *means.*

While many of the articles emphasize either the Jewish or pagan "connection," others reflect the complex historical fact that influences and interactions were mixed. In fairness to this complexity (and doubtless to the dismay of the systematic mind), we have arranged the contributions alphabetically by author.

The publication of this volume was possible only through the willing cooperation of many people. Albert C. Sundberg, Jr., Krister Stendahl's first Harvard doctoral student, was a prime mover for the Festschrift and helped to plan the volume. Norman A. Hjelm, then director of Fortress Press, supported the project from the beginning, and his successor, Harold W. Rast, has helped in many ways. Authors enthusiastically agreed to write. Special thanks are due Helmut Koester of the *Harvard Theological Review.* In recognition of Krister's tenure as editor of the journal, he has accepted this as a special triple issue of the *Review.* I would like to express my appreciation to Pamela Chance, the managing editor of the *HTR*, who oversaw the copyediting, typesetting, and production; to the editorial assistants of *HTR*, Christopher Matthews, Daniel Schowalter, and Karen Wood; to John P. Boyle, director of the University of Iowa's School of Religion, for providing office help and editorial assistance; and to Randal Argall, my research assistant. As their part in this tribute to one whom they know a little and like a lot, Marilyn, Jeanne, and Michael have allowed husband and father the time and space for another, special editorial commitment.

In a very specific way, the untimely death of Krister's long time colleague, George W. MacRae, tempers the celebration appropriate to this Festschrift. George was to have written the dedication, and he was uniquely qualified to do so. That special presence will be missed in this tribute to Krister, but George's contribution remains, intangibly, in the many ways that he readily and cheerfully provided counsel, support, and help in the planning and preparation of the book.

George W. E. Nickelsburg

Iowa City, Iowa
October 1985

DEDICATION

Theologians can be characterized according to a number of categories which describe their contributions: ministers, scholars in specialized fields, ecclesiastical or academic administrators, writers and editors, preachers and lecturers, missionaries, church leaders and—perhaps— prophets. This volume is dedicated to a theologian whose work belongs to almost all of these categories. But to determine the quality and significance of Krister Stendahl's contributions simply by the standards of these categories would leave in our hands but fragments, however precious. In the course of duty in a political career in ancient Rome the servant of the *res publica* was assigned to a variety of civil and military offices. Similarly, Krister Stendahl's career has been devoted to service in the many offices that constitute the universe of theology and religious community—each of these offices contributing to the experience, maturity, and wisdom of a true statesman. This volume honors Krister Stendahl, statesman of the *res ecclesiastica* and expresses our gratitude to him for his creative, fair, and dedicated conduct of office.

When I arrived in this country almost three decades ago, Krister, who welcomed our family on the pier in Manhattan, was involved in building a strong faculty in biblical studies. It was his vision that made this faculty not a "school" but a team of scholars from many schools who were committed to a critical and historical study of the Bible that could demand respect in the university community and, at the same time, in the church. Building a strong doctoral program and teaching the New Testament to ministerial candidates were only two of the most important foci of his work at that time.

When he became an academic administrator, Krister's patience was tested early, because his first year as dean of Harvard Divinity School coincided with the beginning of the so-called student revolution at Harvard. But Krister refused to understand the tasks of his office in terms of a defensive protection of the institution; rather, he transformed the momentum of the movement into a force for reform of the ministerial studies program. He also was able to work for the fulfillment of goals which he had expressed much earlier in his career: the preparation of women for ordination as ministers and the inclusion of a Jewish presence into the discourse of theological education and scholarship.

During the final years of his teaching career at Harvard, Krister devoted himself to the creative and patient development of course offerings in the area of theology and education for the ministry. He personified the highest ambition of scholarship in his willingness to apply his rich expertise in a special field to the instruction of students in the areas of greatest concern for modern ministry: ecumenical relations, Judaism and Christianity, spirituality, and preaching.

But Krister Stendahl's course of offices in the ,res ecclesiastica also included service beyond his career as a scholar, teacher, and dean. Only two major commitments can be mentioned here. He held a number of positions in the Society of Biblical Literature; the Society honored him by electing him to the office of president. He devoted much time during the same years to the World Council of Churches.

In these capacities as well as in his academic and other activities, Krister Stendahl became a leading facilitator of the dialogue between Judaism and Christianity. He was always willing to make the sacrifices that would help to maintain the vision of a reconciliation of these two religions that had sprung from a common ancestry.

This journal, Harvard Theological Review, owes Krister a special debt. After the death of its editor Arthur Darby Nock, who had guided its course for several decades, Krister Stendahl assumed the editorship. His declared goal was to continue and to defend the legacy of high quality scholarly publication which he had so much admired in this great history-of-religion scholar who had been his friend and mentor, and for whose sixtieth birthday he had edited a special issue of the journal.

Notwithstanding his forward-looking contributions in so many offices, and notwithstanding his impatience with all repristinations of religious values and theological positions that had served their time, Krister Stendahl remained committed to tradition in an old-fashioned and pious way. It was particularly his spiritual home—the Lutheran church with its piety, its liturgy, and its hymns—where he found the continuing center of his life's work from which he drew strength for his many activities. As he had been ordained as a Lutheran pastor and as he had always openly confessed his identity as a Christian minister of this tradition in public and in the regular celebration of the eucharist, it seems only fitting that the goal of his course of offices in the res ecclesiastica should be the episcopal office. What to others may seem an archaic institution was and is for Krister Stendahl a community of believers in which the seriousness of a religious commitment is tested in the midst of the life of real people. Service in the offices of the *res ecclesiastica* could be meaningful only if it was bound into the life of the people who constitute this *ecclesia.*

It would have been more appropriate had this dedication not been written by me, a fellow Lutheran. When we planned this volume, we asked George MacRae, the Stillman professor of Roman Catholic Studies at Harvard Divinity School, to write this dedication, and he had readily declared his willingness. His words would have represented much more adequately the ecumenicity of church and theology to which Krister Stendahl is committed so fearlessly and without reservation. Because of George MacRae's untimely death the circle of contributors and friends no longer contains the full number of those who wanted to honor Krister on the occasion of his sixty-fifth birthday. It is therefore not without sadness that I am fulfilling my task of dedicating this volume to Krister Stendahl on behalf of the contributors to this volume, on behalf of the community of teachers, students, and members of the staff of Harvard Divinity School, and on behalf of uncounted others whose names do not appear explicitly.

to

KRISTER STENDAHL

leading biblical scholar,

accomplished statesman of the church universal,

teacher, colleague, and friend

Helmut Koester

Cambridge, Massachusetts
January 1986

KRISTER STENDAHL

Curriculum Vitae
Some Milestones

Born 21 April 1921, Stockholm

Teol. kand., University of Uppsala, 1944

Ordained as a priest of the Church of Sweden, 17 December 1944

Curate in the diocese of Stockholm, 1944–46

Married Brita Johnsson, 7 September 1946

Chaplain to students at the University of Uppsala, 1948–50

Teol. lic., University of Uppsala, 1949

Visited the United States, January-February, 1951
   to observe student and youth work and "see the Lutheran Church
   in a country where it was not an established part of the state."

Studied in Cambridge, England and Paris, 1951

Priest at the Swedish Lutheran Church in Paris, 1951

Instructor in biblical studies, University of Uppsala, 1951–54

Chairman, Inter-European Consultation on Youth Work at the
   World Council of Churches Institute, Bossey, Switzerland, 1953

President, Student Christian Movement in Sweden, 1954

Teol. doc., University of Uppsala, 1954

Docent in New Testament, University of Uppsala, 1954

Assistant Professor of New Testament, Harvard Divinity School, 1954–56

Associate Professor, Harvard Divinity School, 1956–58

Consultant to the Third Assembly of the Lutheran World Federation,
   Minneapolis, 1957

Member, Editorial Committee, *Journal of Biblical Literature*, 1958–61

John H. Morison Professor of New Testament Studies, Harvard Divinity School
   1958–63

Guggenheim Fellow, 1959

Member of Council, World Union of Jewish Studies, 1961–

Fellow, American Academy of Arts and Sciences, 1962
(vice president, 1968–72)

Litt.D., Upsala College, 1963

Frothingham Professor of Biblical Studies, Harvard Divinity School,
1963–68

Editor, *Harvard Theological Review*, 1963–74

Litt.D., Thiel College, 1966

First meeting of the Roman Catholic-Lutheran Working Group, Zurich,
November 1967

Chairman, Committee on Research Projects, Society of Biblical Literature
1968–69

Society of Biblical Literature Delegate to the American Council of
Learned Societies, 1968–69

Member, Executive Council, Lutheran Church in America, 1968–74

Dean and John Lord O'Brian Professor of Divinity, Harvard Divinity School
1968–79

D.D., Colby College, 1970; Whittier College, 1971; St. Olaf College, 1971;
S.T.D., Carthage College, 1971; LL.D., Susquehanna University, 1973

Guggenheim Fellow, 1974

Since Nairobi, a member of the World Council of Churches working
group on Dialogue with People of Living Faiths and Ideologies, 1975–

Moderator, World Council of Churches consultation on the Church and
the Jewish People, 1975–

L.H.D., Miami University (Oxford, Ohio), 1978; Hebrew Union College/
Jewish Institute of Religion, 1980; Brandeis University, 1981

Conducted Bible Studies on the Lord's Prayer, International Conference
on Mission, World Council of Churches Committee on World Mission
and Evangelism, Melbourne, 1981

Andrew W. Mellon Professor of Divinity, Harvard Divinity School,
1981–84

President, Society of Biblical Literature, 1983

Litt.D., Wittenberg University, 1983

Lyman Beecher Lecturer, Yale Divinity School, February 1984

Consecrated as Bishop of Stockholm, 7 October 1984

D.D., Harvard University, 1985

BIBLIOGRAPHY OF THE WRITINGS OF
KRISTER STENDAHL*

Books

Bibelns Mening (Stockholm: SKDB, 1952).

The School of St. Matthew and Its Use of the Old Testament (Uppsala, 1954; 2d rev. ed. Lund: Gleerup, 1967; Philadelphia: Fortress, 1968).

The Bible and the Role of Women: A Case Study in Hermeneutics (Philadelphia: Fortress, 1966). Enlarged edition of the article "Bibelsynen och Kvinnan," in *Kvinnan, Samhället, Kyrkan* (Stockholm: SKDB, 1958).

Holy Week (Proclamation, Series A; Philadelphia: Fortress, 1974). Includes a translation of the Gospel of Peter.

Paul Among Jews and Gentiles—and Other Essays (Philadelphia: Fortress, 1976; London: SCM, 1977). Includes the articles marked below by two asterisks. Swedish translation: *Paulus bland judar och hedningar* (trans. Brita Johnsson Stendahl; Stockholm: Gummessons, 1977). German translation: *Der Jude Paulus und wir Heiden: Anfragen an das abendländische Christentum* (Munich: Kaiser, 1978). Danish translation: *Paulus blandt jöder og hedninger* (Aarhus: Aros, 1978).

Meanings: The Bible as Document and as Guide (Philadelphia: Fortress, 1984). Includes the articles marked below by one asterisk.

Books Edited

The Scrolls and the New Testament (New York: Harper & Bros., 1957; reprinted Westport, CT: Greenwood, 1975) and Chapter One, "An Introduction and a Perspective," 1–17.

---

*The abbreviations used here and throughout this volume are those found in the Instructions for Contributors of the *Harvard Theological Review*.

Immortality and Resurrection: Four Essays [Ingersoll Lectures] by O. Cullmann, H. A. Wolfson, W. Jaeger, and H. J. Cadbury (New York: Macmillan, 1965).

Articles

"Gamla Testamentets föreställpingar om helandet: Rafa'-utsagorna i kontext och ideologi," *SEA* 15 (1950) 5-33.

"Martyr. Ordet och saken. En forskningsöversikt," *STK* 27 (1951) 28-44.

"Neutestamentliche exegetische Dissertationen in Uppsala 1937-1950," *VF* (1951/52) 46-56.

*"Kerygma och kerygmatisk. Om tvetydiga termer i urkyrkans predikan och vår," *Ny Kyrklig Tidskrift* 20 (1951) 167-75. German translation: "Kerygma und kerygmatisch," *ThLZ* 77 (1952) cols. 715-20.

"AXIOS im Lichte der Texte der Qumran-Höhle," *Nuntius* 7 (1952) cols. 53-55.

"The Called and the Chosen: An Essay on Election," in A. Fridrichsen et al., eds., *The Root of the Vine* (Westminster: Dacre; New York: Philosophical Library, 1953) 63-80.

"Lagen som övervakare intill Kristus," *SEÅ* 18/19 (1953/54) 161-73.

"A Report on New Testament Studies 1953-55," *Harvard Divinity Bulletin* 21 (1955/56) 61-80.

"Christology as a Problem of Translation," *The Christian Scholar* 39 (1956) 72-76.

"Alphäus," *RGG* 1 (1956) 247.

"Urkristendomen," *Nordisk Teologisk Uppslagsbok* 3 (1957) cols. 1079-85.

*"Prayer and Forgiveness," *SEÅ* 22/23 (1957/58) 75-86 (Festschrift H. Odeberg).

"The Implications of Form-Criticism and Tradition-Criticism for Biblical Interpretation," *JBL* 77 (1958) 33-38.

*"Kirche: II im Urchristentum," *RGG* 3 (1959) cols. 1297-1304.

"The Dead Sea Scrolls: A Selected Bibliography," *Bulletin of the General Theological Library* 50:4 (1958) 4-12.

"Den nytestamentliga kanonhistoriens huvuddrag" a substantial revision of A. Fridrichsen's section in Lindeskog-Fridrichsen-

Riesenfeld, *Inledning till Nya Testamentet* (2d ed.; Stockholm: 1958) 214–63.

"A Parable of Jesus," *The Pulpit* 30:6 (1959) 6–7.

"Exegetical-Homiletical Notes on the Pericopes of the Church of Sweden (22nd Sunday after Trinity through Sexagesima)," *Svensk Kyrkotidning* 55–56 (1959/60).

"Kan helig skrift översättas?" *Svenska Bibelsällskapets Årsberättelse* 145 (1959); also in *Vr Lösen* 51 (1960) 179–81.

"The New Testament and the Preaching of the Church," *The Lutheran World* 6 (1959/60) 20–32. German edition in *Lutherische Rundschau* 6 (1959/60) 29–35.

"Bibelteologins renässans," *Kristendomslärarnas Förenings Årsbok* 3 (1959) 45–54.

"Paulus och samvetet," *SEÅ* 25 (1960) 62–77.

"Uses and Misuses of the Bible," *Pittsburgh Perspective* 1:4 (1960) 22–32.

"Justification and the Last Judgment," *The Lutheran World* 8 (1960/61) 1–7.

"Theology and Liturgy," in *The Living Liturgy: Papers published by the Department of Worship, United Lutheran Church in America* (1961) 11–15. Reprinted in *Una Sancta* 18:3 (1961) 3–7; *Harvard Divinity Bulletin* 25:3–4 (1961) 1–7.

*"*Quis et Unde*: An Analysis of Matthew 1–2," in Walther Eltester, ed., *Judentum-Christentum-Kirche: Festschrift für Joachim Jeremias*, *ZNW* 26 (1961) 94–105. German translation in Joachim Lange, ed., *Das Matthäus-Evangelium* (Wege der Forschung 525; Darmstadt: Wissenschaftliche Buchgesellschaft, 1980). Also reprinted in G. Stanton, ed., *The Interpretation of Matthew* (Philadelphia: Fortress; London: SPCK, 1983).

"Distance and Proximity: Reflections on the New English Bible," *Virginia Quarterly Review* 37 (1961) 605–12. Reprinted in the *Harvard Divinity Bulletin* 27:1 (1962) 25–30. Swedish translation in *vår Kyrka* 32 (1963).

Commentary on the Gospel of Matthew *Peake's Commentary on the Bible* (ed. M. Black and H. H. Rowley; Edinburgh: Nelson, 1962) 769–98.

"The Apocalypse of John and the Epistles of Paul in the Muratorian Fragment," in W. Klassen and G. F. Snyder, eds., *Current Issues in*

New Testament Interpretation: Essays in Honor of O. Piper (New York: Harper & Bros., 1962) 239–45, 300–302.

*"Sünde und Schuld, IV. Im N.T.," and "Sündenvergebung, II. Im N.T.," *RGG* 4 (1962) cols. 484–89, 511–13.

*"Biblical Theology, Contemporary," *IDB* 1 (1962) 418–32.

*"Hate, Non-Retaliation, and Love: 1QS x, 17–20 and Romans 12:19–21," *HTR* 55 (1962) 343–55.

"Behag," "Dualism," "Kerygma," and "Kyrkotukt," *Svenskt Bibliskt Uppslagsverk*, 1 (2d ed.; 1963).

"Amen," "Aristeasbrief," "Gewissheit," and "Götzendienst," *BHH* 1 (1962).

"Religion in the University," *Daedalus* (Summer 1963) 521–28. Reprinted in *The Church Review* 22:2–3 (1964) 11–13. Polish translation: "Religia e Murach Universytetu," *Tematy* 10 (1964) 26–35.

**"The Apostle Paul and the Introspective Conscience of the West," *HTR* 56 (1963) 199–215. Reprinted in S. H. Miller and G. E. Wright, eds., *Ecumenical Dialogue at Harvard: The Roman Catholic-Protestant Colloquium* (Cambridge: Belknap, 1964) 236–56. Earlier Swedish edition: "Paulus och samvetet," *SEÅ* 25 (1960) 62–77. Cf. *JSSR* 1 (1962) 261–63.

*"Messianic Liscense," in Paul Peachey, ed., *Biblical Realism Confronts the Nation* (Nyack, NY: Fellowship of Reconciliation, 1963) 139–52.

*"Judaism and Christianity: Then and Now," *Harvard Divinity Bulletin* 28:1 (1963) 1–9. Reprinted in Sanford Seltzer and Max L. Stack-house, eds., *The Death of Dialogue and Beyond* (New York: Friend-ship Press, 1972) 105–19; F. E. Talmage, ed., *Disputation and Dialogue: Readings in the Jewish Christian Encounter* (New York: KTAV, 1975) 330–42.

"In Memoriam A. D. Nock," *Numen* 10 (1963) 236–37.

"Himmel," and "Himmelfahrt," *BHH* 2 (1964) cols. 719–21.

"The Bible in Catholic and Protestant Scholarship," *Outlook* (Duxbury, MA: Divine Word Seminary, 1964) 2–7.

"The New Testament View of Membership in the Body of Christ" (printed from unedited tape recording), *Brethren Life and Thought* 9 (1964) 100–108.

"Lord's Prayer," *Encyclopaedia Britannica* (1965) 14. 311.

"Method in the Study of Biblical Theology," in J. Ph. Hyatt, ed., *The Bible in Modern Scholarship* (Nashville: Abingdon, 1965) 196–209.

"The Bible—The Road to Unity," in *Rediscovery of Scripture* (Franciscan Sisters Educational Conference, 1965) 275–88.

"Church or Christianity," *Bulletin of Crozer Theological Seminary* 58:1 (1966) 7–9, 18–19.

"One Baptism for the Forgiveness of Sins," *Worship* 40 (1966) 272–75.

"Introduction," to Leo Baeck, *The Pharisees and Other Essays* (New York: Schocken, 1966) vii–xxi.

"Jesus and the Kingdom," *Alumni Bulletin* (Bangor Theological Seminary) 42:2 (1967), 6–14.

"Religion, Mysticism, and the Institutional Church," *Daedalus* (Summer 1967) 854–59.

"Foreword" to Johannes Munck, *Christ and Israel: An Interpretation of Romans 9–11* (Philadelphia: Fortress, 1967) 7–10.

*"Judaism and Christianity II—After a Colloquium and a War," *Harvard Divinity Bulletin* n.s. 1:1 (1967) 2–9. Reprinted as "Judaism and Christianity: A Plea for a New Relationship," *Cross Currents* 17 (1967) 445–50. German translation: "Judentum und Christentum: Plädoyer für die Erneurerung ihres gegenseitigen Verhältnisses (trans. Rolf Rendtorff; short introduction added and footnotes omitted).

Introduction to "Papers from the Colloquium on Judaism and Christianity held at Harvard Divinity School, October 17–20, 1966," *HTR* 61 (1968) 81–85.

"The Future of Theology," *Nexus* (Alumni Magazine of Boston University School of Theology) 13 (1970) 11–14, 26f.

"The Role of the Bible in the Theology of the Future," in J. Papin ed., *The Dynamic in Christian Thought* (Villanova: Villanova University Press, 1970) 44–51.

*"The New Testament Background for the Doctrine of the Sacraments," in *Oecumenica: Jahrbuch für ökumenische Forschung 1970: Evangelium und Sakrament*, 41–49.

"Biblical Studies in the University," in Paul Ramsey and John F. Wilson, eds., *The Study of Religion in Colleges and Universities* (Princeton: Princeton University Press, 1970) 23–39.

"Women in the Churches: No Special Pleading," *Soundings* 53 (1970) 374–78.

"Foreword," to Merle Severy, ed., *Great Religions of the World* (New York: National Geographic Society, 1971).

"On Earth as It Is in Heaven: Dynamics in Christian Eschatology," in J. Papin, ed., *The Eschaton: A Community of Love* (Villanova: Villanova University Press, 1971) 57–68.

"Foreword" to Anton Fridrichsen, *The Problem of Miracle in Primitive Christianity* (Minneapolis: Augsburg, 1972) 5–9.

*"Immortality is too much and too little," in John D. Roslansky, ed., *The End of Life: A Discussion at the Nobel Conference Organized by Gustavus Adolphus College, St. Peter, Minnesota, 1972* (Amsterdam/London: North Holland, 1973).

(With Emilie T. Sander) "Biblical Literature," Parts VI–VIII (New Testament), *Encyclopaedia Britannica* (1974), Macropaedia, 2. 875–77, 938–72.

Die biblische Auffassung von Mann und Frau," in Elisabeth Moltmann-Wendel, ed., *Menschenrechte für die Frau: Christliche Invitiativen zur Frauenbefreiung* (Grünewald: Kaiser, 1974) 147–61 (a translation of a section of *The Bible and the Role of Women*).

**"[Glossolalia:] The New Testament Evidence," in Michael P. Hamilton, ed., *The Charismatic Movement* (Grand Rapids: Eerdmans, 1975) 49–60. Reprinted in J. Jervell and W. A. Meeks, eds., *God's Christ and His People: Studies in Honor of Nils Alstrup Dahl* (Oslo: Universitets-forlaget, 1977) 12–28.

"Kvinnan i Bibeln och Kyrkan," *Svensk Kyrkotidning* 71 (1975) 474–82 and *Religion och Kultur* 46:4 (1975) 1–15.

*"The Question Concerning the Gospel as Center and the Gospel as Totality of the New Testament Witness," in H. Meyer, ed., *Evangelium-Welt-Kirche: Schlussbericht und Referate der römisch-katholisch/evangelisch lutherischen Studien-kommission "Das Evangelium und die Kirche"* (Frankfurt am Main: Otto Lembeck und Josef Knecht, 1975) 97–109.

"Foreword" to Eva Fleischner, *Judaism in German Christian Theology since 1945* (ATLA Monograph Series 8; 1975) xiii–xvi.

"The Charismatic Movement and the New Testament," in Th. Runyon, ed., *What the Spirit is Saying to the Churches* (New York: Hawthorn, 1975) 17–28.

"Towards World Community," in *Jewish Christian Dialogue* (Geneva:

World Council of Churches, 1975) 59–63. Reprinted in F. von Hammerstein, ed., *Von Vorurteilen zum Verständnis* (Frankfurt: Lembeck, 1976) 70–75.

"In No Other Name (Acts 4:5–12)," in A. Sovik, ed., *Christian Witness and the Jewish People* (Geneva: Lutheran World Federation, 1976) 48–53.

"Widening the Perspective of Jewish Christian Relations," *Face to Face* 1 (Winter/Spring 1976) 17–18.

"Saint Paul and the Jews," in *Engage/Social Action* 3:12 (1976) 19–25.

"Words, Signs, and Wonders in the Bible," in D. H. Pokorny and R. C. Hohenstein, eds., *The Word in Sign and Wonders: A Collection of Papers Delivered at the Second International Training Seminar on Christian Ministry Among the Deaf, 1976* (New York: Arno, 1977) 13–24.

"The New Pentecostalism: Reflections of an Ecumenical Observer," in Russell P. Spittler, ed., *Perspectives on the New Pentecostalism* (Grand Rapids: Baker , 1977) 14–20.

"The Celebration of God's Victory (Lk. 24:1–11)," *In Season* III:31 (1977).

"Responsible Scientific Investigation and Application: A Response to Wernher von Braun," in H. Ober Hess, ed., *The Nature of a Humane Society: A Symposium on the Bicentennial of the U.S.A.* (Philadelphia: Fortress, 1977) 146–61.

"Rooted in the Communities of Faith: A Reaffirmation of a Learned Ministry," *Theological Education* 13:2 (1977) 61–72.

"A Community of Scholars in a Community of Faith," in "Collegium," a Supplement to *Kairos* No. 6 (1977).

"The Priority of the Church," *Proceedings of the 1977 Christian Life Commission Seminar on Priorities* (Nashville: Southern Baptist Convention, 1977) 55–58.

"Theology and Law: Responsibilities of Vocation. Notes for a Future Agenda," *National Institute for Campus Ministries Journal* 2:3 (1977) 108–12.

"New Styles of Life in Faith Communities," in Joseph Gremillion, ed., *Food/Energy and the Major Faiths* (Maryknoll, NY: Orbis, 1978) 216–25.

"Faith That Enlivens the Mind," in Waldo W. Braden, ed., *Representative American Speeches 1976–77* (New York: Wilson, 1977) 168–73.

"En annorlunda Paulus," *Religion och Kultur* 48:4 (1977) 32–36.

*"The Sermon on the Mount and Third Nephi," in Truman G. Madsen, ed., *Reflections on Mormonism: Judaeo-Christian Parallels* (Provo, UT: Brigham Young University Press, 1978) 139–54.

"A Tribute to Amos Wilder," *Harvard Divinity Bulletin* 9:2 (1978/79). Reprinted as a Preface to J. Dominic Crossan, *A Fragile Craft: The Work of Amos Niven Wilder* (Missoula: Scholars Press, 1981).

"Exegesis of Theme Text (2 Cor 5:16–6:2)" (Lutheran Church in America, Division of Parish Services, 1978).

"Humör på allvar," *Vår Kyrka* 51/52 (21 December 1978) 8–9.

"Jesu liknelser och judisk humör" (Krister Stendahl talar om Jesu liknelser), *Vår Kyrka* 51/52 (1978) 8–9.

"A Response" to E. P. Sanders' critique of *Paul Among Jews and Gentiles*, *Union Seminary Quarterly Review* 33 (1978) 189–91.

"Church Priorities for '79," *Christianity Today* 23:7 (1979) 21 (404).

"Såsom i en spegel: En debattbok en Paulusbilden och kristendomstolkningen" (a discussion of *Paul Among Jews and Gentiles*, with a response by Krister Stendahl: "Which Paul May We Interpret?" (Svenska Kyrkans Kulturinstituts Dialog, serie 17; Stockholm: SKEAB, 1980).

*"Paul at Prayer," *Int* 34 (1980) 240–49.

"On College Preaching," *National Institute for Campus Ministry Journal* 5:4 (1980) 66–70.

"The Jewishness of Jesus and His Gentile Followers," The Birks Lectures at the Faculty of Religious Studies, McGill University, 1979. Summary published in *ARC* 7:2 (1980) 66–71.

"Your Kingdom Come: Notes for Bible Study," in *Your Kingdom Come: Mission Perspectives.* Report on the World Conference on Mission and Evangelism in Melbourne, Australia 1980 (Geneva: World Council of Churches, 1980). Reprinted in *Cross Currents* 32 (1982) 257–66.

*"Notes for Three Bible Studies: A Biblical Vision—In No Other Name (Acts 4:12)—The Pitfalls of Universalism," in Gerald H. Anderson and Thomas F. Stransky, C.S.P, eds., *Christ's Lordship and Religious Pluralism* (Maryknoll, NY: Orbis, 1981) 7–18.

"Ancient Scripture in the Modern World," in F. E. Greenspahn, ed., *Scripture in the Jewish and Christian Tradition* (Nashville: Abingdon, 1982) 201–14.

"Judaism and Islam in the Perspective of Christianity," in Isma'il Raji al Faruqi, ed., *Trialogue of the Abrahamic Faiths* (Washington, DC: International Institute of Islamic Thought, 1402/1982).

"Preaching from the Pauline Epistles," in James W. Cox, ed., *Biblical Preaching: An Expository Treasury* (Philadelphia: Westminster, 1983) 306–26.

"The Territorial Dimension of Judaism" (comments on W. D. Davies' book by that title) *Midstream* (March 1983) 39–40.

"Det finns en förväntan i landet," *Aktiva i Svenska Kyrkan-En Livsstilsstudie* (Stockholm: Verbum, 1983) 143–50.

"To Have and To Hold," in Roger A. Johnson, ed., *Views from the Pews: Christian Beliefs and Attitudes* (Philadelphia: Fortress, 1983) 157–65.

"The Bible as a Classic and the Bible as Holy Scripture," *JBL* 103 (1984) 3–10.

"A Friend and His Philo-Connection," in F. E. Greenspahn, ed., *Nourished with Peace: A Memorial Volume for Samuel Sandmel* (Chico: Scholars Press, 1984).

Book Reviews

E. Schweizer, *Das Leben des Herrn in der Gemeinde und ihren Diensten,* *STK* 24 (1948) 192–94.

W. G. Kümmel, *Das Bild des Menschen im Neuen Testament, STK* 25 (1949) 59–63.

T. W. Manson, *The Church's Ministry, STK* 25 (1949) 70–72.

B. Noack, *Satanas und Soteria,* U. Gräsbeck, *Bergspredikan och Jesu verksamhet*; A. Corell, *Consummatum est: Eskatologi och Kyrka i Johannesevangeliet, SEÅ* 15 (1950) 115–26.

N. Johannsson, *Bibelns värld och vår. Vår Kyrka,* 15 (1950).

E. Lövestam, *Äktenskapet i N.T.,* and H. Ljungman, *Guds barmhärtighet och dom, Stockholmstidningen* (6 October 1950).

K. G. Kuhn, *Achtzehngebet und Vaterunser und der Reim, STK* 27 (1951) 61–64.

A. Déscamps, *Les justes et la justice dans les évangiles, STK* 27 (1951) 283–88.

N. Adler, *Taufe und Handauflegung, STK* 27 (1951) 288–90.

S. G. F. Brandon, *The Fall of Jerusalem and the Christian Church, Kyrkohistorisk Årsskrift* 51 (1951) 288–89.

G. Lindeskog, A. Fridrichsen, H. Riesenfeld, *Inledning till Nya Testamentet, Årsbok for Kristen Humanism* 14 (1952) 85–88.

E. Brunner, *Das Missverständnis der Kirche, STK* 28 (1952) 38–43.

K. H. Schelkle, *Die Passion Jesu, STK* 29 (1953) 133–38.

A. Ackermann, *Jesu; Seine Botschaft und deren Aufnahme im Abendland, Kyrokohistorisk Årskrift* 53 (1953) 204–5.

A. Runeberg, *Jesu Korsfästelse i religionshistorisk belysning, Finsk Tidskrift* (Abo) 153 (1953) 92–94.

C. Spicq, *Agapé, JBL* 75 (1956) 64–65.

E. Nielsen, *Oral Tradition, Harvard Divinity Bulletin* 20 (1954/55) 127–29.

J. Knox and Gerald R. Cragg, *The Interpreter's Bible*, vol. 9: *The Epistle to the Romans*, ibid., 124–37.

W. E. Bundy, *Jesus and the First Three Gospels*, ibid., 137f.

J. N. Geldenhuys, *Supreme Authority*; and F. F. Bruce, *Are the New Testament Documents Reliable?*, 138f.

R. Leivestad, *Christ the Conquerer*, ibid., 140–42.

V. Taylor, *The Life and Ministry of Jesus*, ibid., 142f.

C. H. Dodd, *New Testament Studies*, ibid., 143–47.

L. E. Froom, *The Prophetic Faith of Our Fathers*, ibid., 151–53.

(The Reviews of Taylor, Bundy, Knox-Cragg, and Dodd also appear in Swedish translation in *SEÅ* 20 [1955] 69–79.)

A. Schlatter, *The Church in the New Testament, Christian Century*, 73 (1956) 556.

J. Jeremias, *The Eucharistic Words of Jesus, Harvard Divinity Bulletin* 21 (1955/56) 187–92; a shorter form of the review in *TToday* 12 (1956) 534–37

A. M. Hunter, *Interpreting Paul's Gospel*, ibid., 192–95.

J. M. Allegro, *The Dead Sea Scrolls*; Ch. T. Fritsch, *The Qumran Community, Harvard Divinity Bulletin* 22 (1956/57) 93f.

E. R. Goodenough, *Jewish Symbols in the Greco-Roman Period*, vols. 5–6, ibid., 96–98.

W. R. Farmer, *Maccabees, Zealots, and Josephus*, ibid., 98–99.

B. H. Kelly and D. G. Miller, *Tools for Bible Study*, ibid., 100–104.

W. F. Arndt, *The Gospel According to St. Luke*, ibid., 112–14.

J. Martin, *Did Jesus Rise from the Dead?*, ibid., 114–15.

J. F. Bethune-Baker, *Early Traditions about Jesus*, ibid., 115–16.

L. E. Elliott-Binns, *Galilean Christianity*, ibid., 116– 17.

D. F. Rowlingson, *Introduction to New Testament Study*, ibid., 119–20.

F. E. Wilson, *Jesus Christ the Risen Lord*, ibid., 121–23.

P. S. Minear, *Jesus and His People*, ibid., 123–25.

J. Lowe, *Saint Peter*, ibid., 125–26.

J. Reider, *The Book of Wisdom*, Harvard Divinity Bulletin, 23 (1957/58) 113.

B. M. Metzger, *An Introduction to the Apocrypha*, ibid., 118–19.

F. F. Bruce, *Second Thoughts on the Dead Sea Scrolls*, ibid., 120.

A. Parrot, *The Temple of Jerusalem*; idem, *Golgatha and the Church of the Holy Sepulchre*, ibid., 120–21.

E. Würthwein, *The Text of the Old Testament*, ibid., 121.

J. B. Phillips, *The Book of Revelation*, ibid., 124.

Th. S. Kepler, *The Book of Revelation*, ibid., 125.

V. Taylor, *The Epistle to the Romans*, ibid., 125.

F. C. Grant, *The Gospels*, ibid., 129–30.

W. Barclay, *A New Testament Wordbook*, ibid., 130–31.

H. N. Ridderbos, *When the Time Had Fully Come*, ibid., 136.

Ph. Carrington, *The Early Christian Church*, vols. 1–2, ibid., 139–41.

J. Knox, *The Integrity of Preaching*, ibid., 173–75.

E. Stauffer, *New Testament Theology*, Christian Century, 74 (1957) 1169–70.

O. Cullmann, *The Early Church: Studies in Early Christian History and Theology*, TToday, 14 (1957) 127–32.

Th. Gaster, *The Dead Sea Scriptures in English Translation*, JBR 25 (1957) 145–48.

A. S. Kapelrud, *Dödehavsrullene*, JBL 76 (1957) 328–29.

N. Q. Hamilton, *The Holy Spirit and Eschatology in Paul*, JBL 77 (1958) 275–76.

A. E. Sims and G. Dent, *Who's Who in the Bible*, Harvard Divinity Bulletin 25:2 (1961) 17.

B. M. Metzger, *Index to Periodical Literature on the Apostle Paul*, ibid., 17–18.

F. F. Bruce, *The New Testament Documents—Are They Reliable?* ibid., 18–19.

F. W. Danker, *Multipurpose Tools for Bible Study*; W. M. Smith, *Treasury of Books for Bible Study*, ibid., 19.

V. A. Tcherikover and A. Fuks, *Corpus Papyrorum Judaicarum* vols. 1–2, ibid., 21–22.

M. Black, *The Scrolls and Christian Origins*, *The Living Church* (22 October 1961) 16–17, 26.

E. P. Blair, *Jesus in the Gospel of Matthew*, *Int* 16 (1962), 461–64.

G. Baumbach, *Qumran und das Johannesevangelium*, *JSS* 8 (1963) 85–86.

R. V. G. Tasker, *The Greek New Testament: Being the text translated in the New English Bible 1961*, *Harvard Divinity Bulletin* 29:2 (1965) 51–52.

(with Brita Stendahl) Mary Daly, *Beyond God the Father*, Boston Sunday *Globe* (13 January 1974).

"Sissela Bok: A Student of 'Hard Cases'" (review of Bok, *Lying: Moral Choice in Public and Private Life*), *Harvard Magazine* 80:7 (September/October 1978).

Pinchas Lapide, *The Resurrection of Jesus: A Jewish Perspective*, Book Newsletter of Augsburg Publishing House, March/April 1984.

Miscellaneous

Six meditations for the Swedish Radio. Published in E. Arbin, *Vid dagens port* (Stockholm, 1945) and *Det trygga order* (Stockholm, 1946).

Något om Kinseyrapporten (Stockholm , 1948).

"Eight Meditations," *Vår Kyrka*, 1948.

"Att vara präst," *Sveriges Kristliga Gymnasiströrelse*, 1950.

"Att gå till bikt," *Svensk Kyrkotidning*, 16 (1950).

Two articles on Women and the Ministry of the Church of Sweden, *Vår Kyrka* 40 and 42 (1950).

"Himlen och förnuftet," (an article on contemporary issues in the philosophy of religion, *Vår Lösen* 41 (1950) 89–93.

Three articles on The Ecumenical Movement at and after Evanston with special reference to the non-cooperating groups, *Vår Kyrka* (1954).

"Bibelföklaring vid missionärskonferensen i Uppsala i januari 1954,"

Svenska Kyrkans Missionsstyrelses Arsbok (1954) 8–17.

"Eukaristien i himmelen" and "Ett offerliv i Jesu efterföljd," in H. Blennow, ed., *Eukaristi: Beredelse för den heliga nattvarden* (1955).

"Bibeln och ekumeniken," *Vår Kyrka* (1955); cf. *Credo* 36 (1955).

"Amerikansk och svensk förkunnelse," *Stockholms Stiftsbok* (1956) 37–44.

"Qumran Documents Recreate Original Issue of Christianity," Boston *Herald* (19 October 1956).

Five Sunday Meditations in B. Hallgren, ed., *100 Söndagar* (Uppsala: Lindblads, 1958).

"Nativity," *Lutheran Life* (December 1959) 14–15.

"Nya vägar för ekumeniken," *Svenska Dagbladet* (28 January 1960). Review of O. Cullmann, *Katholiken und Protestanten: Ein Vorschlag zur Verwirklichung christlicher Solidarität* (Basel, 1958); M. Villain, *L'Abbé Couturier* (Paris, 1957); and idem, *Introduction à l'oecumenisme* (Paris, 1958).

"Kyrkans Kris," *Svensk Kyrkotidning* 7 (1960).

Address at the Memorial Service for Werner Jaeger (22 October 1961), published at Harvard University, 1961.

"Beyond Pragmatism," *Unity* (1961) 43.

"Was Jesus a Pacifist?" *Frontiers* 14:5 (January 1963) 18–22.

Memorandum on the use of Elizabethan English in liturgical language in Ministers Information Service, Lutheran Church of America, April 1964.

"Would Space Creatures Shake Religious Beliefs," Boston *Globe* (4 April 1965).

"Teologi till vänster," *Vår Lösen* 59 (1966) 128–33.

"I Make All Things New," in *Arena* (Student edition of *The Mennonite*) (October 1969).

"Afterthoughts and Forethoughts," *Harvard Divinity Bulletin* n.s. 3:1 (1969) 1–5.

"Revolution: Rhetoric and Reality" (Commencement Address, 4 June 1969) *Princeton Seminary Bulletin* 62 (1969) 20–23.

"Thoughts of a Recent Immigrant," *American Swedish Historical Foundation Yearbook* (1969–70) 1–4.

"Katekes for 70-talet," *Linköpings Stiftsbok* 65 (1970) 168–73.

"Creative Piety and Theology," in *When Yesterday Becomes Tomorrow: 125th Anniversary Celebration, Congregation Emanu-El of the City of New York 1845–1970* (New York, 1971) 64–79.

"Ministry without Fear," *Concordia Theological Monthly* 42 (1971) 390–96.

"A Non-Denominational View of the Section on Ecumenism," in E. Van Antwerp, S.S., ed., *Seminary Department Relevant Report* (April 1971) 8–9.

"Religionen i en pluralistisk värld," *Vår Lösen* 62 (1971) 301–7.

"Framtidens Kyrka," *Kristet Forum* 5–6 (1972) 24–29.

"Life Beyond Earth and the Mind of Man," in R. Berendzen, ed., *Symposium* (Washington, DC: NASA, 1973).

"Less Baggage and More Faith," *Lutheran Standard* (4 September 1973).

"The Gifts of the Greek Orthodox Church (A Summary)," *The Byzantine Fellowship Lectures* 1 (Brookline, MA: Holy Cross Theological School Press, 1974) 81–83.

"Enrichment or Threat?—When the Eves Come Marching In," in Alice L. Hageman, ed., *Sexist Religion and Women in the Church: No More Silence!* (New York: Association, 1974) 117–23.

"The Future Role of the Universities in the Education for Religious Ministries," in D. N. Freedman and A. Th. Kachel, eds., *Religion and the American Scene* (Waterloo: Council on the Study of Religion, 1975) 25–34.

"En Trettondagspredikan (Lk 11:29–36)," *Svensk Missionstidskrift* 63 (1975) 65–67.

"Ethics and Journalism: Comments," *Nieman Reports* 30:1 (1976) 27–28.

"Divinity School Governance within University Structure: A Private U.S. University Perspective," *Theological Education* 12:1 (1975) 40–43.

"Angelägen teologi—teologi om viktiga ting. Samtal mellan Krister Stendahl och Lars Gyllensten," *Vår Lösen* 67 (1976) 349–54.

"Were Christ (and Muhammad) Illiterate?" *Harvard Magazine* (September-October 1980).

"Stendahl om predikan," *Vår Kyrka* 8 (1982).

"The Rainbow," in Ronald J. Sider and Darrel J. Brubaker, eds., *Preaching on Peace* (Philadelphia: Fortress, 1982) 52–53.

"Söndagsruta," *Dagens Nyheter* (3 April [Easter Sunday] 1983).

Translations

(with Brita Stendahl), Joachim Jeremias, *Okända Jesusord* (*Unbekannte Jesusworte*; Stockholm: SKDB, 1951).

Kristus-Världens Hopp (The Final Report of the Advisory Commission on the Main Theme of the W.C.C. General Assembly in Evanston, 1951; Stockholm: SKDB, 1955).

Interviews

"Varför är vi så negativt kritiska?" *Vår Kyrka* (1960).

"Stendahl on Religion in Higher Education," *Ecumenical Newsletter* [New England] (May 1966).

Major interviews in connection with the election of an Archbishop in the Church of Sweden, 1967: *Expressen* (19 February); *Kvällsposten* (27 March); *Idun-Veckojournalen* (21 April); *Sydsvenska Dagbladet Snällposten* (23 April); *Expressen* (13 August).

An interview by Rune Pär Olofsson with Brita and Krister Stendahl on Love and Marriage, *Vecko Journalen* (August 1968).

"Almost an Archbishop," *The Lutheran* (20 September 1972).

"Theologian-Administrator at Harvard," by K. B. Cully in *The New Review of Books and Religion* 2:9 (1978) 3.

"Ecumenism with a Sting," by Laurence Cohen, *Ecumenism Today* [New Britain Area Conference of Churches] (1978) 4-7.

Interview with James Franklin, Boston *Sunday Globe* (26 March 1978); Richard M. Harley, *Christian Science Monitor* (7 June 1978); Maria Salomon, *Stockholms Stift Informerar* 9:8 (1977).

"En öppen lutheran som vill nynna med änglarna," *Vår Kyrka* 11 (1979) 4-5.

"Conversation with Stendahl," interview by Richard E. Koenig, *Partners* 3:1 (1981) 7-9, 19.

"Antisemitism: Christians Have a Responsibility," interview with Richard M. Harley, *The Christian Science Monitor* (4 June 1981).

"Roboten tvingar fram ny livssyn," interview with Hans Werner, *Ny Teknik* 50 (1981) 48.

"Krister Stendahl, alltid effektiv: Friade efter tre dagar," interview with Lennart Lundberg, *Kyrkans Tidning* (30 March 1984).

"Vi kristna ar Guds försokskaniner," interview with Elisabeth Frankl, *Expressen* (24 April 1984).

Mimeographed and Manuscript Material

(Available in the Vertical File in Andover-Harvard Theological Library, Harvard Divinity School)

"They Were More Than Free: Bible Studies in Preparation for the Lutheran World Federation Assembly in Minneapolis (1957). Abridged edition published in *Youth Programs* (Joint Youth Publications Council for the Luther Leagues; 1956).

"The Content of the Dead Sea Scrolls" (Lecture at the Alumni Institute at Harvard Divinity School; 17 January 1956).

"Some Notes on Reinhold Niebuhr's Use of the Bible" (1958).

"Teologens syn på naturvetenskapen" (1960).

Articles on the *New English Bible* (1961).

Lecture (2 February 1967) in the Packard Manse Course in Jewish-Christian Relations.

Cambridge Forum on Religion in the Year 2000 (22 March 1978).

"The Theological Context of Health and Healing in the Lutheran Tradition and Experience," distributed by the Division for Mission in North America, Lutheran Church in America (1983).

CHRISTIANS
AMONG JEWS AND GENTILES

THE USES OF ANTITHESIS IN HEBREWS 8 – 10

Harold W. Attridge
University of Notre Dame

The interaction between early Christianity and the Judaism from which it emerged took many and diverse forms, and Christians' attitudes toward their Jewish heritage varied considerably. The Epistle to the Hebrews represents a particularly complex case of both the appropriation and the rejection of that heritage. This ambivalent attitude reaches its climax in the central expository section of the text, where the significance of the death of Christ is explored using primarily the analogy of the Yom Kippur sacrifice. This portion of Hebrews is replete with exegetical difficulties which cannot be resolved here. What this essay will attempt is an analysis of the literary techniques through which the model of the Yom Kippur ritual is appropriated.

The examination needs to begin with a consideration of what the boundaries of the central expository section are. For while many commentators recognize 8:1 – 10:18 as a single literary unit, some divide this material into discrete blocks. Most influential among the latter is Albert Vanhoye.[1] Using a variety of indices, he articulates the central expository section of Hebrews into three segments: 7:1 – 28; 8:1 – 9:28; and 10:1 – 18. To construe the surface structure in this fashion obscures the literary dynamics of Hebrews' key argument.

---

[1] Vanhoye's preliminary works on the structure of Hebrews ("Les indices de la structure litteraire de l'Épître aux Hébreux," *StEv* II [TU 87; ed. F. L. Cross; Berlin: Akademie Verlag, 1964] 493 – 507 and "De structura litteraria Epistolae ad Hebraeos," *VD* 40 [1962] 73 – 80) culminated in *La structure litteraire de l'Épître aux Hébreux* (StudNeot 1; Paris: Desclée de Brouwer, 1963), issued in a slightly revised edition in 1976. References here will be to that second edition. On the response to his analysis see his "Discussions sur la structure de l'Épître aux Hébreux," *Bib* 55 (1974) 349 – 80. Vanhoye is not alone in separating 10:1 – 18 from what precedes. See also Otto Michel, *Der Brief an die Hebräer* (MeyerK 13; Göttingen: Vandenhoeck & Ruprecht, 1966) 329.

A review of Vanhoye's analysis and its weakness[2] will suggest an alternative. Vanhoye first finds in Heb 5:9–10 an announcement of the themes of the chapters which follow.[3] The participle "perfected" ($\tau\epsilon\lambda\epsilon\iota\omega\theta\epsilon\acute{\iota}\varsigma$) announces the theme of perfection to be developed in 8:1–9:29. The designation of Christ as the "cause of eternal salvation" ($a\check{\iota}\tau\iota\sigma\varsigma$ $\sigma\omega\tau\eta\rho\acute{\iota}a\varsigma$ $a\grave{\iota}\omega\nu\acute{\iota}\sigma\upsilon$) prepares for the theme of 10:1–18. The reference to the order of Melchizedek ($\kappa a\tau\grave{a}$ $\tau\grave{\eta}\nu$ $\tau\acute{a}\xi\iota\nu$ $M\epsilon\lambda\chi\iota\sigma\acute{\epsilon}\delta\epsilon\kappa$) prepares for chap. 7. Vanhoye's third "announcement" is beyond dispute and chap. 7 is clearly a discrete unit. The other "announcements" are, as we shall see, problematic.

In support of a division of 8:1–9:28 from 10:1–18 Vanhoye invokes other structural indices. Both segments are, he claims, marked by inclusions involving various forms of the verb "to offer" ($\pi\rho\sigma\sigma\phi\acute{\epsilon}\rho\omega$) at 8:3; 9:28; 10:1; and 10:18. Next Vanhoye finds that the two sections are distinguished by characteristic vocabulary, terms such as "offer, gifts and sacrifices, sanctuary, tabernacle, blood and covenant" for the first and "offering, sanctification and sacrifice" for the second. Finally, Vanhoye finds a catchword association between the two sections in the terms for offering, $\pi\rho\sigma\sigma\epsilon\nu\epsilon\chi\theta\epsilon\acute{\iota}\varsigma$ at 9:28 and $\pi\rho\sigma\sigma\phi\acute{\epsilon}\rho\sigma\upsilon\sigma\iota\nu$ at 10:1.[4]

We may consider these structural indices in reverse order. First, the proposed catchword is hardly a good example of this device which certainly does play a role elsewhere in Hebrews.[5] Here the audial dissimilarity and distance between the supposedly interlocking terms suggest that their presence serves no structural function. Of equal importance is the fact that we are dealing here with a verb which is ubiquitous in the central chapters of Hebrews. This fact diminishes its value as a structural index of any sort.

Second, the supposedly distinctive vocabulary of the two segments is hardly that at all. Of six items assigned by Vanhoye to 8:1–9:28, four also appear in 10:1–18. Of nine items assigned to 10:1–18, six appear

---

[2] Despite its wide acceptance, Vanhoye's analysis has had its critics. See esp. John Bligh, "The Structure of Hebrews," *HeyJ* 5 (1964) 170–77; Jukka Thurén, *Das Lobopfer der Hebräer: Studien zum Aufbau und Anliegen von Hebräerbrief 13* (Acta Academiae A-boensis A, 47, 1; Abo: Akademie Verlag, 1973); Michel Gourges, "Remarques sur la structure centrale de l'Épître aux Hébreux," *RB* 84 (1977) 26–37; James Swetnam, "Form and Content in Hebrews 1–6," *Bib* 53 (1972) 368–85; and idem, "Form and Content in Hebrews 7–13," *Bib* 55 (1974) 335–48. Space does not permit a full treatment of these and other proposals about the overall structure of Hebrews.

[3] See Vanhoye, *La structure*, 42.

[4] The suggestions of inclusions at 8:3 and 9:28 and of a catchword link at 9:28–10:1 are new elements in Vanhoye's second edition.

[5] Cf. e.g., $\grave{a}\gamma\gamma\acute{\epsilon}\lambda\omega\nu$ at 1:4–5 and $\pi\iota\sigma\tau\acute{\sigma}\varsigma$ at 2:17–18.

in 8:1–9:28. Forms of προσφέρω, which Vanhoye curiously lists as distinctive of each segment, appear with roughly equal frequency in both, five times in 8:1–9:28 and seven times in 10:1–18.

Third, the inclusions, all involving προσφέρω, are as unpersuasive as the catchword. If offering language by itself is to be taken as an inclusion, its appearance at 8:3 and 10:18 could function as such.

Finally, the announcement of the themes at 5:9–10 is quite artificial. A minor problem is that the order of the themes as they are later developed appears in the "announcement" as 2, 3, 1. In a text such as Hebrews, which so often displays neat parallelisms and chiastic arrangements, this is jarring. More significantly, 8:1–9:28 has a rather tenuous relationship with the theme of perfection, announced by τελειωθείς at 5:9. Verbally the only links are τελειῶσαι τὸν λατρεύοντα at 9:9 and τελειοτέρας σκηνῆς at 9:11. In other cases of themes announced and developed the explicit verbal connections are more explicit.[6] The other portions of the central expository section 7:1–28 and 10:1–18 have such verbal links[7] and are equally relevant to the development of this complex theme.[8] In chap. 7 there is a presentation of Christ in his perfected or exalted state, culminating in the participle τετελειωμένον at 7:28, which encapsulates what it means for Christ to be a priest "according to the order of Melchizedek." In chaps. 8 through 10 as a whole there is a development of the process by which Christ attains that exalted state, a process which in turn "perfects" his followers (10:2, 14).

Structural indices of the sort which Vanhoye uses appear in Hebrews, but they clearly point to the unity of 8:1–10:18. Motifs which are prominently developed in that section are anticipated or announced in chap. 7. These motifs include the reference to the weakness of the priests of the old order, noted at 7:23 and 28 and reaffirmed at 9:6–10, 9:25, and 10:1–3; and the reference to the covenant, mentioned at 7:22 and developed in 8:6–13; 9:15–20; and 10:16. But if there is anything which announces the overarching theme of 8:1–10:10, it is the phrase of 7:27, "he did this, having offered himself for all."[9] This is the first reference to Christ's self-sacrifice in Hebrews. This theme is extensively and explicitly explored throughout the next three chapters.

---

[6] The most obvious major "announcements" are at 1:4; 2:17–18; and 10:36–39.

[7] Cf. 7:19, 28; 10:1, 14 for forms of τελειοῦν.

[8] On the perfection theme in general, see most recently David Peterson, *Hebrews and Perfection: An Examination of the Concept of Perfection in the Epistle to the Hebrews* (SNTSMS 47; Cambridge: Cambridge University Press, 1982).

[9] The point is well made by Bligh, "Structure," 175.

An inclusion also marks off those chapters. In fact the most obvious case of this device in Hebrews is the repetition at 10:16–17 of part of the quotation from Jer 31:31–34, first cited at 8:8–12. Another small but significant item marks the boundaries of 8:1–10:18. The section begins at 8:1 with an allusion to one of the key scriptural texts of Hebrews, Ps 110:1 and its image of Christ "seated at the right hand." The repetition of the material from Jeremiah is introduced with another allusion to the same text at 10:12, the first such allusion since 8:1.

In the review of Vanhoye's discussion of vocabulary characteristic of the material from 8:1 to 10:18, it became clear that the language of offering was a common feature of these chapters. It is also significant that the verb προσφέρω appears in what has emerged as the "announcement" of this section, 7:27. Another element of that verse occurs regularly and emphatically in these chapters, the adverb ἅπαξ or ἐφάπαξ. The vocabulary characteristic of the section is thus closely connected with another major structural index.

A further structural index—alternation of genre—which Vanhoye uses to analyze Hebrews elsewhere, he does not find relevant to the articulation of the central section. Indeed, the section does not alternate between exposition and exhortation as does Hebrews as a whole. Nonetheless, the section marked by the other structural indices which we have considered does have a formal generic identity which merits consideration. Like other well-defined blocks of material in Hebrews, 8:1–10:18 consists basically of a citation from scripture and comments related to that citation.

The closest formal parallel to the section under consideration is 3:1–4:13, well analyzed by Vanhoye.[10] That pericope begins with a brief introductory paragraph (3:1–6), contrasting Moses and Christ as examples of fidelity in different capacities. The paragraph serves as a transition from the portrait of Christ as a faithful high priest (2:17–18) to the exhortation to be faithful, based on the events of the Exodus. There follows a lengthy quotation from Psalm 95 (3:7–11), then a hortatory exposition and application of the text (3:12–4:11). This exposition concludes with a rhetorical flourish on God's word (4:12–13),[11] which balances the quotation from the Psalm. The text moves on with a resumptive paragraph beginning at 4:14 with the phrase "having

---

[10] See Vanhoye, *La structure*, 93–104.

[11] This pericope is seen by Wolfgang Nauck as a key structural element: "Zum Aufbau der Hebräerbriefes," *Judentum, Urchristentum, Kirche: Festschrift für Joachim Jeremias* (ZNW Beiheft 26; ed. W. Eltester; Berlin: Töpelmann, 1960) 199–206. At this point Vanhoye's analysis is more persuasive. See his "Discussions," 366.

therefore a great high priest."

The central expository section, 8:1–10:18, is a unit much like the block of material focused on Psalm 95. The pericope begins with a transitional introduction (8:1–6) summarizing the image of Christ as an exalted or heavenly high priest which emerged from chap. 7. There follows a lengthy quotation from Jeremiah 31 (8:7–13), then an exposition of the themes enunciated in the introduction and the quotation (9:1–10:10). The exposition concludes with a rhetorical flourish explicitly recalling the beginning of the unit (10:11–18). The text then moves on at 10:19 with an expression similar to that used at 4:14, "having therefore boldness."[12]

A striking feature of the central expository unit, as it has emerged from this analysis of the surface structure of Hebrews, is the deployment throughout of certain fundamental antitheses. Some of these, the opposition of flesh and spirit, earth and heaven, many and one, already appeared in chap. 7 and these will continue to operate in 8:1–10:18. To them will be added antitheses of old and new and external and internal. The force of the exposition will depend to a large extent on the way in which the poles of these antitheses are interrelated, that is, on how the spiritual, heavenly, and unique act of Christ is seen to be new and interior. That much is often recognized by commentators.[13] What is not usually observed is how at a decisive point there is a reversal in the polarity of the antithetical pattern and how the spiritual, unique and new, is seen to be earthly as well as heavenly. The text will suggest that precisely because Christ's sacrifice is such a combination of opposites it is the sort of act which can inaugurate the covenant promised by Jeremiah. A review of the central section will illustrate how the antitheses function.

In the introduction (8:1–6), the opposition between earth and heaven comes to the fore. Christ is a priest of the true, heavenly tabernacle (8:2) of which the desert sanctuary is but a shadowy imitation (8:3). These affirmations draw on widespread imagery of the heavenly tabernacle[14] and recall elements of the description of the eternal τάξις

---

[12] Vanhoye (*La structure,* 104) prefers to see 4:14 as the conclusion of the section beginning with 3:1, but that division is quite artificial. See Swetnam, "Hebrews 1–6," 383 and Peterson, *Hebrews and Perfection,* 74.

[13] See, e.g., William R. G. Loader, *Sohn und Hohepriester: Eine traditionsgeschichtliche Untersuchung zur Christologie des Hebräerbriefes* (WMANT 53; Neukirchen: Neukirchener Verlag, 1981) 172–73.

[14] In general see Otfried Hofius, *Der Vorhang vor dem Thron Gottes: Eine exegetisch-religionsgeschichtliche Untersuchung zu Hebräer 6,19f und 10,19f* (WUNT 14; Tübingen: Mohr-Siebeck, 1972); George W. MacRae, "Heavenly Temple and Eschatology in the

to which Christ as high priest belongs; they require little comment.

In the next segment (8:7–13), the author introduces the scriptural text which serves as the basis for the following exposition, Jer 31:31–34. The introductory and concluding comments (8:7, 13) articulate the second major antithesis, that of old and new. The manifest function of the citation and its framing comments is to show that the first covenant was not blameless and that a second "was sought." The citation also has another important function, to indicate what are the "better promises" (8:6) on which the new covenant is based.[15] These promises are implicit in the two verses of the citation from Jeremiah which are repeated at 10:16–17. The first promises that the new covenant will be an interior affair (8:10; 10:16); the second that in the new covenant sin will be effectively forgiven (8:12; 10:17). These two promises are intimately related, as the exposition of chaps. 8–10 makes clear. Moreover, the first suggests a new antithesis, between external and interior, which will be the pivotal element in what follows.

In the first section of exposition (9:1–10), the author focuses on the earthly pole of the earth-heaven antithesis and offers a description of the κοσμικόν or "worldly" sanctuary, the "copy and shadow" mentioned at 8:5. Elements of other antitheses are brought into play in this exploration of the earthly and its weakness. The opposition of old and new is alluded to in the references to "the present time" (9:9) and the "time of correction" (9:10). The many-one antithesis surfaces in the allusion to the annual sacrifice by the high priest (9:7). The most significant connection of the various antitheses, however, occurs in the further play on external versus internal. To equate old with external and new with internal the author has recourse to yet another antithesis, that of flesh and spirit which first emerged in 7:16. Here the old, earthly cultic system is seen to be operative only on the surface, since it consists of "regulations of the flesh" regarding "foods, drinks and washings" (9:10). As such it cannot effect the interior of the worshiper, the realm of συνείδησις or conscience (9:9).

The next segment (9:11–14) presents a mirror image of the preceding, focusing on the heavenly pole of the basic antithesis, through the image of the "greater and more perfect tent" (9:11; cf. 8:2). The image has been interpreted in various allegorical ways,[16] but those need

---

Letter to the Hebrews," *Semeia* 12 (1978) 179–99; and Loader, *Sohn*, 182–84.

[15] Vanhoye (*La structure*, 143) sees the function of the citation as purely negative. See also Peterson, *Hebrews and Perfection*, 132.

[16] The σκήνη has frequently been taken as a symbol for the body of Christ in one or another sense. For a review of such interpretations, see Loader, *Sohn*, 166–67; Peterson, *Hebrews and Perfection*, 140–44; and Franz Laub, *Bekenntnis und Auslegung: Die*

not concern us here. For our purpose it is sufficient to note that the heavenly pole of the earth-heaven antithesis is clearly evoked. The positive poles of several other antitheses are now associated with this "heavenly" pole. The heavenly is the realm of the absolutely unique, where Christ entered "once for all" (ἐφάπαξ, 9:12). It is, as opposed to the realm of flesh (9:13), the setting in which Christ makes an offering "through eternal spirit" (9:14). This phrase has also occasioned much interpretive comment, which need not be expanded upon here.[17] It is sufficient to note the evocative function of the language of "spirit" in establishing the equivalence of the positive poles of the antithesis. While the old and earthly dealt merely with fleshly externals, the new and heavenly operates in the realm of the spirit, which is by implication the realm of the heart and mind mentioned by Jeremiah. This association is further solidified by the note that Christ's sacrifice effectively "cleanses conscience" (10:14).

The next pericope (9:15–22) forms the midpoint of the expository comments inaugurated by Jer 31:31–34, and it is framed by two sets of balanced pericopes. At this central juncture the antithesis of old and new is emphatically deployed. Christ is the mediator of a "new covenant" which effects "redemption from the transgressions under the first" (9:15). The covenant theme from the Jeremiah passage is reintroduced and, in the play on διαθήκη which follows, an important principle is introduced by appeal to the events at Sinai (Exod 24:8; Heb 9:20). The inauguration of a covenant requires bloodshed. What remains to be explained in working out the equivalences of the antithetical pattern is how an earthly, quite fleshly act such as bloodshed can be associated with a heavenly and spiritual event.

The next segment of the exposition (9:23–28) picks up the development of the antitheses where they had been left before the pivotal passage on the covenant, by reverting to the heavenly realm which had been discussed in 9:11–14. The focus on this pole is clear from the introductory remark (9:23) that as the imitations need cleansing, so too do the heavenly or true (ἀληθινά) realities themselves. Here is another crux and various interpretations have been offered about what

---

paränetische Funktion der Christologie im Hebräerbriefes (Biblische Untersuchungen 15; Regensburg: Pustet, 1980) 196–200.

[17] For a review of earlier options, see John J. McGrath, *"Through Eternal Spirit": An Historical Study of the Exegesis of Hebrews 9:13–14* (Rome: Pontificia Universitas Gregoriana, 1961).

"heavenly realities" the author ultimately has in mind.[18] The earlier association of the positive poles of the antitheses suggests that the author now indeed is using the imagery of the heavenly tabernacle symbolically and that heavenly archtypes need cleansing because they are in fact interior realities—the heart, mind, and conscience. Yet rather than resolving the question of the referent of the author's probably symbolic language, it is important to note the function of his comment on the heavenly pole of the basic antithesis. The note that what is heavenly needs cleansing sets up an almost intolerable paradox. This is, however, only a stage in the author's exposition, a preparation for the even greater paradoxical affirmation of the final segment of the exposition.

Before examining that pericope it is worth noting that here (9:11–14) the author establishes even more firmly than had been the case previously that the "heavenly" act of Christ is such because it is absolutely unique. Note the insistent repetition of ἅπαξ in 9:26, 27, and 28. This insistence on the uniqueness of Christ's act prepares for the following pericope verbally by way of contrast with the multiplicity of the old priestly sacrifices (10:1–3), and thematically by suggesting that the once-for-all event is qualitatively unique.

The final segment of the exposition (10:1–10) serves not as an appendage or separate repetitive comment, but as the climactic point in the author's argument. The introductory verses (10:1–4) suggest two of the antitheses. First that of new and old is evoked by the reference to the "good things to come" of which the Law is but a "shadow." It is interesting that in this phrase a linkage of the spatial and temporal antitheses is suggested, since "shadow" had previously (8:5) been part of the description of the relationship of earthly to heavenly tabernacles. The phrase has played a key role in debates about the author's eschatological perspectives. Yet to focus on that issue is to miss the full import of the text's dramatic play on its antithetical patterns.

The exposition continues with the citation of and exegetical comment on Ps 40:7–9. The introductory phrase is significant. There (10:5) Christ is said to utter this psalm "upon coming into the world" (εἰσερχόμενος εἰς τὸν κόσμον). The phrase thus evokes the earthly pole of the heavenly-earthly antithesis, recalling the designation of the earthly sanctuary as κοσμικόν at 9:1. That evocation completes the thematic balance in the pericopes which follow the citation of Jeremiah

---

[18] See, e.g., Aelred Cody, *Heavenly Sanctuary and Liturgy in the Epistle to the Hebrews* (St. Meinrad, IN: Grail, 1960) and most recently, Lincoln D. Hurst, "Eschatology and 'Platonism' in the Epistle to the Hebrews," *SBL 1984 Seminar Papers* (Chico, CA: Scholars, 1984) 41–74.

and which surround the reference to the new covenant at 9:15–22. The first (9:1–10) was dominated by the earthly pole; the second (9:11–14) by the heavenly; the third (9:23–28) by the heavenly; now in the last (10:1–10) the earthly again comes to the fore.

Two elements stand out in the quotation of the Psalm (10:5–7). The first is in the second verse, where the LXX offers a variant from the MT. Instead of "ears you have hollowed out for me" there appears "a body (σῶμα) you have prepared for me."[19] The variant suits the author's purpose well. Once again what is earthly is emphasized. It becomes clear that precisely here, in the κόσμος, indeed in a σῶμα, the decisive covenant inaugurating act is carried out.

That this should be the case is understandable given the requirement that blood is necessary for a covenant. Yet once again, how can a cosmic, somatic act accomplish the spiritual cleansing and interior renewal which our author takes as promises enunciated in Jeremiah? Here the other significant element in the quotation comes into play. As 10:7 indicates, Christ came "to do your will, O God." The repetition of this phrase in the exegetical comment of vs 9 suggests its significance for our author and the exultant summary of vs 10 indicates what that significance is. It is "by that will," that is, the will of God to which Christ has conformed himself, that "we" are sanctified. Yet that will is *embodied*, for the sanctification occurs, as the climax of 10:10 states, "through the offering of the body of Jesus Christ once for all."

Hence the opposition between the basic antitheses is overcome. Interior and external, heavenly and earthly are united in the action of Christ. Because his sacrifice is made in the body it can, figuratively, cast a shadow (10:1). Less imagistically, it fulfills the requirement for establishing a lasting covenant relationship between human beings of "blood and flesh" (2:14) and God. Yet because that bodily act is a unique act of conformity to God's will it is the sort of act that establishes the interior and effective covenant promised by Jeremiah.

The application of the model of the Yom Kippur ritual to the death of Christ in Hebrews is a complex and subtle hermeneutical effort. In the process of that application, Christ's death, traditionally interpreted as an atoning sacrifice, is seen in a new light as Yom Kippur becomes blended with Sinai as a covenant inaugurating event. The catalyst for this theological chemistry is exegetical rhetoric, a rhetoric which delights in exploiting and resolving antithetical oppositions. The transforming fusion produced by that catalyst creates a powerful new Christian compound.

---

[19] See Friedrich Schröger, *Der Verfasser des Hebräerbriefes als Schriftausleger* (Biblische Untersuchungen 4; Regensburg: Pustet, 1968) 172–77 and Kenneth J. Thomas, "The Old Testament Citations in Hebrews," *NTS* 11 (1965) 303–25.

THE FAITHFULNESS OF GOD AND THE PRIORITY OF ISRAEL IN PAUL'S LETTER TO THE ROMANS

J. C. Beker
Princeton Theological Seminary

I

It is a joy for me to contribute to a volume of essays dedicated to Krister Stendahl. I owe him a particular debt of gratitude. From the time that I—an immigrant from Holland—started to teach at Union Theological Seminary in New York in 1955 until today, Krister has been a model for me of what it means to be not only a conscientious scholar but also a Christian theologian. Through the turbulent years of the sixties and early seventies he always found time to counsel and guide me—however much we were geographically separated from each other.

Throughout his career Krister has wrestled with the problem of the relationship of Judaism to Christianity. The fact that the Jewish-Christian dialogue has flourished in recent years is in no small way due to him. I will attempt in this essay to make a small contribution to Krister's central concern.

II

A. I have contended for some time that Paul is a hermeneutic theologian rather than a systematic theologian. Paul must be viewed primarily as an interpreter of the early Christian tradition and not as a builder of Christian doctrine. The texture of his hermeneutic calls for special attention. Paul is able to translate the abiding Word of the gospel in such a manner that it becomes word on target for his congregations. And so his hermeneutic is characterized by the reciprocal interaction between the constant of the gospel and the variables of historical circumstance. I call this interaction the dialectical relation between the coherence of the gospel and the contingency of the situations to which the gospel is addressed.

This dialectical hermeneutic applies as well to Paul's most systematic letter, the letter to the Romans. Although the tendency persists to view Romans as a dogmatics in outline, or as a version of a *compendium doctrinae Christianae* (Melanchthon), Romans is actually a profoundly occasional letter. And the challenge to the interpreter of Romans is to clarify—in this, Paul's most systematic letter—the peculiar interaction between coherence and contingency, that is, between universality and particularity.

B. This challenge pertains especially to the "Jewish question" in Romans 9–11. The relation between universality and particularity has frequently been distorted with respect to these chapters. Romans 1–8 was considered to be the systematic-universal core of Romans, whereas Romans 9–11 was relegated to a Pauline afterthought, too particular and awkward to be awarded any theological weight. Rudolf Bultmann,[1] C. H. Dodd,[2] William Sanday and A. C. Headlam,[3] and Robin Scroggs[4] all essentially concur in their own way with F. W. Beare's judgment:

> We have left out of consideration three chapters (9–11) of this letter, chiefly because they do not form an integral part of the main argument. They are a kind of supplement in which Paul struggles with the problem of the failure of his own nation. We cannot feel that the apostle is at his best here, and we are inclined to ask if he has not got himself into inextricable (and needless) difficulties by attempting to salvage some remnant of racial privilege for the historic Israel—Israel "according to the flesh"—in despite of his own fundamental position that all men are in the same position before God.[5]

This statement contains two fundamental errors: (1) it disturbs the unique texture of Paul's hermeneutic by simply disjoining the coherent-universal elements of his thought from their contingent-occasional counterparts; and (2) it misconstrues the purpose and theological thrust of Paul's letter to the Romans.

---

[1] *Theology of the New Testament* (trans. Kendrick Grobel; New York: Scribner's, 1955) 2. 132.

[2] *The Epistle of Paul to the Romans* (New York/London: Harper, 1932) 148–49.

[3] *A Critical and Exegetical Commentary on Romans* (New York: Scribner's, 1926) 225.

[4] "Paul as Rhetorician: Two Homilies in Romans 1–11," in Robert Hamerton-Kelly and Robin Scroggs, eds., *Jews, Greeks and Christian Religious Cultures in Late Antiquity* (SJLA 21; Leiden: Brill, 1976) 271–98.

[5] Francis Wright Beare, *St. Paul and His Letters* (London: A. & C. Black, 1962) 103–4.

C. Although the two issues are closely related, I will concentrate my remarks on the last one because it will also unmask the first mentioned error.

The occasion for Paul's letter to the Romans is a convergence of several factors, which explains its occasional, yet "systematic" form. There are at least four such factors:

1) When Paul writes Romans, he finds himself in a new situation. Since the mission work in the east has been accomplished, he is eager to go to Spain and to be supported in this endeavor by Rome (Rom 15:24).

2) Paul's forthcoming visit to Jerusalem with the collection from the Gentile churches preoccupies him. Indeed, the collection visit occupies center stage in Romans 15, especially vss. 30–32. The Jerusalem visit focuses on the "Jewish question" because it expresses symbolically the eschatological unity of the church of "Jews" and "Gentiles" in the purpose of God as the fulfillment of Paul's apostolic mission.

3) Paul had written Galatians just prior to Romans. Again the "Jewish question" had troubled him there in the form of the judaizing opposition. And it is likely that Paul had lost his case with the Galatian churches. Moreover, the repercussion of his letter to the Galatians could only have worsened his relations with Jerusalem. For in Galatians, Paul had created the impression that the place of the Jew in salvation history was a purely negative one and had in fact become obsolete with the coming of Christ. And so Romans attempts to discuss the "Jewish question" within the context of the special situation in Rome.

4) The situation in Rome—although quite unlike that in Galatia— necessitates as well a solution to the "Jewish question." For in Rome there is the threat of disunity caused by the tension between the weak and the strong, between a minority of Jewish-Christians and a majority of Gentile-Christians (Rom 14:15).

D. Romans then is directed to a particular church with particular problems by an apostle who is faced by particular historical challenges. However, the occasionality of the letter does not deprive it of universal importance. Indeed, the contingency of its motivation and address is radically interwoven with the coherent structure of Paul's gospel, that is, the continuity of the gospel with God's promises to his covenant people Israel. In other words, the "Jewish question" in Paul's former missionary territories, heightened both by his forthcoming visit to Jerusalem and by the threat of disunity in the church at Rome, compels him to reflect on the relationship of Judaism to Christianity, on its continuous and discontinuous dimensions.

III

The theme of the letter (Rom 1:16–17) revolves around four inter-related issues: (1) the gospel reveals the righteousness of God; (2) the righteousness of God is apprehended by faith; (3) the gospel is the "power of God for salvation to everyone who believes, to the Jew first and also to the Greek"; (4) the righteousness of faith in the gospel is the confirmation and fulfillment of the Old Testament promise of Hab 2:4.

Tracing Paul's development of the theme, we notice that, notwith-standing preliminary climactic statements along the way (4:24–25; 5:9–11; 5:20–21; 8:38–39), the basic climax is reached prior to the paraenesis of Romans 12–15 in 11:32: "For God has consigned all people to disobedience, that he may have mercy upon all," followed by a hymnic conclusion in 11:33–36. The climax of the letter seems to sug-gest that the πᾶσ argument carries the day so that the universal pitch of the gospel ("to everyone") seems to drown out the emphasis on the particularity or the priority of the Jew in the thematic statement of Rom 1:16.

However, this first impression is quite mistaken. Why? How is Paul able to maintain both the priority of Israel and the equality of Jew and Gentile in Christ on the basis of justification by faith alone (cf. Rom 3:28–31)?

A. In the first place, it is important to recognize that although Paul uses the terminology of *anthrōpos* (3:28) and *pas/pantes* (11:32), he never loses sight of the fact that Jews and Gentiles are two distinct peo-ples who even in Christ cannot be fused into one general category of *homo universalis*. Just as Paul's notion of the body of Christ is charac-terized by "many members in one body" (Rom 12:3), this same con-cept of unity amidst diversity applies to his discussion of Jew and Gentile. In other words, Paul's emphasis on equality of Jew and Greek in the body of Christ does not nullify the distinctiveness of both peo-ples. Therefore, there is no contradiction for Paul when he juxtaposes the universal equality of the believer and the particular priority of the Jew in Rom 1:16. Just as Karl Barth and Ernst Käsemann are wrong in characterizing the Jew in Romans as the *homo religiosus* in general, so it is wrong to suppose that the emphasis on *pas* or *anthrōpos* blots out the ethnic specificity of two different peoples, Jews and Gentiles.

Paul intends to stress not uniformity, but unity in diversity. The pluralistic diversity of peoples in their ethnic and cultural variety is maintained, although in Christ this pluralism becomes nevertheless a unity.

B. It is essential for Paul to maintain the priority of the Jew in the gospel, not only for the sake of the Jew, but especially for the sake of the Christian. What is at stake is nothing less than the faithfulness of God. If it could be argued that God has rejected the people of the election, Israel, and that therefore God's promises to Israel have become null and void, how are the Gentiles to trust the confirmation of these promises to them through God's righteousness in Christ? Could it not be said in that case that there is arbitrariness on God's part (Rom 9:14) and that God is not to be trusted—even the God who justifies us in Christ? In other words, the gospel cannot have any authentic validity or legitimation apart from the people of Israel because the theological issue of God's faithfulness (Rom 3:3) and righteousness determines the truth of the gospel.

Moreover, such a rejection of Israel by God would simply cut the connection of the gospel to its foundation in the Hebrew Scriptures and degrade the God of Jesus Christ into the God of Marcion—a "new God" who has no relation either to creation or to Israel's salvation history.

Therefore, it is crucial for Paul to confirm the faithfulness of God as an inalienable dimension of the righteousness of God and to emphasize that the protological election of Israel in the Old Testament will be confirmed by the eschatological priority of Israel at the time of the parousia and the establishment of the triumph of God.

Paul's struggle with this issue comes to a climax in Rom 11:26–32. If, as I have argued, Rom 11:32 is the climax and crown of Paul's argument, its emphasis on the universal embrace of God's mercy ("that he may have mercy upon all") occurs in a context which affirms the particularity of Israel's eschatological priority (Rom 11:25–26). Thus Rom 11:26–32 confirms the thesis of the theme of Rom 1:16–17 where both the equality of Jew and Gentile and the priority of Israel are accepted. In other words, the total sweep of the argument of Romans is held together by the theme of the peculiar interaction between Israel's particularity and the universality of the gospel for the Gentiles.

C. In the third place, as is well known, Paul uses the phrase *dikaiosynē theou* (righteousness of God), with the exception of 2 Cor 5:21, only in Romans and here in such a central way that it must be characterized as the key term for the letter as a whole (cf. Rom 1:17; 3:5, 21, 22, 25, 26; 10:3). According to Käsemann, the "righteousness of God" has a consistent apocalyptic meaning. As God's eschatological salvation power, it claims the creation for God's lordship and sovereignty which the Christ-event has proleptically manifested. It denotes the victory of God and his cosmic act of redemption. As such, it not only acquits the sinner but also abolishes the power of sin by transferring us to the dominion of the lordship of Christ. Within the context of the theme of Romans the *dikaiosynē theou* must be understood in terms of its theocentric focus and in its overarching significance as connoting the full range of God's soteriological activity.

The theocentric focus of the phrase *dikaiosynē theou* points to the hermeneutical field in which it functions. The term gathers up in itself the rich connotations of Israel's covenant terminology: *hesed* (steadfast love), *emet* (truth), and *zedakah* (righteousness), especially in its eschatological dimensions as documented, for instance, in 2 Isaiah and the Psalms.

In other words, in Romans the *dikaiosynē theou* comprises a hermeneutical field in which it is correlated with terms like *pistis theou* (faithfulness of God, Rom 3:3), *alētheia theou* (truth of God, Rom 3:7; 15:8; cf. 3:4), and *eleos theou* (mercy of God, cf. Rom 11:31–32; 15:9).

In this function the *dikaiosynē theou* must be understood both as God's faithfulness to himself and as his redemptive activity in accordance with his faithfulness.

Concretely speaking, the *dikaiosynē theou*—now manifested in Christ—points backward to God's promises to Israel and forward to God's full realization of his promises in the apocalyptic hour when Israel, along with the Gentiles and the whole created order, shall "live" in the *gloria dei*, when God will triumph over everything that resists his will—the moment in which the promise of "life" according to Hab 2:4 (Rom 1:17) will be fully realized and the *dikaiosynē theou* will be synonymous with the order of cosmic peace (*shālōm*), salvation (*sōtēria*), and life (*zōē*) that has been proleptically manifested in Christ.

D. As we have seen, the priority of Israel is the necessary consequence of God's character as being faithful to himself and as manifesting this faithfulness in his saving actions. This fundamental-coherent dimension of Paul's gospel has direct contingent relevance both for his audience in Rome and for his own immediate plans.

1. Paul is about to travel to Jerusalem to deliver the collection of his Gentile churches to the Jerusalem church. And as he reports, the Gentile churches "were pleased to do it, and indeed they are in debt to them (i.e., the saints in Jerusalem), for if the Gentiles have come to share in their spiritual blessings, they ought also to be of service to them in material blessings" (Rom 15:27). In other words, the Roman church is asked to acknowledge the priority of the Jew in the gospel by the apostle to the Gentiles, Paul.

2. The situation in the Roman congregation demands an urgent solution (Romans 14–15). "To a church that seems split between a

Gentile majority and a Jewish minority, Paul argues for the unity of that community. Paul stresses the salvation-historical priority of the Jew while also arguing for the right of the Gentiles to belong to the people of God."[6] It is in this context that the prevalent theme of "boasting" in Romans must be heard. In Romans 11 Paul explicitly condemns the Gentile majority in Rome for its boasting which is directed at the Jewish minority (Rom 11:17–18; cf. 11:25).

Earlier in the letter Paul had likewise castigated Jewish boasting which served as a fundamental reminder to Jewish Christians in Rome of what constitutes the true and the false claim to the priority of the Jew in the gospel (Rom 2:17–23; 3:27; 4:2). Indeed, true boasting can only be an act of gratitude for God's gift of grace in Christ (Rom 5:2, 3, 11).

The Christ-event makes clear the true nature of Israel's priority. It does not lie in Israel's "boasting," that is, in its empirical achievement of "covenant keeping" or in Israel's elitist awareness of its exclusive status before God, but solely in God's faithfulness to his promises, that is, in God's grace. But the Christ-event also makes clear that the Gentiles cannot boast to have supplanted Israel simply because they represent the majority in the Christian church.

3. In this context the Gentiles must hear that the Gentile church has no authenticity or identity unless it realizes that it "is grafted, contrary to nature, into a cultivated olive tree," that is, into Israel, "beloved for the sake of their forefathers" (Rom 11:24–28). Therefore Paul is careful in Romans to argue the unity of two distinct peoples in the gospel. Contrary to Galatians 3, Romans 4 maintains the distinctiveness of Jew and Gentile as Abraham's seed (4:12–16). Moreover, Paul corrects in Romans 9–11 the argument of Galatians 3 (and even Romans 4?), where Israel seems simply absorbed into the church. Thus Paul argues in Romans against any conception of the church as the "true Israel." By so doing he protects not only the priority and separate identity of Israel in the gospel, but also the full range of his conception of the faithfulness of God.

---

[6] C. D. Myers, Jr., "The Place of Romans 5:1–11 within the Argument of the Epistle" (Th.D. diss., Princeton Theological Seminary, 1985) 234.

AN ARABIAN TRINITY

G. W. Bowersock
Institute for Advanced Study
Princeton

K.S. olim collegae semper amico

In 1875 the collector and scholar Wilhelm Froehner published a short text incised on a gem of red jasper that had been offered to him in Nazareth for possible purchase.[1] Of the six lines of this text only the first three have been much cited because they consist of three gods' names, and reference has customarily been not to Froehner's original publication but to Louis Robert's quotation from it in his *Collection Froehner* of 1936.[2] In making an apposite allusion to the Froehner gem in her excellent study of the cults of the Hawran in the Roman period, Dominique Sourdel was under the impression that the great nineteenth-century collector had actually acquired the piece;[3] but Froehner himself reports unambiguously that he refused to pay the dealer's price. The object has therefore been lost to the world of scholarship. Nonetheless Froehner's transcription, entirely baffling to him in its second half, is worth resurrecting in the light of more recent discoveries in the Roman Near East. It bears upon several important cults among the inhabitants of *provincia Arabia*.

---

[1] Wilhelm Froehner, *Mélanges d'épigraphie et d'archéologie* (Paris: Detaille, 1875) 52–53.

[2] Louis Robert, *Collection Froehner* (Paris: Éditions des Bibliothèques Nationales, 1936) 1. 115 n. 3, cited in Dominique Sourdel, *Les cultes du Hauran à l'époque romaine* (Paris: Imprimerie Nationale, 1952) 77 n. 2, and in G. W. Bowersock, "The Arabian Ares," *Tria Corda: Scritti in onore di Arnaldo Momigliano* (Como, 1983) 44 n. 3.

[3] Sourdel, *Les cultes*, 77 ("recueilli jadis par Froehner").

As given by Froehner the text on the Nazareth jasper was as follows:

APHC
ΘEANΔPOC
ΔOYCAPH
NOYAEMIΘ
HPACΘH
PABON

The first three lines name three gods, one per line. The name Ares poses no orthographical difficulty, but the next two names are both slightly defective. Theandrios is a divinity well known to students of the Hawran in southern Syria and northern Jordan. His name appears consistently as Theandrios, not Theandros, until it gives way to the late antique form, Theandrites.[4] Since the first two names appear on the gem in the nominative case, one would expect the third to do the same, and accordingly it looks as if Froehner's transcription should be corrected to Δουσάρη[s], the Greek form of the Nabataean Dushara. If Froehner's eye (or indeed the light in which he was shown the piece) misled him in line three, we might also wish to consider reading line two as Θεάνδρ[ι]ος. As far as I am aware the three final lines have not ever been discussed by anyone, including Froehner himself.

To judge from the first three lines, each line of this text contains a single word. The fifth appears to conform to this pattern (ἠράσθη) and suggests a magical use for the gem in an erotic context. The fourth and sixth lines, however, seem at first glance impenetrable, but PABON deserves closer scrutiny. The god Theandrios points specifically to the region of the Hawran, and Dusares, the chief god of the Nabataeans, while by no means confined to that territory, was important there (notably at Bostra).[5] It happens that Rabbos (or Rabos) is well attested in precisely the Hawran as a proper name and thus fits well the indication of the divine names.[6] More striking still is the description of Theandrios on several inscriptions, according to Sourdel's convincing interpretation, as θεὸς Ραββου.[7] The god was apparently associated with

---

[4] For full documentation on Theandrios/Theandrites see ibid., 78–81.

[5] For Dusares, see Sourdel, *Les cultes*, 59–68 and, most recently, A. Kindler, *The Coinage of Bostra* (Warminster: Aris & Philips, 1983) 79–83.

[6] Sourdel, *Les cultes*, 78–81. Cf. Jean Cantineau, *Le nabatéen* (2 vols. in 1; Paris: Leroux, 1932) 2. 145 and Maurice Sartre, *Inscriptions grecques et latines de la Syrie*, vol. 13: *Bostra* (Bibliothèque Archéologique et Historique 113; Paris: Geuthner, 1982) nos. 9084 and 9370.

[7] Sourdel, *Les cultes*, 78–80.

a certain Rabbos and might therefore have been appropriately invoked by others bearing that name.

The primary significance of the second half of the text is thus the appearance of Rabos, confirming the Hawran provenance implied by the divine names. The syntax of the last lines is a separate matter, but some modest speculation may be permissible here. The bizarre fourth line is unlikely to be magical nonsense in view of the perfectly comprehensible words that follow. Since Froehner's transcription cannot be, as we have already noted, wholly accurate, it is legitimate to suspect error in line four; and suspicion falls first upon the alpha, situated oddly between two other vowels. Alpha and lambda are commonly misread (A and Λ), and if we read Λ here the sequence -λεμιθ resembles the termination of a Semitic proper name for a woman (-lmt). The preceding vocalization represented by -ou- imposes šlmt, Shulamith, or in Greek Σουλεμιθ. If Froehner had misread a sigma as a nu at the beginning of this line, he probably did so because the letter was squeezed close to the edge. The incision may have been similarly confusing at the right edge in line six, where one would not readily accept the barbarism of an accusative after ἡράσθη. On the other hand, reading Pαβος would supply the verb with a subject and leave the indeclinable feminine name as the object of ἡράσθη in an understood genitive. Hence, we may postulate (Σ)ουλεμιθ | ἡράσθη | Pαβο(ς).

However that may be, we are left with a magical gem of Hawran origin naming a triad of divinities, including the principal Nabatean god (Dusares) and another that was traditionally tied to the name of Rabbos (Theandrios). The third god is the Arabian Ares, who is also associated particularly, but not exclusively, with the Hawran and Jebel Druz. Memories of Ares in this region lingered on, to be reflected in Nonnus's account of Dionysus among the Arabs.[8] Ares was regularly assimilated in Syria and Transjordan to the camel-riding war god Arṣu,[9] and it is presumably Arṣu who is represented by Ares on the Nazareth gem. As a camel-rider he appears on the coinage of Bostra,[10] and as a

---

[8] See Bowersock, "Arabian Ares."

[9] Javier Teixidor, *The Pantheon of Palmyra* (Leiden: Brill, 1979) 69–71 with pl. XXI.1. A full and admirable account of Arṣu by Pascale Linant de Bellefonds may be found in *Lexicon Iconographicum Mythologiae Classicae*, 2. 615–18.

[10] The figure on the reverse of the coin which is no. 34 (p. 117) in Kindler's catalogue (above, n. 5) has been universally identified as Dusares, but comparison with the iconography of Arṣu, as it can be conveniently studied in the plates of the *LIMC* article (above, n. 9), proves incontrovertibly that he is the camel-rider. I make this point at greater length and with illustrations in my contribution to a Symposium on Caravan Cities (September 1985 at Petra).

warrior he dominates the coinage of Areopolis (Rabbathmoba), whose Greek name reflects the assimilation of Ares/Arṣu with the eponymous god of Ar. The Arabic Arṣu was momentarily incorporated into the name of the city during the reign of Elagabalus, when coins proclaim Arsapolis in place of the conventional Areopolis.[11] At Bostra, the capital of *provincia Arabia* and the most important city of the Hawran during the life of the province, the Nabataean Dusares was the recipient of a major cult that had its origins under the Nabataean kings. The god is commemorated on the city's coinage in both aniconic and anthropomorphic representations. The traditional representation had been a baetyl, but under hellenized Roman rule a handsome Semitic face was created for Dusares, at least from the age of Commodus onwards.[12] But the baetyl also continued to be worshiped at Bostra, and coins of Elagabalus, Decius, and Herennia Etruscilla inscribed with the name of Dusares depict it in company with two smaller baetyls.[13] It has been generally acknowledged in recent years that the Dusares of Bostra formed part of a trinity of gods, but a satisfactory identification of the other two has never been made.

Milik proposed that Dusares' companions were baetyls of Allath and the deified city of Bostra,[14] but, despite Milik's argument for a baetyl of a goddess Bostra at Petra, it remains unlikely that so Hellenic a goddess as *polis* or *tyche* appeared in aniconic form, even granted the assimilation of *tyche* with the Semitic *gad*. Naster, by contrast, has recently suggested al-'Uzza as a substitute for Bostra in the trinity,[15] but there is no supporting evidence for annexing this goddess, who is the Arabian Aphrodite, to Dusares and Allath. The Froehner gem is the only testimony, so far as I know, for a trinity of Hawran divinities including

---

[11] In "Arabian Ares" I emphasized the novelty of the Arsapolis types in the coinage of Rabbathmoba but had not realized at that time that the element "Arsa" simply represented the Semitic name of the god Arṣu, which was pronounced locally as "Arsa." For the pronunciation see J. T. Milik, *Dédicaces faites par des dieux* (Paris, 1972) 49.

[12] No. 18 (p. 110) in Kindler.

[13] No. 33 (p. 116), no. 47 (p. 122), no. 52 (p. 124) in Kindler. Coins of Philip show an anthropomorphic Dusares: Kindler no. 43 (p. 121). The simultaneity of the aniconic and anthropomorphic forms can be seen in two coins of Caracalla from 209/10, one with an anthropomorphic Dusares (Kindler no. 29 [p. 114]), the other with an aniconic Dusares (Kindler no. 30 [p. 115]). The obverse die for the two coins is probably the same: Augusto Spijkerman, *The Coins of the Decapolis and Provincia Arabia* (Jerusalem: Franciscan, 1978) Bostra, 76 (nos. 37 and 38).

[14] J. T. Milik, "Nouvelles inscriptions nabatéennes," *Syria* 35 (1958) 227–51 esp. 248.

[15] P. Naster, "Le culte du dieu nabatéen Dousarès reflété par les monnaies d'époque impériale," *Proceedings of the Ninth International Congress of Numismatics, Berne, September, 1979* (Wetteren, 1982) 1. 399–408, esp. 404.

Dusares, and it would accordingly be reasonable to assume that the god's companions there are the same as those on the Bostra coins. It follows that the two smaller and adjacent baetyls on those coins should represent Ares/Arṣu and Theandrios.

According to Damascius,[16] Theandrites, as Theandrios was called in late antiquity, was worshiped among the Arabs in masculine form (ἀρρενωπὸν ὄντα θεόν). But that is no impediment to an aniconic form earlier, and it is quite possible that, just as in the case of Dusares, aniconic and anthropomorphic representations existed simultaneously. The very name Theandrios deserves attention because it is the only divine name on the Froehner gem for which we cannot be sure of a Semitic equivalent. In dedications to Theandrios set up by Arabs in Pannonia and Mauretania (Volubilis) this god is associated with a north-Arabian deity, Manaf,[17] but it is clear that Manaf is a πάρεδρος (associate) of Theandrios and not identified with him. The Greek word Theandrios is itself remarkable, because, together with related forms, it was used in Christian Greek to express the nature of Christ. Lampe is, however, demonstrably wrong in asserting in his lexicon that the Christians invented the word for this purpose.[18] Sourdel justly remarks, "On ne comprend pas comment ce nom, employé par les Chrétiens pour désigner le Christ, a pu d'abord être appliqué à un dieu dont l'origine arabe ne semble pas douteuse."[19]

We may conclude that at least in the Roman Hawran the Arabs worshiped the traditional Nabataean deity Dusares as part of a trinity. The coins of Bostra prove that two other gods shared the cult with him, and with the help of the Froehner gem those gods may be identified as Theandrios and the Arabian Ares.

---

[16] Damascius, *PG* 103.1290. Cf. the good article on Theandrios by Höfer in Roscher's *Lexicon.*

[17] *ILS* 4349 (Pannonia); L. Robert, *REG* 49 (1936) 1–6 (Volubilis), reprinted in his *Opera Minora Selecta* 2. 939–44. On Manaf see also Sourdel, *Les cultes*, 84–85.

[18] *LPGL*, p. 615 *s.v.* θεανδρίτης: "word coined to describe Christ as a compound being."

[19] Sourdel, *Les cultes*, 78 n. 2.

JEWISH WOMEN'S HISTORY IN THE ROMAN PERIOD:
A TASK FOR CHRISTIAN THEOLOGY

Bernadette J. Brooten
Harvard Divinity School

As a teacher, as a scholar, as a dean, and as a churchman, Krister Stendahl has worked for decades to further Jewish-Christian relations and to promote women's studies and women. It is out of gratitude to him that I present these theses, which I see as a continuation of his work.

The Task

1. Writing the history of Jewish women in the Roman period is an urgent task for Christian theology. By recognizing and working with ambivalence within our tradition, we can lay the groundwork for a society based on the dignity and equality of all human beings. Much of past and present Christian theology has not proceeded from the dignity and equality of all human beings. For example, Christian men have often drawn upon Christian theology to support the subjugation of Jews, of other non-Christians, and of Christian women. Both at the level of religious motif—Jews as Christ-killers, women as daughters of the seductress Eve, and at the systemic level of theological reflection—salvation through Christ alone, the masculine as more spiritual than the feminine—Christian theology has often supported the religious and civic subordination of Jews, heathens, and Christian women to Christian men. Anti-Judaism, anti-paganism, and anti-feminism still live on in the Christian churches.

The Prevailing Approach

2. A prevalent view among church people and Christians theologians is that Jewish women in the first centuries CE were more oppressed than early Christian women. I believe that Christian feminists who are in anguish at how deeply rooted within Christianity female subordination is find hope in the possibility that its roots might actually lie else-

where.[1] I further believe that many Christian men wish to create equality within Christianity for women and to enable women to remain within the church. Seeing Jesus and the early church as revolutionary in their attitudes towards women allows such men to call for changes within the church today without departing from the authority of scripture.[2]

Difficulties with the Prevailing Approach

3. *Historically*, the comparative situation of women in ancient Judaism and in early Christianity is very unclear. For example, some argue that the church should not take Jesus' strict prohibition of divorce (Matt 5:31–32; 19:9; Mark 10:11–12; Luke 16:18; 1 Cor 7:10–11) literally, because the prohibition is actually progress for women when compared with ancient Jewish divorce practice.[3] Or one might argue that the command to women to be silent in the church (1 Cor 14:34) need no longer apply today because cultural, especially Jewish constraints were what gave rise to the prohibition.[4] Such arguments are on shaky ground historically.

4. *Theologically*, such arguments represent an avoidance of thorny theological questions: What does a Christian do who disagrees with an

[1] See Rachel Conrad Wahlberg, *Jesus and the Freed Woman* (New York: Paulist, 1978); Virginia Ramey Mollenkott, *Women, Men and the Bible* (Nashville: Abingdon, 1977); Rachel Conrad Wahlberg, *Jesus According to a Woman* (New York: Paulist, 1975); Alicia Craig Faxon, *Women and Jesus* (Philadelphia: United Church, 1973). On this and the following points I have not attempted to give exhaustive references, but rather only examples.

[2] See Robert Jewett, "The Sexual Liberation of the Apostle Paul," *JAARSup* 47 (1979) 55–87, and the literature cited there; Leonard Swidler, *Biblical Affirmations of Woman* (Philadelphia: Westminster, 1979); Ronald W. Graham, "Women in the Pauline Churches: A Review Article," *Lexington Theological Quarterly* 12 (1976) 25–34; Leonard Swidler, *Women in Judaism: The Status of Women in Formative Judaism* (Metuchen, NJ: Scarecrow, 1976); Robin Scroggs, "Paul and the Eschatological Woman: Revisited," *JAAR* 42 (1974) 532–37; idem, "Paul and the Eschatological Woman," *JAAR* 40 (1972) 283–303.

[3] On the debate on Jewish women's right to divorce in antiquity see Bernadette Brooten, "Konnten Frauen im alten Judentum die Scheidung betreiben? Überlegungen zu Mk 10,11–12 und 1 Kor 7,10–11," *EvTh* 42 (1982) 65–80; Eduard Schweizer, "Scheidungsrecht der jüdischen Frau? Weibliche Jünger Jesu?" *EvTh* 42 (1982) 294–300, esp. 294–97; Hans Weder, "Perspektive der Frauen?" *EvTh* 43 (1983) 175–78; Bernadette J. Brooten, "Zur Debatte über das Scheidungsrecht der jüdischen Frau," *EvTh* 43 (1983) 466–78.

[4] See T. R. W. Longstaff, "The Ordination of Women: A Biblical Perspective," *ATR* 57 (1975) 316–27; Marco Adinolfi, "Il silenzio della donna in 1 Cor. 14,33b–36," *BeO* 19 (1975) 121–28.

undisputed saying of Jesus (e.g., on divorce)? How can one maintain a traditionally understood authority of scripture after discovering female subordination at all levels of the NT tradition (undisputed letters of Paul, deutero-Pauline letters, possible interpolations, etc.)? How does Judaism's bearing the burden for Christian female subordination differ from more traditional Christian anti-Jewish arguments?

5. Many theologians have distinguished between the time-bound, culture-bound precepts of the NT and its eternal message. For example, James Crouch has argued that Christians today need not follow literally the command in Colossians that wives and slaves be subordinate (Col 3:18-4:1), because our society—unlike that of the first century—does not demand the subordination of women and slaves. For Crouch, the timeless message is: "The *Haustafel* calls one, therefore, to give oneself to one's neighbor within the limitations which the social order places on the relationship."[5] This schema of time-bound precepts versus an eternal message requires a particular historical reconstruction. One must assume that the NT writers were, in essence, forced by their culture to make statements which in our culture they would not have made. In order to uphold this assumption, one must assume or establish: (1) a radical dissimilarity between the two cultures, and (2) that the principal in question enjoyed universal or at least general acceptance in the cultural environment of the NT (i.e., that female subordination was an unquestioned societal norm).

6. The distinction between time-bound and eternal causes within NT historical research a focus on evidence for female subordination in antiquity. For example, evidence for female non-subordination in the first-century Mediterranean world in general or in Judaism in particular undercuts the theory of female subordination as a cultural necessity. In the course of time NT scholars have recognized the diversity of female experience in the non-Jewish Greco-Roman world.[6] The category

---

[5] James E. Crouch, *The Origin and Intention of the Colossian Haustafel* (FRLANT 109; Göttingen: Vandenhoeck & Ruprecht, 1972) 160. Ronald W. Graham notes how scholars have explained and defended Paul: "A distinction can and should be drawn between what is of the everlasting order of things, e.g., 'male and female' (Gal. 3:28) and what is the product of history and therefore, given time, can and should be changed, e.g., 'wives, be subject to your husbands' (Col. 3:18)" ("Women in the Pauline Churches," 34).

[6] Robert Jewett proposes as possible influences on the sexual liberation of Paul (1) Roman influence, given the relative freedom and emancipation of Roman women; (2) the Apostolic Conference with its move away from the Jewish Law; (3) an androgyny campaign in Corinth during the time of the Corinthian correspondence ("Sexual Liberation of Paul," 75-76).

"time-bound" becomes especially problematic in the face of a similar diversity within Judaism. If women in the Judaism of this period were not only powerless, but also leaders, not only legally disadvantaged, but also in enjoyment of certain rights, then it is no longer clear why a NT writer *had* to call upon women to be subordinate to their husbands or to be silent.

7. Much of the work on Jewish women at the time of Jesus is currently being done by Christians who wish to learn more about the background of the NT.[7] It is usual to compare the respective positions of women in Judaism and in early Christianity, focusing especially on Jesus' attitudes towards women or Paul's statements on women. This manner of comparison and its results are historically questionable.[8] The category "position," similar to the categories "status" and "role," do not allow for the variety of Jewish women's experience. Using Judaism as a background often means foreshortening and oversimplifying. Further, before meaningful comparisons can be drawn, many more detailed historical studies of Jewish and Christian women's lives and of cultural understandings of the female in this period need to be written.

8. It is now known that women were missionaries and prophets in some early Christian communities,[9] and that some early Christian women were writers.[10] In Judaism, some women served as leaders in

---

[7] See Ross S. Kraemer, "Bibliography: Women in the Religions of the Greco-Roman World," *Religious Studies Review* 9 (1983) 127–39, esp. 130.

[8] See Judith Plaskow, "Christian Feminism and Anti-Judaism," *Cross Currents* 28 (1978) 306–9, reprinted as "Blaming the Jews for the Birth of Patriarchy," *Lilith* 7, 11–13, and in Evelyn Torton Beck, ed., *Nice Jewish Girls: A Lesbian Anthology* (Watertown, MA: Persephone, 1982) 250–54; Bernadette J. Brooten, Jüdinnen zur Zeit Jesu: Ein Plädoyer für Differenzierung," *ThQ* 161 (1981) 281–85.

[9] Elisabeth Schüssler Fiorenza, *In Memory of Her: A Feminist Theological Reconstruction of Christian Origins* (New York: Crossroad, 1983) esp. 160–204; idem, "Word, Spirit and Power: Women in Early Christian Communities," in Rosemary Ruether and Eleanor McLaughlin, eds., *Women of Spirit: Female Leadership in the Jewish and Christian Traditions* (New York: Simon and Schuster, 1979) 29–70; idem, "Women in the Pre-Pauline and Pauline Churches," *USQR* 33 (1978) 153–66; Roger Gryson, *The Ministry of Women in the Early Church* (trans. Jean Laporte and Mary Louise Hall; Collegeville, MN: Liturgical, 1976).

[10] See John Wilkinson, *Egeria's Travels to the Holy Land* (Jerusalem: Ariel, 1981); Patricia Wilson-Kastner, et al., *A Lost Tradition: Women Writers of the Early Church* (Washington, DC: University, 1981); Elizabeth A. Clark and Diane F. Hatch, *The Golden Bough, The Oaken Cross: The Virgilian Cento of Faltonia Betitia Proba* (AARTS 5; Chico: Scholars Press, 1981).

the ancient synagogue,[11] and some Jewish women were well educated.[12] How can one compare these women and their respective positions within their communities?

Or how can one compare and weigh Jewish and Christian misogynist statements? Is it the quantity that counts? The vindictiveness or vehemence? The system of thought behind the individual statements? No clear methods of comparison are currently in use.

9. The relative status of women is the subject of much comparison, but not that of such other societal groups as men, children, slaves, day laborers, or non-Jews/non-Christians. A history of the comparative work on women in ancient Judaism and women in early Christianity is required. I posit that in this country it began, or perhaps increased in momentum, when nineteenth-century women's rights advocates began criticizing Christianity more vocally. That is, I suggest that Christians usually employ the comparison to defend Christianity.

10. Seeing Judaism as a primary source of Christian women's oppression has been present in U.S.-American feminist thought since at least Elizabeth Cady Stanton's *The Woman's Bible*.[13] Today, Christian feminists are faced with the dilemma of sexism within the very roots of Christianity, the New Testament. Judith Plaskow has insightfully spoken of projection onto "the Other" of that which we cannot acknowledge in ourselves. She writes:

> Feminist research projects onto Judaism the failure of the Christian tradition unambiguously to renounce sexism. . . . This is the real motive behind biased presentations of Jesus' Jewish background: to allow the feminist to present the "true" Christian tradition as uniquely free from sexism.[14]

Differentiated, detailed historical research on women's history and on understandings of the female in both Judaism and Christianity is the first step towards acknowledging and working with the ambiguity in our religious tradition.

[11] See Bernadette J. Brooten, *Women Leaders in the Ancient Synagogue: Inscriptional Evidence and Background Issues* (BJS 36; Chico: Scholars Press, 1982); Shaye J. D. Cohen, "Women in the Synagogues of Antiquity," *Conservative Judaism* 34:2 (1980) 23–29.

[12] Philo describes the *therapeutrides* and *therapeutai*, ascetics who devoted their lives to the study of the Torah, in *De vita contemplativa*. See also Brooten, *Women Leaders*, 94–95; David Goodblatt, "The Beruriah Traditions," *JJS* 26 (1975) 68–85.

[13] Elizabeth Cady Stanton, *The Woman's Bible* (1895–98; reprinted New York: Arno, 1972).

[14] Plaskow, "Blaming the Jews," in *Nice Jewish Girls*, 253.

New Ways of Proceeding

11. One must distinguish between the history of Jewish women and the history of Jewish men's attitudes towards women. Not distinguishing leads to applying such attitudinal categories as "positive" and "negative" to historical phenomena. "Positive" and "negative" are inadequate for describing such complex phenomena as Jewish women's religious and community activities, their economic situations, their daily lives, their beliefs and their struggles. One might add that studying attitudes, such as Philonic or rabbinic thinking about women or about the feminine, also requires more sophisticated categories.

12. To study Jewish history not only as background to Christian history, but also as an alternative to it, can lead to a deeper understanding of both.[15] Judaism and Christianity were both thriving religious movements in the Roman and early Byzantine periods, and the evidence for female conversions suggests that women found both religions attractive.[16]

13. Studying Judaism and Christianity as alternatives to each other implies developing historical categories, especially periods, appropriate to each. For example, the phrase "Jewish women at the time of Jesus" assumes a Christian frame of reference. It is not false. It is simply no more appropriate to Jewish history than a study of Christian women at the time of Rabbi Judah the Prince would be to Christian history. The historian of Jewish and Christian women must also ask whether the traditional male categories, "Apostolic Age," "Early Rabbinic Period," "Patristic Period," are suited to women's history.

14. Jewish women can provide insights into Jewish women's history that others will less easily be able to provide. The work of such historians as Ross Kraemer, Ellen Umansky, Marion Kaplan, Charlotte Baum, Paula Hyman, or Sonya Michel constitutes significant progress in understanding.[17] If possible, a Christian's descriptions of Jewish

---

[15] For an analysis of the framework that led to the invisibility of the postbiblical history of Jewish men, see Gaven I. Langmuir, "Majority History and Post-Biblical Jews," *Journal of the History of Ideas* 27 (1966) 343–64.

[16] See Brooten, *Women Leaders*, 144–47. Ross S. Kraemer is currently working on a longer study of this topic. She has presented preliminary results of her research at the Society of Biblical Literature Annual Meeting, Dallas, December 1983 and at the Sixth Berkshire Conference on the History of Women, Smith College, June 1984.

[17] On Ross S. Kraemer, see n. 16. The larger scope of her research is women in Greek-speaking Jewish communities in antiquity. Ellen M. Umansky, *Lily Montagu and the Advancement of Liberal Judaism: From Vision to Vocation* (Studies in Women and Religion 12; New York: Mellen, 1983); a collection of Montagu's sermons edited by Umansky is forthcoming; Marion A. Kaplan, *The Jewish Feminist Movement in Germany: The*

women's history should not be left to stand alone—in a series of papers, an anthology, a lecture, or lecture series. There should also be at least one paper, lecture, etc. on the topic by a Jewish woman. We should follow the same model for all cross-cultural and interreligious feminist work.

15. Researchers of all backgrounds, both women and men, can contribute to our knowledge of *any* group in the history of humanity. However, when studying oppressed minorities or oppressed majorities, researchers belonging to the class of the oppressors, historical or present, must be aware of their presuppositions and of how their research results can be used. All historians need to be conscious of how attitudes and experience may influence the understanding of historical documents and artifacts. For example, a Christian scholar will probably have attitudes towards dietary or purity laws which differ from those of a religious Jewish feminist scholar. It might be difficult for a non-Jewish feminist to understand how a first-century Jewish woman may not have seen Paul's advice on Jewish dietary laws to be liberating. Historical writing is best when one's stance on such matters is expressly stated and when scholars from a variety of backgrounds have the opportunity to comment on the same historical source or question.

16. Christians have nearly always employed descriptions of Jewish patriarchy for anti-Jewish purposes. For this reason, non-Jews should be extremely cautious in analyzing patriarchal structures within Judaism. For the moment, in my view, Jewish feminists are the most suitable persons to analyze such structures.[18]

17. The history of Jewish women implies exploring every avenue of historical knowledge. We need to draw upon all available literary and non-literary sources to understand the religious, cultural, economic, political, and legal aspects of their lives. Archaeology can teach us about women's housing circumstances and daily lives. Inscriptions and

---

Campaigns of the Jüdischer Frauenbund, 1904–1938 (Westport, CT: Greenwood, 1979); Charlotte Baum, Paula Hyman, and Sonya Michel, *The Jewish Woman in America* (New York: Dial, 1975).

[18] For such analyses, see Susannah Heschel, ed., *On Being a Jewish Feminist: A Reader* (New York: Schocken, 1983); Beck, *Nice Jewish Girls*; Blu Greenberg, *On Women and Judaism: A View from Tradition* (Philadelphia: Jewish Publication Society, 1981); Roslyn Lacks, *Women and Judaism: Myth, History, and Struggle* (New York: Doubleday, 1980); Liz Koltun, ed., *The Jewish Woman: New Perspectives* (New York: Schocken, 1976); Sally Priesand, *Judaism and the New Woman* (New York: Behrman, 1975); and also Ora Hamelsdorf and Sandra Adelsberg, *Jewish Woman and Jewish Law: A Bibliography* (Fresh Meadows, NY: Biblio, 1980); Aviva Cantor, ed., *On the Jewish Woman: A Comparative and Annotated Listing of Works Published 1900–1979* (Fresh Meadows, NY: Biblio, 1979).

papyri can yield information about life expectancy, birth rates, family arrangements, women in positions of leadership, law as it functioned in practice, women and property ownership, and so on. An especially promising body of material is the Archive of Babata, a group of around 40 documents in Greek, Aramaic, and Nabatean dating to the early second century CE and found near the Dead Sea in 1961. When published they will provide scholars with extensive documentation on the life of this Palestinian Jewish woman and those associated with her.[19] In addition to detailed work with the sources, one needs to place Jewish women's history of this period within the context of non-Jewish women's history, as well as of Jewish men's history.

Questions in Need of Further Study

18. The study of Jewish and Christian women in the Roman period urgently requires greater knowledge of women in other Greco-Roman religions. Because these religions have not survived and do not have advocates from within, one might not see the relevance of studying them for interreligious dialogue. The history of Christianity's relations with other religions can help us today in developing interreligious understanding. Further, the cavalier use of "neo-pagan" as a charge against feminist theology should inspire us to come to an accurate and thorough understanding of pagan women in the Roman and other periods.[20]

19. Emphasizing the special contributions that Jewish women can make to Jewish women's history is not to imply an unbroken continuity in Jewish women's experience. The question of historical continuity is a very difficult one. For example, a twentieth-century Palestinian Muslim woman may live in greater historical continuity with a second-century Palestinian Jewish or Christian woman than does a North American Christian or Jewish woman. Historical lines are so complex that tracing one's own origins may lead to discovering that other groups are also—or even more properly—the heirs of one's ancestors. Analyzing our ethnic and racial images of Christians and Jews in antiquity, and.

---

[19] Initial reports appeared in 1962: Yigael Yadin, "Expedition D—The Cave of the Letters," *IEJ* 12 (1962) 227–57; H. J. Polotsky, "The Greek Papyri from the Cave of the Letters," *IEJ* 12 (1962) 258–62. See also idem, "Šlwš tʿwdwt mʾrkywnh šl bbth bt šmʿwn," *E. L. Sukenik Memorial Volume* (1899–1953), *Eretz-Israel* 8 (1967) 46–51; Joseph A. Fitzmyer and Daniel J. Harrington, *A Manual of Palestinian Aramaic Texts* (BibOr 34; Rome: Biblical Institute, 1978) 162–63, 217 (nos. 61–63); *BAR* 7:4 (1981) 12.

[20] See Kraemer, "Women in the Religions," esp. 131–33.

testing these against historical evidence, will lead to greater precision in assessing racial and ethnic, and thereby cultural, continuity or discontinuity between researchers and the subjects and documents studied.

Goals

20. The history of women must be the history of all, not just of white, Christian-born, non-poor, U.S.-American and North European women. Further, Christian theology needs women's history in order to articulate a theology which takes Christian women's experience into account and which allows non-Christian women to live their lives fully and in peace. Understanding something of Jewish women's past can help us to understand and live together with Jewish women in our society today.[21] The same is true for the history of women of other religious traditions.

[21] For discussion of further issues of Jewish-Christian feminist dialogue, see Deborah McCauley and Annette Daum, "Jewish-Christian Feminist Dialogue: A Wholistic Vision," *USQR* 38 (1983) 147–90.

GENTILES, CHRISTIANS, AND ISRAELITES
IN THE EPISTLE TO THE EPHESIANS

Nils Alstrup Dahl
Oslo

Most early Christians perceived the world in which they lived as a world of Jews and Gentiles. Ephesians speaks most impressively about the unity of the two parts in the church, which is the body of Christ. Studies of Ephesians have very often concentrated on the idea of the church and the relationship between ecclesiology, christology, and soteriology. Some scholars have paid special attention to the relationship between the church and Israel, Christians and Jews. Statements about the Gentiles have received much less attention, but for reasons which will become apparent in the course of this article, I prefer to begin with them.*

The Gentiles

Ephesians contains four somewhat detailed descriptions of the Gentiles, their status and their way of life (2:1–3, 11–12; 4:17–19; 5:3–13). The term τὰ ἔθνη refers to the non-Jewish part of humanity, not to a plurality of nations. Non-Jewish Christians may or may not be reckoned among the Gentiles (3:1; 4:17). Those who do not believe

---

*Lack of time and space has made it impossible for me to supply this article with notes. Much of what should have been in the notes can be found in earlier articles of mine: "Der Epheserbrief und der verlorene, erste Brief des Paulus an die Korinther," in Otto Betz, Martin Hengel, and Peter Schmidt, eds., *Abraham unser Vater: Juden und Christen im Gespräch über die Bibel* (*AGJU* 5; Leiden: Brill, 1963) 65–67; "Das Geheimnis der Kirche nach Eph. 3,8–10," in Edmund Schlink and Albrecht Peters, eds., *Zur Aufer-bauung des Leibes Christi* (Kassel: Stauda-Verlag, 1965) 63–75; "Cosmic Dimensions and Religious Knowledge (Eph 3:18)," in E. Earle Ellis and Erich Grässer, eds., *Jesus und Paulus* (Göttingen: Vandenhoeck & Ruprecht, 1975) 57–75; "Ephesians, Letter to the," *IDBSup*, 268–69; "Interpreting Ephesians: Then and Now," *TD* 25 (1977) 305–15; "Dåpsforståelsen i Efeserbrevet," in Siegfried Pedersen, ed., *Dåben i Ny Testamente* (Aarhus: Aros, 1982) 141–60.

are outsiders, "the other ones" (οἱ λοιποί, 2:3), and are regarded as the "sons of disobedience" (2:2; 5:6). Because they lacked the sign of the covenant on their bodies, Gentiles were collectively called "the foreskin" (ἀκροβυστία, 2:11). The term "those far off" (οἱ μακράν, 2:17; cf. 2:13) is derived from Isa 57:19, but in the context of Ephesians it indicates not geographical distance but exclusion in terms of sacred Law. The situation of those who were "far off," foreigners and/or aliens, is spelled out in Eph 2:12: they had no share in Christ and were excluded from the commonwealth (πολιτεία) of Israel. That is, they did not enjoy the privileges of citizenship but were aliens to the dispensations of the promise of God. No hope for the godless! (ἄθεοι).

Other passages describe the mindset which is supposed to be characteristic of idolaters: futility, obscured thought, a callous heart, and moral insensitivity. As a consequence, the Gentiles have become captive to their own vices, which they practice without inhibition. Offenses against sexual morality hold first place among their sins and desires, but unfair gain at the expense of others (πλεονεξία) is not considered a lesser evil (see esp. 4:17–19; also 2:3; 4:22; 5:3–6). Within the framework of a cosmic dualism, Gentiles side with death and darkness, and with the prince that holds sway over the sublunar sphere of the air, the devil (see esp. 2:1–3; 5:8, 11–12). The eschatological wrath will certainly come upon such sinners and their associates (2:3; 5:5–6).

To a considerable degree this picture of the Gentiles and their way of life draws upon Jewish and Christian stereotypes. The descriptions of the consequences of idolatry in Eph 4:17–19 have many features in common with Rom 1:18–32. But in Romans Paul gives his argument a special twist in order to prove that there is no distinction between Jews and Gentiles. Ephesians uses the description in a more conventional way, as a warning not to act as the Gentiles do. No shades of gray modify the dark picture. Nothing is said about Gentiles who have some knowledge of God and of what the Law requires, and who may even happen to do it. Neither is anything said about civil authorities who have their power from God, so that Christians ought to obey them and intercede for them.

Both the explicit statements and the absence of modifying factors contribute to the impression that Ephesians represents an excessively negative attitude toward non-Christian Gentiles, but this negative picture provides a foil for the demonstration of the rich grace and the immense power of God, who in Christ has granted salvation to the condemnable Gentiles (2:1–10, 11–22). The dualism is counterbalanced by use of universalistic, not to say monistic, language to talk about the universal lordship of Christ and about God, the Father of all, who performs all that his will has decided (see, e.g., 1:10, 11, 19–23; 3:10, 15–16; 4:6, 8–10, 15–16). Ephesians also makes use of cosmological terminology to speak about the church as the body of Christ (esp. 1:23; 4:16).

A tension between exclusivity and universalism is present in many varieties of biblical religion, Jewish and Christian. In Ephesians it is conspicuous and not modified by any allusion to the origin of idolatry, an original fall, or the subjection of creation to futility, as it is in Romans (1:18–28; 5:12–19; 8:19–23). Ephesians contains almost no theological discussion but blames the Gentiles for their sins and praises God and what he has done in Christ, and does both things in order to extol the lot of those Gentiles who have been called by God and have become members of the church of Christ.

Christians among the Gentiles

Like other Pauline epistles, Ephesians does not talk about "Christians," but about the "saints" (e.g., 1:1, 15). Other designations are rarely used—"the brethren" in 6:23, "we who believe" in 1:19. The audience is addressed by second person plural forms in 3:1 (cf. 2:11) as "you (the) Gentiles," while an inclusive "we" or "all of us" refers to Christians in general, both Jews and Gentiles. The alternation of first and second person plurals may reflect a combination of epistolary style and devotional language.

Ephesians uses a complex imagery to praise the action of God in Christ which has radically altered the situation of the Gentiles who have heard the gospel, been baptized, and received the seal of the Spirit. Together with all Christians they have received all kinds of spiritual blessings (1:3–14). The gift aspect is complemented by transfer terminology: those who were dead have been made alive in Christ and given seats of honor in the high heavens. Once excluded as aliens, they have received reconciliation and peace, gained free access to the Father, and become fellow citizens and members of God's household (2:1–10, 11–22). Once darkness, they are now light in the Lord (5:8).

The specific paraenesis in Eph 4:25–5:21 is introduced by two thematic headlines, one negative ("not like the Gentiles," 4:17–19), the other positive ("you have been taught . . . to put off the old human being . . . and put on the new human being," 4:21–24). To paraphrase the metaphors, the shift from the old to the new implies a shift of identity as well as of role. What this means for the conduct of daily life is spelled out through alternating pairs of negative and positive instructions, some of them moral commonplaces, with appended reasons which are more specifically Christian (4:25–5:21). At this point there is a striking difference between Ephesians and Colossians. In Colossians the exhortations are not contrasted with the vices of the Gentiles but with ritual and ascetic precepts advocated by adherents of some kind of mystical "philosophy." The juxtaposition of positive and negative prescriptions is, however, a common pattern which Paul uses in Romans 12–13.

Ephesians does not only call for a clean break with the pagan past but also tells Christians not to associate with the Gentile sinners among whom they live: "Do not become their partners. . . . Do not take part in the unfruitful works of darkness" (5:7, 11). These are moral imperatives, analogous to the version of the later commandments of the Decalogue in Palestinian targumim (e.g., "You shall not be murderers, nor friends nor partners of murderers. . . . You shall not be coveters, nor friends nor partners of coveters," *Frg. Tg.* Exod 20:13, 17)—not strict rules of discipline like those of the sectarian documents from Qumran (e.g., 1QS 5.9–20). Most likely Ephesians reproduces a current paraenetic topic, as Paul apparently did in an early, now lost letter to the Corinthians. In the first of the canonical letters Paul modifies what he had written and gives various specific pieces of advice about what Christians should avoid or may do in their social intercourse with outsiders (1 Cor 5:9–12; 6:1–6; 7:12–16; 8:7–13; 10:23–33). In Ephesians the prescriptions are so general that it is impossible to know whether or not the author really wanted to recommend sectarian isolation, or how he envisaged the relationship between Christians and Gentiles in everyday life.

Ephesians no doubt presupposes that the mission to the Gentiles continues, probably carried on by special "evangelists" (cf. 4:11), but not exclusively by them. All Christians are to put on the whole armor of God and—as imitators of God—resist and fight the powers of evil, not only with defensive weapons but also equipped with the "gospel of peace" and using the "sword of the Spirit, which is the word of God" (Eph 6:11–17; cf. Isa 59:17–18; Wis 5:17–21, and Eph 4:24; 5:1). A missionary aspect is probably also present in Eph 5:11: "Take no part in the unfruitful works of darkness, but instead expose them" (μᾶλλον δὲ καὶ ἐλέγχετε). The exhortation could possibly apply to mutual correction among Christians, but the context makes it more natural to think of the shameful things which Gentiles do in secret: if their evil deeds are exposed by the light, Gentiles may awake from the sleep of death, so that Christ will shine upon them as the light of a new day upon those who awake in the morning. But even if this interpretation is correct, the concern of Ephesians is the organic growth of the church in faith and knowledge, in truth and mutual love, much more than an increasing 1number of members (see esp. 4:1 – 16).

It is not any special action but the existence of the church as the one body in which Gentiles have been united with the Israelites which makes the manifold wisdom of God known to the powers and principalities who, apparently, had assumed that they were forever to rule over various parts of a fragmented world (Eph 3:10). Ephesians represents Paul as the mediator of revealed knowledge who through his mission to the Gentiles made the secret plan of the creator become public reality (3:1 – 13). In this context the Christian Gentiles are considered representatives of the entire non-Jewish part of humanity. Their incorporation accords with the mystery of God's will, to "recapitulate" all things in Christ (Eph 1:10). The relationship of Gentile believers to outsiders is thus seen from two points of view, as separation and as representation. What both points of view have in common is that it is a very special privilege to belong to those Gentiles who have been chosen to become partners of the Israelites.

The Israelites

Ephesians never uses the term "the Jews" (οἱ ᾽Ιουδαῖοι). In contrast to uncircumcised Gentiles the Jews are said to have been called "the circumcision" (ἡ λεγομένη περιτομή, 2:11). In contrast to the Gentiles who, apart from Christ, were far off, the Jews were "the near ones" (οἱ ἐγγύς, 2:17): they enjoyed the full rights and privileges which the dispensations of the promise granted to citizens of Israel. In order to express this privileged status, I use the term "the Israelites," as Paul does in Rom 9:4. In Rom 9:4 – 5 Paul enumerates the advantages of the Jews; the analogous list in Eph 2:12 speaks about privileges which Gentiles did not have.

Ephesians never speaks about Jews except in statements about Gentiles and Israelites. Overcoming cosmic duality, Christ has made both parts one new human being (2:14 – 16). The designation "the saints" (οἱ ἅγιοι) is not reserved for Israelites, but when Gentiles are said to have become "fellow citizens of the saints" we are primarily to think of Christian Jews. First person plural forms include all Christians, Gentiles and Jews (2:3 – 7, 14, 18), but are never to be understood as meaning "we Jews" (not even in 1:11 – 12). In short, the Israelites appear in Ephesians as the heirs of the promise from whom the Gentiles were once separated but with whom the Gentiles have been united in Christ.

The separation is mentioned only in statements about the past time which came to an end when Christ abolished the Law and reconciled both parts with God. Ephesians maintains what Paul denied, that the Law had been abrogated (Eph 2:15; Rom 3:31). Without spelling out any doctrine of the Law, Ephesians seems to operate with concepts which are more akin to those of Hebrews than to Romans and Galatians. The commandments of the Law are envisaged as a set of rules for common life and worship, a fence around Israel and a dividing wall that kept aliens outside and became a cause of hostility. The theme of the key section Eph 2:11–22 is that Gentiles who were once "far off" have now "come nearby in the blood of Christ." Nevertheless it becomes quite clear that the abrogation of the Law and the reconciliation of the two parts with one another and with God changed the situation of the Israelites as well.

The designation the "so-called circumcision" carries disparaging connotations which are reinforced by the pejoratives "in the flesh" and "made with hands" (2:11). The unexpressed contrast is the circumcision of the heart, or the "circumcision of Christ" (cf. Rom 3:29; Col 2:11). Another contrast is suggested by the positive statements that through Christ "we both have access to the Father in the Spirit" and that "all that is built ($\pi\hat{\alpha}\sigma\alpha$ $o\hat{\iota}\kappa o\delta o\mu\acute{\eta}$) is joined together and grows into a holy temple in the Lord" (Eph 2:18, 21). The Law, we may supply, only gave the Jews access to the temple which was made with hands. In any case, the text of Eph 2:11–22 implies that the atoning death of Christ had a double consequence: the exclusion of the Gentiles came to an end, and both they and the Israelites were created anew and transferred from an earthly existence "in the flesh" to the new age of the Spirit.

Other texts confirm that all Christians, Jews and Gentiles, have received the same spiritual blessings and been made alive in Christ, without whom they were all dead in their trespasses, "children of wrath like the rest of mankind" (1:3–14; 2:1–7). As Christian Gentiles represent the non-Jewish part of humanity, it is reasonable to think of Christian Jews as representatives of all Israel, but the strange fact is that Ephesians does not say a single word about a split within Israel. We hear nothing about Jews who pursued a righteousness of their own and took offense at the crucified Christ, nor about Jewish instigators of persecutions of Christians, locally or in Judea.

In general, Ephesians yields very little information about the Israelites with whom the Gentile Christians have been united. If there were Christians of Jewish origins among the addressees, the author takes no account of them. He insists that the mystery of the unification of

Gentiles and Israelites is at the basis of Christian congregations among the Gentiles, but the paraenesis simply exhorts the addressees to preserve the "unity of the Spirit" among themselves, by means of mutual love, tolerance, and forgiveness (see esp. 4:1–6).

After the time of Paul and of Ephesians several authors still found it necessary to warn Christians against the adoption of "Judaizing" customs. Ephesians does not. In the later years of Paul the most controversial matter was not circumcision of Christian Gentiles but the problem of which concessions, if any, Christian Jews might make in order to preserve the unity with their non-Jewish brothers and sisters (see Gal 2:11–14; Acts 21:20–21). Controversies on this issue were a major reason for a split which made the unity of Jews and Gentiles in the church break down. The issue must have been burning at the time of Ephesians, especially on the theological premises of the epistle itself: if Christian Jews continued to observe the Law, how could their unity with Christian Gentiles be manifested in practice? If not, how could the Jews inside the Christian church still be authentic representatives of Israel? We don't know what the author of Ephesians would have answered because the issue is not a concern of his.

One thing is clear: the addressees have heard about Paul, certainly also about his Jewish past (Eph 3:1–2). We can also safely assume that the "foundation of the apostles and prophets" was laid within Israel (2:20). Ephesians represents Paul as the one who preached the gospel to the Gentiles and thereby made the mystery of the unification of Jews and Gentiles become a public reality. But Paul did not act on his own—the mystery of the inclusion of Gentiles was also revealed in God's "holy apostles and prophets" (3:4–7). The full concord between Paul and the foundational authorities of the church (in Jerusalem?) provides the evidence for the unity of Israelites and Gentiles in the church. I see no way to avoid the conclusion that the author of Ephesians had a keen interest in the Jewish roots and origin of the church but failed to show any concern for the relationship of his audience to contemporary Jews in or outside the church.

In comparison with nearly contemporary writings, it is remarkable that Ephesians contains no expression of anti-Jewish sentiments. The author did not embrace the idea that Israel had been rejected and replaced by the Christian church as the people of God. The vision of unification in Christ is a modified version of a point of view which is likely to go back to the earliest years of Christian history: through the death and resurrection of Jesus, the Christ, God confirmed his promise and redeemed his people Israel, with the consequence that Gentiles who believed in Christ were added as associates (see, e.g.,

Rom 15:7-12; Acts 3:25-26; 15:13-18). This notion did not cause great problems as long as Christian Gentiles were a tiny majority. Ephesians has updated it to fit a setting in which a majority of Christians were of Gentile origin.

Ephesians envisages the incorporation of Gentiles in a way that corresponds to Paul's image of Israel as the fine, cultivated olive tree into which wild olive branches have been grafted, but does not take account of the peculiar way in which Paul elaborates the image in Rom 11:16-24. In Romans Paul attests his deep concern for his fellow Jews and warns Gentile Christians not to feel safe and boast at the expense of Jews who have failed to believe in their own Christ. Ephesians simply reminds Christian Gentiles of their former status as excluded aliens in order to demonstrate the magnitude of the blessings which God in his mercy has extended to them.

The Epistle to the Ephesians

Ephesians is a sublime yet elusive document. There are almost no references to specific times, places, or persons, or to events after the baptism of the addressees. The epistle portrays the church as one and universal but says nothing about "ecumenical" relations between geographically separated churches. The picture of social contacts between the addressees and their pagan environment, or with Jews inside or outside the church, remains equally vague. This vagueness is one among several indications of pseudonymous authorship. The author, I think, was a personal disciple of Paul who lived in Asia Minor at a time when many winds of doctrine caused fragmentation and the Pauline heritage was in danger of being lost. In this situation the anonymous author composed a letter in the name of Paul which, taken at face value, was addressed to some recently founded congregation(s), and reminded young Gentile Christians of the implications of their faith and baptism, and exhorted them to live up to their calling.

The real function of this "letter from Paul" was to make the apostle present to Christians of a later generation, and to call them back to the beginnings of Gentile Christianity, the mission of Paul, and their own baptism. The author alludes only in passing to burning issues of his own time but exceeds all alleged revelations of secret knowledge by means of a laudatory description of the mystery of God's will and its enactment in Christ. Christians of a Gentile background are to understand that their own existence in Christ, as equal partners of the Israelites, is at the core of the mystery of Christ.

The double, fictional, and real setting of Ephesians provides an explanation for the treatment of the unification of Gentiles and Israelites as the basis for all Gentile Christianity and, at the same time, the greatest of mysteries. The epistle spells out what consequences this should have for the unity and holiness of the church, in a setting in which Christians lived as a minority in a pagan environment and paternalistic households were constituent parts of the Christian community. But the vision of Ephesians has consequences that reach far beyond the horizon of the author and the first recipients of the epistle.

ONESIMOS

David Daube
University of California, Berkeley

When Paul deems conversion to imply a "new creation," he is in line with the Jewish tenet—valid to this day—which assigns a convert the position of a "child just born."[1] One consequence is that a pagan family coming over *en bloc* is in principle unaffected by incest taboos: they are no longer related. Still, the Rabbis, lest the unthinking might conclude that incest was being taken lightly, impose a restriction, pragmatic and variable—banning such unions as are illicit in the surrounding culture. Along with the maxim, Paul also adopts this proviso: he tells the Corinthians that their pride in their novel state must not lead to marriage with a stepmother, "fornication not found among the gentiles" (1 Cor 5:1). No tenet, he urges, not even one so fundamental, so cherished, as that of re-creation, is to be turned into a fetish. Glory becomes vainglory when the resultant actions are the opposite of beneficial to the individual, the opposite of upbuilding for the church. I am going to suggest that some passages in his Epistle to Philemon may have to be read bearing in mind the same counterpointal interplay: on the one hand, a radical concept of conversion; on the other, moderation from considerateness as an individual as well as from dedication to the church's welfare.

All writers on the Epistle observe that Paul does not ask Philemon to manumit Onesimos, yet does ask him to receive him not as a slave but as a brother. The explanation is that the man baptized by Paul is no longer the man that was owned by Philemon. Paul actually speaks of

---

[1] *b. Yebam.* 22a; 2 Cor 5:17. For details, see my following works: *The New Testament and Rabbinic Judaism* (London: University of London, Athlone Press, 1956; reprinted New York: Arno, 1973) 113; "Pauline Contributions to a Pluralistic Culture: Re-creation and Beyond," in Donald G. Miller and D. Y. Hadidian, eds., *Jesus and Man's Hope* (Pittsburgh: Pittsburgh Theological Seminary, 1971) 2. 223ff.; "Biblical Landmarks in the Struggle for Women's Rights," *Juridical Review* 90 n.s. 23 (1978) 184ff.; and *Ancient Jewish Law: Three Inaugural Lectures* (Leiden: Brill, 1981) 8, 14ff.

him as "my child whom I have begot": echo of the rabbinic idiom mentioned above, and let us recall the dictum—applied to Abraham, prototype of proselytizers—that "anyone who brings a gentile near is as though he had created him."[2] Philemon, of course, himself guided into the faith by Paul, will understand this well. Possibly, the remark that Onesimos, now a beloved brother to Paul, should be this "all the more to Philemon, both in the flesh and in the Lord," is intended to emphasize the completeness of the change. The very body that was once subject to Philemon is no more; the present Onesimos is a different being in every respect. In any case, the main part of the letter opens with the reminder that Paul could simply direct Philemon in Christ to renounce his hold. Surely, what is envisaged here is not an arbitrary demand but one that would be fully warranted by the transformation that has occurred.

So much for the principle. There is, however, a great deal in mitigation. For one thing, Paul clearly expects Onesimos patiently to accept whatever decision Philemon will make. Though free—and also, it should be added, not accountable for wrongs of the former Onesimos—if Philemon cannot let go, he is to submit. For another thing, movingly, the apostle himself, in this matter of great concern to him, sets an example of self-restraint. He beseeches instead of ordering. He appeals to love and partnership. He will be content with what is tendered willingly rather than exact the utmost. In fact, should Philemon feel strongly about it, he volunteers to bind up the breach and make good any loss. To be sure, throughout, he leaves no doubt as to what he hopes will be Philemon's response. But this does not detract from the genuineness of his approach. Philemon has a choice. If he makes the wrong one, no irreparable harm is done and Paul will go on trying. If, as is likely, the right one, the positive effects will be enormous all around. From Col 4:7 it would appear that Philemon did come through.

A brief return to 1 Corinthians may be helpful. I have already adverted to the section on "incest"—in inverted commas—between converts. Another one (1 Cor 7:12–16) deals with converts whose spouses do not join them. Since the convert is a new person, the marriage is dissolved and he or she is at liberty to wed someone else. (This proposition, when its roots were forgotten, came to be mistaken for an infringement on Jesus' teaching and was named *privilegium Paulinum.*)

---

[2] *Gen. Rab.* on 12:6. The biblical text puzzlingly reports a "making" of souls. For the midrash, this is an allusion to a gathering in of heathens which, indeed, equals a making, a giving life.

Nevertheless, once again, the principle is not carried to extremes. If the unbeliever is prepared to stay on, that is to be welcomed. Cohabitation will bring about a fresh marriage, preferable to a casting off, in the interest both of peace and of the chance that, ultimately, the unbeliever will be won over. There follows a disquisition on the basic irrelevance of external callings: circumcision or uncircumcision, slavery or freedom. Commentators are distinctly uneasy about a lack of connection with what precedes: the designation "excursus" is common. But the meaning, the proper understanding, of re-creation is a very substantial link. The child just born need not, should not, trouble about whether he is circumcised or not. Moreover, even if in his preconversion existence he was a slave, he is that no longer, though circumstances may be such—yet another instance of adjustment—that he ought to put up with being kept in servitude. In a previous publication[3] I claimed that 1 Corinthians has far greater thematic unity than is generally recognized. This "excursus" provides further support. And it is in perfect agreement with the doctrine of the Epistle to Philemon.

How widely shared this construction was, how long it persisted, will not here be investigated. I confine myself to pointing out that in a number of the other Epistles, while they contain nothing irreconcilable with re-creation in its fullest sense, the weight is all on the conduct worthy of the holy community. Both slave and master are exhorted to it in Ephesians and Colossians, the former alone in 1 Timothy, Titus, and 1 Peter.[4]

Two thoughts in conclusion. First, if my view is correct, any lingering scruples as to the authenticity of the Epistle to Philemon may safely be dismissed. The mix is so unique. Second, one could imagine that Paul's extraordinary preoccupation with the miraculous power of conversion has to do with his own extraordinary experience. In both 1 Cor 15:8 and Gal 1:15, short as the accounts are, they contain references, couched in intense language, to his natural birth and his higher one. It may be asked why, starting out afresh, he should feel as contrite as he does about his previous stubbornness. But logic has its limitations. He was very special to God from his mother's womb, yet went to fearful lengths in denying his election. Some Rabbis are exercised by the sufferings of proselytes who have not yet had time to sin in their

---

[3] "Pauline Contributions," 227.

[4] Eph 6:5–9; Col 3:22–4:1; 1 Tim 6:1–2; Tit 2:9–10; 1 Pet 2:18. Similarly, whereas the duties of both spouses are outlined in Ephesians, Colossians, and 1 Peter, only the wife's are in 1 Timothy and Titus; see Edward Gordon Selwyn, *The First Epistle of St. Peter* (London: Macmillan, 1946) 182.

new life. An old answer is that what counts against them is a too long hesitation to embrace the truth after becoming aware of it.[5] Near enough. In Acts 9:8 there is no mention of birth but, instead, of blindness and starvation for three days, reminiscent of the tomb.

I am profoundly grateful for the opportunity of offering this note to Krister Stendahl, whose generosity and warmth will never allow the growth of a fetish.

---

[5] b. Yebam. 48b; Josephus Ant. 2.2.4; see Daube, Ancient Jewish Law, 17–18.

REFLECTIONS ON THE MORMON "CANON"

W. D. Davies
Texas Christian University

This essay might seem inappropriate for this volume, but it is not. Krister Stendahl is particularly distinguished by a catholicity of mind and spirit which enables him to look with understanding, sympathy, and empathy on all sorts and conditions in what he once unpejoratively called "God's menagerie of religions." That Mormons do not belong to the main bodies of Christians does not exclude them from his purview. But apart from this, the Mormons are in fact highly germane to the theme of this volume. Uniqueness is always hard to substantiate: Christians, Jews, and Gentiles have been related in many varied and complex ways. But there seems to be no parallel to the way in which Mormons—while claiming to be Christians—assert as well that they are genealogically connected with Jews and that they are therefore physically a rediscovered, restored, and reinterpreted "Israel." As far as I am aware they constitute a very special, if not unique, case of Christians among Jews and Gentiles since by implication they have redefined all three of these terms.[1] This is the justification for the inclusion of this essay in this volume. We here reflect on one aspect of Mormon life: their fixation of their own "canon."[2]

The attitude of the Church of Jesus Christ of Latter-day Saints, or the Mormons, to scripture is unusual—undeniably radical if not unique. Certain factors govern the way in which Mormons have been led to their formation of their own canon of scriptures which is both similar to

---

[1] See W. D. Davies, "Israel, the Mormons and the Land," in *Reflections on Mormonism, Judaeo-Christian Parallels* (Provo, UT: Brigham Young University Press, 1977) 79–97.

[2] The term canon as applied to Mormonism is not without difficulty. That is why I have placed the term canon in quotation marks in the title and introduction. Hereafter these marks are omitted, except where otherwise necessary.

and different from Protestant, Roman Catholic, and Orthodox canons of scripture.

There can be no question that Mormons regard themselves as Christians. They affirm that they have Jewish roots and belong to and emerge within the tradition which is rooted in the OT and the NT. Both Testaments are explicitly stated to be canonical for them. The *Articles of Faith* of the Mormon Church were published on 1 March 1842, twelve years after the organization of the Church, as "The Wentworth Letter."[3] The eighth article reads: "We believe the Bible to be the word of God as far as it is translated correctly." By the term "Bible" is meant the Hebrew Bible and the NT. The Apocrypha, accepted as canonical by the Roman Catholic Church but about which the Greek Orthodox Church is ambiguous, is not canonical but is nevertheless valuable. The prophet Joseph Smith, the founder of Mormonism, is reported to have prayed to know whether the Apocrypha contained God's holy word. On 9 March 1833, at Kirtland, Ohio, he received the following reply by revelation: "Verily thus saith the Lord unto you concerning the Apocrypha. There are many things contained therein that are true, and it is mostly translated correctly. There are many things therein that are not true, which are interpolations by the hands of men" (*D&C* 91.1–2; see below, 51, for an explanation of this abbreviation). For this reason it was decreed by Joseph Smith that it was not necessary that the Apocrypha should be translated again (*D&C* 91.3), and it did not become a part of the Mormon canon.[4]

---

[3] In *Times and Seasons* 3 (1842) 706–19.

[4] On the Apocrypha, see the fascinating article by J. M. Ross, "The Status of the Apocrypha," *Theology* 82 (May 1979) 183–91. I am also indebted to the (unpublished) paper of one of my students, Father Dimitri Cozby, on "Orthodox Christian Views of the Disputed Books of the Old Testament," in which bibliographical data are given. He confirms the view that

> the dominating view among Orthodox theologians is that the disputed books rightfully belong in the OT and are in some sense divinely inspired, but that they are to be distinguished from the books of the short canon. The precise implications of this distinction are not spelled out, however, though it does not apparently preclude their reading in public worship as well as for private edification. One should also remember that this position lacks official sanction and universal acceptance and is questioned by Orthodox theologians of repute. Regarding terminology, both "deuterocanonical" and "*anagignoskomena*" seem to be acceptable designations, but the latter is perhaps preferable due to its Patristic origin.

Truman G. Madsen, professor at Brigham Young University, in a private note of 20 June 1985 and orally, reminds me, however that "considerable care was taken to include the Apocrypha with the biblical materials placed in the cornerstone of the Nauvoo Tem-

The Bible as the Mormons knew and spoke of it was the English translation known as the *King James Version* (*KJV*), published in 1611. But in the eighth Article of Faith, already cited, the Bible is accepted as canonical only "as far as it is translated correctly." This qualification is important. On 15 October 1843, Joseph Smith declared that "I believe the Bible as it read when it came forth from the pen of the original writers. Ignorant translators, careless transcribers, or designing and corrupt priests have committed many errors."[5] This is not surprising. Earlier, in June 1830, Joseph Smith had already reported that God had revealed to him that many things had been taken from the words that Moses himself had written, but that some of these were to be recovered. The OT, as it stands, is therefore lacking in many ways. Convinced that he was inspired by the spirit of the ancient prophets, Smith believed that he could seek to detect by the gift of discernment what was not in accordance with the Spirit in the Bible and also recognize that much that was originally in it had been either taken away from it or lost.

This conviction lies behind the claim to his having had an early divine commission to revise the Bible. In *D&C* we read of a revelation given at Kirtland, Ohio, on 7 March 1831. This revelation concerning the future repeats much of the apocalyptic teaching of the NT. It reaches a point where the following words occur: "And now, behold, I say unto you, it shall not be given unto you to know any further concerning this chapter, until the New Testament be translated, and in it all these things shall be made known; Wherefore I [God] give unto you [Joseph Smith] that ye may now translate it, that ye may be prepared for things to come" (*D&C* 45.60–61). The implication was that the

---

ple. And Joseph Smith is reported to have said of the Apocrypha that 'it required much of the Spirit' to discern the truths within it." See Edward L. Stevenson, *Reminiscences of Joseph the Prophet* (Salt Lake City: private publication, 1893). Madsen goes on to say:

> The declaration that "there are many things contained therein [the Apocrypha] which are true and it is mostly translated correctly" has been sometimes extended by Mormons to apply to other extra-canonical materials. With the Dead Sea Scrolls came the discovery that *many biblical books* have earlier Hebrew and Aramaic texts. The question has been raised again "Are they scripture or important supplements?" Typically, Mormons deny such volumes canonical status while tending to the view that in some cases they precede and in others echo authentic biblical materials. They are sympathetic to the view that many extra canonical writings may reflect inspired source materials.

[5] In *The History of the Church of Latter Day Saints* (1902; 2d ed. with Introduction and Notes by B. H. Roberts; Salt Lake City: Deseret, 1964) 6. 57 (henceforth *HC*). The *HC* is the history of Joseph Smith, the prophet, by himself.

KJV as it stood was regarded as inadequate. Accordingly (under the guidance of revelation) Smith began to revise the Bible. The exact date when he began this revision is not known. Presumably it was begun after 7 March 1831, but was interrupted, because on 1 December 1831, Smith recorded that "I resumed the translation of the scriptures, and continued to labor *in this branch of my calling* with Elder Sidney Rigdon as my scribe." There are references to this work of revision in his revelations recorded for 16 February 1832, 8 March 1833, and 6 May 1833. Smith called his work of revision that of "translation." The work was carried on intermittently till July 1833. The Book of Genesis was first revised in the fall and winter of 1830. After 7 March 1831, Smith began the NT and after this resumed work on the OT. By 2 July 1833, most of the revision was completed but revisions and alterations continued up till Smith's death in 1844. An edition of Joseph Smith's Bible (i.e., the Bible, the *KJV* which he used) was published in 1867, and in 1944 a "New Corrected Edition" appeared.[6] This latter contained only a few adjustments and changes. In probably only 352 verses does the edition of 1944 differ from that of 1867. The Mormons think of Smith's version of the biblical texts he translated as "inspired," but it has never been accepted as canonical as a whole, although the revision of Matt 23:39 and Matthew 24 was so accepted.[7]

So far we have noted the biblical contents of the canon of the Mormon Church. Our discussion revealed acceptance and criticism of the Christian canon as normally understood in Protestantism and largely in Roman Catholicism and Orthodoxy. The criticism centered on the character of the *KJV* as a translation that required revision and as a corruption of God's original revelation caused by ignorance or deliberate priestly intent. Emphasis seems to be put most on omissions from what God originally had revealed.[8] Not surprisingly, then, the Bible was revised although the *KJV* retained preeminence. Equally it is not surprising, since the Bible was regarded as inadequate, that the Mormon Church claimed to have had further revelations which are to

---

[6] The most significant changes in the Joseph Smith translation are now footnoted in the new (1979) Mormon edition of the *KJV*. The lengthiest additions are presented in a separate section of the Appendix. Their net effect is threefold: (1) to trace the messianic and christological understanding of various OT texts to an earlier date than most scholars allow; (2) to resolve contradictions or conflicting readings; and (3) to clarify the timebound and obscure passages (so T. G. Madsen).

[7] See *Pearl of Great Price*, 43–46.

[8] See on this esp. the provocative article by Hugh W. Nibley, "The Forty-day Mission of Christ—The Forgotten Heritage," *VC* 20 (1966) 1–24.

be taken as scripture. In the first place, these revelations are those believed to have been given to Smith at various intervals. We may now surmise those documents, which in addition to the NT and the OT (without the Apocrypha), are regarded as canonical in Mormonism.

There is, first, the Book of Mormon[9]

Responding to words in Jas 1:5, and troubled by the war of words and tumult of opinions among the religious denominations of his day, Joseph Smith retired to the woods to ask wisdom of God. His petition was answered. On 21–22 September 1823,[10] two heavenly personages appeared to him. According to Smith, they were the Father and the Son. They advised him to join no denomination but to prepare himself for a great task. There followed a series of reported revelations. These included the miraculous discovery and translation of a set of gold plates.[11] Joseph Smith claimed that they were revealed to him by the counsels of Moroni, an angel, who identified himself as the son of Mormon, the original compiler of the plates. After four years of trial and temptation, on 22 September 1827, Joseph Smith was given charge of the plates. A portion of these plates he then claimed to have translated as the Book of Mormon. It was published in 1830. The Book of Mormon purports to be a history of pre-Columbian America (from 600 BCE to 400 CE), its settlement by some Hebrews and their subsequent destiny and apostasy. The translation was made possible by means of two special stones set in rims to which a breastplate was attached. This instrument was called the "Urim and Thummim"—a term which refers to certain elements in the accoutrements of the High Priest in the OT (Exod 28:30; Lev 8:8; Deut 38:8; Ezra 2:63; Neh

[9] The Book of Mormon is regarded by Mormons as a divinely inspired record covering generally the period 600 BCE to 400 CE, made by the prophets of the people who inhabited the Americas centuries before Christ. In Mormon belief, this record was made known to Joseph Smith by Moroni, the last of those pre-Columbian prophets on the American continent, and was translated by Smith. In the judgment of Krister Stendahl "the laws of creative interpretation by which we analyze materials from the first and second Christian centuries operate on and are significantly elucidated by works like the Book of Mormon and by other writings of revelatory character." He insists that "such authentic writing should not be confused with spurious gospel forgeries, many of which are discussed in *Strange Tales about Jesus* (Philadelphia: Fortress, 1983)." See Krister Stendahl, *Meanings, The Bible as Document and as Guide* (Philadelphia: Fortress, 1984) 99. This judgment calls for scrutiny: we find it more provocative than convincing.

[10] See James E. Talmage, *A Study of the Articles of Faith* (1890; Salt Lake City: The Church of Jesus Christ of Latter-day Saints, 1976) 255.

[11] Moroni revealed that the plates were buried in a hill, called Cumorah or Ramah near Palmyra in western New York state, not far from Joseph Smith's home.

7:65). In time Joseph Smith, through the instruction of the heavenly personage, showed the plates to his close associates—Oliver Cowdery, Martin Harris, and David Whitmer. These three men signed a sworn affidavit declaring "with words of soberness, that an angel of the Lord came down from heaven, and he brought and laid before our eyes, that we beheld and saw the plates, and the engravings thereon." Later eight other witnesses swore that "Joseph Smith, the translator of this work, has shown unto us the plates of which hath been spoken, which have the appearance of gold, and as many of the leaves as the said Smith has translated we did handle with our hands; and we also saw the engravings thereon." They added that they had "seen and hefted" the plates: they did so with "words of soberness." According to Mormons all eleven of these first witnesses remained steadfast in their testimony until they died.[12]

According to the eighth of the *Articles of Faith*, Mormons believe the Book of Mormon to be the word of God. "The elders, priests and teachers of this church shall teach the principles of my gospel, which are in the Bible and the Book of Mormon, in which is the fullness of the gospel" (*D&C* 42.12). The Book of Mormon "contains the truth and the word of God" (*D&C* 19.26). It was recognized, however, that, like the Bible, the Book of Mormon also was a translation, not the original text.[13] Thus the original text itself was an abridgment of a more original record. At this point the contents of the Book of Mormon need not detain us. It is made up of 15 books, one being a kind of editorial note. In all, in the current edition of the Mormon Church, it contains 522 pages. Nor again need we seek to "explain" the Book of Mormon, as has been done, in terms of a pious fraud or forgery, or of psychological or historical causes. All such explanations do not affect believing Mormons, who claim the Book of Mormon to be revealed

---

[12] As far as I am aware, the fact that—apart from Smith himself—the witnesses numbered exactly eleven has escaped comment. Can it be that there is here a contrast and parallel intended with "the Twelve" who formed the inner circle of the disciples of Jesus in the NT? One of the Twelve did not remain steadfast so that the effective witnesses were eleven. Perhaps Smith himself was the twelfth. See 1 Cor 15:5, where the Greek text of Nestle gives "the Twelve" (τοῖς δώδεκα), but some MSS—D*, G, and the Latin and Syriac versions—read eleven (τοῖς ἕνδεκα). Did the risen Lord appear to Judas? The textual evidence favors reading "the Twelve"—as does the theology of the early church. There is no evidence to support this conjecture and it must remain only such.

The constraint of evidence has led several encyclopedias to reverse their earlier allegations that the three witnesses "later denied their testimony." See, R. L. Anderson, *Investigating the Book of Mormon Witnesses* (Salt Lake City: Deseret, 1981) 67–78.

[13] Note esp. the full title as given in Talmage, *Articles of Faith*, 257f.: *The Book of Mormon: An Account written by the hand of Mormon upon plates taken from the plates of Nephi.*

truth. It was therefore canonized and regarded as the direct fulfillment of the prophecy of Isa 29:4. It is a parallel testimony with that of the Bible in fulfillment of Ezek 37:16–19.[14] Joseph Smith has brought the restored dispensation of the fullness of time anticipated by Paul in Eph 1:9, 10.[15]

The Pearl of Great Price

In addition to the OT and the NT and the Book of Mormon, there are other documents regarded as canonical which have been gathered into one volume called *The Pearl of Great Price*. A selection from the Revelations, Translations and Narrations of Joseph Smith, First Prophet, Seer and Revelator to The Church of Jesus Christ of Latter-day Saints.[16]

1) *The Book of Moses* in eight chapters, giving visions revealed to Joseph Smith in June 1830. These visions are in part derived from Smith's revision of Genesis. While chap. 1 was not from the Book of Genesis, chaps. 2–8 were revelations received while Smith was "translating" or revising the book (see *HC* 1.98–101); chap. 6, vss 45–68 and chap. 7 are an extract from the prophecy of Enoch.

2) *The Book of Abraham*. According to Smith, this is derived from two rolls of papyri from the "catacombs of Egypt" sold to the Mormons at Kirtland, Ohio, in July 1835 by one Michael Chandler. It purports to be the history of Abraham written by Abraham with his own hands in "characters of hieroglyphics" (*HC* 2.236).

3) The revised form of Matt 23:39 and 24, as "translated," that is at some points reworded and in some verses expanded, by Joseph Smith.

4) *Extracts from the History of Joseph Smith, the Prophet*.

5) *The Articles of Faith of the Church of Jesus Christ of Latter-day Saints*.[17]

---

[14] Talmage, *Articles of Faith*, 20–21.

[15] Ibid., 21. Timothy L. Smith has argued that the appeal of the Book of Mormon in the first generation, to converts as to inquirers, was essentially its confirmation of the biblical witness of Christ. Its role as supplementary scripture was, he concludes, secondary. He adds that no doctrine of any prominence in the Book of Mormon is without biblical precedent. See Timothy L. Smith, "The Book of Mormon in a Biblical Culture," *Journal of Mormon History* (1982) 3–21. One hesitates to confirm this view without further examination.

[16] Salt Lake City: Church of Jesus Christ of Latter-day Saints, 1979.

[17] The *Articles of Faith* are in the *Pearl of Great Price* but according to T. G. Madsen, "neither Joseph Smith nor his successors viewed the Articles of Faith as scriptural or even as 'creedal' in status. For Joseph Smith, creeds were to be viewed as 'suggestive' not 'as setting up stakes" and were not to rank as scripture." One of the *Articles of Faith*

We have given the contents of the *Pearl of Great Price* in the edition published at Salt Lake City by the Church in 1979. Another section reads *The Doctrine and Covenants of the Church of Jesus Christ of Latter-day Saints, Containing Revelations given to Joseph Smith, the Prophet, with some Additions by his Successors in the Presidency of the Church.* (The French translation speaks of a "choix," a selection from the revelations.) The edition of 1979 when compared with the previous editions of 1833, 1876, 1879, 1921, shows change. In earlier editions, from 1851 to 1902, a hymn called "Truth" known familiarly as "Oh Say, What Is Truth" appeared. It was then dropped (section 77 of the *D&C* first printed in *Times and Seasons* in 1844) and was first included in the 1876 edition of the *D&C*.[18]

So far we have dealt with documents that have already been given canonical status by the Mormon Church. In addition to those already indicated, certain other writings of the Mormon Church, composed of utterances which have continued into the present, are esteemed as scripture. In *D&C* 68.2–4 we read:

> And, behold, and lo, this is an ensample unto all those who were ordained unto this priesthood, whose mission is appointed unto them to go forth—And this is the ensample unto them, that they shall speak as they are moved upon by the Holy Ghost. And whatsoever they shall speak when moved upon by the Holy Ghost shall be scripture, shall be the will of the Lord, shall be the mind of the Lord, shall be the work of the Lord, shall be the voice of the Lord, and the power of God unto salvation.

This revelation indicates that brethren may speak without being "moved upon by the Holy Ghost." But when they do so speak (when moved upon by the Holy Ghost), their words become scripture. How

---

(the eighth) says "many great and important truths are yet to be revealed." Madsen finds here an official statement "to assure that neither the Articles of Faith nor the canon is final if that means complete."

[18] On all this, see Milton R. Hunter, *The Pearl of Great Price* (Salt Lake City: Bookcraft, 1951) 240–48. Concerning the Prophecy of Enoch, Matthew Black, whose great work on 1 Enoch has just appeared, orally informed me that he finds no trace of its influence in the Mormon texts. But see also J. H. Charlesworth, "Messianism in the Pseudepigrapha and the Book of Mormon," in *Reflections on Mormonism* (Salt Lake City: Publishers Press, 1978). As a parallel in the Enochic corpus, George Nickelsburg has called my attention in correspondence to 4QEnGiants⋯⋯ 8.3: *prsgn lwḥ' tny[n]* ("the copy of the sec[on]d tablet"; J. T. Milik, *The Books of Enoch* [Oxford: Clarendon, 1976] 314–15). Nickelsburg has also noted the idea in *Jubilees* 8 and the Nag Hammadi treatise *The Three Steles of Seth.*

52   Essays in Honor of Krister Stendahl

was it to be determined whether a particular speech or writing were by
the Holy Ghost? Two criteria were to be observed. One is expressed
by Brigham Young as follows:

> Were your faith concentrated upon the proper object, your
> confidence unshaken, your lives pure and holy, everyone fulfilling
> the duties of his or her calling according to the Priesthood and
> capacity bestowed upon you, you would be filled with the Holy
> Ghost, and it would be as impossible for any man to deceive and
> lead you to destruction as for a feather to remain unconsumed in
> the midst of heat.[19]

> I am more afraid that this people have so much confidence in their
> leaders that they will not inquire for themselves of God whether
> they are led by Him. I am fearful they settle down in a state of
> blind self-security trusting their eternal destiny in the hands of
> their leaders with a reckless confidence that in itself would thwart
> the purposes of God in their salvation, and weaken what influence
> they could give to their leaders, did they know for themselves, by
> the revelations of Jesus, that they are led in the right way. Let
> every man and woman know, by the whispering of the Spirit of
> God to themselves, whether their leaders are walking in the path
> the Lord dictates, or not.[20]

In these passages the burden of proof for the "scriptural," that is,
canonical character of any utterance, is placed upon the hearer. A Mormon knows whether another Mormon has spoken "when moved upon
by the Holy Ghost" when he himself is moved upon by the Holy Ghost
in response to his brother's words.

But Joseph Smith had previously provided another criterion.
According to *D&C* 18.1–4, citing a revelation given in early June 1829
through Smith himself to the Elders of the Church at Kirtland, Ohio:

> 1. Now behold, because of the thing which you, my servant Oliver
> Cowdery, have desired to know of me, I give unto you these
> words:
> 2. Behold, I have manifested unto you, by my Spirit in many
> instances, that the things which you have written are true; where-
> fore you know that they are true.
> 3. And if you know that they are true, behold, I give unto you a
> commandment that you rely upon the things which are written;

---

[19] *Journal of Discourses* (Liverpool: R. D. and S. W. Richards, 1854–56) 7.2.
[20] Ibid., 9. 150.

4. For in them are all things written concerning the foundation of my church, my gospel, and my rock.

Here the reference to what Cowdery had written is to the Book of Mormon. When Joseph Smith urges reliance on "the things that are written" it means the Book of Mormon. Cowdery and, by implication, all Mormons were not to rely on their own ideas or concepts. The written word was also stressed later on 7 June 1831, through a revelation to Smith at Kirtland, Ohio. Certain people—Joseph Smith, Sidney Rigdon, John Corrill, John Murdock, Hyrum Smith, Jr.—are to journey "preaching the word by the way, saying none other things than that which the prophets and apostles have written and that which is taught them by the Comforter through the power of prayer" (*D&C* 52.9; cf. 52.36). They are to go two by two (cf. *D&C* 52.10) presumably so that individual utterances—among other things—might be "checked." One test for prayer, speech, and humility is given in *D&C* 52.15–18— obedience to the ordinances (cf. *D&C* 6.9). Another test of the spirit is understanding (*D&C* 50.12–24), and further, the Spirit of Truth witnesses to itself; it is received by the Spirit of Truth in the hearer (*D&C* 50.14–19; cf. 50.31). The operative verses are:

> Therefore, why is it that ye cannot understand and know, that he that receiveth the word by the Spirit of truth receiveth it as it is preached by the Spirit of truth? Wherefore, he that preacheth and he that receiveth, understand one another, and both are edified and rejoice together. And that which doth not edify is not of God, and is darkness. That which is of God is light; and he that receiveth light, and continueth in God, receiveth more light; and that light groweth brighter and brighter until the perfect day. (*D&C* 50.21–24)

In the passages cited, the discussion of how words uttered in the present could be taken for scripture applied to missionaries in the early days of the Church (though there is no indication that these words were therefore to be written down, so that the term "scripture" is ambiguous). Later the same privilege was extended to other utterances which were not strictly missionary. Persons of the First Presidency and the Quorum of the Twelve were commissioned with a special calling and gift. These—prophets, seers, and revelators—had a special spiritual endowment in connection with their teaching of the people. Subject to the authority of the President of the Church, this group had the "right, power and authority" to declare the mind and will of God to his people. Only to this group is this special gift given. Over and above them stands the President of the Church, who has a further, special endowment. He is The Prophet, The Seer, The Revelator. He alone has the right to receive revelations for the people either new or "corrective" of previous revelations. He alone can give authoritative interpretations of scriptures that are binding on the Church. He alone can change the doctrines of the Church. He alone is the mouthpiece of God to his people in the sense that he alone can declare to and for the entire Church the mind and will of God. Anyone seeking to act in any such matters, unless authorized by the President to do so, can be known to be out of order and not to have been moved by the Holy Ghost. See D&C 20.1–4 for the commissioning of Joseph Smith and Oliver Cowdery as first and second elders of the Mormon Church; 20.9–12 for the inspiration and confirmation of the translation of the Book of Mormon by men and angels "proving to the world that the holy scriptures [here the Bible and Book of Mormon are meant] are true and that God does inspire men and call them to his holy work in this age and generation, as well as in the generations of old, thereby showing that he is the same God yesterday, today and forever, amen" (D&C 20.11).[21] However, the elevation of the President[22] did not make it impossible for him on rare occasions to teach and preach when he had not been "moved upon by the Holy Ghost" (HC 5.265). Asked if a prophet was always a prophet, Smith quickly affirmed that "a prophet was a prophet only when he acted as such" (see HC 5.265; 2.302).

The processes whereby the added scriptures of Mormonism came into being we can only touch upon. There have been various approaches to the experience of Joseph Smith which led to the Book of Mormon. Abnormal psychology and sociological pressures have been appealed to for explanation. As we noted earlier, for our present purposes such attempts are not important because, however explained, believing Mormons took the experience of Joseph Smith as valid communications from God: they were of divine origin. But this did not preclude much consideration of the style and structure of the messages of Smith.

Particular emphasis was placed on the First Vision to Smith. In Moses 1.9–10 (given years after Smith's first theophany), Smith recounts the experience of Moses on Mt. Sinai. After his experience of being in the presence of God, and after that presence had been

---

[21] For the kerygma, see D&C 20.21ff; 107.7, esp. 107.18, 64–67, 91–92 (the comparison with Moses); 115:19 (on loyalty to the President 117.13); 124.125 (but see also 124.126).

[22] On which see D&C 90.1–4; 107.8, 64–67, 91–92; 124.123; HC 11.477; 6.363.

withdrawn from him, "as he was left to himself, [Moses] fell to the earth. And it came to pass that it was for the space of many hours before Moses did again receive his natural strength like unto man; and he said unto himself: 'Now, for this cause I know that man is nothing, which thing I had never supposed.'" It is sometimes said that Smith seems to have reenacted this experience in his own first and later visions. After the third visit of "the personage," from beyond at his bedside, the "heavenly messenger" who revealed to him the location of the plates from which the Book of Mormon was to emerge in translation, he writes that "I found my strength so exhausted as to render me entirely unable. . . . I fell helpless to the ground, and for a time was quite unconscious of any thing."[23] But caution is necessary. There is no direct parallel with the biblical account of Moses' experience on Sinai. There is in the *Origin of the Book of Mormon* no reference to Moses falling to the ground. On the contrary, it is the exultation of Moses in the presence of the Lord that is emphasized: his face shone. On the other hand, in Exodus Moses cannot be allowed to see the "fullness of the glory" of God. But there is no such restraint in the account Smith gives of the visit of Moroni. Smith's fear soon left him after Moroni first came but there is little of the Promethean character of the biblical Moses in the Smith of this vision. More similar to that of Smith is the outcome of the revelation recorded in Daniel 8. This ends in 8:26–27 as follows: "And the vision of the evening and the morning which was told is true; wherefore shut thou up the vision; for it shall be for many days. And I Daniel fainted, and was sick certain days; afterward I rose up, and did the king's business" (*KJV*). Paul's vision near Damascus was more violent than that of Smith. According to Acts 9:3f., Paul fell to the ground, was blinded by the light of the vision for three days during which he took no food or drink (cf. Acts 22:6–11). Reference is sometimes made to parallels with the account of the Transfiguration (Mark 9:2ff. and parallels). But the only common element is the reference to the light on Jesus' face. The references to the fear of the disciples, and to their falling on their faces are not parallel to anything in the *Origin.* One might conclude that the account of Smith's vision owes little to the biblical tradition except for the use of certain forms that have become traditional in the descriptions of visions.[24] For the conventional visionary language, the reader is

---

[23] Preface to the Book of Mormon, *Origin of the Book of Mormon*, unpaginated.

[24] Richard L. Bushman, in his *Joseph Smith and the Beginnings of Mormonism* (Urbana: University of Illinois Press, 1984) chap. 1, shows that the first visions were part of Joseph Smith's familial and environmental setting.

referred to a rich discussion of the parallels between the accounts of Paul's conversion and materials in the Pseudepigrapha and the OT.[25] The account of Smith's vision is more extensive than those of the Bible and possibly the Pseudepigrapha, but the same phenomena emerge in Mormon visions or revelation as in the biblical and pseudepigraphic documents, for example, voices (*Enoch* 5.10; *D&C* 88.1; 76.1–66). The Spirit, unless by implication only, is surprisingly absent from the first vision; but note references to the Spirit in *D&C* 8.1. In this passage the revelation is connected with understanding and meditation as well as with the Spirit. In *D&C* 8.2–3 the mind and the heart are the media, through the Holy Ghost, of revelation or the spirit of revelation (cf. *D&C* 110.1–4). One manner of revelation as experienced by Smith is described by Parley Parker Pratt.[26]

The belief that there are books in heaven which record (1) registers of actual Israelite citizens with a right to temporal blessedness and also (in Dan 12:1) to an immortality of blessedness, and (2) the record of good and evil deeds, emerges clearly in the OT and the Pseudepigrapha and in later rabbinic sources. These documents also contain the notion of heavenly tablets containing God's plans (laws?), for example, Exod 25:9, 40; Dan 10:21 ("what is written in the Book of Truth"). Here the context refers to "future events which have already happened." The convention of heavenly tablets presenting divine mysteries is, then, an ancient and well established one. It was revitalized powerfully by Joseph Smith. The currents by which the convention had reached him, apart from the OT and the Pseudepigrapha, we probably cannot trace. It may be significant that the first translation of *1 Enoch* from the Ethiopic was published in 1821, just before the rise of Joseph Smith to prominence, and that references to heavenly tablets in that work may have contributed to the form that Joseph Smith's vision assumed. Another pseudepigraphic work, *The Book of Abraham*, which became part of the Mormon Canon, is declared to have been translated by Joseph Smith from "some ancient Records that have fallen into our hands from the catacombs of Egypt" (*HC* 2.235–351).[27]

---

[25] See Johannes Munck, *Paul and the Salvation of Mankind* (trans. Frank Clarke; London: SCM, 1959) chap. 1.

[26] See the Appendix at the end of this article.

[27] Is it without significance that William Blake, the great visionary, died in 1827, and that the decade in which Joseph Smith saw visions saw also the appearance of some of Blake's work of vision and of the reinterpretation and correction of the Christian tradition? As far as I am aware, this question has not been posed. Did the *Zeitgeist* favor visions?

The Mormon Canon, then, is made up of biblical and nonbiblical documents and of utterances recognized as under the influence of the Spirit. What is the relative weight attached to these various components of the Canon? The answer has been clearly given. As we have seen, appeal to the writings in the detection of the presence of the Spirit in given utterances is emphasized. But the Presidents of the Mormon Church have made it clear that primacy is to be given not to the written words from the past, however sacred, but to the living word of God. The following quotation from Wilford Woodruff needs no comment:

> I will refer to a certain meeting I attended in the town of Kirtland in my early days. At that meeting some remarks were made that have been made here today, with regard to the written word of God. The same principle was presented, although not as extensively as it has been here, when a leading man in the church got up and talked upon the subject, and said: "You have got the word of God before you here in the Bible, Book of Mormon, and Doctrine and Covenants; you have the written word of God, and you who give revelations should give revelations according to those books, as what is written in those books is the word of God. We should confine ourselves to them." When he concluded, Brother Joseph turned to Brother Brigham Young and said, "Brother Brigham I want you to take the stand and tell us your views with regard to the written oracles and the written word of God." Brother Brigham took the stand, and he took the Bible, and laid it down; he took the Book of Mormon, and laid it down; and he took the Book of Doctrine and Covenants, and laid it down before him, and he said: "There is the written word of God to us, concerning the work of God from the beginning of the world, almost, to our day." "And now," said he, "when compared with the living oracles those books are nothing to me; those books do not convey the word of God direct to us now, as do the words of a Prophet or a man bearing the Holy Priesthood in our day and generation. *I would rather have the living oracles than all the writing in the books.*" That was the course he pursued. When he was through, Brother Joseph said to the congregation, "*Brother Brigham has told you the word of the Lord, and he has told you the truth.*" . . . The Bible is all right, the Book of Mormon is all right, the Doctrine and Covenants is all right, and they proclaim the work of God and the word of God in the earth in this day and generation until the coming of the Son of Man; but the Holy Priesthood is not confined particularly to those books, that is, it did not cease when those books were made.[28]

---

[28] Wilford Woodruff, *Conference Report* (October 1897) 22–23.

In a Conference Report for April 1955, Marion G. Romney states: "There are other prophets who will talk to you during this conference. . . . [They] are prophets as much as any men who ever lived upon the earth have been prophets. I plead with you to hear their voices. . . . These men will preach and teach the gospel of Jesus Christ as he himself defined it." The implication is that the written canon can be subordinated to the present experience of being "moved upon by the Holy Ghost." Harold B. Lee, eleventh President of the Church, states the position without ambiguity and deserves quotation.

> Sometimes we get the notion that if it is written in a book, it makes it more true than if it is spoken in the last general conference. Just because it is written in a book does not make it more of an authority to guide us. President John Taylor goes on with this same idea and explains why *the scriptures of the past are not sufficient for us today*:
> "The Bible is good; and Paul told Timothy to study it, that he might be a workman that need not be ashamed, and that he might be able to conduct himself aright before the living church [there is that word "living" again], the pillar and ground of truth. The church-mark, with Paul, was the foundation, the pillar, the ground of truth, the living church, not the dead letter. The Book of Mormon is good, and the Doctrine and Covenants, as land-marks. But a mariner who launches into the ocean requires a more certain criterion. He must be acquainted with heavenly bodies, and take his observations from them, in order to steer his barque aright. Those books are good for example, precedent, and investigation, and for developing certain laws and principles. But they do not, they cannot, touch every case required to be adjudicated and set in order.
> "We require a living tree—a living fountain—living intelligence, proceeding from the living priesthood in heaven, through the living priesthood on earth. . . . And from the time that Adam first received a communication from God, to the time that John, on the Isle of Patmos, received his communication, or Joseph Smith had the heavens opened to him, it always required new revelations, adapted to the peculiar circumstances in which the churches of individuals were placed. Adam's revelation did not instruct Noah to build his ark; nor did Noah's revelation tell Lot to forsake Sodom; nor did either of these speak of the departure of the children of Israel from Egypt. These all had revelations for themselves, and so had Isaiah, Jeremiah, Ezekiel, Jesus, Peter, Paul, John, and Joseph. *And so must we, or we shall make a shipwreck*".[29]

---

[29] Harold B. Lee, *Stand Ye in Holy Places* (Salt Lake City: Deseret, 1974) 34. Italics added.

I do not know a stronger statement, and I have gone back enough generations to quote a prophet. I might have said the same thing myself in the same language, and you, because you have more faith and are better grounded in believing in a living oracle today, perhaps, would have believed. But I have gone back enough generations to President Taylor so that probably it has more "epical" authority than if I had said it in my own language today. But you see the point that he makes.[30]

The Mormons' need for living adaptability and flexibility in the present created a need for present revelation and ensured the priority of living prophets as they are "moved by the Spirit" even over the written scriptures.

This leads to the question of how the emergence and development of the Mormon Canon compares and contrasts with the process of canonization in early Christianity. Certain contrasts leap to the mind.

First, then, the Mormon Canon is far larger than the traditional Christian one. Apart from the OT and NT, the Mormons have canonized the Book of Mormon (522 pages), the Doctrine and Covenants (270 pages), and the *Pearl of Great Price* (60 pages), a massive amount of materials—not as large as the Bible but of considerable size. This volume itself is certainly far larger than the NT—the traditional specifically Christian part of the Canon. Certain factors may account for this. The initial experience of Joseph Smith, which gave birth to Mormonism, was in the form of a revelation of *documents* to be translated. This committed Mormonism from the beginning to a substantive addition to the traditional Canon. The Book of Mormon became a basic document of Mormonism far more immediately than did the NT to the early church. Similarly, the form of Joseph Smith's experience of successive revelations demanded their preservation in writing, as did the form of the revelations given to subsequent Presidents of the Mormon Church. Eventually these also had to be recorded in written form because most of them were originally spoken. Contrast with all this the simple fact that Jesus never wrote anything. (He is simply recorded to have written on the sands once, John 9:6–8.)

[30] Idem, "The Place of the Living Prophet, Seer, and Revelator" (Address to Seminaries and Institutes of Religion Faculty, Brigham Young University, 8 July 1964) 9.

[31] T. G. Madsen explains: "Catholicism distinguishes biblical theology from sacred tradition. Since the Vatican Council, both are regarded as 'historically conditioned.' For the Mormons the living word of the living leadership may *become* sacred tradition. But it only becomes *canon* by the double process of prophetic presentation and common consent."

No known document of revealed truths and histories and command-ments came from His hands. Moreover, apart from the Book of Reve-lation (1:10, 19), no document in the NT claims to have been written at the direct command or dictation of the Deity. In this sense Mor-monism is a far more "bookish" movement than other movements in Christianity from the beginning. That is of its essence.

This "bookishness" in itself gave an impetus to a rather speedy development of a canon in Mormonism. The canon begins to be defined in the very earliest stages of the history of the movement. With this speed went a certain readiness to add to the canon with con-siderable flexibility and a readiness to subordinate past "canonical" documents to the present experience of revelation under the Spirit. Contrast again the slow and chequered fixation of the canon of the NT. It was not finally fixed until the end of the fourth century. Moreover, although the Church Fathers had pondered and elaborated on the faith, their important letters and utterances did not achieve canonization. The need for restraint in the early church governed the limitation of the canon, whereas the need for flexibility in Mormonism led to its expansion comparatively more freely and more rapidly. There is here a paradox. The early church, beginning without a revealed book (apart from the OT), only gradually sought a book, the NT, to be its "rule" or "canon." The Mormon Church, on the other hand, beginning with the Bible and a complete revealed book, comparatively quickly added many more "revelations."[32] Is there an explanation for this? Perhaps it lies in the attitude of the early church and of Mormonism to the tra-ditions within which they respectively emerged. One suggestion is that the criticism of Mormonism by the major churches of Christendom—Protestant and Roman Catholic—with whom the Mormons had to react was initially far more violent than was the criticism of the early Chris-tian movement by Judaism. The need for self-definition and,

---

[32] In the NT women are among the witnesses to the significance of the birth of Jesus and to the empty tomb (Mark 16:1f.; Luke 23:55–24:1–11, 22; Matt 28:1–10; John 20:1–10). In John 20:11–18 a woman, Mary Magdalene, sees the risen Jesus. At first sight, such a role for women does not appear in the accounts of the revelations to Joseph Smith in the Mormon tradition, i.e., they are not presented as witnesses. But T. G. Mad-sen insists that Mormon women (e.g., Joseph's wife Emma) were witnesses to many of the origin-events of the Church and were immediately given voting or "sustaining" rights with the men in all matters of church leadership. A woman, Sister Mary Whitmer, was privileged to see the plates of the Book of Mormon. See *LDS Biographical Encyclo-pedia*, compiled by Andrew Jenson (Salt Lake City: Deseret, 1901) 1. 283. And women were made joint heirs with men to all the blessings of the gospel including the higher blessings of the temple.

therefore, for the canonization of certain texts, was more immediately felt by Mormons than by early Christians. It should not be overlooked that early Christians lived in a milieu and at a time before the appearance of "cheap" printing, while the nineteenth century in the United States was a period when religious tracts of all kinds were abundant, so that the publishing of and concentration on religious documents was not only easier but more usual and expected than in the first and subsequent centuries during which the NT came to be fixed.[33]

Secondly, we offer a general reflection, prompted by the history of the Samaritans. The Samaritans chose to accept only the five books of Moses (that is, the Pentateuch) as their canon, excluding all else. But the Samaritans exercised little if any influence upon either Judaism or the pagan world around them. Unlike the early church, which did wrestle with the question of adding new documents to the OT, and spread into the Gentile world, the Samaritans remained in the small region of Palestine and gradually became more and more numerically diminished. Is there, one may ask, a correlation between the smallness of the Samaritans' canon and their very limited influence? The Mormons, by way of contrast, have today dispersed to traverse the entire world. Is their canon, ever augmented, a sign or a symbol of the vitality and inclusiveness of their faith? What began as a small American sect has become worldwide in its range and influence.

Thirdly, it is necessary to state that the Mormon view that the OT has been corrupted has its parallel among certain Jewish Christians of the first centuries of the Christian era.[34] Schoeps has maintained that certain Jewish Christian sects claimed that ideas in the primitive Jewish tradition concerning the Temple, sacrifice, and the cult had been changed when the Bible was assembled. On this point the Mormons—perhaps without being aware of it—revert to a Jewish criticism of the OT left behind and neglected by the Christian tradition. It should be emphasized, therefore, that the notion that the Bible is corrupted is not peculiar to Mormons.

[33] On the fixation of a canon as a function of self-definition, see James A. Sanders, *Torah and Canon* (Philadelphia: Fortress, 1972). Most important for the extent to which the Jewish group could go in changing the Torah is p. 90.

[34] See Hans Joachim Schoeps, *Theologie und Geschichte des Judenchristentums* (Tübingen: Mohr-Siebeck, 1949) 148–87. Particularly important is now the (unassessed) approach of Ben Zion Wacholder (*The Dawn of Qumran: The Sectarian Torah and the Teacher of Righteousness* [Cincinnati, Hebrew Union College Press, 1983]) to the attitude of the sectarians to the written Torah.

Fourthly, Mormon utilization of nonbiblical documents is not unique. We have stated that for the Mormons the extrabiblical tradition has become as important as the biblical writings. *Mutatis mutandis,* one finds a similar development in rabbinic Judaism, for which the oral tradition—*torah shebe'al peh*—has sometimes been even more important than the OT.[35] Without overstatement, one may claim that for rabbinic Judaism the oral tradition preserved in the Mishnah, and developed later in the Talmud and elsewhere, has become the rule of life for religious Jews. The relation between the Mishnah and the OT is one of the most difficult questions in Judaism. There are knowledgeable Jews who emphasize that the oral law developed independently of the OT. See, for example, the work of Ellis Rivkin who writes: "The Mishnah when set alongside the Pentateuch starkly reveals not a logical progression, but a quantum jump. *By any measure the Mishnah is incongruent with the Pentateuch.*"[36] In Rivkin's view there are between the Mishnaic system and the Pentateuch profound discontinuities that are the result of a Pharisaic revolution. At this point the Mormons are like the rabbinic Jews: in a veritable revolution—like that of the Pharisees—they elevate their own tradition above the Christian and Jewish canons. Although that tradition is plastic, as is the rabbinic, it is arguable that the links between the OT and the *Doctrine and Covenants* with *The Pearl of Great Price* of the Mormons are perhaps better preserved than the links between the Tanakh and the Mishnah.

However, as we saw, the new revelations received by the Mormons were written down immediately. The Rabbis, on the contrary, chose very deliberately not to write down the oral law until the second century CE. Perhaps the reason why the Mormons wrote the revelations and commandments of Joseph Smith immediately was simple. For them it was not necessary to establish their oral tradition against the Pentateuch through a long period, as it was for the Jews, because in Christianity the OT had already been subordinated to the NT. It was against the Christian churches of their time, not against the scriptures, that the Mormons sought to establish their identity. To do this they needed to compose new scriptures.

But, finally, one may ask whether one may truly use the word "canon" to describe all the scriptures that the Mormons have accepted as revelation and the future scriptures which they are likely, on their

---

[35] On this see W. D. Davies, *Jewish and Pauline Studies* (Philadelphia: Fortress, 1984) 14, where I cite *m. Sanh.* 11.3.

[36] Ellis Rivkin, *The Hidden Revolution* (Nashville: Abingdon, 1978) 223. Italics added. Davies, *Jewish and Pauline Studies,* 10–14.

theological premises, to adopt as such. The word "canon" implies that there is a list of books, fixed or set in order and authorized, and accepted by a religious community as the norm for its own understanding of itself. For such a community the truth has already been given in the selected scriptures. Revelations received after a canon has been fixed served simply to explicate the same canon: they are in accord with that canon, not revolutionary or independently revelatory. For Saint Paul, for example, the Gospel had been given "according to the scriptures," that is, according to the canon of Judaism. Subsequently in Protestantism and Catholicism and Orthodoxy every interpretation of the Gospel is understood to be according to the scriptures (*kata tas graphas*). Paul's own letters could eventually become canonical because they, too, were understood not to contradict the scriptures. But for the Mormons the scriptures of the Bible are apparently subordinated to the revelations given to Joseph Smith and to the succeeding Presidents of the Church.[37]

It agrees with this that in their theological writings, the Mormons seldom speak of their "canon" but of what they call "the Standard Works of the Church."[38] In the indices to their work one does not often find the word canon. One may translate the phrase "standard works" by "classical writings" or by "definitive works." In a dictionary of the Bible,[39] published by the Mormons in 1979, there is a treatment of the word "canon," but even that account emphasizes the notion of a progressive revelation.[40] That notion is in tension with the definition of a canon in the strict sense. This is why Mormonism must be represented as a radical movement, despite its continuity within

[37] This notion is not to be confused with that of the apostolic succession in Roman Catholicism. That doctrine is primarily concerned with the preservation of the continuity of the tradition, whereas the Presidents in Mormonism are not only agents of continuity but more perhaps of newness of revelation.

[38] Talmage, *Articles of Faith*, 7.

[39] "Bible Dictionary in *The Holy Bible*, authorized *KJV* with explanatory notes and cross references to the standard works of the Church" (Salt Lake City: The Church of Jesus Christ of Latter-day Saints, 1979) 519–792.

[40] T. G. Madsen comments on this as follows: "Mormons are often characterized as Biblical literalists and even as verbal infallibilists. Both characterizations are misleading. The initial Mormon acknowledgment of translational and transmissional error has already been noted. In addition, writers within the standard works themselves, including the Book of Mormon, speak of the faults and the mistakes of men." Stendahl observes that to say this of and in a sacred book strengthens rather than weakens respect ("The Sermon on the Mount and Third Nephi in the Book of Mormon," *Meanings*, 101). Joseph Smith himself made clarifying revisions in most of the documents he himself wrote or translated.

Judaism and Catholicism. The issue raised by the attitude of Mormons to their "canon" is fundamentally this: at what point does the notion of progressive or continuous revelation, as they understand it, fall outside "the limits of tolerance" of those churches that submit themselves to the traditional canon—Protestant, Roman Catholic, or Orthodox? Mormons have raised acutely the question of the nature of revelation within the Jewish and Christian traditions: is "Revelation" to be controlled by a fixed canon or is it open to development and even revision in terms of subsequent "revelations"? Progressive and continuous revelation is certainly an attractive notion, but equally certainly it is not without the grave danger of so altering or enlarging upon the original revelation as to distort, annul, and even falsify it. This is the fundamental question which all the more traditional Christian communions and—indeed, the NT itself—pose to Mormonism.[41]

It has been one of the great privileges of my life to have had Krister Stendahl as φίλος and συνεργός, especially in Matthean, Pauline, and Jewish studies. For all that he and Brita (for we join her name inseparably with his) have been across the years, and continue to be, we salute them with gratitude, admiration, and affection.

Appendix

Elder Parley P. Pratt (speaking of the revelation, now printed as Section 50 of the *Doctrine and Covenants*, given in May 1831) describes how the Prophet worked when receiving revelations. He says:

> After we had joined in prayer in his translating room, he dictated in our presence the following revelation:—(Each sentence was uttered slowly and very distinctly, and with a pause between each,

[41] Another question faces Mormonism more acutely than other Christian communions. The tradition of connecting revelation with divinely commissioned and divinely inspired and even written stones or documents has been questioned radically in recent discussion. The revelation to Moses as recorded in the OT can hardly be taken literally as an event in which the Divine handed over or dictated to Moses Ten Commandments written on stone. Aetiological and liturgical elements are now recognized to have entered into the presentation of what happened. The account of the giving of the Torah *witnesses* to the revelation of God on Sinai in the experience of Israel but is not to be taken literally. However, Mormonism demands that the account of the announcement and discovery of the Book of Mormon by Joseph Smith be taken factually and literally, not merely as an attempt, necessarily inadequate, to witness to a revelation. It must be asked whether in Mormonism conventional modes of describing revelation found in the OT and the Pseudepigrapha have been so literally taken over as fact as to give a facticity to what was intended as symbolic. As noted, other communions face this difficulty, but it is peculiarly contemporary and acute in Mormonism.

sufficiently long for it to be recorded, by an ordinary writer, in long hand).

This was the manner in which all his written revelations were dictated and written. There was never any hesitation, reviewing, or reading back, in order to keep the run of the subject; neither did any of these communications undergo revisions, interlinings, or corrections. As he dictated them so they stood, so far as I have witnessed; and I was present to witness the dictation of several communications of several pages each. . . .)[42]

It seems clear that on this occasion there was no audible voice, though the opening sentence of the revelation reads: "Hearken unto me, saith the Lord your God." However, President B. H. Roberts points out that when some of the early revelations were published in the Book of Commandments in 1833, they

> were revised by the Prophet himself in the way of correcting errors made by the scribes and publishers; and some additional clauses were inserted to throw increased light upon the subjects treated in the revelations, and to paragraphs added, to make the principles or instructions apply to officers not in the Church at the time some of the earlier revelations were given. The addition of verses 65, 66 and 67 in section xx of the Doctrine and Covenants is an example.[43]

At Montrose, Iowa, in August 1842 (there is some uncertainty as to the exact date), the Prophet, attending a Masonic ceremony, prophesied that the Saints would be driven to the Rocky Mountains and declared events incident to the move. Brother Call describes this scene as quoted in his biography by Tullidge, as follows:

> Joseph, as he was tasting the cold water, warned the brethren not to be too free with it. With the tumbler still in his hand he prophesied that the Saints would yet go to the Rocky Mountains; and, said he, this water tastes much like that of the crystal streams that are running from the snow-capped mountains. We will let Mr. Call describe this prophet scene: "I had before seen him in a vision, and now saw while he was talking his countenance change to white; not the deadly white of a bloodless face, but a living brilliant white. He seemed absorbed in gazing at something at a great distance, and

---

[42] Parley P. Pratt (fils), ed., *Autobiography of Parley Parker Pratt* (Salt Lake City: Deseret, 1938) 62.

[43] *HC* 1.173, n.

said: 'I am gazing upon the valleys of those mountains.' This was followed by a vivid description of the scenery of these mountains, as I have since become acquainted with it. Pointing to Shadrach Roundy and others, he said: 'There are some men here who shall do a great work in that land.' Pointing to me, he said, 'There is Anson, he shall go and shall assist in building up cities from one end of the country to the other, and you,' rather extending the idea to all those he had spoken of, 'shall perform as great a work as has been done by man, so that the nations of the earth shall be astonished, and many of them will be gathered in that land and assist in building cities and temples, and Israel shall be made to rejoice.'[44]

"It is impossible to represent in words this scene which is still vivid in my mind, of the grandeur of Joseph's appearance, his beautiful descriptions of this land, and his wonderful prophetic utterances as they emanated from the glorious inspirations that overshadowed him. There was a force and a power in his exclamations of which the following is but a faint echo. 'Oh the beauty of these snow-capped mountains! The cool refreshing streams that are running down through those mountain gorges!' Then gazing in another direction, as if there was a change of locality: 'Oh the scenes that this people will pass through! The dead that will lay between here and there.' Then turning in another direction as if the scene had changed: 'Oh the apostasy that will take place before my brethren reach that land!' 'But,' he continued, 'the priesthood shall prevail over its enemies, triumph over the devil and be established upon the earth, never more to be thrown down!' He then charged us with great force and power, to be faithful to those things that had been and should be committed to our charge, with the promise of all the blessings that the Priesthood could bestow. 'Remember these things and treasure them up. Amen.'"[45]

---

[44] Note here the equation of Mormons with "Israel."

[45] In Tullidge's *Histories*, vol. 2: *History of Northern Utah and Southern Idaho, Biographical Suppplement*, 271ff. *HC* 7.85 n.

MATTHEW 27:51 IN EARLY CHRISTIAN EXEGESIS

M. de Jonge
University of Leiden

General Remarks

This article deals with Matthew's account of the rending of the temple veil. Matt 27:51 will be interpreted in its context: in vss 51–53 the incident is one of several taking place between Jesus' death and the centurion's confession. At the same time the verse under discussion will be considered against the background of the interpretations in early Christian literature which very often take Matt 27:51–53 as a starting point.

The rending of the temple veil has been interpreted in many ways. No consensus as to the meaning of the incident has been reached so far, as is shown, for instance, in recent work on Mark 15:38.[1] One of the interpreters, Paul Lamarche, begins his article[2] by listing no less than six interpretations in ancient and modern authors, and it would be easy to distinguish even more if we take into account a number of nuances and combinations put forward by a number of individual authors. Yet it would seem that a number of approaches which have been popular until the present day will not lead to satisfactory results.

First: The Gospel accounts do not seem to be interested in the question as to which of the two curtains of the temple is meant.[3] It is only Hebrews (particularly the reference to the second curtain in 9:3)

---

[1] Cf., e.g., Rudolph Pesch, *Das Markusevangelium* (HTKNT II,2; Freiburg: Herder, 1977) 498–99 (literature, 502–3); Frank J. Matera, *The Kingship of Jesus* (SBLDS 66; Chico: Scholars Press, 1982) 137–40, plus nn. on 197–98 referring to different opinions; Harry L. Chronis, "The Torn Veil: Cultus and Christology in Mark 15:37–39," *JBL* 101 (1982) 97–114.

[2] "La mort du Christ et le voile du temple selon Marc," *NRTh* 106 (1974) 583–99, survey of interpretations, 583–86. See also M. De Jonge, "De berichten over het scheuren van het voorhangsel bij Jezus' dood in de synoptische evangliën," *NedThTs* 21 (1966–67) 90–114.

[3] A hotly debated issue in commentaries. See Matera, *Kingship*, 197 n. 63.

which introduces the distinction between the two; the Gospels do not seem to feel the need to specify. This question should, therefore, not be discussed in the exegesis of the texts in (each of) the Synoptic Gospels. As will be seen presently, the matter was not brought up before Origen, who used it in the context of a very specific theological interpretation.

Second: Scholars have studied the biblical accounts of the tabernacle and the temple of Solomon, and the descriptions of the second temple by Philo and Josephus with a view toward the names, functions, and outward appearance of the curtains.[4] This is of doubtful value because it is not evident that the Gospel writers were aware of these details or expected their readers to understand their reference to the rending of the temple veil in this light.

Third: Scholars who interpret the rending of the temple veil as a sign of the coming destruction of the temple often point to Josephus *Bell.* 6.288–31 which records a number of portents, prophecies, and oracles. One of these has received special attention. At the time of the feast of unleavened bread (§ 290)

> the eastern gate of the inner court . . . was observed at the sixth hour of the night to have opened of its own accord. The watchmen of the temple ran and reported the matter to the captain, and he came up and with difficulty succeeded in shutting it. . . . The learned understood that the security of the temple was dissolving of its own accord and that the opening of the gate meant a present to the enemy, interpreting the portent in their own minds as indicative of coming desolation. (*Bell.* §§ 293–96)[5]

This report has been connected with rabbinic statements in *y. Yoma* 6, 43c; *b. Yoma* 39b[6] about portents occurring forty years before the actual destruction of the temple and with the accounts in the Synoptic Gospels. Some have pointed especially to Jerome's reference to a "Gospel

---

[4] See A. Pelletier, "La tradition synoptique du 'voile déchiré' à la lumière des réalités archéologiques," *RevScRel* 46 (1958) 161–80, one of several articles by him. The latest survey of the material is that by S. Légasse, "Les voiles du temple de Jérusalem: Essai de parcours historique," *RB* 87 (1980) 560–89 (with a survey of recent literature, including the article by Pelletier, 560 n. 2).

[5] LCL, 3. 461–63.

[6] See, e.g., Str-B 1. 1043–46 and 3. 733–36 (a contribution by Heinrich Laible). Very informative is Excursus XIII, "Das Osttor des inneren Tempelbezirkes (6, 293)," in Otto Michel and Otto Bauernfeind, *Flavius Josephus, De Bello Judaico—Der Jüdische Krieg* (Darmstadt: Wissenschaftliche Buchgesellschaft, 1969) 183–84; see also further nn. on 179–92.

in Hebrew characters" which did not report the "rending of the temple veil but the collapse of the astonishingly big lintel of the temple" (non velum templi scissum, sed superliminare templi mirae magnitudinis conruisse).[7] Now Jerome does refer to Josephus's list of portents,[8] but significantly only to the one recorded in *Bell.* 6.300. "Moreover, at the feast which is called Pentecost, the priests on entering the inner court of the temple by night . . . reported that they were conscious, first of a commotion and a din, and after that of a voice as of a host: 'We are departing hence.'"[9] Jerome follows here Eusebius[10] who, as far as I have been able to find, is the first to refer to this particular incident in Josephus's list (and *not* to the one about the doors), in keeping with earlier Christian interpretations of the incident with the temple veil in terms of departure of angels or the Spirit from the temple (to be discussed below).

Matt 27:51 in Its Matthean Context

In Matt 27:51a the rending of the temple veil is described with the words found (in different order) in Mark: the curtain "was torn in two, from top to bottom." The rent is irreparable, definitive.[11] In the preceding vs 50 Matthew uses the expression "he yielded up his spirit," suggesting that Jesus gave it up voluntarily (cf. Luke 23:46 and John 19:30; 10:17–18). The connection between vss 50 and 51 is closer than between the corresponding vss in Mark; the καὶ ἰδού

---

[7] *Ep.* 120.8 *ad Hedybiam* (ed. Isidorus Hilberg; CSEL 55, 1912); cf. Jerome *Comm. in Matt.* on 27:51 (SC 259): "The infinitely big lintel was broken and divided" (superliminare templi infinitae magnitudinis fractum esse atque divisum). See also section 3 below. Th. Zahn ("Der zerrissene Templevorhang," *NKZ* 13 [1902] 729–56) used these and other data for an ingenious but entirely unacceptable reconstruction of the actual events in order to indicate the historical reliability of the accounts in the Gospels.

[8] Both in his *Ep.* 120.8 and his *Comm. in Matt.* 27:51 (see further 300 n. 100 in the ed. of Bonnard).

[9] Cf. also Tacitus *Historiae* 5.13.

[10] See his *Hist. eccl.* 3.8.1–9; *Dem. ev.* 19; *Ecl. proph.* 3.48; *Comm. in Luc.* (*PG* 24. 605b), etc.

[11] This is emphasized by David Daube, *The New Testament and Rabbinic Judaism* (Jordan Lectures, 1952; London: Athlone, 1956) 23–26. He refers to 2 Kgs 2:12 from which the Rabbis concluded that in certain cases a rent garment may never be repaired. As to the rending of the veil of the temple, Daube remarks: "It is safe to find here an allusion to the rite practised as a sign of deepest sorrow. We need not decide whether the death of Jesus is likened to that of a teacher of Torah or to the destruction of the temple." He also mentions a possibility "that those responsible for the crucifixion are the real blasphemers, and not Jesus at whose words the High Priest had rent his clothes" (24).

suggests that the series of events beginning with the rending of the veil follows immediately upon Jesus' voluntary and obedient death.

The rending of the temple curtain is accompanied by a shaking of the earth and the splitting of the rock (vs 51b). By repeating the ἐσχίσθη of the veil in ἐσχίσθησαν of the rocks Matthew suggests connection and continuity between the various happenings.[12] The splitting of the rocks introduces the opening of the tombs which, in turn, is connected with the resurrection of many of the saints after the resurrection of Jesus himself. This, again, is followed by a reference to their entrance into the holy city and their appearance to many (vss 52–53). Then, finally, the centurion is mentioned. Matthew describes his reaction *and* that of his companions as one of great fear after seeing "the earthquake and what took place." The confession of this group agrees almost verbatim with that found in Mark (vs 54).

Modern interpreters[13] have noted that Matthew—by adding "if you are the Son of God" in vs 40 and the taunt of the chief priests, scribes, and elders: "he trusts in God, let God deliver him now, if he desires him; for he said: I am the Son of God" in vs 43 (cf. Ps 22:9; Wis 2:13, 18–20)—his readers of the temptation story (4:1–11) and accentuates the opposition between the reaction of the Jewish authorities and that of the centurion and his men. The former ask for definite proof of Jesus' identity and challenge him to show that God is on his side. Humankind does not receive any sign until immediately after Jesus' death. The reaction of the centurion and his men is one of awe in the presence of God appearing and acting on earth (note the *passiva divina!*) and they rightly confess the crucified Jesus as the Son of God.

Reinhard Kratz, following earlier interpreters, compares the events recorded in vss 51–54 with *prodigia* occurring at the death of famous persons and with descriptions of the theophanies in the Old Testament and later Jewish literature. He particularly points to Psalm 18 which mentions a cry for help (vs 7), a theophany (vss 8–16) leading to the deliverance of the one who prays (vss 17–20), a man living in perfect

---

[12] See Pelletier, "La tradition synoptique," 174.

[13] See Reinhard Kratz, *Auferweckung als Befreiung: Eine Studie zur Passions- und Auferstehungstheologie des Matthäus (besonders Mt 27,62–28, 15)* (SBS 65; Stuttgart: KBW, 1973) esp. 38–47; and idem, σεισμός, *EWNT* 3 (1983) 563–66; Donald Senior, "The Death of Jesus and the Resurrection of the Holy Ones (Mt 27:51–53)," *CBQ* 38 (1976) 312–29; Wolfgang Schenk, *Der Passionsbericht nach Markus* (Gütersloh: Mohn, 1974) 74–82; Maria Riebl, *Auferstehung Jesu in der Stunde seines Todes? Zur Botschaft von Mt 27,51b–53* (SBB 8; Stuttgart: KBW, 1978).

obedience to the Lord (vss 21–25).[14] Donald Senior stresses the influence of Ezek 37:1–14 (earthquake, vs 7; the opening of the graves, vs 12; the reference to resurrection, vs 12; cf. vs 13; entrance of the saints into the holy city / the land of Israel, vs 12). "The vivid orchestration of most of these elements (i.e., those found in Matt 27:51b–53) in Ezekiel 37 and the use of this text in intertestamental Judaism as an expression of messianic hope make it probable that Matthew himself drew on this particular tradition for his inspiration."[15] Wolfgang Schenk tries to prove that Matthew took over a Jewish apocalyptic hymn dealing with the resurrection, inspired by Ezekiel 37. Senior has rightly criticized him on this point, but he follows Schenk in assuming apocalyptic elements derived from Ezekiel 37 *and* perhaps from Psalm 22.[16] Maria Riebl also assumes a tradition connecting Jesus' death with Ezek 37:12–14. She thinks that Jesus' death is presented here as the beginning of his resurrection, the proof of his divine power and the decisive new beginning in salvation history.[17] The authors just mentioned unfortunately concentrate completely on Matt 27:51b–54 and seem to regard vs 51a as an element taken over from Mark which is connected with, but need not necessarily fit into, the apocalypticizing description of events which is peculiar to Matthew. Schenk, however, sees vs 51a as a judgment on Israel and its temple (cf. 23:38), which is the counterpart of the salvation described in the following phrases.[18] Senior follows him with some hesitation, but does not really discuss the point;[19] the others do not express an opinion.

---

[14] See also Kratz, *Auferweckung als Befreiung*, 56: "Bei allen besprochenen Stellen, an denen Matthäus den Begriff 'Erdbeben' einführt (8,24; 21,10; 27,51.54) handelt es sich jeweils um die Übertragung eines Theophanie-motivs auf die Person Jesu. Dadurch wird seine göttliche Macht demonstriert und seine wahre Gottessohnschaft erwiesen."

[15] Senior, "Death of Jesus," 320–21. Like others, he points to the parallels between Matt 27:51b–53 and the scene on the Ezekiel panel of the resurrection at the synagogue of Dura Europos; see Harald Riesenfeld, *The Resurrection in Ezekiel XXXVII and the Dura-Europos Paintings* (UUA 11; Uppsala, 1948) 27–38.

[16] "The expansion of 27:51b–53 by means of the Ezekiel tradition and the chorus of faith on the part of the soldiers echo the triumphant conclusion of Ps 22 and even reflect the primitive apocalyptic that seems to emerge in the concluding portion of the Psalm (22:28–32)" (Senior, "Death of Jesus," 324).

[17] Riebl, *Auferstehung Jesu*, 75–77.

[18] Schenk, *Der Passionsbericht*, 80–81. According to him already in a pre-Markan "Sieben-Stunden-Apokalypse" the rending of the temple veil indicated the end of the temple: "Nicht erst die spätere Zerstörung sondern die durch den Todesschrei Jesu erfolgte Profanierung ist als das eigentliche Ende des Tempels anzusehen" (45–48, esp. 47).

[19] Senior, "Death of Jesus," 324 n. 34; cf. 328 and n. 47.

There is, indeed, not much to go on. Twenty years ago[20] I, like Schenk, pointed to Matt 23:37–39 and connected this pericope with the preceding vss 29–36. After the death of Jesus, who is God's most important and final envoy in the long series of divine messengers to Israel, God initiates his judgment starting with the temple.

Related Apocryphal Gospels

We mentioned already the reference to a gospel in Hebrew characters in Jerome's *Comm. in Matt.* 27:51, and his *Ep.* 120.8, which presupposes an earthquake to have caused the breaking of the very big "lintel of the temple." Philipp Vielhauer[21] and Kurt Aland,[22] also mention the medieval *Historia Passionis Domini* (fol. 65^r) which refers to the "evangelium Nazaraeorum," but seems to be dependent on Jerome since it not only mentions the incident with the lintel, but also refers to Josephus *Bell.* 6.300. Scholars have put forward ingenious theories to explain the reading in this gospel as a variant to the Matthew text,[23] but it is not at all sure that Jerome is a reliable witness. In his *Ep.* 18.9 (*ad Damasum*) he comments on Isa 6:4 (LXX, καὶ ἐπήρθη τὸ ὑπέρθυρον); he remarks: "that the lintel was lifted up and the house was filled with smoke, is a sign of the destruction of the Jewish temple and the total conflagration of Jerusalem" (quod autem sublatum est . . . superliminare et domus impleta est fumo, signum est templi Judaici destruendi et incendii universae Hierusalem). According to some this took place "when the veil of the temple was rent and the entire house of Israel was confused by the cloud of error" (quando velum templi scissum est et universa domus Israhel erroris nube confusa). Then, again Jerome refers to Josephus *Bell.* 6.300! Does he refer here, implicitly, to the source mentioned in the two earlier instances? If so, we have yet a different wording of the relevant text. It should also be mentioned that *Ep.* 120.8 says that the gospel referred to did not speak about the curtain but about the lintel, whereas in *Ep.* 18.9 "superliminare" and "velum" are connected. Jerome is not very precise, to say the least.[24] Either Jerome or his source seems to have

---

[20] See de Jonge, "De berichten," 110–11.

[21] "Das Nazaräerevangelium," *NTApoc* 1. 90–100, frg. 36.

[22] *Synopsis Quattuor Evangeliorum* (9th ed.; Stuttgart: Deutsche Bibelstiftung, 1976) 489.

[23] See Walter Bauer, *Das Leben Jesu im Zeitalter der neutestamentlichen Apokryphen* (Tübingen: Mohr, 1909) 230–33.

[24] See also M. de Jonge, "Christelijke elementen in de Vitae Prophetarum," *NedThTs* 16 (1961–62) 161–78, which mentions further details on pp. 172–74 and points to *Vit. Hab.* 12: τότε ἄπλωμα φησι τοῦ Δαβὴρ εἰς μικρὰ ῥαγήσεται, καὶ τὰ ἐπίκρανα τῶν δύο στύλων ἀφαιρεθήσονται (recensio anonyma; Theodor Schermann, ed., *Prophetarum Vitae*

meditated freely on Isa 6:4 (or Amos 9:1?) and introduced an interesting variant in the picture found in the Synoptic Gospels.[25]

Gos. Pet. 19–20 presents us with another problem. Here the rending of the veil in vs 20 is directly connected with Jesus' last words: καὶ ὁ Κύριος ἀνεβόησε λέγων· Ἡ δύναμίς μου, ἡ δύναμις, κατέλειψάς με· καὶ εἰπὼν ἀνελήφθη. Καὶ αὐτῆς ὥρας διερράγη τὸ καταπέτασμα τοῦ ναοῦ τῆς Ἰερουσαλὴμ εἰς δύο (And the Lord cried out: My power, (my) power, have you left me? And after he had said that, he was taken up. And at that moment the veil of the temple was rent in two.")[26] The αὐτῆς ὥρας (MS αὐτοσωρας) has the same function as the καὶ ἰδού in Matthew.[27] What the close relationship between vs 19 and vs 20 implies for the meaning of the latter verse depends on the meaning of the former—which is by no means clear.[28] In the *Gospel of Peter* there are very few other clues. In vs 25, "the Jews and the elders and the priests" regret the evil they have brought upon themselves and declare: "the judgment and the end of Jerusalem have drawn nigh."[29] In vs 26 "Peter" and his friends hide themselves because they fear they will be arrested as evildoers who want to set fire to the temple; finally, in vs 28 we are told that all the people were murmuring and beating their breasts, saying: "If these very great signs have occurred

---

Fabulosae [Leipzig; Teubner, 1907] 87; comparison with the other recensions on pp. 21, 14f.; 33, 11f.; 58, 12f.; 102, 20f). Charles Cutler Torrey, *The Lives of the Prophets* (SBLMS 1; 1946) 44 translates: "Then, he said, the veil of the inner sanctuary will be torn to pieces, and the capitals of the two pillars will be taken away." The preceding verse announces that the end of the temple will be brought about by a western nation.

[25] See also Bauer, *Das Leben Jesu,* 232; and Vielhauer, "Das Nazaräerevangelium," 93: "eine novellistische Weiterbildung."

[26] See M. G. Mara, *Évangile de Pierre* (SC 201; Paris: Cerf, 1973).

[27] The same (or very similar) expression is found in syr[s] and syr[p] on Matt 27:51, the Pal. Syriac lectionary, and a number of gospel harmonies; see W. L. Petersen, *Die Diatessaron and Ephrem Syrus as Sources of Romanos the Methodist* (Diss. Utrecht, 1984) 74–76. Petersen regards it as a "Diatessaronic" reading. See, however, Origen *Comm. in John.* 19.16 mentioned below, n. 46. It seems natural to emphasize the close connection in time between the two events. Here it should be noted that Petersen finds two further Diatessaronic readings in Matt 27:52–53 (pp. 76–91); these two together with the variant just mentioned are regarded as representing an earlier stage of the text than that found in the canonical Matthew.

[28] See, e.g., Léon Vaganay, *L'Évangile de Pierre* (Paris: Gabalda, 1930) 255–59; Mara, *Évangile de Pierre,* 132–41; Jürgen Denker, *Die theologiegeschichtliche Stellung des Petrusevangeliums: Ein Beitrag zur Frühgeschichte des Doketismus* (Europäische Hochschulschriften XXIII, 36; Bern/Frankfurt: Lang, 1975) 73–75, 118–20. Much depends on the meaning of δύναμις and ἀνελήφθη in the context of the christology of this gospel.

[29] Cf. the additions to Luke 23:48 in g[1] and sy[s.c.].

at his death, behold how righteous he is!"[30] Vs 17, καὶ ἐπλήρωσαν πάντα καὶ ἐτελείωσαν κατὰ τῆς κεφαλῆς αὐτῶν τὰ ἁμαρτήματα (and they fulfilled everything and heaped the full measure of their sins upon their heads), suggests that this gospel portrays the rending of the "veil of the temple *of Jerusalem*" as punishment for the sins of the Jewish leaders and announcement of the coming destruction.

Second- and Third-Century Christian Writers on the
Rending of the Temple Veil

The early Christian interpretations of the event under discussion usually show acquaintance with the account in Matthew and treat the rending of the temple veil in the context of the darkening of the sun, the earthquake, and the resurrection of the saints. We find an astonishing variety of points of view.

To mention only one example falling outside the period to be discussed here: Ephraem Syrus, in his *Comm. in Diatess.* 21.4–6, written between 363–73,[31] gives a long list of possible interpretations of the rending of the veil, moving freely from one interpretation to another and without really choosing one of them. No doubt he had found many of these explanations in the works of earlier writers; some of them, however, were surely the outcome of his own meditation on the theme. The very lack of distinctiveness in the biblical accounts (which early Christian authors studied together, and not separately) invited ingenious explications of the supposed implicit message.[32] This also applies to the interpretations found in the works of Christian authors of the second and third centuries. One can distinguish a number of recurring elements—departure of the Spirit (to the Gentiles); indignation and mourning of the temple (together with the rest of God's creation); mourning of an angel living in the temple, and departure of that angel from it; revelation to all new believers (outside Israel) of that which was hidden—but we find many combinations of these elements, and

[30] Cf. Luke 23:47–48.

[31] See Louis Leloir, *Ephrem de Nisibe: Commentaire de l'Évangile concordant ou Diatessaron* (SC 121; Paris: Cerf, 1966) 376–78. On the date of the composition see 25.

[32] On the early Christian material see Martin Werner, *Die Entstehung des christliche Dogmas problemgeschichtlich dargestellt* (Bern/Leipzig: Haupt, 1941) 88–98; Pelletier, "La tradition synoptique"; M. De Jonge, "Het motief van het gescheurde voorhangsel van de tempel in een aantal vroegchristelijke geschriften," *NedThTs* 21 (1966–67) 257–76; Lamarche, "La mort du Christ." See also M. de Jonge, "Two Interesting Interpretations of the Rending of the Temple Veil in the Testaments of the Twelve Patriarchs," *Bijdragen.* For this last article, as for the present one, use could be made of *Biblica Patristica* 1–3 (Paris: CNRS, 1975–80).

there is great variety in detail.

Melito of Sardes in his *In Pascha* 98 contrasts the imperturbability of the people at Jesus' death with the quaking of the earth and the terror of the heavens. He adds, "when the people did not tear their clothes, the angel tore his." [33] In New frg. 2.11, preserved in Georgian, we read: "the angels, horrified, quit the temple. ... the veil was torn," but M. Richard found a corresponding Greek text reading ἄγγελος ἐξήλατο τεταραγμένος τοῦ ναοῦ, περιεσχισμένου τοῦ καταπετάσματος τοῦ οἴκου, σκότος ἐπλήρωσε τὴν γῆν ("an angel jumped out of the temple, terrified, after the veil of the house had been rent [as a garment]; darkness covered the earth"). [34] Melito clearly refers to Matthew, including vss 52–53, which he interprets as a descent to Hades (*In Pascha* 101–2; New Frg. 2.12). We also find this descent followed by an ascent in *T. Benj.* 9 where, however, the rending of the temple veil is a sign of the departure of the Spirit of God to the Gentiles. [35] When the descent to Hades is referred to in *Sib. Or.* 8.305–11 the rending of the temple veil is connected with this revelation: "For no longer with secret law and temple must one serve the phantoms of the world. That which had been hidden was again made manifest when the eternal sovereign came down to the earth." [36]

---

[33] Stuart George Hall, *Melito of Sardes on the Pascha and Fragments* (Oxford: Clarendon, 1979) 54–55. Some MSS have here the plural "angels" (cf. New frg. 2.11). One should compare here Daube's article mentioned in n. 11 (which only refers to *Ps. Clem. Recog.* 1.14.3 listed below).

[34] Hall, *Melito of Sardes*, 90. The Greek is based on Ps.-Chrysostom *In ascensionem hom.* 3 (*PG* 52, 797). For details see Hall, *Melito of Sardes*, 90 n. 27 and pp. xxxx and l. The plural "angels" is in keeping with the exegesis of Eusebius and others who refer to Josephus *Bell.* 6.300 (see above) and, therefore, *lectio facilior.*

[35] For details see de Jonge, "Two Interesting Interpretations," section 2.1. There also *T. Levi* 4.1 is mentioned, a description of God's final judgment containing a number of reminiscences of Matt 27:45, 51–53. Kratz mentions it (*Auferweckung als Befreiung*, 43) as a pre-Christian text in his section "Erdbeben als Theophaniemotiv." The expression σκυλεύειν τὸν ᾄδην which occurs here is a typical Christian expression; see the examples mentioned in Harm W. Hollander and M. de Jonge, *The Testaments of the Twelve Patriarchs: A Commentary* (SVTP; Leiden: Brill, 1985) on this verse. To these may be added the description found in Jacques Liebaert, *Deux Homélies Anoméenes pour l'Octave de Paques* (SC 146; Paris: Cerf, 1969) 1. 27 (... ἐταφή καὶ τὸν ᾄδην ἐσκύλευσεν ...).

[36] So the translation by J. J. Collins in James H. Charlesworth, ed., *The Old Testament Pseudepigrapha* (Garden City: Doubleday, 1983) 425. This passage is quoted by Lactantius *Div. Inst.* 4.19.5 but without an interpretation of the rending of the veil; in the introduction to the quotation he writes, however, "and the temple veil that separated the two tents was rent in two pieces" (et velum templi quod separabat duo tabernacula scissum est in duas partes" (ed. Samuel Brandt; CSEL 19, 1890). Cf. also *Sib. Or.* 1. 372–79 which speaks about a great sign effected by the temple of Solomon.

Tertullian, in *Adv. Marc.* 4.42, speaks about the breaking out of the angel, who deserted the daughter of Sion, but in *Adv. Iud.* 13.15, commenting on Matt 27:51–53, he remarks that the Holy Spirit does not dwell in the synagogue of the Gentiles "as he dwelt in the temple, in the past, before the advent of Christ who is the true temple of God" (ut in praeteritum in templo commorabatur ante adventum Christi qui est veri dei templum).[37] In the Syriac *Did. Apost.* 23, God is said to have abandoned the Jewish people and to have deserted the temple. "And He rent the curtain and took away from it the Holy Spirit, and poured Him upon those who believed."[38] In the third-century Ps.-Cyprian *Adv. Iud.* 4, the immobility of the people is, again, contrasted with the commotion of the entire creation; the author adds "The angel fled in shame after having torn the veil, the people remained standing, their clothes undamaged, without trembling" (Angelus in paenitentiam conscisso velamine refugit, plebs sine pavore integra veste permansit).[39]

Other texts do not speak of an act of the Spirit or the angel of the temple, but see the rending of the veil as an act of the temple itself. In *Ps. Clem. Recog.* 1.41.3[40] we find another description of the cosmic commotion at Jesus' death following Matt 27:51–53, in which we read, "The veil of the temple was rent, as if lamenting the imminent end of the place" ("Velum templi scissum est, velut lamentans excidium loco imminens." Ps(?)-Hippolytus *In Pascha* 55.2, describing this commotion as a sign that the elements recognize the man on the cross, introduces the veil as "suffering with (Christ) and indicating the true heavenly high priest" (συμπάσχον καὶ μηνύον τὸν οὐράνιον ἀληθῶς ἀρχιερέα).[41] Ps.-Cyprian *De laude martyrii* 29, in a similar description, writes "The veils which hung before the doors were rent, the entire temple moaned" (scissa quae foribus dependebant vela, templum omne

---

[37] (ed. Hermann Tränkle; Wiesbaden: Steiner, 1964). Cf. Hilary of Poitiers *Comm. in Matt.* 33:7 (ed. Jean Doignon; 2 vols.; SC 258; Paris: Cerf, 1979): "Together with the watch of the protecting angel the honor of the veil was removed" (veli honor cum custodia angeli protegentis aufertur). In *Trac. in Psalm.* 57:10 (ed. Anton Zingerle; CSEL 22, 1891) he speaks of a "spiritual protector": "As if a spiritual guard broke away from there" (tamquam custodia illinc spiritali erumpente).

[38] (trans. Arthur Vööbus; CSCO 408=Script. Syr. 180, 1979) 210–11. Cf. *Ap. Const.* 6.5.4.

[39] (ed. G. F. Diercks; CCL 4, 1972).

[40] (ed. Bernhard Rehm and Franz Paschke; GCS 51, 1965).

[41] (ed. Pierre Nautin; SC 27; Paris: Cerf, 1950). On the question of authorship see Maurice Geerard, *Clavis Patrum Graecorum I* (Turnhotti: Brepols, 1983). In Hippolytus *C. Noetum* 18.8 we find a description inspired by Matthew 27 which mentions the rending of the veil without any further explanation.

mugiit)[42] while in Ps.-Cyprian *De montibus Sina et Sion* 8, the events in Matt 27:51–53 bring the Jews to repentance: "All those who stood before the cross, some in sorrow, others, however, blaspheming and deriding, fell on their faces and lay down, trembling and as if dead. Then the Jews understood that they had offended God and turned to mourning; and there was bitterness" (omnes qui stabant ante lignum alii dolentes allii vero blasphemantes inludentes prostrati in faciem iacuerunt trementes tamquam mortui. Tunc Iudaei intellexerunt se offendisse Deum et in luctum conversi sunt; et fuit exacerbatio).[43] A singular view is expressed in *T. Levi* 10.3 where Levi tells his sons that they will act lawlessly with Israel, "so that he (the Lord) will not bear Jerusalem because of your wickedness, but will rend the covering of the temple so as not to cover your shame."[44]

In Origen *Frg. on Matt.* no 560, the rending of the temple veil is compared with the rending of clothes by people in mourning, without a specification as to whether Origen thinks here of the temple itself, or an angel living there (ἢ καὶ ὡς ἐπὶ θανάτου καὶ πένθους ὅπου περιεσχίζονται οἱ ἄνθρωποι τὰς ἐσθῆτας).[45]

This interpretation comes as an alternative after an earlier one which stresses that the curtain was rent completely in order that the believers from the gentiles would see the holy things, which they had not been able to see "hindered by the thickness of the letter" (τῇ τοῦ γράμματος παχύτητι ἐμποδίζοντο). This, in turn, is an additional note to yet another interpretation, the one usually found in Origen with which the fragment begins: "It makes symbolically clear that the hidden things of the law were revealed in Christ, through his suffering" (συμβολικῶς δηλοῖ τὰ κρύπτα τοῦ νόμου ἐν Χριστῷ διὰ τοῦ πάθους

[42] (ed. Wilhelm von Hartel; CSEL 3,3, 1881) 50.

[43] Ibid., 112–13. Berthold Altaner and Alfred Stuiber (*Patrologie* [8th ed.; Freiburg/Basel/Wien: Herder, 1978] 177) date both writings in the third century. Cyprian himself in *De bono patientiae* 7 (ed. C. Moseschini; CCL 3, A, 1976) uses elements from Matthew 27 in a description of the passion as perfect obedience.

[44] On this difficult passage, see de Jonge, "Two Interesting Interpretations," section 2.

[45] (ed. Erich Klostermann, Ernst Benz, and Ursula Treu; GCS Origenes 12, 1941). Cf. *Fragm. on Luke* no. 250 (ed. Max Rauer; 2d ed.; GCS Origenes 9, 1959) on the darkness: "when the air there thickened, because it, too, was filled with sorrow about what had happened" (ἢ τοῦ ἐκεῖσε ἀέρος παχυνθέντος συμπενθοῦντος καὶ αὐτοῦ τῷ γεγονότι. In his *Comm. on John* ([ed. Erwin Preuschen; GCS Origenes 4, 1903] 19, 16; § 103) Origen connects Matt 17:51a directly with vs 50 (εὐθέως τὸ καταπέτασμα τοῦ ναοῦ ἐσχίσθη κτλ (cf. *Gos. Pet.* 20 and parallels). He tells us that this happened because a king left his body and accomplished with power and authority what he wanted.

αὐτοῦ ἀποκαλύπτεσθαι). This leads, here and elsewhere,[46] to a discussion of the question of which of the two veils of the temple is meant here. Origen's allegorical interpretation comes out most clearly in his *Comm. in Matt.* 27:50–54.[47] Here Origen treats Matt 27:51–54, commenting "Thus, when he gave up the spirit, signs took place concerning him and omens testifying to his dignity in the following fashion: 'and, see, the veil of the temple was rent in two, from top to bottom'" (ideo eo spiritum emittente signa facta sunt super eum et prodigia testificantia dignitatem eius hoc modo: et ecce velum templi scissum est in duas partes a summo usque deorsum). He points out that before Jesus' death the temple veil covered the interior of the temple: "It was fitting that these things were veiled, until the only one who could reveal them should make them manifest to those who wanted to see them, in order that those who had been liberated from death through the death of Jesus Christ who destroys the death of the believers, would be able to behold what is inside the veil" (oportebat enim ea velari, donec ille qui solus poterat revelare manifesta faceret ea videre volentibus, ut per mortem Jesu Christi destruentis credentium mortem, qui liberati fuerunt a morte possint aspicere quae sunt intra velum). True insight is granted to those whose death has been destroyed by the death of Christ.

Next, Origen distinguishes between the two veils of the temple, "which were images of the holy tabernacle which the Father has prepared from the beginning" (quae figurae erant tabernaculi sancti quod praeparavit ab initio pater). At Jesus' death the outer veil was rent. The second veil will follow, "when that which is perfect will have come . . . in order that we may see also those things which were hidden inside the second veil . . . the innermost mysteries" (quando venerit quod perfectum est (1 Cor 13:10) . . . ut videamus etiam quae intra secundum velum sunt occultata . . . interiora mysteria). The true disciples will be able to see the "interiora mysteria" with spiritual eyes (here Origen alludes to Heb 7:17, 21; 9:4–5).

In his comments on vss 51b–53 Origen gives a similar "spiritual" interpretation. The rocks are the Law and the prophets; they are rent "in order that we may see the spiritual mysteries hidden deep in them" (ut in profundis eorum posita spiritualia mysteria videamus). The tombs are the bodies of sinful souls who are dead to God. Vss 52–53

---

[46] See *Fragm. in Luke* nos. 151 and 251 (ed. Max Rauer; 2d ed.; GCS Origenes 9, 1959) and cf. the *Commentary on the Song of Songs* (ed. Wilhelm Adolf Baehrens; GCS Origenes 8, 1925) 162–63.

[47] (ed. E. Klostermann and Ernst Benz; 2d ed.; GCS Origenes 11, 1976) 284–92.

are interpreted in the light of John 5:25: these souls must be "raised to faith" (suscitatae ad fidem), the bodies must become bodies of saintly souls. By the grace of God people may now follow him who rose from the dead, in order to walk in newness of life.

Origen concentrates on the theme of revelation and true spiritual interpretation of the Old Testament, made possible by the death of Christ. The Gospel itself also can only be properly understood by divine illumination: "The Spirit, however, which surpasses the nature of the letter, with movements of a more divine nature has given a greater enlightenment to those people for whom the Gospel is not veiled . . . for he who sees because the veil of Scripture is rent from top to bottom and sees what is inside it, becomes full of higher knowledge" (Spiritus autem qui supergreditur litterarum naturam, divinioribus motibus magis eos illuminavit quibus evangelium non est velatum . . . maiori enim repletur scientia qui videt, quod conscinditur velum scripturae [2 Cor 4:3] a sursum usque deorsum [Matt 27:51], et videt quae sunt intra eum).

Space does not permit us to compare Origen's views with the ideas about revelation and salvation laid down in *Gos. Phil.* 69.14–70.9 and 84.20–85.21.[48] Nor are we able to discuss the possible relationship between the notion of the angel rending his garment and similar statements concerning the demiurge found in Eznik of Kolb *De Deo* 358 (writing about the Marcionites) and *Treat. Seth* 58.20–33.[49]

By now it will have become clear that the variety of interpretations found in early Christian literature is at least as great as that found in the works of scholars working with modern exegetical methods. Interpreters belonging to the latter category have explicitly taken over some elements from those belonging to the former; in other cases the text itself inspired parallel or similar conclusions. Our survey of the material suggests, however, that it is very unlikely that "the" meaning of Matt 27:51a will ever be established beyond doubt. Perhaps, however, the scrutiny of the early Christian material will induce modern exegetes to review their own interpretations critically and to present them with utmost modesty. Many of them are not all that new, and all of them are tenuous.

---

[48] See Jacques Ménard's commentary on *Sentences* 76–77 and 125 in his *L'Évangile de Philippe* (Diss. Strasbourg; Paris, 1967). Cf. also de Jonge, "Het motief," 272–76.

[49] For some details see de Jonge, "Het motief," 263–64 and idem, "Two Interesting Interpretations," n. 39.

JEWISH-GENTILE CONTINUITY IN PAUL: TORAH AND/OR FAITH? (ROMANS 9:1-5)*

Eldon Jay Epp
Case Western Reserve University

Judging from his relatively few surviving letters, Paul—whether as Jew or Christian—was a person with both outer and inner conflicts. We know much less than we would like about these external confrontations and inner struggles, but time and again his letters show evidence of his wrestling with one or another serious ambivalence. Actually, it is not often a present struggle that is portrayed or revealed, for Paul writes with a remarkable maturity and with the confidence of one who has moved well beyond the tossing and turning of a continuing inner struggle. Yet at times, most notably in Romans 9-11, Paul's simple statement of a mature judgment still evokes, in the very restating of his conclusions, the intensity of the original ambivalence and conflict. A further indication that Paul was this kind of person is found, if only incidentally, in his dialectical mode of thinking: if he mentions "death," at once he thinks of "life"; if he refers to "flesh," immediately "spirit" crosses his mind, or if he speaks of "slaves" or "slavery," then "sons" or "freedom" is instantly present.

This essay focuses on one of these Pauline inner struggles—perhaps the leading example if one is to judge by the intensity of expression and emotion. It concerns the relationship between Paul's beloved Israel

---

*Krister Stendahl, who served as major adviser for my Ph.D. program and to whom I owe so large a debt, was accustomed to characterize modern biblical scholarship as the transference of footnotes from other books and articles to our own (or words to that effect). A plea of "no contest" to such a charge would be automatic from this quarter, for my own publications are replete with the traditional scholarly apparatus of footnotes and endnotes; therefore, as a tribute—however inadequate—to Professor Stendahl, the present essay eschews entirely that genre. This is not to say that I owe nothing to others; far from it, though here I shall claim only to have employed standard reference works and to have looked again at Stendahl's provocative *Paul Among Jews and Gentiles* (Philadelphia: Fortress, 1976).

and his new-found Gentile-Christian community, which together comprise the people of God and—to the extent that "Israelites" are Christians—constitute the body of Christ. To state it more sharply and more precisely, Paul struggled with the rationale for continuity between Israel and the church. The depth of the conflict comes out in his highly impassioned—almost pathetic—yearning over his fellow Jews, willing himself to be damned (Rom 9:3) if only his "brethren," "Israelites" could be saved (Rom 10:1). The classical passage is Rom 9:1 – 5:

> I am speaking the truth in Christ, I am not lying; my conscience bears me witness in the Holy Spirit, that I have great sorrow and unceasing anguish in my heart. For I could wish that I myself were accursed and cut off from Christ for the sake of my brethren, my kinsmen by race. They are Israelites, and to them belong the sonship, the glory, the covenants, the giving of the Law, the worship, and the promises; to them belong the patriarchs, and of their race, according to the flesh, is the Christ. God who is over all be blessed for ever. Amen.

For Paul, the Jew, who was now also a Christian, something had gone wrong. The strong language of these verses in Romans 9 is not accidental, the pathos is not contrived, and the solemn doxology is not routinely or idly inserted. The noun, ὀδύνη (anguish), occurs only here in Paul, though its verbal form is found in Luke-Acts with reference to the rich man tormented in Hades (Luke 16:24 – 25) and in describing the feelings of the elders of the church at Ephesus in reaction to Paul's final farewell—"that they should see his face no more" (Acts 20:38). Thus, it is the anguish of final separation, and Paul in Rom 9:2 feels its piercing intensity as he faces the fact that his fellow Jews by and large are not "in Christ." How could this be? After all, to the Jews belong the adoption as sons, the glory, the covenants, the giving of the Law, the worship, the promises, the patriarchs, and the Christ—all of these are rightfully and naturally theirs. It is Paul's assumption, of course, that these items are also—perhaps even preeminently—the possessions of those who are "in Christ." Yet the Jews—Israel—are not "in Christ." This is unthinkable, for all the ingredients of consonance between Israel and Christianity have long been present and should have acted to sustain this important continuity. These ingredients require more careful analysis:

1. *Sonship.* This parent-child relationship between God and Israel, literally "adoption," is evident all the way from the Exodus ("Israel is my first-born son; . . . let my son go"—Exod 4:22; "Out of Egypt have I called my son"—Hos 11:1) to the coming of the Son of God. God's

gracious, parental actions down through the ages were directed toward and for the primary benefit of his adoptive children, his one people. The only other uses of the term "sonship" (i.e., "adoption as sons") in Paul speak of the "spirit of sonship" in terms of the intimate, inner cry of "Abba! Father!" that identifies the "children" and "heirs of God" as "fellow heirs with Christ" (Rom 8:14–17, specifically vs 15; cf. the very similar language of Gal 4:4–7) and of an inward groaning for "adoption as sons" (Rom 8:23). In this Romans 8 passage, incidentally, Paul has the Exodus in view when he says "For all who are led by the Spirit of God [recalling the leading of the pillars of cloud and of fire] are sons of God" [as is Israel] (8:14), an imagery confirmed by the reference to "slavery" in vs 15. Therefore, in his employment of this terminology of "sonship," Paul ties together (1) the sonship of Israel (Rom 9:4), (2) the sonship of Jesus Christ ("born of a woman, born under the Law"—that is, a Jew—Gal 4:4), and (3) the sonship of Christians ("so that we might receive adoption as sons," Gal 4:5). Paul, by quoting from Hosea in Rom 9:25–26, makes the same point: "not my people" shall be "my people"; "not my people" shall be "sons of the living God." He does the same also in Gal 3:26—in the context of "there is neither Jew nor Greek" (3:28)—when he affirms that "in Christ Jesus you are all sons of God." Similarly, in the context of "neither is circumcision anything, nor uncircumcision," he invokes "peace and mercy . . . upon the Israel of God" (Gal 6:16), a clear reference to God's "son," that is, to his one continuous people, Jewish or Christian.

Thus, the continuity of the one people of God is clear enough in "sonship," but Israel, for the most part, now has withdrawn from this relationship and the long-standing connection seems not to have held.

2. *The glory.* This is *kabod*, closely related to the *shekinah*, and refers to the "radiance" of God and to the epiphany that actualizes his presence and his claim to kingship. This assurance of God's presence was given to Israel from the time Moses received Torah ("The glory of the Lord settled on Mount Sinai," Exod 24:16 and 33:17–23) and down through the periods of the tabernacle and the Temple, but most recently affirmed (according to Paul) in the appearance of the "Lord of glory" who was crucified (1 Cor 2:8), who provides "knowledge of the glory of God" (2 Cor 4:6), and who is "our hope of sharing the glory of God" (Rom 5:2). But Paul might have written over Israel "Ichabod"—"the glory has departed from Israel" (1 Sam 4:21–22), for Israel has not appropriated this final self-manifestation of Yahweh's *kabod*, and the continuity provided by the "glory" has been broken.

3. *The covenants.* Paul speaks of two covenants, the "old" and the "new" (2 Cor 3:6, 14; cf. 1 Cor 11:25), and the plural form, which is the "harder" reading, is probably correct (though "covenant" is the more strongly attested reading). The steadfast covenant-love of the Lord God down through countless ages issued ultimately in the Christ: Paul, in a context explicitly treating the continuity between Israel and Gentiles, combines two OT quotations: "The Deliverer will come from Zion, he will banish ungodliness from Jacob"; "and this will be my covenant with them when I take away their sins" (Rom 11:26-27). Paul elsewhere makes it clear that "covenant" refers to the "promises to Abraham" (Gal 3:17 and context; cf. 4:22-28). But a "hardening has come upon part of Israel, until the full number of Gentiles come in" (Rom 11:25), and the covenants, both of which are Israel's rightful possession, have been abrogated and the continuity has been broken.

4. *The worship.* λατρεία and its corresponding verbal form are words almost absent from Paul; elsewhere he speaks only of "spiritual worship" (Rom 12:1; 1:9; Phil 3:3; cf. "idol worship" in 1 Cor 10:14) or of worship of the "creature rather than the Creator" (Rom 1:25). The most obvious reference for the term in Rom 9:4, however, would be to Deut 10:12 and its context (especially through 11:25), where the requirement placed upon Israel is "to serve (LXX: λατρεύειν) the Lord your God with all your heart and with all your soul." As the accompanying historical survey of the "acts of God" shows (Deut 10:21-11:1), this is the (one and only) God to whom belong heaven and earth, but who has chosen this one people "above all peoples" (Deut 10:14-15). That the "worship," according to Paul, belongs to Israel is to recognize and affirm this unique relationship of a unique people with the unique God. Paul himself, in his life and ministry, continues in that worship of God, "whom [he says] I serve (λατρεύειν) with my spirit in the gospel of his Son" (Rom 1:9; cf. Phil 3:3), but Israel, by and large, does not worship and serve God in this way, and, therefore, this aspect of the continuity between Israel and its new synagogue of Christians has lost its force.

5. *The promises.* The age-old promises to Abraham that "in thee shall all the nations be blessed" (Gen 12:3; 18:18; cited in Gal 3:8) were clearly fulfilled when the "seed" of Abraham appeared (Gal 3:16) and Gentiles received him as the Christ. As Paul notes elsewhere, "all the promises of God find their Yes in him [Christ]" (2 Cor 1:20). The promises also recall faith, for "Abraham believed God and it was reckoned to him as righteousness" (Gen 15:6; cited in Gal 3:6). So, for Paul, the continuity with Israel is maintained when "those who are people of faith are blessed with Abraham who had faith" (Gal 3:9);

however, "not all who are descended from Israel belong to Israel, and not all are children of Abraham because they are his descendants" (Rom 9:6–7). Again, the continuity—the linkage between Jews and Christians—that should have issued from the promises to Israel has been broken.

6. *The patriarchs.* The term actually is "fathers," with the clear flavor of our term "patriarchs," and Paul is affirming the obvious, that all the patriarchs, those ancestral forebearers who attest to God's faithfulness past and present, belong to Israel. Incidentally, in an autobiographical note Paul refers to his own extraordinary zeal for the traditions of his "fathers" (Gal 1:14), thus personalizing his links with Moses, Ezra, and the teachers of Judaism who followed. Actually, however, Paul speaks sparingly of the patriarchs in his letters, with the notable exception of Abraham, so this reference to patriarchs in Rom 9:5 really serves to reinforce the points made through his use of "covenants" and "promises" above. For example, Paul speaks of the "promises given to the patriarchs [fathers]" in Rom 15:8 in the context of how those promises apply to the Gentiles, and often when Abraham is referred to specifically as "father" and when the term "descendants" is in the context, "promise" and "faith" are also to be found (e.g., the entire fourth chapter of Romans; cf. Gal 3:14). Other patriarchs invoked by Paul in a generally similar way are Isaac (Rom 9:7–12; Gal 4:28—Paul's only references to Isaac); Jacob (Rom 9:13—his only reference to Jacob as an individual); Benjamin (Rom 11:1); Moses (Rom 9:15); and David (as the ancestor of Christ, Rom 1:3; or with reference to faith, 4:6; or of grace and hardening, 11:9—all of Paul's references to David). Paul does not, however, mention Rachel, Joseph, Aaron, Joshua, Saul, Solomon, Daniel, Ezra, or others who might come to mind. Paul's point, though, is clear: to Israel belong the fathers, whose response to God was faith and from whom the faithful have descended—including the Christ himself, but—once again—this continuity of patriarchal faith and of the acceptance of the Messiah who issued from them has been broken.

7. *The Christ.* The final item on Paul's list. Here the reference is to the literal continuity, consisting in the actual line of descent "according to the flesh," that brought the Messiah—this too belongs to Israel. But the genealogical "root" from which Israel and the Christ grew has experienced the loss of its "natural branches" (Rom 11:17–22), that is, Israel, so that even this natural or physical continuity now has been destroyed by Israel's unbelief (Rom 11:20).

The result so far is that both the natural and the spiritual continuity of God's one people—the continuity between Israel and the church—

has been broken, and this has occurred in spite of the overwhelming evidence of the inherent continuity between Israel and the Christian synagogue that Paul can point to, and in spite of all the sustaining factors that have favored its continuation down through the ages. Israel has been "broken off" and the Gentiles have been "grafted in."

Paul's litany of continuity, however, contains another item that has been omitted purposely from the preceding analysis, an item that might well have settled the matter.

8. *The giving of the Law*. To the Jews belongs "the giving of the Law," or Torah, which—in good Pharisaic tradition—was viewed as created before the world (*Sipre Deut.* 11.10, § 37 [76a–b]; *Pesaḥim* 54a; *Zebaḥim* 116a), was the daughter of God (*Lev. Rab.* 20.7 [120a]; *Sanh.* 101a *bar.*), was intimately identified with God—it "lay on God's bosom" (ˀ*Abot R. Nat.* 31 [8b]), and was active with God in creation (*Gen. Rab.* 1.1; ˀ*Abot* 3.15). Given its prominence ever since the time of Ezra and the "Men of the Great Synagogue," Torah should have functioned for Paul the Pharisee as the dominant link between Israel and the newly emerging "body of Christ." After all, Paul describes himself "as to the Law a Pharisee" (Phil 3:5). Torah, the instruction of God, the revelation of his will, which provides opportunities both to praise the Almighty and to obey him (the more laws, the more opportunity to please God), should have provided the parameters within which all the heirs of God—Jews and Christians—would find their pattern of life. In addition, Torah—of all the items in Paul's list—is by far the most effective, active, and practical link to draw the past and present together; it has been practiced for generations. In reality, it is the only item in the list that could function in this fashion, for the "old" covenant between God and Israel was subsumed under Torah as the generations passed, and at least the priestly worship in the Temple was, since the exile, effectively overshadowed by Torah, for after Ezra a Jew was no longer defined as one whose worship centered in the Temple and its sacrifices but as one who submitted to Torah. Moreover, the other factors mentioned—sonship, glory, promises, patriarchs, the messianic lineage—are abstract or theoretical in nature, as well as more detached from everyday life and practice. Also, if one looks at "covenants" and "worship" in their broader dimensions, as described in points (3) and (4) above, they too lose their concrete force and take on more abstract and theoretical meanings, thereby diminishing their "down-to-earth," everyday effectiveness as continuing links. So, of all the items in Rom 9:4–5 it is Torah that should have formed the basis of continuity for Paul, the Pharisee; it was Torah that should have remained preeminently the connecting tissue of the old and yet newly

emerging "people of God," now also to be called the "body of Christ."
Yet, recognizing Paul's numerous critical statements toward Torah, it
may seem surprising that "Law" is included in the list at all. Did he
not describe the Law as entailing a "curse" (Gal 3:13) and seek to
break away from its constraints (Rom 7:1, 5–7; Gal 3:23–26)? That is
a vast subject not to be explored here, but the point is that Paul does
include "the giving of the Law" as one of the possessions of Israel that
connect it with the one, all-encompassing "people of God." Yet the
continuity Paul envisioned was not effectual, for at an even faster pace
than Israel was failing to believe in Christ, Gentiles were rushing into
the church. It soon became obvious—probably because of sheer
numbers—that it was not practical to require that these Gentiles first
become Jews if they were to become Christians. Such a practice, if it
had been normative, would have maintained the continuity that Paul
expected between "Torah" and "promise" and thus between Israel and
the church—or, to state it more accurately, such a "Judaizing" practice
would have maintained the continuity within the new Judaism-
Christianity of which Paul and other early Christians found themselves
a part.

This pressure at the practical level to permit Gentile converts to
relax or to forego the halakic regulations of Torah may have been the
occasion for rather tumultous conflicts within Paul. These, however,
were inner, intellectual conflicts, rather than outer conflicts, for Paul's
confrontation with Peter after the so-called Jerusalem Council was not
over the issue of "Judaizing" itself, that is, over the substance of the
issue whether Gentiles must first become Jews in order to become
Christians, but rather over Peter's hypocrisy and inconsistency, as
clearly indicated in Paul's own account of it in Gal 2:11–18. The outer
conflict, according to Paul's account (and also Acts 15, despite the
reference there to "much debate"), seems to have been quite quickly
resolved on very practical, matter-of-fact grounds:

> When they saw that I had been entrusted with the gospel to the
> uncircumcised, just as Peter had been entrusted with the gospel to
> the circumcised, . . . and when they perceived the grace that was
> given to me, James and Cephas and John . . . gave to me and Bar-
> nabas the right hand of fellowship, that we should go to the Gen-
> tiles and they to the circumcised. (Gal 2:7–9)

The preceding verses in Galatians 2 confirm the fact that Paul's position on the evangelization of the Gentiles was well established and was
not to be altered (vss 2–5)—there was no debate in his mind about the
necessity of circumcising Gentile converts, for that was not to be

required and that question was settled. At the risk of redundancy, it can be said that Paul was confident in his call to preach to the Gentiles and to impose neither circumcision nor food laws upon them; this was his trust (vs 2) and divine calling, and no further justification was required. If the practicalities of the situation required accommodations for these Gentiles, that too demanded no elaborate rationale, "for Christ is the end/fulfillment of the Law, that every one [Jew or Gentile, as the context shows] who has faith may be justified" (Rom 10:4; cf. 9:30ff), and that was rationale enough as far as the Gentiles were concerned. After all:

> Is God the God of Jews only? Is he not the God of Gentiles also? Yes, of Gentiles also, since God is one; and he will justify the circumcised on the ground of their faith and the uncircumcised because of their faith. Do we then overthrow the Law by this faith? By no means! On the contrary, we uphold the Law. (Rom 3:29–31)

The continuity of Israel and the church from the Gentile standpoint, then, is clear: they come in through faith, in accordance with the "promises," but, at the same time, for Paul the continuity of the Law is also upheld.

Paul's inner conflict, however, while still concerned with the continuity between Israel and the Gentile Christians, focused on Israel, and not on the Gentiles. The question was not how Gentiles could come in, but how it happened that Jews could be left out. The one God (1 Cor 8:6; Gal 3:20), the "one man, Jesus Christ [Messiah]" (Rom 5:17), and God's one people ("one body—Jews or Greeks," 1 Cor 12:13; cf. Rom 12:5) should have encompassed Israel automatically, but that had not occurred. Paul reports his struggles over this issue in Romans (particularly chaps. 3–4 and 7–11) and in Galatians (especially chaps. 2–5), where the issue of Torah and/or faith is explored.

It was not, however, a polarity between the "giving of the Law" and the possession of the "promises" (Torah versus faith, so to speak) that Paul saw as responsible for the discontinuity, nor was this how he explained the breaking off of Israel. Both terms ("Law" and "promises") are in the same list, both are rightful possessions of Israel, both fall under the doxology of Rom 9:5b. "Is the Law then against the promises of God? Certainly not" (Gal 3:21). After all and despite anything else he might have said about Torah, for Paul "the Law is holy, and the commandment is holy and just and good" (Rom 7:12), it is "spiritual" (7:14), and Paul "delights" in it (7:22). Doubtless Paul had assumed that both the Law and the promises could operate in juxtaposition in Christianity as they had (or should have) operated in Judaism—at least as Paul understood Judaism.

Furthermore, the discontinuity between Israel and Christianity was not created by Paul by his own "conversion" (or "call") or even by the conversion of Gentiles to the new sect of Judaism (Christianity), but it was created by Israel's rejection of Christ as Messiah. How was Paul to cope with the repeated rejection of Christ by Jews, a rejection reinforced every time Paul entered a new city and proclaimed his message first in the local synagogue? How was he to identify the expected continuity between God's people (Israel), to whom the age-old promises had been both made and fulfilled in Christ, and the Gentiles, to whom the promises were only secondary—through Israel—but who so readily embraced the Christian message? Each rejection in each synagogue, followed by new Gentile converts, exacerbated the problem: the gap was becoming wider and wider between two groups of what should have been God's one people. There were far fewer Jews than expected and far more Gentiles than expected, and the latter entered without a full enforcement of the *halakot.* Paul knew that continuity between these two groups existed—or must exist—but how was it to be rationalized (in the best sense of that term) so that Torah still functioned in some meaningful fashion as an aspect of the linkage?

If the scheme of things had been functioning properly ("In thy seed all the nations of the earth shall be blessed"), Gentiles should be coming to the one true God through his people Israel—a universalism operating through a particularism. But the crucial link seems to have broken down: Gentiles were coming, but were bypassing Israel (i.e., they were entering apart from the natural link of Torah—which did not bother Paul particularly) when, at the same time, Israel was bypassing Christ (which did bother Paul very much). The continuity, then, was broken on both sides: by Gentiles not keeping Torah and by Jews not recognizing the messianic descendant of their fathers.

When the expected scheme failed to function, what was Paul to do? Though Israel had been "cut off," God had not rejected Israel (Rom 11:1), and neither could Paul. After all, the continuity was there—as evidenced in Paul's litany of links—even though it had been broken down by Israel's unbelief. Paul felt compelled to reconnect Israel and Gentile Christianity, and a rationale had to be found. Judging from the solution he finally reached, Paul apparently sought as that rationale the oldest possible basis for continuity. This eliminated the command to worship and to serve the Lord God with all of heart and soul, which was neither sufficiently ancient nor concrete. Sonship, however, was an old link, for it extended back to the very formation and concept of the nation at the time of Jacob (= Israel); it might have been selected as the dominant connection between all of God's people, though Paul did not choose it. Actually, it was Torah—again—that should have been the winner "hands down," for Torah, according to the Rabbis, was among those seven items created before the world was created (*Pesaḥim* 54a). Like Wisdom, with which it was identified, Torah was present and active with God at the creation (*Tanhuma, Ber.* 1 [6b]; *Gen. Rab.* 1.1). All of this should have left Torah, without question, as the oldest link and therefore Paul's logical basis for continuity.

Yet, assuming that Paul the Pharisee knew these traditions about the preexistence of Torah (it is hard to imagine that he did not), Paul chose not to appeal to them. (Of course, he really could not choose this option, for then he would have had to insist that Gentiles follow all aspects of Torah—but the sluice had been opened to Gentiles without the detailed requirements of Torah, and it was no longer either practical or possible to recall the spilled water.) Rather, Paul made a most interesting move: in his list of connecting links, he did not refer simply to "Law" (which would have invoked the rabbinic traditions about Torah's extreme antiquity), but he spoke pointedly and specifically of "the *giving* of the Law." That formulation emphasized Torah's extension back (only) to the time of Moses and his actual receipt of the Law (that occasion when he caught merely a glimpse of the glory of God). Thus Torah, when described as the *giving* of the Law, was an old link, though certainly not the oldest, and not even as old as "sonship." In speaking of the giving of the Law, therefore, Paul introduced a limitation upon Torah that permitted him to diminish its otherwise logically preeminent place among the factors of continuity for God's people, though without diminishing the "good" and "holy" nature of Torah. This latter point, too, was one of importance to Paul—his letters show no anti-Torah motif and he had no intention of ruling out Torah; rather, he wanted to define its proper place and role (see Gal 3:24).

Confirmation of all this comes, of course, when Paul's rationale for Jewish-Gentile continuity is heard. Fortunately it was close at hand for him and readily to be found in the "promises" and in the "covenant(s)"—which for Paul encompassed the "promises"—and in the "patriarchs," specifically in Abraham. Paul drew out of these the simple solution: The promises to Abraham and Abraham's response of faith take temporal precedence and spiritual priority over all else, and "the Law, which came 430 years afterward [i.e., after Abraham], does not annul a covenant previously ratified by God, so as to make the promise void" (Gal 3:17). Indeed, "the scripture . . . preached the gospel beforehand to Abraham" (Gal 3:8)—before the giving of the Law.

In this connection, it is of more than passing interest that Paul, by using rabbinic methods of interpretation, carried Christ back into the early history of Israel—even prior to the giving of the Law: In 1 Cor 10:4 he argued that Moses and the Israelites on their Exodus journeys "drank from the supernatural [or spiritual] Rock which followed them, and the Rock was Christ" (cf. Exod 17:6 and Num 20:8–11). So not only did the promises precede the giving of the Law, but Christ himself was present in and with Israel prior to the Law-giving, and it might be said that, for Paul, even Christ was a more ancient and continuous link than was Torah. Faith, however, still held the position of priority and preeminence.

The conclusion, then, is that through Paul's rationale for the continuity of God's people the breach once again had been closed: Israel's earliest relationship to God was through faith (represented by Abraham), and that continued wherever faith was found; Jewish-Christians in Paul's day were related to God by faith, and Gentile-Christians likewise. The continuity of God's people had been restored and it could and would go on. It is not a continuity based on *either* Torah *or* faith, but one based on *both* Torah *and* faith, though faith by virtue of its temporal priority has assumed the preeminent place. Jews and Gentiles—who by natural Pharisaic expectations should have been bound together by Torah—in fact find their continuity in faith. And that made all the difference for Paul—and for Christianity.

JEWS, GENTILES, AND SYNAGOGUES IN THE BOOK OF ACTS

John G. Gager
Princeton University

Modern criticism of the book of Acts began with a hyper-Cartesian decision to doubt everything simultaneously. The author was not to be trusted as a reliable reporter on any issue of significance—the character and fate of the believers in Jerusalem, the status and role of Peter, the teaching of Paul, and so on. Recently, a former student of Krister Stendahl, A. T. Kraabel, has proposed that we should extend our skepticism to yet another area of Acts, to wit, the presence of Gentiles in all of the synagogues visited by Paul on his missionary journeys.[1]

Against the prevailing consensus, Kraabel has argued that those Gentiles depicted in Acts as present in synagogues where Paul preaches his gospel are nothing more than Luke's invention, introduced for the purpose of showing "how Christianity had become a Gentile religion legitimately and without losing its Old Testament roots."[2] Furthermore, just as the presence of the Gentile "god-fearers" in Acts is to be accounted for solely in terms of Luke's theological needs, so there is no solid evidence for their existence in the surviving material evidence from the broader Greco-Roman world. Kraabel offers the following arguments in support of his position:

—whereas Luke uses the terms φοβούμενος and σεβόμενος to describe such Gentiles, these terms never appear in inscriptions;[3]

---

[1] A. T. Kraabel, "The Disappearance of the 'God-fearers,'" *Numen* 28 (1981) 113–26; see also idem, "The Roman Diaspora: Six Questionable Assumptions," *JJS* 33 (1982) 445–64; and idem, "Greeks, Jews, and Lutherans in the Middle Half of Acts," in this volume.

[2] Idem, "Disappearance," 120.

[3] It must be noted that the phrase σεβόμενοι θεὸν ὕψιστον appears in three inscriptions from Tanais, northeast of the Black Sea. They are discussed by E. Schürer in "Die Juden im bosporischen Reiche und die Genossenschaften der σεβόμενοι θεὸν ὕψιστον ebendaselbst," SPAW (Berlin, 1897) 200–25. Whether these inscriptions have anything to do with Judaism is another matter. The presence of terms like σεβόμενοι, θεὸν ὕψι-

there the term customarily taken as referring to "god-fearers" is
θεοσεβής and it refers exclusively to Jews;
—there is no hint from the material evidence that Jews were
interested in a missionary outreach of any kind;
—the literary evidence, Christian and other, concerning "god-
fearers" has been over-determined by Luke's now discredited
presentation in Acts.

These are interesting arguments. They raise certain issues which
have not received adequate attention in previous studies. What is
more, if Kraabel is correct, we will need a fundamental reappraisal of
the current consensus with regard to relations between synagogues and
Gentiles in the Greco-Roman world. But first we must consider
whether Kraabel's arguments are convincing.

Initially, there can be no doubt concerning the appropriateness of
Kraabel's insistence that most treatments have failed to heed the
material evidence. Against the accepted view, he objects that Luke's
terms, φοβούμενος and σεβόμενος, never show up in the inscriptions.[4]
Yet we must also ask whether the respective media—inscriptions and
literary texts—might not only produce but require different usages.
Furthermore, as others have pointed out, there is a significant time-lag
between the majority of the inscriptions, which date from the third century and beyond, and Luke who stands somewhat earlier. Thus, if θεοσεβής does designate Gentile sympathizers of one kind or another, it
may well have developed as a technical, or semi-technical term during
the intervening period. In this connection it is important to recall that
θεοσεβής is in effect little more than an adjectival contraction of the
Lukan phrase, σεβόμενος τὸν θεόν (16:14; 18:7). Also, we should not
make the mistake of regarding Luke's terminology itself as rigidly fixed
or formulaic: in 10:2, the term is εὐσεβὴς καὶ φοβούμενος τὸν θεόν;
in 13:16 it is φοβούμενος τὸν θεόν; in 14:1 it becomes Ἕλληνες and
several verses later ἔθνη (14:5); in 17:4 the phrase is σεβόμενοι
Ἕλληνες; and so on. In short, whether Luke invented the category of
Gentiles described by these terms or was simply reporting a common
phenomenon, he follows no consistent pattern of usage.[5] Indeed, as

---

στον, and πρεσβύτερον point toward a positive answer.

[4] See, however, the texts cited in the previous note.

[5] That the phrase, σεβόμενος τὸν θεόν, is not a Lukan invention is made plain by
Josephus Ant. 14.110, where it also appears to designate Gentiles: πάντων τῶν κατὰ τὴν
οἰκουμένην Ἰουδαίων καὶ σεβομένων τὸν θεόν.

B. Lifshitz,[6] Stern,[7] and others have suggested, the variety of terms, including the *metuens* in Juvenal[8] and a number of Latin inscriptions, may reflect nothing more than different counterparts to *yir'ê shāmayim*, which in several rabbinic texts designates Gentile "God-fearers" as distinct from Jews and full proselytes.

With these observations in mind, we may return to the significance of the literary evidence, apart from Acts, which speaks of Gentiles who were attracted to Judaism and to various forms of participation in the life of diaspora synagogues. There is no need to rehearse here the large number of texts which speak of such Gentiles.[9] Their weight and number cannot be ignored. Furthermore, there can be little doubt that these texts refer primarily to Gentiles who were not full converts. They were certainly not regarded as full Jews. Yet they were welcomed, as were Christians at a later date, by many synagogues. Indeed, they appear to have been designated by a recurrent, if unofficial set of terms, and to have been the intended audience for a body of Jewish literature.[10] In short, far from it being the case that the many literary texts have been read in the light of Acts, one must say that an interpretation of Acts that ignores them must be said to lack plausibility.

Next, Kraabel raises the intriguing issue of the symbolic function of diaspora synagogues and concludes that they reveal "no hint that these Jews were reaching toward their Gentile neighbors."[11] The first question one must ask here is just what kind of evidence would count one way or the other. Inscriptions would, of course, be relevant but they remain to be treated later. One important symbolic manifestation of

---

[6] "Du nouveau sur les 'sympathisants,'" *JSJ* 1 (1970) 82–83. For other works of Lifshitz on the Jewish inscriptions see his *Prolegomenon* to *CII* (New York: Ktav, 1975) 1. 21–107 and idem, *Donateurs et fondateurs dans les synagogues juives* (Paris: Gabalda, 1967).

[7] *Greek and Latin Authors on Jews and Judaism* (Jerusalem: Israel Academy of Sciences and Humanities, 1980) 2. 103–7.

[8] The use of *metuens* in Juvenal *Sat.* 14.96 is particularly interesting, for it refers specifically to a father who observed some Jewish customs and beliefs, whereas his son becomes a full convert and undergoes circumcision. Cf. also the famous account of Izates of Adiabene who eventually became a full convert to Judaism but was originally advised that it was possible τὸ θεῖον σέβειν without circumcision (Josephus *Ant.* 20.41).

[9] Among others, J. G. Gager, *The Origins of Anti-Semitism: Attitudes toward Judaism in Pagan and Christian Antiquity* (New York: Oxford University Press, 1985).

[10] So E. R. Goodenough, in his *Introduction to Philo Judaeus* (New York: Barnes & Noble, 1962) 33–34 with respect to certain treatises of Philo; and John J. Collins, *Between Athens and Jerusalem: Jewish Identity in the Hellenistic Diaspora* (New York: Crossroad, 1983) with respect to a broad range of Hellenistic Jewish literature.

[11] Kraabel, "Disappearance," 117.

outreach is location. Sardis offers an instructive example. The synagogue is an enormous building, located in the very heart of the city. In his excellent survey of the synagogue and its significance for the study of ancient Judaism in general, Kraabel says the following:

> The upper walls and roof of the building must have been clearly visible above the shops and road colonnades. The interior of the building could be seen by gentiles walking by when the doors were open. The Forecourt may have contained a municipally licensed fountain and may have been accessible to all. . . . The evidence from epigraphy buttresses the evidence from architecture.[12]

At the level of religious symbolism, this description sounds very much like an openness and an outreach to Gentiles. As Kraabel himself remarks, "It is hard to avoid the conclusion that the building was intended to be a showplace of Judaism for Sardis gentiles. . . . We believe that was by design.[13]

Of course, there is also literary evidence for a Jewish mission of some kind; the Jewish merchant, Ananias, who combined business travels with a successful effort to convert the royal house of Adiabene;[14] the Pharisees of Matt 23:15 who are said to cross sea and land to make a single proselyte;[15] and Juvenal's Jewish woman who interpreted dreams for a fee.[16] In sum, our lack of information about how Jews reached Gentiles should not be read as evidence that they failed to do so. In the second, third, and early fourth centuries, Christian missionary activity was seldom a public affair and its techniques are not well attested. And yet many Gentiles were attracted during that period. What we do know, ironically, is that Christians in the city of Antioch in the late fourth century found their way to the synagogue(s) with sufficient regularity and in sufficient numbers to provoke a vitriolic tirade against them from no less a figure than John Chrysostom.[17] In brief, the cumulative evidence, literary and material, points toward the

---

[12] A. T. Kraabel, "Impact of the Discovery of the Sardis Synagogue," in George M. A. Hanfmann, ed., *Sardis from Prehistoric to Roman Times: Results of the Archaeological Exploration of Sardis, 1958–1975* (Cambridge: Harvard University Press, 1983) 184.

[13] Ibid., 188.

[14] Josephus *Ant.* 20.34–48.

[15] Kraabel ("Disappearance," 123) rather implausibly dismisses the passage due to its polemical tone.

[16] *Sat.* 6.542–47.

[17] See the discussion in Wayne Meeks and Robert Wilken, *Jews and Christians in Antioch in the First Four Centuries of the Common Era* (Missoula: Scholars Press, 1978) 25–36.

conclusion that many synagogues were well-known local institutions, often situated centrally, and open to outsiders with varying degrees of involvement.

Most important of all for the argument that the material evidence fails to sustain the picture given in literary texts is the assertion that the numerous synagogue inscriptions give no hint of Gentile "God-fearers." "If we had only the synagogue inscriptions as evidence, there would be nothing to suggest that such a thing as a God-fearer had ever existed."[18] This means, of course, that all instances of θεοσεβής and *metuens* in the inscriptions must refer to Jews; the terms themselves simply mean "pious" and have no technical meaning at all.[19] This is a highly controverted position. It is not shared at all by Lifshitz and Stern and only in part by Feldman,[20] Leon,[21] and others. However, the chief authority behind Kraabel's position is Louis Robert, the most authoritative voice in all of modern epigraphy and the editor of the first synagogue inscriptions from Sardis.[22] Any attempt to contest the view represented by Kraabel and Robert must reckon with formidable opposition.

As we shall see presently, there is new evidence to suggest that this skeptical view is no longer tenable. For the moment, however, the issue is whether it was tenable in the first place. In his review of the θεοσεβής inscriptions, Robert takes a strong stand: Polyippos and Eulogios, donors cited in the synagogue at Sardis and described as θεοσεβής, were full members of the community, which must mean either full proselytes or Jews with Greek and Roman names; Eustathios, mentioned as a donor in an inscription from Philadelphia (Lydia) and described as ὁ θεοσεβής, was not a sympathizer;[23] the well-known inscription in the theater at Miletus, reserving places with the formula τοπος ειουδεον των και τηεοσεβιον (*sic*),[24] must mean that the group in question is the Jews who are also called pious; and Latin

---

[18] Kraabel, "Disappearance," 117.

[19] Kraabel refers to Lifshitz, *Donateurs*, although it must be said that Lifshitz's views regarding the reference of these terms are antithetical to Kraabel's.

[20] See his article, "Jewish 'Sympathizers' in Classical Literature and Inscriptions," *TAPA* 81 (1950) 200ff.

[21] *The Jews of Ancient Rome* (Philadelphia: Jewish Publication Society 1960) esp. 247, 251ff.

[22] *Nouvelles Inscriptions de Sardes* (Paris: Maisonneuve, 1964).

[23] *CII* 754.

[24] *CII* 748; see the discussion in Lifshitz, *Donateurs*, 25–26; and Robert, *Nouvelles*, 41–42.

inscriptions which include transcriptions of θεοσεβής[25] do not indicate the presence of a technical formula.[26] In sum, θεοσεβής cannot possibly designate a pagan Judaizer.[27] It can only be used to signal the piety of a member of the community.[28]

Overall, Robert's argument is somewhat puzzling, for it adduces no evidence from the inscriptions themselves to justify the claim that they must all refer to Jews. With Kraabel, too, the case rests largely on extrinsic considerations relating to the term itself. The critical factor with Robert is his assertion that the term θεοσεβής was too honorable, dignified, and elevated to have been applied to non-Jews. Kraabel's reasoning is somewhat different, though based on the same assumption that θεοσεβής must designate an exalted status. More troublesome for him is the implication drawn by some that the presence of non-Jewish sympathizers or "God-fearers" in some fashion demonstrates the fundamental inadequacy of Judaism in this period.

Martin Hengel in particular has spoken in such terms.

> The large number of semi-proselytes standing between Judaism and paganism . . . show the insoluble dilemma of the Jewish religion in ancient times. As it could not break free from its nationalistic roots among the people, it had to stoop to constant and ultimately untenable compromises.[29]

This is an astonishing statement, as offensive to reason as it is unjustified by the facts. Kraabel is entirely correct in treating it with contempt. But surely the correct response is to attack the fallacious reasoning and the unfounded assumptions that underlie the argument, as Kraabel has done admirably in his article on the significance of the Sardis synagogue, rather than to dismiss the data.[30] For it is not the data that are responsible for the bad interpretation but the unreliable interpreter.

---

[25] *CII* 228 and 619a.

[26] So F. Siegert ("Gottesfürchtige und Sympathisten," *JSJ* 4 [1973] 157) who adopts a skeptical stance toward the evidence of the θεοσεβής inscriptions but is otherwise inclined to the view that Gentile sympathizers were a regular feature of synagogues.

[27] It must be noted that Robert is inclined to connect all epigraphic occurrences of the adjectival θεοσεβής with synagogues; so *Nouvelles*, 44. In his "θεοσεβής" (*TDNT* 3 [1965] 124–25) G. Bertram lists a number of Greek Jewish texts where the adjective is applied to Jewish and biblical figures. In general, he notes, its usage in Jewish literary texts is rare.

[28] Robert, *Nouvelles*, 45.

[29] Martin Hengel, *Judaism and Hellenism* (2 vols.; Philadelphia: Fortress, 1974) 1. 313.

[30] Kraabel, "Impact," 178, 185.

If the underlying reasons for the skeptical view of the θεοσεβής inscriptions are thus extrinsic and essentially irrelevant, we must now ask whether these inscriptions sometimes or even regularly refer to Gentile sympathizers, that is, those who chose to affiliate themselves with synagogues in various ways without becoming full converts. Certainly this possibility has been recognized by numerous students of these texts—Frey,[31] Feldman,[32] Leon,[33] and Lifshitz.[34] The two donors called θεοσεβής at Sardis may be Gentiles after all. Certainly Cornelius, the φοβούμενος τὸν θεόν in Acts 10, is depicted as a donor; so is Julia Severa, a (former?) pagan priestess, who co-sponsored the construction of a synagogue in Acmonia.[35] Eustathios, who donated a basin to "the most sacred synagogue of the Hebrews" in Philadelphia, may well have chosen a technical term when he presented himself, with the definite article, as ὁ θεοσεβής.[36] And the category to which he belonged may well be mentioned in an inscription from the Crimea (Kertsch) which speaks of "the synagogue τῶν Ἰουδαιων καὶ θεὸν σεβον."[37] This would certainly be the case if the final phrase were to be emended, as Lifshitz and others have proposed, to read θεοσεβον.[38] Finally, the much-debated theater inscription from Miletus, even if not emended so as to read τοπος ειουδεον και τον θεοσεβιον, most likely stems from local authorities who may well have been uncertain of the distinction between Jews and sympathizers.[39]

There remains one further piece of evidence to consider, a set of inscriptions from ancient Aphrodisias in Caria, not far removed from Sardis and other cities with Jewish populations. Inasmuch as these inscriptions are not yet published, I must limit myself to a few brief remarks concerning their relevance for the debate about the "God-fearers."[40] Both texts are carefully inscribed on a tall, rectangular piece

[31] In his original edition of the *CII* (Rome, 1936) passim.
[32] "Jewish 'Sympathizers,'" esp. 208.
[33] *Ancient Rome*, 251ff.
[34] "Du nouveau," 77ff., where he discusses previous interpretations.
[35] *CII* 766; discussed by Lifshitz in *Donateurs*, 35–36.
[36] *CII* 754; discussed by Lifshitz in *Donateurs*, 31.
[37] See Lifshitz, *Prolegomenon* to *CII*, 65–66.
[38] Ibid., 65.
[39] See Lifshitz, "Du nouveau," 81–82; *Donateurs*, 25–26; and Siegert, "Gottesfürchtige," 159–60. The emendation was first proposed by Frey, *CII* 748.
[40] I am indebted to the editors of the Aphrodisias synagogue inscriptions, Joyce Reynolds and Robert Tannenbaum, both for their permission to make use of their contents and for their openness in discussing them with me. I am also grateful to G. W. Bowersock for providing me with a copy of a public lecture in which he discusses the inscriptions at some length.

of marble. The first contains some sixty lines of personal names, many of them with identifying professions, for example, Rouben the confectioner. The first and last lines are missing. Approximately at the mid-point of the text, there is a break of some five lines. The text recommences with the following heading: καὶ ὅσοι θεοσεβις (*sic*). The remaining twenty-five or so lines contain personal names and identifying professions, for example, Prounikios the fuller. This first nine of these names are identified as city councillors (βουλευτής). Before the break at the mid-point, the names are a mix of Jewish (Eusabbathios), biblical (Ioseph), and common Greek and Roman types, while following the break there are no biblical or Jewish names.

The second text, inscribed on an adjoining face of the same stone, and dating from a later period, contains some twenty-five lines, of which more than twenty contain personal names and a variety of further identifiers. As in the first text, the names are a mixture of Jewish, biblical, and Greco-Roman types. Several of the biblical names, for example, Samouel, are identified as proselytes; two of the Greco-Roman names are identified as θεοσεβής.

It is no exaggeration to propose that these inscriptions represent the most important epigraphic evidence from the world of Greco-Roman Judaism. They will be the center of debate for years to come. Yet even at this point, certain results seem assured. θεοσεβής designates a separate category of persons associated with the synagogue; it is used in a technical fashion as a title; the category itself is distinct from both proselytes and other Jews; it appears to cover Gentiles, whether exclusively or not.

Beyond Aphrodisias, these preliminary results would seem to undermine the skeptical view that θεοσεβής cannot be used of non-Jews. The older view, according to which "God-fearers" or sympathizers were a prominent feature of synagogue life in the Jewish diaspora, has now received a source of support that it hitherto lacked. The epigrahic data may be seen as corroborating the literary evidence in this regard. Of course, this does not prove that every reference to a θεοσεβής designates a Gentile sympathizer. Nothing would prove that. But the likelihood is now significantly increased that the term was used widely in epigraphic contexts to designate Gentiles who were not full converts to Judaism but nonetheless played an active and officially recognized role in many synagogues.

Regarding the book of Acts, it would appear that Kraabel's argument must be modified in one, but only one respect. I agree entirely that Luke uses the "God-fearers" for his own theological purposes, specifically to justify his view that Gentiles have replaced Jews as the chosen people of God. For whereas the Jews reject God's chosen messiah and persecute his followers, Gentile "God-fearers," that is, those who had already confessed the true God of the Bible, recognize the fulfillment of the biblical promises in Jesus and embrace the Christian movement. As indicated by both the external evidence from literary and epigraphic sources and the internal inconsistencies in Acts itself, since not all Jews reject the message even in Luke's text (e.g., 28:25), Luke's invention is not the category of "God-fearers" as such but rather their immediate and total abandonment of Judaism for Christianity. Apart from Acts, there is no support for this claim whatsoever. Against it stands the continued vigor of synagogue communities like Sardis and Aphrodisias, long after the time described by Acts; and against it stands the continuous tradition of Gentile Christian Judaizers, as attested by John Chrysostom's sermons at Antioch in the late fourth century and by the prohibitions against similar practices issued by the Council of Laodicea—located in close proximity to Sardis and Aphrodisias—in the mid-fourth century. Against it also stand the θεοσεβής inscriptions, many of which give us direct testimony of the ways in which Jews and Gentiles interacted in their shared environment. For it now seems likely that the θεοσεβής was, in some meaningful and official sense, a member of the Jewish community.

WHO IS THE TRUE PROPHET?*

Dieter Georgi
Johann Wolfgang Goethe-Universität, Frankfurt/Main
Harvard University

Krister Stendahl and the colleagues assembled around him at Harvard Divinity School have contributed to the fact that the history-of-religion approach has taken a sure foothold in NT studies in the United States. In the countries of its origin this approach is in sad decline, even in the homeland of the "History-of-Religion School." A major part of the heritage of that school has been the refusal further to abuse biblical studies for apologetic reasons lest one make the biblical environment merely a negative foil to the claim of superiority for the experience and message of Jesus and the primitive church. The attack on Christian triumphalism in exegesis and the insistence on the integrity of the historically particular, indeed of the peculiar, has been one of Krister Stendahl's hermeneutical contributions to the exegetical pursuit.

Krister helped me to realize the need for fairness to the dead, to acknowledge the original excitement, challenge, and tribulation of the dialogue of 2000 years ago, and not to make it a mere extension of our own interests and agitations. The participants in that dialogue of old are not copies of us but have an integrity of their own, their identity being often vastly different from that of their alleged heirs. The fact that many of the dead in the NT tradition and its "Christian," Jewish, and pagan environment have no heirs is not to be held against them.

---

*Twelve years ago I gave a paper at the Chicago meeting of the Society of Biblical Literature comparing the *Carmen saeculare* of Horace and Revelation 18. The following essay is a revision of this yet unpublished Chicago address incorporating further research and thought. It is the enlarged form of the essay "Zwei eschatologische Perspektiven" mentioned in my essay "Die Visionen vom himmlischen Jerusalem in Apk 21 and 22," in Dieter Lührmann and Georg Strecker, eds., *Kirche: Festschrift für Günther Bornkamm zum 75. Geburtstag* (Tübingen: Mohr-Siebeck, 1980) 351–72, esp. nn. 10 and 54. In honoring Krister I also think of our common predecessor as Frothingham Professor, and Krister's predecessor as editor of *Harvard Theological Review*, Arthur Darby Nock.

The challenge Krister has brought to us, his colleagues, can be condensed in the famous phrase of Tacitus: *sine ira et studio.* That this methodological ideal does not diminish adrenalin is proven by Tacitus and Krister alike.

A history-of-religion approach appears most necessary vis-à-vis the concept of eschatology because no other concept has been so misused in biblical studies in recent decades. The History-of-Religion School, in discovering the eschatological aspects of Jewish and early Christian thought and literature, experienced this as a shocking encounter with strange phenomena. Meanwhile "eschatological" has become a household word in biblical studies, a term which now denotes what is peculiarly and uniquely Christian, "our" property as it were, "us" over against "them;" "us" being early and modern Christians together, "them" being all others, including post-first-century Jews. And "eschatological" has also become synonymous with what is a-material, a-political, and frequently "dialectical," but now in a sense neither Hegel nor Marx would have associated with it, namely, "neutral." Thus an adjustment of our focus on eschatological texts of NT times appears to be in order. The inclusion of some unexpected worldly material will be of help, for part of the reason for the apologetic triumphalist abuse of the "eschatological" has been the isolation of the biblical connection from its "pagan" and "apocryphal," even its diaspora, environment, contrary to the History-of-Religion School's branching out and its subsequent discovery of strange bedfellows.

It is rather curious that students of the NT, particularly those making eschatology a battle cry, never mention certain highly eschatological texts contemporary with Jesus and Paul—namely, Roman texts—despite the fact that they reflect the origin and consequences of a rather lively propaganda in NT times, a propaganda which extended far beyond Italy. The only text some will mention here is the Fourth Eclogue of Virgil, and then only to say that the poem is a strange and curious text, rather foreign in its environment; and since no one really knows how to interpret this *alienum* the text is dropped again. But Virgil's Fourth Eclogue is not a strange and singular bird, but the expression of a much more general and pervasive mood ranging from Cicero's *Somnium Scipionis* to the poems of Statius.[1] The fact that the

---

[1] Besides the texts of Horace mentioned below and the Fourth Eclogue of Virgil there are other texts of Virgil which have eschatological overtones, not just the *Nekyia*, the descent into Hades in the sixth book, or the description of the divine shield in lines 626–728 of the eighth book of the *Aeneid*, but many more passages of this famous epic. Among the Eclogues, the First, the Fifth, the Sixth, and the Ninth should be mentioned too, as well as certain passages of the *Georgics*, e.g., lines 24–42 and 498–514 of the first

book of Revelation in chap. 13 describes the Caesar religion as a prophetic one deserves more attention.[2]

I would like to single out an "official" Roman text and its context, a text written by one of the major contributors to the Augustan cultural renaissance but also, besides Virgil and Augustus himself, the major theologian/prophet of the budding Caesar religion, the prophetic religion John of Patmos attacks. I am speaking of the *Carmen saeculare* of Horace. This poem is relatively contemporary with the NT. It originated at a time when the gospel according to Augustus had the world spellbound. Because there is not space here to produce a detailed textual analysis of that ode,[3] I will limit myself to certain observations and considerations which are relevant for the understanding of eschatology in NT times.

The *Carmen saeculare* was commissioned for the official celebration of the secular games, the official jubilee for the founding of the republic.[4] This was not an annual affair but was meant only for the end of a

---

book, 136–76 and 458–541 of the second, 1–49 of the third, 315–558 of the fourth. The two fragmentary Eclogues of the Einsiedeln Manuscript, the Caesar Eclogues of Calpurnius Piso, and the Caesar poems of Statius are further examples of Roman eschatology in NT times.

[2] The Harvard Th.D. dissertation of Steven Scherrer, "Revelation 13 as an Historical Source for the Imperial Cult under Domitian" (1979), presents excellent material for this comparison.

[3] See in particular the commentary on Horace by Adolf Kiessling, *Q. Horatius Flaccus: Werke* (10th ed.; rev. by Richard Heinze; Berlin: Weidmann, 1960) 1. 466–83 (on odes and epodes). See also the epilogue to this volume by Erich Burck with a detailed and annotated bibliography, 569–647. Important also is Eduard Fraenkel, *Horace* (Oxford: Oxford University Press, 1957). On 467–70 Kiessling gives the text of the oracle and of the records for and of the respective games. Relevant texts are also found in Viktor Ehrenberg and Arnold Hugh Martin Jones, *Documents Illustrating the Reigns of Augustus and Tiberius* (2d ed.; Oxford: Clarendon, 1955) nos. 30–32 (pp. 60–61). See also below n. 11.

[4] On the secular games see further Martin Nilsson, "Saeculares ludi," *PW* 1 A 2, 1696–1720; Lily Ross Taylor, "New Light on the History of the Secular Games," *AJP* 55 (1934) 101–20; Ronald Syme, *The Roman Revolution* (Oxford: Oxford University Press, 1952) 84, 218, 443–44; Franz Altheim, *A History of Roman Religion* (New York: Dutton, 1938) 72, 287–91, 353, 382, 390, 394–407, 442, 458–60; Kurt Latte, *Römische Religionsgeschichte* (Handbuch der Altertumswissenschaften; Munich: Beck, 1960) 248, 298–300; Robert E. A. Palmer, *Roman Religion and Roman Empire: Five Essays* (Philadelphia: University of Pennsylvania Press, 1974) 102–8; J. Gagé, "Beobachtungen zum Carmen Saeculare des Horaz," in Hans Oppermann, ed., *Wege zu Horaz* (Wege der Forschung 99; 2d ed.; Darmstadt: Wissenschaftliche Buchgesellschaft, 1980) 14–36. These authors give more primary data and secondary literature.

saeculum.[5] The origin as well as further occurrences of the games are a matter of dispute.[6] The length of a *saeculum* was not firmly established and was open to local variety and political manipulation. The date of the games certainly fell in the province of political expediency, and was therefore easy prey for convenient adjustments. Major occurrences and catastrophes, like the outbreak of the civil war, could also influence the calendar. The games were supposed to propitiate for past sins.[7]

Since Octavian understood himself as the savior of the republic, a celebration of the turn (revolution) of a *saeculum* as centenary of the initial republic fit well into his program. He had the secular games, long overdue, very carefully prepared.[8] Most probably he planned them immediately after the decisive battle of Actium, but then delayed them for political reasons.[9] Like his politics in general his final arrangement showed respect for tradition together with conscious modifications. In fact, his reform of the secular games "veränderte ihren Charakter völlig, indem sie den Akzent von der Sühnung der Vergangenheit auf den Beginn einer neuen Epoche verlegte."[10]

The relationship of the *Carmen saeculare* to the games has been a matter of dispute since the discovery of the records of the games and Theodor Mommsen's commentary on them.[11] But it seems certain that Horace's poem played a liturgically important role, that it "einen einzigartig wirksamen Ritus darstellte, die Götter gnädig zu

---

[5] The idea of a *saeculum* and its use as an instrument for dividing epochs cultically and institutionally seem to have come from the Etruscans. The lengths of these periods were and still are matters of debate. Prodigies played a role. On the concept and the debates see n. 4 and Gerhard Radke, "Saeculum," *Der kleine Pauly* 4. 1492–94. Here also further bibliography and further evidence about the games.

[6] Different opinions concerning age and further occurrences of these games in Taylor, "New Light," and Latte, *Römische Religionsgeschichte*, 246, esp. n. 4; new considerations in Palmer, *Roman Religion.*

[7] This is the opinion of Latte, *Römische Religionsgeschichte*, 248 n. 3.

[8] On these preparations see, e.g., ibid., 298–300.

[9] So, with good arguments, Harold Mattingly, "Virgil's Golden Age: Sixth Aeneid and Fourth Eclogue," *Classical Review* 48 (1934) 161–65.

[10] Latte, *Römische Religionsgeschichte*, 248. This official eschatological concept of the new age as political reality is presented in a fascinating way in the famous letter of the proconsul of the province of Asia, and in accompanying decrees on the new calendar. A copy was found in Priene, then also in Apamea, Eumeneia, and Dorylaeum (*OGIS* 458 and *SEG* 4. 490, reprinted in Ehrenberg-Jones, no. 98 pp. 81–83; cf. also the inscription from Halicarnassus, *IBM* 4. 1, no. 894; Ehrenberg-Jones, no. 98a, pp. 83–84).

[11] For the text of the official records of the Augustan games see *CIL* VI 32323 = *ILS* 5050; and Theodor Mommsen's commentary on them in *Ephemeris epigraphica* 8 (1891) 225–309. Also important is his article, "Die Akten zu dem Säulargedicht des Horaz," in *Reden und Aufsätze* (Berlin: Weidmann, 1905). See also above n. 3.

stimmen."[12] In Ode 4.6, which is contemporary with this "centennial song," Horace describes the situation of origin of the festival hymn. Here he defines his own mission as inspired by Apollo.[13] Horace dedicates this ode as well as the *Carmen saeculare* to the Delphic god who has a temple on the Palatine Mount.[14] The poet of the ode, "Parcus deorum cultor et infrequens,"[15] takes the gods not as a mere foil of poetic hyperbole. Gods for him are a presence laden with power as his ode "Bacchum in remotis carmina rupibus"[16] also demonstrates. Viktor Pöschl has described the bacchantic inspiration of Horace in an essay which is also instructive for the student of the NT.[17] In his discussion of this ode Pöschl observes a certain phenomenon of composition which is important for the *Carmen saeculare*: "Der Mythos als Gipfel und Zusammenfassung des Ganzen erscheint auch sonst gelegentlich in Horazgedichten."[18]

---

[12] Gagé, "Beobachtungen," 33. This observation appears correct although some of Gagé's hypotheses concerning models for Horace, i.e., earlier "carmina," may be debatable. In any case the festival song contributed to the efficacy of the rites. Hellenistic religion in general and Roman religion in particular kept the ancient conviction that the word, here the poem, is magically effective. The idea of Horace's poem as a mere melodramatic accompaniment of the festivities, intended only for aesthetic enjoyment, is a typically modern thought, foreign to the ancient mind.

[13] "'Twas Phoebus lent me inspiration, Phoebus the art of song, and gave me the name of poet" (lines 29–30). All quotes of texts and translations are from LCL.

[14] Also to the sister of Apollo, Diana/Artemis.

[15] "I, a chary and infrequent worshipper of the gods" (1. 34).

[16] "Bacchus I saw on distant crags" (2.19).

[17] "Dichtung und dionysische Verzauberung in der Horazode III 25," reprinted as "c. 3,25: Quo me Bacche," in Viktor Pöschl, *Horazische Lyrik: Interpretationen* (Heidelberg: Winter, 1970) 164–78. The tradition about Dionysiac ecstasy of the poet, which likens him to the Maenads, is already known to Plato. In NT times this idea was still present as Philo shows. See Hans Leisegang, *Der Heilige Geist* (Leipzig: Teubner, 1919) 126–231, 236–37; Hans Lewy, *Sobria Ebrietas* (ZNW 9; Berlin: De Gruyter, 1929) 3–72; Hans Jonas, *Gnosis und spätantiker Geist* (Göttingen: Vandenhoeck & Ruprecht, 1954) 2. 92–107. Philo proves that Judaism had also become acquainted with this idea.

[18] "Dichtung," 169 n. 2. Since the 2d century BCE, a movement towards remythicizing was much stronger than the tendency towards rationalization, religious uncertainty, or even decomposition. Some of the most impressive examples were Apocalypticism, Gnosticism, and Neopythagorean philosophy. As Lucretius's poem shows, even Epicurean philosophy, so important for Horace, was not untouched by this mythicizing tendency. In *Horaz und die Politik* (2d ed.; Sitzungsberichte der Heidelberger Akademie der Wissenschaften, Phil.-hist. Kl; Heidelberg: Winter, 1963) Pöschl writes: "Horaz bedient sich der Formeln und Symbole der früheren Poesie—sie umgestaltend und steigernd—, um seiner Aussage grössere Würde und Monumentalität zu geben, wobei auch der römische Glaube an die Autorität des Vorbildes hineinspielt, und, was für die Entwicklung römischer Poesie und Rhetorik besonders wichtig ist und einer Untersuchung wert wäre, die römische Überzeugung von der magischen Kraft geprägter Formen" (16).

It speaks for this high degree of self-estimation of Horace that he calls himself *vates*[19] as does Virgil. It is most probable that these poets follow the opinion of Varro concerning the meaning of the Latin term. This antiquarian, so important for Augustan reform, had assumed a false etymology and claimed that *vates* originally meant the poet.[20] Virgil and Horace both took this term to mean the inspired singers of ancient times. But then they used the term to refer to themselves, thus putting their own function and importance on the same level as the bards of old.[21]

The poet belongs to the sphere of the extraordinary, the miraculous. According to the ode "Non usitata nec tenui ferar,"[22] the poet is more successful than Icarus because he has turned into a heavenly bird, has turned immortal during his lifetime, and his immortal song has made funeral songs unnecessary.[23] According to Horace's Augustus Epistle,[24] the poet is not merely an educator of youth and comforter of the poor and the sick but also effective in prayer. In these lines from the letter to Augustus the "song" means first of all the *Carmen saeculare*; but it also stands for the poetry of the singer in general. His word is

---

[19] In Ode 4.6.44 and frequently elsewhere.

[20] See on this esp. Hellfried Dahlmann, "Vates," *Philologus* 97 (1948) 337–53; further Dietrich Wachsmuth, "Vates," *Der kleine Pauly*, 5. 1146–47.

[21] In the *Augustus Epistle* (*Ep.* 2.1.18–49[89]) Horace scolds those who would like to admit and appreciate *only* the old poets and show contempt for the modern ones.

[22] "On no common or feeble opinion shall I soar in double form through the liquid air" (2.20).

[23] "Let dirges be absent from what you falsely deem my death, and unseemly show of grief and lamentation! Restrain all clamour and forgo the idle tribute of a tomb" (lines 21–24). Of the miraculous inspiration of the poet I have spoken before. Horace also narrates a wondrous preservation during his early youth (Ode 3.4; see below) as well as a rescue from the attack of a wolf (Ode 1.22). On these and other miraculous events, and on the idea of the miraculous in Horace, see E. Zinn, "Erlebnis und Dichtung bei Horaz," in Oppermann, *Wege*, 369–88, and esp. the enumeration of Horace's accounts of wondrous events in his life, 377. Zinn says of the poet (based on Ode 1.22): "So kann er aus Faktum und Deutung die Konsequenz einer entschlossenen Bereitschaft ziehn: immer und überall dem Beklemmenden und Drohenden standzuhalten und liebender Dichter, dichtend Liebender zu bleiben" (383). Zinn writes (based on the research of Otto Weinreich): "Bei Horaz erscheint keine Religiosität einer reinen Innerlichkeit, sondern die Fülle einzelner *sacra* als Konkretionen des Göttlichen, das eben an den konkreten, faktischen Rettungen und Gaben, die man ihm verdankt, als übermenschlich, als göttlich erfahren wird" (686). I agree with Zinn (here and in his study "Aporos Soteria," in Oppermann, *Wege*, 220–57 esp. 247 n. 37) against Pöschl that Horace does not want to express himself merely figuratively, but that he has concrete experiences in view. I would, however, like to stay away from using the term "Faktizität."

[24] *Ep.* 2.1.126–38.

powerful, not only among humans but also among the gods. It has a relationship to prayer, magically invoking the gods, imploring and interceding for the purpose of winning the good and averting the bad.[25] In short, the divine and the human meet on the territory of the song.[26] Bringing this about is the function of the poet as *vates*.[27] His mission thus gains soteriological dimensions. Horace utilizes here the associations of *vates* during his time, namely, that of seer and magician.[28]

The glorification of the *princeps* and of the time of Augustus is not mere courtly poetry. Horace sees it as the immediate fulfillment of a heavenly order and as the execution of divine inspiration. The motif of ecstatic rapture, comparable to the "sweet" danger of the communion of the poet with Dionysus,[29] alludes to the situation at the composition of his song in honor of Augustus. As the poet wants to put the Caesar among the gods he does not speak as courtly sycophant but as peer, as one who himself belongs to the immortal ones.[30] In fact, it is the power of the poet's word which places the Augustus among the gods.

When people discuss the relationship of Horace to Augustus they often overlook this proud self-estimation of the singer. In the fourth Roman Ode (3.4) the divine protection of Horace and of Augustus are put side by side.[31] Horace sees both in the context of the mythical triumph of divine wisdom and moderate rest. The immediate miraculous experiences of the poet are extensively described, those of the Caesar are only hinted at (37–40). The narrative of the wondrous events of Horace's life is steeped in the light of eschatological myth: of paradise

---

[25] "Their chorus [that of the boys and girls at the centenary] asks for aid and feels the presence of the gods, calls for showers from heaven, winning favour with the prayers he [the *vates* mentioned before] has taught, averts disease, drives away the dreaded dangers, gains peace and a season rich in fruit" (*Ep.* 2.1.134–37). Here the poet gives a more general description of his function as *vates*.

[26] Cf. the *presentia numina sentit* in the passage just quoted, and then the following lines: "Song wins grace (*carmine placantur*) with the gods above, song wins it with the gods below" (137–38).

[27] "Vatem ni Musa dedisset" (*Ep.* 2.1.133).

[28] See on this association, Altheim, *Roman Religion*, 381–93.

[29] Ode 3.25: "Whither, O Bacchus, dost thou hurry me, o'erflowing with thy power? Into what groves or grottoes am I swiftly driven in fresh inspiration (*velox mente nova*)? In what caves shall I be heard planning to set amid the stars, and in Jove's council, peerless Caesar's immortal glory? I will sing of a noble exploit, recent, as yet untold by other lips" (25.1–8).

[30] In Ode 1.2 Horace speaks of Augustus as a savior who has come down from heaven. See Ernst Doblhofer, *Die Augustuspanegyrik des Horaz in formalhistorischer Sicht* (Heidelberg: Winter, 1966) 113–14. On the deification of Augustus in this song see also Pöschl, "Lyrik," 165–67.

[31] *Descende caelo* ("Descend from heaven").

in the case of the protection of the boy (9–20), of demonic terror at the ends of the earth, of hope for future preservation (29–35). In between Horace mentions the miracle of rescue during the battle of Philippi but also the wonders of protection from a falling tree and from the waves of the sea (25–28). Caesar and his troops are given rest by the Muses with whom the poet is in intimate conversation throughout his work. They give counsel, too, and through whom but the poet, so divinely saved and thus adorned? Imperial campaign, rest, and poetic counsel to the Caesar then are put into the context of the primordial myth of the rebellion of the Titans and Jupiter's miraculous victory over them (42–80). The recurrence of the mythical past in the end-time is a major tenet of Apocalyptic thought.

This ode proves how closely related personal quietude, idyll, and world peace are for Horace. Peace is not merely seen as political status but is put into the light of cosmic processes. Election, inspiration, experience, and linguistic magic all are personal realizations of this cosmic process. The Ode to Maecenas[32] shows in an impressive manner that for Horace the experiences of rest and of composed serenity are divine gifts, miracles indeed, when they happen during hopeless situations. They are comparable, yes superior, to the military and administrative securing of the empire (the business of Maecenas).[33]

The political and the private for Horace are not two separate spheres as Viktor Pöschl claims in his essay "Horaz und die Politik"; rather they constantly interconnect. The Ode to Maecenas demonstrates this. In this poem, which is so private in one way, Horace also gives political counsel to his patron. These suggestions are summarized in the μηδὲν ἀγάν.[34] Horace wants to be an exemplary Roman in this connection of the political, the religious, and the private. He hopes to restore old civic virtues in contrast to the individualistic tendencies of the previous decades. Horace sees different roles or functions in each of these areas,

---

[32] Ode 3.29, *Tyrrhena regum progenies* ("Scion of Tuscan kings").

[33] See Zinn, "Aporos Soteria," 246, about the miraculous aspect of the protection of the poet in the last two stanzas of the poem. Zinn says, "Es ist derselbe Mensch, der seinen Besitz—wenn das Schicksal es will—gelassen preisgibt, und dessen innerer Unanfechtbarkeit auch von aussen, von Natur und Gottheit her, Schutz und Rettung erwidert. Indem Horaz dies Geschehen für sich selbst im Indikativ fester Zuversicht prophezeien kann, verbindet sich in den Schlussversen des Gedichtes eine äusserste Selbstbescheidung mit äusserster Selbsterhöhung—das schlichte Abtun aller 'indifferentia' mit der 'Anmassung' eines Bewusstseins der Auserwähltheit." On the interpretation of the ode see also Pöschl, *Lyrik*, 198–245.

[34] In his interpretation of Ode 1.37 (*Nunc et bibendum*) Pöschl (*Lyrik*, 78) rightly says: "Wieder klingt die für Rom so charakteristische Verflechtung des politischen und des religiösen, des privaten und des öffentlichen Bereiches an."

but they do intersect. Interpreters have exposed the work of Horace again and again to questions about personal conviction and consistency. But these questions are conditioned by an image of personality as developed in the nineteenth century, an image unknown to people of the first century BCE or the first century CE. Even today this concept of personality is not a realistic one. It is an everyday experience still that the same persons play different roles and serve various functions at the same time. In compliance with such roles and functions they follow varying requirements, often expressing themselves in different, even contradictory utterances and behaviors. Even in all his various statements Horace appears to be more consistent and unified than many modern academicians.

The Epistle to the Pisones, usually called *Ars poetica*, and written about the same time as the *Carmen saeculare*,[35] shows the opposition Horace feels to something like pure poetry. Poetry for Horace transcends mere private satisfaction or the enjoyment of aesthetically minded small audiences. Poetry is an ethical, a political task. Indeed, according to lines 391–407 it has the function of creating and maintaining culture.

In the Augustus Epistle (2.1), one of, if not the last, works of Horace, poetry is described as an essential instrument of political education. Thus the attention that great men of politics pay to great men of the word is very appropriate. Poetry and military-administrative achievements are different expressions of wisdom and, therefore, should appreciate each other.[36] The beginning of this poem sees the *princeps*, the semi-gods, and the singers as colleagues. All are θεῖοι ἄνδρες.[37] The poet has the advantage that fame and name, that is, the

---

[35] Extensive discussion of this Epistle and its date can be found in Carl Becker, *Das Spätwerk des Horaz* (1963) 64–112, 232–37; cf. also ibid., 246–47 on its relationship to the *Carmen saeculare*.

[36] Future research will have to study further the relationship between the various forms of interest in wisdom in the Hellenistic world. The connection between Jewish and Hellenistic eschatology discussed in this essay seems to be but one part of the connection.

[37] On the θεῖος ἀνήρ see Dieter Georgi, *The Opponents of Paul in 2 Corinthians* (Philadelphia: Fortress; Edinburgh: T. & T. Clark, 1986) esp. the Epilogue with reference to further literature. On the socio-economic dimensions see idem, "Socioeconomic Reasons for the 'Divine Man' as a Propagandistic Pattern," in Elisabeth Schüssler Fiorenza, ed., *Aspects of Religious Propaganda in Judaism and Early Christianity* (Notre Dame/London: University of Notre Dame Press, 1976) 27–42. The development of the Hellenistic θεῖος ἀνήρ concept in Jewish missionary theology and its successful integration into worldwide missionary practice added to the attraction of the concept for Roman theologians and practitioners of the first century BCE. The Jewish missionaries proved the potential of the concept. Its interplay of tradition, law/morality, plurality, purpose, competition, and

real divine eternity of the *princeps* and other divine men, depend on the poet's reporting and eternalizing them.

Even the Sixteenth Epode in which Horace contemplates surrendering Rome must not be read as an escapist poem.[38] On the contrary, it is a political sermon.[39] The chaos prevailing in the Roman empire at the end of the forties and beginning of the thirties was tremendous, as was the corresponding loss of hope. The later savior of the republic, Octavian, was in his early twenties. Rome was about to commit suicide. On the surface it appears as if Horace completely concurred with the many predictions of doom circulating at the time.[40] But the reference to certain catastrophe serves as a foil for the banner of bright hope the poet raises.[41] He calls for emigration across the sea. The closing of the epode alludes to the migrations and colonizations of the epic period, but does not mention directly the most logical example, that of the flight of Aeneas. The reference to the Phoceans (line 17), who fled Persian rule, indicates that Horace is led by the idea of emigration for political and religious reasons.[42] The isolation of a *melior pars* (line 39)

---

merit showed success, provided motivation, and promised control. Any radical democracy (grass roots oriented and participatory) was feared as anarchy. But a consensus structure was needed which transcended the capital, Rome, and was able to stimulate local activities and loyalties beyond the confines of Roman citizenship, military force, and administration. Caesar's attitude towards the Jews had ingratiated them and set the pattern for the future. Collaboration was the consequence. Even the Jewish *Sibylline Oracles* did not propagate fundamental opposition. Hellenistic-Jewish missionary theology on the whole appreciated the Augustan reform, thus providing a trans-Italian support structure which helped to tie the provinces to Rome.

[38] In her study (*Der junge Horaz und die Politik* [Heidelberg: Winter, 1971]) Doris Ableitinger-Grünberger sees in the Sixteenth Epode a decisive turning away from political life for Horace. She emphasizes even more strongly than Pöschl a polarity between Horace's life and poetry on the one hand and the political world on the other. Even in the late Horace she sees at most an approximation towards a certain sacred synthesis which intends the propitiation of the political sphere, but never a real exchange. She claims that Augustus is praised for giving the possibility of existence to the sphere of the poet within the real world. Her ideas of reality and spirituality would seem to be foreign to Horace.

[39] The outline of the poem imitates the form of a speech in the people's assembly introducing a motion. So Richard Cornelius Kukula, *Römische Säkularpoesie* (1911) 13–14.

[40] On this see Latte, *Römische Religionsgeschichte*, 288–89.

[41] The majority of interpreters rightly think that the Sixteenth Epode is not ironic and the projected voyage not a journey into a fool's paradise as Kukula has claimed. See, e.g., Ableitinger-Grünberger, *Der junge Horaz.*

[42] On the motif of emigration see Harald Fuchs, *Der geistige Widerstand gegen Rom in der antiken Welt* (2d ed.; Berlin: De Gruyter, 1964) 9–13.

shows a familiarity with thoughts of contemporary sectarian circles which cherished the motif of emigration. Naturally, this idea of emigration associates easily with the expectations of eschatological doom and salvation. [43]

The Sixteenth Epode betrays acquaintance with Jewish motifs, especially those of an eschatological nature.[44] They can be traced back to biblical prophecy which Horace probably knew by way of Jewish missionary propaganda.[45] This Jewish missionary theology contained a vivid eschatology, found, among other places, in the Jewish *Sibylline Oracles.*[46] The Sibyl(s) and the Sibylline books were not an originally Jewish phenomena but the Jewish (and then Christian) literature in question picked up on the popularity of the Sibyl and of collections of

---

[43] The Essenes (at least their radical community in Qumran) are well known for an ideology of world flight and a corresponding organized isolation, as are the Therapeutae and Hermetic groups.

[44] Cf., e.g., Isidor Levy, *Horace, le Deutéronome et l'Évangile de Marc: Études horatiennes* (Brussels, 1937) 147–52; Franz Dornseiff, *Verschmähtes zu Vergil, Horaz und Properz* (Berichte über die Verhandlungen der sächsischen Akademie der Wissenschaften zu Leipzig, Phil.-hist. Kl. 97.6; Berlin: Akademie Verlag, 1951) esp. 44–63 (on Virgil's Fourth Eclogue), 57–60 (on the connections between Horace's Sixteenth Epode and the *Sibylline Oracles*), 64–72 (on Jewish elements in Horace's satires), 72–91 (on relations between Horace's odes, Virgil, and the LXX), 97–104 (on the Jewish influence on the fourth book of odes); Rudolf Hanslick, "Die Religiosität des Horaz," *Das Altertum* 1 (1955) 230–40, esp. 238 (on the influence of Jewish messianic ideas on Ode 1.2); Ableitinger-Grünberger, *Der junge Horaz*, 16–17, 67, 73–79; see also the more general discussion of analogies between Roman and Israelite-Jewish ideas in Otto Seel, *Römertum und Latinität* (Stuttgart: Klett, 1964) 103–37, 167–88.

[45] Dornseiff (*Verschmähtes*, 60–62) has drawn attention to the similarity of the passages in Jer 9:1–2 and 8:1–2 (not 8:17 as printed) to Epode 16.1–14, esp. 16.13 and 14. Dornseiff has argued that Horace's father was at least a proselyte, if not a born Jew, and that the son knew the LXX and the *Sibylline Oracles* of Jewish origin (65). The resemblances of Jewish motifs in Horace given by Dornseiff (see previous note) are often striking indeed. Although this specific biographical argument seems unwarranted, the acquaintance with Jewish missionary activity and its theology appears evident, and thus also an indirect familiarity with biblical motifs. On this Jewish propaganda see Georgi, *Opponents*, 41–60, 69–151, 174–217, esp. 148–51.

[46] On the *Sibylline Oracles* as part of that propaganda and of that eschatology see ibid. John Collins has given good arguments (*The Sibylline Oracles of Egyptian Judaism* [SBLDS 13; Missoula: Scholars Press, 1974) for dating and locating major portions of the third and fifth books of the *Sibylline Oracles*, the major Jewish parts of the whole collection. But he does not deal sufficiently with the missionary aspects of these Jewish oracles, which are, in my opinion, of primary importance even in the fifth book. The extant Jewish *Sibylline Oracles*, remainders of a larger corpus, thrived among many competitors. On the interest in such literature, particularly in Rome and among Romans of the late republic and the early principate, see further Gerhard Radke, "Sibyllen," *Der kleine Pauly*, 5. 158–61.

Sibylline oracles throughout the Mediterranean world. Their popularity did not rest on their mild language. On the contrary, heavy amounts of dirge and gore together with cryptic language added to the attraction of these oracles.

The many oracles going under the name of individual sibyls or of *the* Sibyl (the majority not extant) were of varying origins, character, and authenticity. In the majority, *ecstatic* prophetic and oracular phenomena were described with such terms. The official Roman Sibylline books of legendary origin were *ritual* prescriptions and regulations. According to Dionysius of Halicarnassus (*Ant.* 4.62.6) they were destroyed in the fire of the temple of Jupiter on the capitol in 83 BCE. Then a curious decision was made to restore this collection by "carrying together (oracles) from many places" (εἰσι συμφορητοί [χρησμοί] . . . ἐκ πολλῶν . . . τόπων), i.e., from all over the Mediterranean world, including the Near East. This was accomplished not only by official delegates but also by private persons who offered what they claimed to be transcripts. The obvious expectation was that from all of that mass of material (with apparent ἐμπεποιημένοι [χρησμοί] τοῖς Σιβυλλείος [χρησμοῖς]) one could restore the authentic ones. As to tendency the new collection followed the more common notion of the Sibyl and her oracles as being outright prophetic, although the new oracles (established, stored, and thus made secret, on the capitol starting from 76 BCE) were also consulted by the appropriate institution of interpreters (the *quindecimviri*) on ritual matters, such as the secular games. The reinstitution of the Roman Sibylline Books did not stop their further edition, nor the circulation of their sources, nor the production and circulation of new oracles. This is clearly demonstrated by the many quotes and the history of tradition of the Sibylline Oracles. Tacitus (*Ann.* 6.12) attests that under Augustus many of such oracles circulated (*multa vana sub nomine celebri vulgabantur*). Augustus felt compelled to order all Sibylline Oracles known to the public to be delivered to the urban praetor up to a set deadline after which any private ownership would become illegal. He concluded his own sifting and collating of oracles and editing of the Sibylline Books with their transfer to the temple of Apollo on the Palatine (Suetonius *Augustus* 31.1). Under Caligula even official attempts were still made—though unsuccessfully—to add new Sibylline books to the canon of 76 BCE.

Following Franz Dornseiff,[47] Moses Hadas[48] compares two passages, one of Horace, one of the Jewish Sibyl.

[47] See above n. 44.
[48] *Hellenistic Culture: Fusion and Diffusion* (New York: Norton, 1972) 242.

Already a second generation is being ground to pieces by *civil war*, and Rome through her own strength is tottering. . . . The savage conqueror shall stand, alas! upon the *ashes* of our city, and the *horseman shall trample it with clattering hoof*, and (impious to behold!) shall scatter wantonly Quirinus' bones that now are sheltered from the wind and sun.[49]

Upon thee, Italy, no warfare of foreign foes shall come, but *civil bloodshed* lamentable and *of long continuance* shall ravish thee, thou famous land, for thy shamelessness. And thou, stretched prone among the burning *ashes*, shalt slay thyself, in thy improvident heart. Thou shalt be no mother of good men, but a *nurse of wild beasts*.[50]

On the one hand there is the great mass, the *indocilis grex* (the "unconvertable crowd"). On the other, there is the *melior pars* (the "better part"), the two forming the *omnis exsecrata civitas* (the "entire self-condemning state").[51] This is reminiscent of the division of Israel by the prophets into the just and the unjust, particularly of the motif of the holy remnant. Like the prophets, Horace addresses the entire people, but he expects only the truly pious to follow his call.[52]

The proposed voyage will go to the isles of the blessed, the Greek Elysion, an individualized golden age.[53] Traditionally this eschatological place is accessible for common mortals only after death. But heroes may reach it before they die (that is, they become immortal). Horace realizes this eschatological concept but not, as expected, in the manner of Hellenistic utopian literature where, in attempts to realize eschatology, the islands of the blessed had become the place for institutions, laws, customs, offices, peoples, or societies. It was an anticipation of the return of the golden age in the collective sense of that motif.[54] This

---

[49] Horace, Epode Sixteen. I have italicized parallels between this and the subsequent quotation.

[50] *Sib. Or.* 3.464–69 from the translation of H. N. Bate, *The Sibylline Oracles: Books III–V* (New York: Macmillan, 1918).

[51] *Ep.* 16.36–37. On *exsecrata* as *unter Selbstverwünschung schwören* ("swearing by cursing oneself" not "cursed") see Ableitinger-Grünberger, *Der junge Horaz*, 37–40.

[52] On *pius* and *pietas*, so important for the later Augustan reform, see Latte, *Römische Religionsgeschichte*, 39–40, 238–39; Theodor Ulrich, *Pietas (pius) als politischer Begriff im römischen Staate bis zum Tode des Kaisers Commodus* (Historische Untersuchungen 6; Breslau: Marcus, 1930); H. D. Weiss, "Piety in Latin Writers in Early Christian Times" (Ph.D. diss., Duke University, 1964).

[53] "Let us seek the Fields, the Happy Fields, and the Islands of the Blest" (lines 41–42).

[54] On utopian literature see Hans Volkmann, "Utopia," *Der kleine Pauly*, 5. 1083–84. Unfortunately Volkmann does not acknowledge the indebtedness of Roman literature of

is all the more surprising since Horace does not stick to the traditional concepts of the Elysion, although he uses some key words.[55] The idyll described in lines 43–62 resembles the notion of peaceful paradise returned as found in biblical prophecy and translated into sermons and treatises of Jewish missionary theology.[56] But this Jewish theology has visions of an exemplary society, too. Thus Horace wants to border on such utopian thoughts, including their pacifist tendencies, without committing himself to any social concreteness. He commits only his will to utilize the heroic, immortalizing dimensions of the Elysian concept in order to undergird the call to immediate political action. Those following Horace's appeal, that is, the morally sound who still have political courage, are promised the place of immortal heroes *now.* The other utopian dimensions remain just beyond the horizon.[57]

Horace tries to influence the socio-political reality with a dialectic blend of prophetic criticism and hope in the concept of flight (*fuga*, 66). The desperate situation makes him concentrate on the critical side of this dialectic. This can be interpreted in the sense of critical distance, but not in the sense of resigning to inner emigration. The poet sees himself as the head of another emigration to a mythical west like the founder of Rome, Aeneas. A threat also resides in the poet's suggested flight, namely, the remaining republic will lack the creative word of the poet-prophet and the morally sound core of the people who follow him. Rome, alas Italy, will be doomed like Troy. Its only future will be with the emigrants in another Rome, another Italy.

Rome, torn asunder by the strife of civil war, has turned into an incarnation of the myth of the catastrophic end of the iron age, just at the threshold of the return to the new age. Horace presents a mythicized form of the move away from the city, here radicalized into a

---

the first centuries BCE and CE to Greek and Hellenistic utopian thought. See also Robert von Pöhlmann, *Die Geschichte der sozialen Frage und des Sozialismus* (3d ed.; Munich: Beck, 1925); Reimar Müller, *Die epikureische Gesellschaftstheorie* (Schriften zur Geschichte und Kultur der Antike 5; 2d ed.; Berlin: Akademie Verlag, 1974); idem, "Zur sozialen Utopie im Hellenismus," in *Die Rolle der Volksmassen in der Geschichte der vorkapitalistischen Gesellschaftsformationen* (Veröffentlichungen des ZIAGA der Akademie der Wissenschaften der DDR 7; Berlin: Akademie Verlag, 1975) 277; idem, "Sozialutopien der Antike," *Das Altertum* 23 (1977) 227.

[55] The concepts *divites insulae* and *arva beata* are found together in Pindar's Second Olympian Ode (55–83) and Hesiod's *Erga* (167–70).

[56] On the description of a future of bliss in missionary texts of Hellenistic Judaism see Georgi, *Opponents*, index under eschatology. The most extensive representations are in Philo *De praemiis et poenis* 79–126, 152–72.

[57] Horace shares this "teasing" approach to the symbolic-allegorical with the eschatology of Jewish missionary theology, as Philo's tractate *De praemiis et poenis* shows so well.

move away from Italy altogether. The civil war seems to have proven the end of a civilization sold on urbanization. This had led to an extreme overpopulation in major cities, especially in Rome, with devastating consequences for the labor and housing market. Mass employment was never contemplated. This dilemma was covered up by the provision of inexpensive or gratuitous grain for the "plebs." This "dole" had turned into an expensive but successful instrument of demagoguery because it created an impression of leisure among the masses, a resemblance of the freedom of the nobility of Rome. Thus it distinguished the recipients of the gift of grain, the *annona*, from social peers elsewhere. Demagogues in the political competition and conflict would promise more such material leisure and nobility in exchange for votes and other support. This made the city all the more attractive and the social pressure of people migrating to the city increased, along with the potential for social and political unrest.

Horace's suggested flight was an extreme form of remedy: counter-migration, flight from the city instead of from the land. This would decrease the overpopulation in the city and thus the economic pressure and revolutionary potential there. Horace shows no awareness that his call to the west gave some ideological support to the practices of richer people who had started to invest heavily outside of Italy. Their interest in better financial returns could not be backed with the excuse of the catastrophic situation in the capital and in Italy. Horace, out of despair for reasons of dramatizing his criticisms of the state of affairs in Rome and in Italy at large, would propose an extreme version of that move to the open country, a migration where the vision of the unknown world would provide more certainty than the chaotic reality of the doomed city.

At the fringe of the dialectic message of the Sixteenth Epode stands the hint of an impossible possibility (lines 25–34):[58] the emigrants swear not to return unless both inanimate and animate nature change in a revolutionary fashion. The cosmic changes described in the oath of those who have been exiled bear eschatological traits and thus concur with the eschatological nature of the goal of the proposed voyage. The enumeration of impossibilities appears to be more than a means of rhetorical style. The conditions for the return expressed in the oath play with the idea of a greater miracle than the voyage to the land of the

---

[58] Horace uses here the stylistic element of accumulating impossibilities (ἀδύνατα). See on this esp. Ernest Dutoit, *Le thème de l'Adynaton dans la poésie antique* (Paris: Budé, 1936). Ableitinger-Grünberger (*Der junge Horaz*, 40–42) has shown that Horace has formed the "adynata" in an original way.

blessed could be: the restoration of the republic. Horace can predict this only in eschatological cosmic dimensions. The return of Rome will be an event which will shake and move the world.[59]

The *Carmen saeculare* celebrates the miracle which occurred in the meantime: the salvation of the republic. The impossible had happened. The hope expressed in the *Carmen* is miraculous, no doubt, but present, indeed fulfilled. The confidence about the realization of what has been desperately expected before is concrete, and the materialism of the expectation indicates the degree of reality. There are many eschatological themes: the eschatological language of *Urzeit-Endzeit*, the ideal of the miraculous return of the golden age and paradise, and even the ideal of the eschatological savior—in line with the heroes of old.[60] All of this is imbedded in a prophetic framework with reference to the Sibyl at the start of the poem and with the conjuration of the divine prophet and protector of the seers, Apollo, in the beginning and at the end. The reference to the prediction is found at the end as well.[61] There is also the prophetic role of the *vates*, the poet himself.

The recently enacted marital legislation of Augustus[62] at first glance

---

[59] The correspondence between the Sixteenth Epode of Horace and Virgil's Fourth Eclogue is one of the more dramatic occurrences in world literature. Scholars differ as to who presupposes and criticizes whom. I follow those who take the Sixteenth Epode to be the earlier poem, with Virgil's Fourth Eclogue opposing his friend's skepticism. Virgil says that the taking to the sea can be an interlude at most (lines 31–37). The impossible, in fact, has already happened: the iron age has ended and the golden age is beginning. This interpretation stands in contradiction to that of, among others, Dornseiff (*Verschmähtes*, 63), Hadas (*Hellenistic Culture*, 243), and Becker (*Das Spätwerk*, 314). Dornseiff bases his argument in part on some other correspondences with Virgil in the entire work of Horace. But the two friends were in dialogue, and that dialogue was mutually influential, at least until the death of Virgil. The golden age hoped for is that of peace, the new age of the eschatological hope of Jewish missionary theology. Virgil's confidence will prove to be in line with economic, social, and political development.

[60] Jewish eschatology of missionary persuasion was attractive to Romans not only because of its inherited soteriological and cosmological breadth and depth, but also because of its utopian dimension with a clear interest in using propaganda to influence present structures of social consent.

[61] Christian theologians and scores of other critics throughout the centuries take exception to the "materialistic" interests expressed in Horace's and similar statements. Their religious integrity is doubted. But this criticism only proves that Christians have used eschatology to dematerialize and thus deconcretize the hope for change.

[62] Using his tribunal power Augustus had initiated in 18 BCE the *Lex Julia de maritandis ordinibus*, legalizing marriages between freeborn citizens and people freed from slavery (senators, however, were excluded from this liberalized practice), thus rewarding marriage and childrearing, and discouraging abstention from marriage and childbirth, and the *Lex Julia de adulteriis coercendis*, making adultery a public crime.

may not appear to be an appropriate subject for a poem of eschatological orientation (lines 13–24). Our readiness to take the ordinary political allusion of Horace seriously is dimmed further by our hindsight: we know of the ultimate lack of success of this legislative measure of Augustus. For the author and the audience of the song, however, the marital legislation of Augustus is a new and impressive symbol of Augustus's efforts to reverse the catastrophe of moral and physical decay, the suicide of the republic. It is a sign that far-ranging change is on its way and its duration is secured.[63] The poem prays for stability, prosperity, and peace with impressive language.[64] The hearer receives sufficient indication that these things are not bloodless dreams but present reality,[65] and that the *Carmen* prays for their increase.

The longest single portion of the song (lines 37–52) invokes the tradition which was only alluded to in the Sixteenth Epode, that of Aeneas. At the time of origin of the secular song this tradition was not yet codified in the public consciousness. The epic of Horace's friend, Virgil, was not yet public property.[66] But the tradition was already part of public education, especially since Augustus had started to take active interest in this Trojan hero.[67] Horace mentions only briefly the flight of the great man from Troy and his subsequent adventures, including those in Italy. He uses the divine interference in these experiences as examples for his own prayer, which asks for further divine actions to improve the education of youth and the security of old age.[68]

Then, in lines 49–52 (60), Aeneas suddenly turns into a contemporary figure who brings about worldwide peace through weapons, threat, and persuasion. The miraculous heroic past has become present epiphany in the activity of Augustus. In Aeneas, the Caesar himself has entered the scene. We hear that the age-old virtues of *pietas*, *pax*, *honor*, and *virtus* have returned. In the same breath *copia* is mentioned as a quality of similar value; it also experiences a return. It is not just a certain good, but a basic value which guarantees the salvation and

[63] Existence and return of the *saeculum*, as such already an eschatological good, depend on this (lines 21–24).

[64] Esp. in lines 19–32, 57–60, and 65–68.

[65] Cf., besides the references to the marital legislation, the double *iam* ("already") in lines 53 and 57.

[66] The *Aeneid* was published after Virgil's death (19 BCE) against the expressed will of the poet but by the request of Augustus.

[67] Augustus suggested the topic of the *Aeneid* to Virgil.

[68] See lines 45–46, obviously connected with lines 33–36. The third recipient of the beneficial assistance of the gods, proven in history, is the entire progeny of Romulus, all of the Roman people (47–48).

duration of the commonwealth.[69] Thus it is not surprising that in the end the song prays not merely for general audition but also for growth of the might and fortune of Rome and Latium (lines 65–68).

The *Carmen saeculare* describes the perfection of the endtime in rural colors. The tones of pastoral idyll as we know them from Virgil's Fourth Eclogue resound in Horace. Although this style fits within the genre of the bucolic poem of Virgil, it is hardly expected in the *Carmen* of Horace. Neither can it be said that eschatological writing requires rural expression. Biblical and Jewish eschatology can work with urban images as the prophecies concerning Zion prove.

Horace does not even offer any harmonization between the rural and the urban image as found in the end of Ezekiel or in Ps.-Aristeas. In these, the harmonization is not a secondary accommodation but an acknowledgment of an important socio-economic problem in antiquity. The antithesis and conflict between urban and rural grew into heavy exploitation of the countryside by the cities during the Hellenistic period. Thus the harmonization in some of the eschatological predictions promised a coming reconciliation of social adversaries and thus the miraculous resolution of a dilemma that history had been unable to solve.

But in the *Carmen saeculare* Horace does not mention the urban world at all. This is striking in a festival song which praises the achievements and blessings of the principate of Augustus, one of the major city builders of the ancient world, and which celebrates the largest city of the age. One of the most important achievements of Augustus was the restoration and improvement of the city of Rome, not merely politically and morally, but also architecturally. In addition, the Augustan reform had brought about a worldwide improvement of urban life, including an increase in the number of cities and of the size of many existing ones. Thus the silence of the *Carmen saeculare* on urban life is very surprising. The traditional interest of Romans in soil and in agriculture is not a sufficient explanation. During the time of Augustus the city of Rome had lost direct contact with the life of farmers and shepherds. In the Hellenistic world in general and especially in Roman society, the city, particularly *the* city, the *urbs* absolute, Rome, had become the central symbol.

---

[69] One is reminded of the southern panel on the eastern side of the altar of Pax Augusta, erected some four years later, where Italy is depicted as a goddess in the midst of signs of agrarian plenty and peace.

There are socio-economic and political reasons for this silence on the city and emphasis on the countryside in the secular song of Horace. These reasons also explain the preference for the idyllic in the preceding works of the two main theologians of Augustus, with Virgil initially being more optimistic than Horace. Although Augustus was the first citizen of the city of Rome and although he very actively improved the image of this city, he still established his own base and his prosperity through Egyptian soil. Under him Egypt grew into a gigantic agricultural domain for the principate. But what developed fully under Augustus had begun before. The trends of Hellenistic society and economy had moved from the direction of worldwide urbanization to that of ruralization.[70] The Romans followed this trend. Augustus built in part on the extraordinary position that agriculture held in Roman tradition, which he wanted to restore. But the restoration of the rural world would not have happened if the socio-economic situation had not been ready for it.

Rome's ideology and social structure had remained basically agrarian. Noble and rural, piety and soil, were always related, if not synonymous. Migration to the countryside for the purpose of farming could create a counterweight to the explosive urbanization, reviving old strategies and their potential for social stability and control.

The land issue had been a major element of the Roman civil war. The popular party, that of the Gracchi, of Caesar, and later Augustus, had taken up the banner of the plight of the ever-increasing urban masses. Their impoverishment was supposed to be helped by distribution of public land, and this was to relieve the socio-economic and political pressures of overpopulation on Rome. But during the civil war the Gracchic reforms were only partially realized, and the population of the city continued to grow, with devastating consequences for the labor and housing markets.

---

[70] Or, as one might call it, paganization, using the Latin term *pagani*, which denotes persons living in a *pagus* (rural country), the hinterland from an urban, "educated," point of view. The *pagani* happened to be more conservative, holding on to their inherited religion. Thus the term later became synonymous with non-Christian. But the irony of history wills that the move of the church towards power-sharing in the state coincided with the church's increasing missionary success in the countryside. The phenomenon of the massive return first of the Roman elite and then of others to the countryside is also the topic of the book by Werner Raith, *Das verlassene Imperium: Über das Aussteigen des römischen Volkes aus der Geschichte* (Berlin: Wagenbach, 1982). But my perception of the character and dimension of the phenomenon and my explanation differ from Raith's.

Despite the distribution of land since Tiberius Gracchus and the settlement of veterans in rural areas in the subsequent century, there was, nevertheless, an increasing hesitation among the masses to leave the city. The socio-economic development of farming moved away from small farms toward large estates aimed at maximizing profits. Worked and administered by slaves, these estates had turned into centers for the production of profitable goods starting with a limited number of profitable agricultural products, but soon taking advantage of the presence of resources and cheap labor to produce other wares.[71]

Thus, since the end of the first century BCE, property in the open country promised to be a better investment of capital with a growing rate of productivity and profit, at least in the case of large agricultural plants. The Ptolemaic system, with its controls and monopolies, had prepared the way for this economic development. Although Augustus provided for the free distribution of wheat to more than 300,000 citizens of Rome, his profit from relatively little expenditure in the Nile valley was tremendous. The principle which worked in rural estates and plants also proved to be a better basis for the expensive, long distance sea trade, which was essential to the economic structure of the empire.[72] This trade needed major capital backing without which it could not survive. It was too expensive and too risky for short term financing. But, literally, in the long run, it could pay off.

Meanwhile, the social pressure on the city had not yet diminished; on the contrary, the big cities, especially Rome, still attracted many lower class people. And the slave-operated estates were driving farmers away, and not attracting free laborers. Therefore, a concerted effort was necessary to allay realistic fears among the lower classes regarding their situation on the land. In addition, more landowners needed to be moved to care for their rural estates personally instead of relying on

[71] E.g., brick, pottery, glass, and even metal. Agriculturally the big estates would concentrate on whatever proved to give the highest financial yield given local circumstances. In Italy this would mean wine, fruit (particularly figs), and oil. In some suitable areas space was also devoted to the large-scale raising of cattle, sheep, pigs, and poultry.

[72] Land routes were too expensive for long distance trading because horse power could not yet be economically "harnessed," in the literal sense of the world. Ox power was too slow, clumsy, and costly. On sea routes much space was preempted by grain imported to Italy, especially to Rome, not just from Sicily, but from Africa, Egypt, and as far as the Black Sea. The remaining freight space could be more profitably used to transport luxuries for the well-to-do. This transportation factor is one of the reasons for the absence of interest in mass production in the city. It would have required extensive systems of distribution, particularly for long distance conveyance. The provision of inexpensive or gratuitous grain to the masses, though expensive to those responsible, was maintained because it proved to be more beneficial politically (see above, 113–14).

slaves. This would work against the disastrous effects of investment in estates outside of Italy and of absentee ownership of land. Having wealthy Romans invest more in Italian estates and be physically present would create confidence among the smaller farmers because of the shared Roman consensus-structure. An invocation of the old Roman virtues, particularly of thriftiness, could induce restraint in the consumption of luxuries among the rich, thus reducing social envy and improving the catastrophically negative balance of trade.

If more lower class free people moved to the countryside landlords might also be attracted to invest still more in their estates because they could count on a better labor market. City people might be attracted to work as farm hands which would tempt small farmers to forego economic risks and turn their plots over to the landlords and take up tenancy as a safer way of farming. This would help the landowners since slavery was becoming increasingly expensive.

Augustus was more a symptom than a cause. He stood for the acceleration of an economic and social momentum which later developed into an avalanche: the rise of the owners of the *latifundiae* ("large estates") into the position of essential and decisive producers and promoters and carriers of trade. The flight from the city would eventually end in the dethroning of Rome as the capital city. The centralizing efforts of the Caesars of the first and second centuries were futile attempts to create a counterweight. They helped neither the empire nor society at large, but aided the deurbanizing decentralization because they tended to make ever larger parts of the empire imperial domains. This turned increasingly larger portions of the populace into an imperial clientele with other investors, proprietors, and producers imitating and competing. Virgil and Horace express the eschatological dimensions of this growing development: the capitalism of the suburbs and of the rural estates as realized eschatology.[73]

---

[73] Augustus, the Augustan religion, and all who helped them, became pacesetters of an economy and society which turned away from the city, of a flight to the countryside. The centralizing efforts of the Caesars of the first century were not really of an economic nature in this respect, but a mere passing stage in a contrary development. The Caesars themselves boycotted their centralizing measures by their own private economic activities, arrangements, and establishments.

As it turned out the development which Virgil and Horace promoted and supported did not happen for the sake of the city of Rome. It did not strengthen the situation of small and moderate farmers either, but of the rich, particularly those willing to invest. The political theology as expressed in the poems of Virgil, Horace, and those sharing their opinion in the end gave encouragement and good conscience to the leading class for leaving the cities to the masses, thus turning them into sources of cheap labor for the future heirs of the big country estates, the coming centers of economy and society.

Idyllic elements appear early, too, in the eschatology of Jewish missionary theology. Although this theology and its practice initially was heavily if not entirely urban, from the start it tended to relate happiness to nature.[74] Whereas initially a reconciliation with the urban was contemplated, this interest later receded into the background. In the *Sibylline Oracles* the positive urban dimension does not go beyond abstract mentions of Jerusalem as the center of the world. In Philo's *De praemiis et poenis* the rural aspects of the future world described prevail. Philo proves elsewhere that he is acquainted with handbooks on agriculture,[75] typical reading for the well-to-do who wanted to establish or improve their investments in rural estates.[76] Jewish missionary theology proved to be in line with socio-economic development. Thus its eschatology—constructively utopian through its biblical heritage— became supportive for the trends highlighted in Roman theological literature,[77] active efforts in social collaboration.

I want to turn now to an author who, towards the end of the first century, had to suffer under the consequences of the confusing trends and policies which the principate and the Caesar religion stood for— John, the author of the Book of Revelation. Whereas in the case of Horace's work the religious and theological sides have not been taken seriously by its interpreters, in the case of John's visions the opposite is true: John's revelation is interpreted at the expense of its relationship to the real life of its addressees. In both cases the interpreters claim a distancing of the respective author from political reality, particularly with respect to social and economic dimensions and consequences.

The work of John has gained the attention of critical exegetes only recently, although it deserved it long ago given its historical and theological importance. The Revelation of John presupposes the genre and theology of Apocalyptic literature, but it pursues interests contrary to Apocalypticism. The author does not use a pseudonym but mentions his name, John. The historical situation of the addressees thus is not veiled and transcended by a legendary past but is spoken to directly and

---

[74] Georgi, *Opponents*, 129–32, 143–46, 149.

[75] *De agricultura* and *De plantatione*, 152–72.

[76] See the handbooks of Cato and Columella.

[77] It is interesting that the Gospel of Mark and the work of Luke, both pro-Roman, show growth of the idyllic element. The trend towards the development of Christianity as a separate entity from its start coincides with the interest to come to an accord with socio-economic tendencies of the leading forces of society. The fact that Mark and Luke both have certain ascetic aspects would not interfere with their acceptability in leading circles since the official Roman ideology stressed a certain degree of discipline, promoting not only social but also economic control.

concretely in the addresses to the seven churches. The format of the heavenly letter, basic for John's work, is known to Apocalypticism, but John has radically modified it through the concrete addresses in the first three chapters and the utilization of the form of the Pauline epistolary prescript (1:4–6).

Because of their interest in calculable prediction of final events, apocalypses usually provide their readers with coded but verifiable information about past and present events as a basis for their eschatological projection. But the continuous delay of the predicted eschaton made adjustments and revisions necessary again and again. This became one of the essential traditional and historical reasons for the literary peculiarity of apocalypses which present themselves more or less as comprehensive and often contradictory compilations of various Apocalyptic sketches and fragments. John imitates this literary peculiarity of apocalypses skillfully. But he uses it to establish a compositional scheme which Victorinus of Pettau described long ago and Günther Bornkamm and Adela Yarbro Collins have recently rediscovered.[78] The author presents in several series[79] a similar sequence of eschatological visions: each new series is slightly more extensive than the previous one, has a two-part key vision precede it, dresses the whole collation of

---

[78] Günther Bornkamm, "Die Komposition der apokalyptischen Visionen in der Offenbarung Johannis," in *Studien zu Antike und Urchristentum* (3d ed.; Munich: Kaiser, 1969) 204–22; Adela Yarbro Collins, *The Combat Myth in the Book of Revelation* (HDR 9; Missoula: Scholars Press, 1976). Yarbro Collins's study has also blazed new trails for understanding the theology and religious context of the book. She has enlarged this in further stimulating studies which are contained or at least reflected in her *Crisis and Catharsis: The Power of the Apocalypse* (Philadelphia: Westminster, 1984). She sees the views of John not as directly politically involved as I do, although she shows well the social orientation of the book's perception of reality and its message to its situation. More emphasis on the political concerns of John is found in Elisabeth Schüssler Fiorenza, "Religion und Politik in der Offenbarung des Johannes," in *Exegetische Randbemerkungen: Schülerfestschrift Rudolf Schnackenburg* (Würzburg: Echter Verlag, 1974) 261–71, and in "Visionary Rhetoric and Social-Political Situation," in her *The Book of Revelation: Justice and Judgment* (Philadelphia: Fortress, 1985) 181–203. All of the other essays in that volume provide further enlightenment for our understanding of John. My own views on some major aspects of the Apocalypse of John can be found in my essay "Visionen."

[79] In *Combat Myth* Yarbro Collins has shown that John presents the same arrangement of the sequence of persecution, judgment, and triumph five times, namely, in chaps. 6 and 7; 8–11 (without 10:1–11:12); 12–15:4; 16:4–19:10; and 20:1–21:8. She proves that there are other, even more intricate correspondences, and that there are interludes in this complex of 6:1–22:5 as well.

visions into a letter format with seven addressees,[80] and finally adds a preface (1:1–3). In the several parts of the epistolary introduction many of the formal and material elements of the main body are already touched upon.[81] By way of his recapitulation scheme John prevents his readers from abusing his visions as objectifying means for defining their privileged place in salvation history and for setting the clock for the end of time. John's concept of history is different, and so is his understanding of the character of the church's situation within it.

John shows himself sufficiently acquainted with Apocalyptic hermeneutics, particularly as it concerns the integration of tradition and symbolism. John is conscious of the creative dimension of language and literary composition. The peculiar Greek style of the book is not an expression of linguistic incompetence or barbarism but proves to be an original creation of a singular language with its own rather consistent grammar, syntax, and vocabulary.[82] John uses this language not, as Apocalypticism does, in order to create another supernatural reality but in order to get hold of historical reality with the help of prophetic magic. Nowhere in the NT do we find a similarly rich collection of heavenly statements. One can even speak of a heavenly authorship of the book, and John is of the conviction that the finished work is holy writ word for word. The heavenly sphere which the seer invokes by his word is not another world, but the concrete basis for the historical reality of congregations as they witness to Jesus in their Sunday worship and in their confession.

John's work is anything but the product of an esoteric quietistic piety. Here a prophetic consciousness which has a hold on historical reality expresses itself. It is ready to call into question the claim of "official" reality which considers itself able to create and control everyone. John challenges the Roman state, in particular the principate. According to chaps. 13 and 17 John sees in the gigantic machinery of the *Imperium Romanum* the demonstration of a prophetic religion

---

[80] The two key chaps. are 4 and 5; the epistolary frame is 1:4–3:22 and 22:6–21.

[81] A few examples include macarisms (which are lacking in Apocalyptic literature with one or two exceptions; rather surprising considering the sapiential development of Apocalypticism since Daniel) which occur in Rev 1:3; 14:13; 16:15; 19:9; 20:6. Παντοκράτωρ appears as a title in 1:8; 4:8; 15:3; 16:7, 14; 19:6, 15; 21:22. The motif of the heavenly temple is found in 3:12; 7:15; 11:1–2, 19; 14:15, 17; 15:5–6, 8; 16:1, 17; 21:22; the white garments in 3:4–5, 18; 4:4; 6:11; 7:9, 13; 19:14; the book of life in 3:5; 13:8; 17:8; 20:12, 15; 21:27.

[82] On the language of the Book of Revelation and its internal regularity see esp. R. H. Charles, *The Revelation of St. John* (ICC; Edinburgh: T. & T. Clark, 1920) 1. cxvii–clix, under the significant heading "A short grammar of the Apocalypse."

fascinating the world. Revelation 13, 17, and 18 testify to the correctness of the analysis of Horace given above, namely, that the political ideology of the principate possessed religious integrity, relevance, and attraction. John is aware of the eschatological dimension of the intentions and actions of the principate although he protests them. For him the Caesar religion is cult and theology of the devil which apes the authentic eschatological conviction, that which is caused by Jesus. It speaks for John's prophetic consciousness, his confidence in having a hold on reality, that he dares to make such anachronistic claims about the imitation of the Jesus faith by the Caesar religion. At the same time the power and persuasiveness of the Augustan religion finds an indirect testimony in John's polemics. John can describe it appropriately only by using high powered categories. The seer feels himself in a dramatic competition with the prophet(s) of the Caesar religion, people like Horace and Virgil and lesser ones. The religion they represent and propagate is a world religion, the religion of a world empire. Therefore the battle with them has to be seen in cosmic proportions.

There is a long section in the Book of Revelation which at first sight seems to be entirely foreign to the rest of the work. It appears to be too secular. I am speaking of chap. 18. It contains the great lament about the fall of Babylon (vss 9–20), the mourning of the allies of the city (vss 9–10), the wailing of the merchants (vss 11–17), and finally the dirge of the captains and sailors (vss 17b–20). There is no doubt that the seer had found a model for this threnody in Ezekiel 26–27, the lament about the fall of Tyre. There the loss of the trade center on the east coast of the Mediterranean is described in a very concrete and technically precise fashion. But there are sufficient differences, which suggest that Ezekiel had prompted John to look at the reality of his own days in the same realistic fashion.

John also has people lament the loss of a world trade center.[83] That center in John's days was Rome, not a port in the strict sense of the word but through its harbor, Ostia, connected with the sea. The commerce of Rome depended on long distance trading. It was indeed ship related. Since the Second Punic War Rome had turned to the sea very consciously, and shortly before the Book of Revelation was written Ostia had experienced major improvements. The elegy in Revelation

---

[83] Ernst Lohmeyer's commentary on the text (*Die Offenbarung des Johannes* [2d ed.; HNT 16; 1953] 151) misses the point: "Die Waren sind die des Transithandels einer orientalischen Stadt, aber sie passen nicht zur Kennzeichnung Roms. Zudem war Rom niemals in irgendeinem hervorragenden Masse Handels—oder gar Seestadt, sondern verdankt seinen Ruhm rein seiner politischen Bedeutung."

18 correctly recognizes the fact previously mentioned that Roman trade had turned particularly to exotic luxury goods as primary freight, in addition, of course, to grain. The recognition of Rome as a world trade center in the Book of Revelation is a new idea in early Christian literature and has no parallels in Jewish apocalypses. The prediction of the decline of Rome as a world trade center, expressed in the prophetic perfect, proves John to be very realistic, at least as much as Horace during his own time. John proves even more clairvoyant with respect to future developments in Rome. The subsequent decades brought about an economic decline of Rome. During the end of the first century Rome experienced an essential reduction of its central commercial role. Certain provincial cities and ports like Ephesus gained renewed or entirely new influence on industry and world trade and tried to increase their importance at the expense of Rome.

With respect to the rural situation Revelation takes a position entirely opposite to that of the *Carmen saeculare*. Despite his attack on Rome, John confirms urban life at the end of his book in a really monstrous fashion. The future world is portrayed as one huge city, and this as Babylon redeemed.[84] This is not a simple reflection of the importance Jerusalem had for biblical and Jewish eschatology.[85] The new Jerusalem of Revelation has nothing to do with the topography of either Jerusalem or Zion.[86] It is also astonishing to note how the issue of Jerusalem *as city* is subordinated in *4 Ezra* and *2 Baruch*, documents contemporary with Revelation. There the new world is not described as an urban world. Neither *1 Enoch* nor the Qumran writings emphasize the urban dimensions of Jerusalem in their eschatological predictions, only the sacred, the Temple.

Revelation reflects the post-Easter decision of the majority of the Jesus movement for the city. Stephen and his friends apparently had concentrated on this already. It is even more unambiguous with Paul. His independent missionary strategy is directed towards major trade centers, particularly harbors—places connected with world trade. The missionary strategy of the early church has to be seen in the context of the competition which the cities of the Hellenistic world carried on

[84] On the seer's concept of Jerusalem as Babylon redeemed see Georgi, "Visionen," 370–72.

[85] The most elaborate discussion on the comparability of John's visions of the heavenly Jerusalem with biblical and Jewish tradition is found in Charles, *Revelation*, 2. 144–80, 200–11. Qumran material on the new Jerusalem esp. in DJD 1.134–35; 3.84–90, 184–93; 211–302.

[86] On the topography of John's heavenly Jerusalem see Georgi, "Visionen," 361–71.

with the city of Rome. In this competition the ports of western Asia Minor were especially successful, among them the addressees of the Revelation of John. But John stands in the shadow of Paul whose epistolary format he uses. Paul had paid particular attention to the most important place of industry and trade on the coast of Asia Minor, Ephesus. Of all his various stays in Hellenistic cities during his independent missionary activity the one in Ephesus was the longest: two and a half years.[87] And the importance of Ephesus grew continuously. John addresses this city in his first circular letter.

The concentration of missionaries of the early church on the east reflects the growing importance of this part of the Mediterranean. The period in which John is writing is informed by a return to ethnic values and groups, among others Greeks and Jews, but all of this still under the universal umbrella of Hellenism. This growing self-confidence of the provinces found manifold expressions, including philosophical and religious ones as well: Apollonius of Tyana, Dio Chrysostom, Plutarch, and the Pharisees are examples of this—not necessarily always in opposition to Rome. Missionizing religious groups like the Jesus groups helped to increase this self-confidence.

As regards the foreseeing of this immediate future John proved to be superior to Horace. He saw the deterioration of Rome ahead of time, particularly the decline of its previously dominant role in world trade. But as to the predictions of the predominance of the rural Horace seems to have been more reality bound, truer to the future. John, on the other hand, was wrong in his prediction of complete urbanization and the final victory over the Caesar. The Caesar finally co-opted the church, and the church of Jesus Christ became basically a rural religion and remains so today. Was this a final triumph of Virgil and Horace over Paul and John?

---

[87] Idem, *Die Geschichte der Kollekte des Paulus für Jerusalem* (ThF 38; Hamburg: Reich, 1965) 94–95.

CARPOCRATIANS AND CURRICULUM:
IRENAEUS' REPLY

Robert M. Grant
The Divinity School
University of Chicago

It seems suitable, when honoring a dean who has become a bishop, to write on an episcopal theologian who thought he could answer Gnostics by discussing curriculum. I doubt that in either office Krister Stendahl would ever have taken such a tack. It is odd to see Irenaeus doing so. Irenaeus's Hellenistic culture was important to him, even when he wrote against Gnostic heresies.[1] It appears in his preface, where he rhetorically claims not to be using rhetoric, and in his references to the authors and themes of Hellenistic education. To be sure, he was no philosopher. His training was not on the level of Apuleius, who called himself a "Platonic philosopher." But he was versed in logical argumentation—"dialectic"—as known to rhetoricians.[2] Here we look at one important aspect of his Hellenistic argument against Gnostics.

The Situation

Irenaeus himself tells us most of what we know about the Carpocratians, apart from exotic details about the life and thought of Carpocrates' son Epiphanes which we owe to Clement. The account seems rather incoherent. Carpocrates taught that the soul of Jesus, "which was strong and pure, preserved the memory of what it had seen in the sphere of the unbegotten Father." After passing through the realms of the archons who made the world, it escaped to the Father. Similar

---

[1] See my article "Irenaeus and Hellenistic Culture," *HTR* 42 (1949) 41–51; W. R. Schoedel, "Philosophy and Rhetoric in the Adversus Haereses of Irenaeus," *VC* 13 (1959) 22–32; idem, "Theological Method in Irenaeus (*Adversus Haereses* 2.25–28)," *JTS* 35 (1984) 31–49.

[2] See the basic article by B. Reynders, "La polémique de saint Irénée: Méthode et principes," *Recherches de théologie ancienne et médiévale* 7 (1935) 5–27.

souls can make the same ascent, for they receive powers enabling them to perform the same actions. These souls when in bodies can perform any deeds they wish, for "good and evil actions exist only by human opinion." So far, so good; the moral doctrine is essentially Cynicism.

Next, however, Irenaeus says that "in their transmigrations into various bodies the souls have to (*oportere*) participate in every [kind of] life and every [kind of] act." They have to experience everything; otherwise they must return to bodies.

He admits that he has doubts as to whether they really live this way, but claims that advice to act thus is to be found in their books.[3] We observe that Justin, whose works Irenaeus knew, expressed similar doubts about Gnostic licentiousness.[4] Both authors were thus able to make charges against their opponents without being responsible for their information.

Irenaeus's Comments

Irenaeus devotes parts of two chapters in his second book (31.2–32.2) to attacks on the behavior of Simonians and Carpocratians.[5]

First he discusses their use of magic and then turns to their demand for libertinism, more accentuated among the Carpocratians.

a) This demand is opposed to the teaching of the Lord, especially as expressed in the Matthaean Sermon on the Mount. The Jesus whose soul they claim to admire taught them not to perform the actions they advocate or to think about them. "If nothing were bad or good, but some things were considered unjust or just because of human opinion alone, he would never have declared in his teaching, 'The just will shine like the sun in the kingdom of their Father.' As for the unjust and those who do not do the works of justice, he will send them into eternal fire."[6]

b) They claim that they must experience everything imaginable. But have they ever "tried to devote themselves to what is related to virtue, what is difficult, what is glorious, what is artistic—in other words, what is considered good by everyone"? Surely Irenaeus here has Phil 4:8 in mind: "whatever is true, whatever is honorable,

---

[3] All this occurs in *Adv. haer.* 1.25.1–5 and is reprinted by Morton Smith, *Clement of Alexandria and a Secret Gospel of Mark* (Cambridge: Harvard University Press, 1973) 301–3.

[4] *Apol.* 1.26.7.

[5] See Adelin Rousseau and Louis Doutreleau, eds., *Irénée de Lyon Contre les hérésies Livre II* (2 vols.; SC 293–94; Paris, 1982) 187–88.

[6] *Adv. haer.* 2.32.1; Matt 12:43.

whatever is just, whatever is pure, whatever is lovely, whatever is gracious, if there is any excellence, if there is any praise, think on these things."[7] There is a commonly accepted standard of good and bad, but the Carpocratians seem to consider only the bad. Their actions thus fail to reach their own goal of complete experience.

c) Now Irenaeus proceeds to indicate their shortcomings. "If one ought to experience every work and activity, it was fitting to learn all the arts without exception, both theoretical and practical or those learned by self-mastery and acquired by effort and exercise and perseverance." The studies he is about to list are the ones that a student would encounter after he studied grammar, probably rhetoric, and possibly dialectic. He would go beyond literature to theory and practice. Thus music dealt with the study of harmony, arithmetic with addition and subtraction and the relations of numbers, geometry with abstract essence, astronomy, like the others, with divine things and their harmony with one another. (Clement adds dialectic with its distinction of genera from species.)[8]

The distinction between theoretical and practical arts, already expressed by Aristotle (*Metaph.* E (vi) 1025b20), is frequently set forth around Irenaeus's time.[9] But all the studies came to be regarded as important, and the tetrad of theoretical studies gradually attracted other areas to itself, as Irenaeus's list itself shows.[10] Marrou notes that the first century polymath Cornelius Celsus gave the title *Arts* to a collection that included only four treatises: agronomy, medicine, rhetoric, and military science.[11]

Galen's treatment of these studies is noteworthy. Like the Gnostic Epiphanes and Origen he was taught by his father, who he says was an expert in "geometry, architecture, practical and theoretical arithmetic, and astronomy.[12] In *Protrepticus* 5 he says that closest to the god Hermes, discoverer of the arts, stand those who practice geometry, arithmetic, philosophy, medicine, astronomy, and literature; in second place there are teachers of grammar, carpenters and architects and stonecutters; after them come the rest of the arts. The list is significant because Galen's own art, medicine, has replaced music (and is above

---

[7] *RSV*, slightly revised.

[8] Clement *Strom.* 6.80.2–3.

[9] Philo *Leg. alleg.* 1.57; Quintilian *Inst. orat.* 2.18; Galen (see below); and Origen *Hom. in Luke* (ed. Rauer; GCS, 9).

[10] H. Fuchs, "Enkyklios Paideia," *RAC* 5 (1965) cols. 365–98.

[11] Henri Irénée Marrou, *Saint Augustin et la fin de la culture antique* (Paris: Université de Paris, 1937) 226–27.

[12] *De probis pravisque alimentorum succis* 6.755 (ed. Kühn); cf. *Libr. ord.* 4.19.59.

his father's architecture) and because in his view all the arts were close to a god. Elsewhere (chap. 14) he returns to the theme and differentiates "mental" arts from "manual" ones. The line is hard to draw, for his first class includes medicine (first of all!), rhetoric, music, geometry, arithmetic, logic, astronomy, grammar, and law. He is willing to add sculpture and painting (architecture has disappeared), but he has no use for merely manual arts. (The point seems to neglect his own emphasis on the role of the hand in *De usu partium.*)

In his *Gymnasticus* the rhetorician Philostratus includes in *sophia* the study of philosophy, rhetoric, poetry, music, geometry, and astronomy, but places military science, medicine, painting, sculpture, and working in stone and metal in a lower rank. Below these come navigation and gymnastics. Similarly in the *Life of Apollonius* he rates poetry, music, and astronomy at the top, rhetoric (if not for pay) below them, and at the bottom painting and sculpture, along with navigation and farming.[13] These examples and others show that Irenaeus's catholic list of sciences and arts was not unique.

1) He begins with "music, arithmetic, geometry, astronomy, and all the other theoretical disciplines." These are the mathematical disciplines generally regarded as the foundation of the so-called *enkyklios paideia* or *liberales artes.*

2) He then turns to the practical or productive arts.[14] "The whole of medicine, the knowledge of herbs [= pharmacy] and all the disciplines developed for saving life."[15]

3) "Painting, sculpture in bronze and marble, and other arts like these." These arts, Galen said, involve toil and pain but make money for the artisan.[16]

4) "Agriculture, the care of horses and of flocks and herds, and all the arts which include others, such as navigation, gymnastics, hunting, military science and kingship." Galen discusses the advantages and disadvantages of such arts in relation to the health of the artist; but horsemanship and hunting had been included in such lists for a long time. We find the former in Teles and, along with hunting, in an old Stoic fragment.[17]

---

[13] *Gymn.* 1; *Vita Apoll.* 8.7.3.

[14] See also the distinctions drawn in Diog. Laert. 3.84, with the discussion of the forms of medicine in 3.85.

[15] Cf. the discussion by Origen in *Hom. in Jer..* frg. from Homer 39 (ed. Nautin, 374) in *Philoc.* 2.2 and my note "Paul, Galen, and Origen," *JTS* 34 (1983) 533–36.

[16] *Comm. II in Hippocr. de humor.* 28 (ed Kühn, 16. 311–12).

[17] Stobaeus 4.34.72; 2.67.5 = *Stoicorum veterum fragmenta* 3. 294.

5) "Without counting all the others, of which they could not learn a ten-thousandth part in a whole life's labor." Ultimately only God possesses such knowledge, as we learn from Wis 7:17–20.[18]

d) Instead of working at any of these arts and sciences, the Carpocratians turn to pleasures, lust, and disgusting deeds. They thus condemn themselves on their own grounds because they lack experience of the matters just discussed.

Irenaeus concludes by returning to his strongest point. These people really profess the hedonistic philosophy of Epicurus and the indifference of the Cynics. They wrongly claim to follow one whose teaching was sharply opposed to theirs.

We note that Irenaeus's argument is not consistent with what Clement of Alexandria tells us about the Carpocratians. He says that the youthful Gnostic Epiphanes, son of Carpocrates, was "educated by his father in the encyclical education and Platonic philosophy."[19] If Clement is right, Irenaeus should have argued not that the Carpocratians knew nothing about the subjects he listed but that they knew only part of them, the theoretical studies. Did he know? or did he care? Presumably he did not know the book by Epiphanes which Clement cited. Its ridicule of both private property and monogamy could hardly have been answered by raising a question about Carpocratian education.

Irenaeus's Use of His Sources

As we have seen, Irenaeus's list of advanced studies is similar to other lists produced or copied by some of his contemporaries, presumably often based on the writings of rhetoricians.[20] Philostratus was himself a rhetorician.

Irenaeus pointed out how much the Gnostics claimed to experience and how limited their experience really was. He has listed items from the higher studies, that is, those going beyond reading books, and has pointed out how difficult it would be to know all these subjects. Sextus Empiricus makes the same point against teachers of literature, and we must suspect that Irenaeus took the idea from some similar source.

> If the grammarian possesses an art capable of discriminating among the things said by poets and prose-writers, he must understand either the words only, or the objects behind them, or both. But it

[18] Cited by Origen *Hom. in Luke.* (ed. Rauer; GCS, frg. 50).
[19] Clement *Strom.* 3.5.3
[20] See Friedmar Kühnert, *Allgemeinbildung und Fachbildung in der Antike* (Deutsche Akademie der Wissenschaften zu Berlin. Schriften der Sektion für Altertumswissenschaft 30; Berlin: Akademie-Verlag, 1961) 71–111.

is evident that they do not understand the objects. For some of
these are physical, some mathematical, some medical, some musical, and he who deals with the physical must of course be a physi-
cist, he who deals with the musical a musician, and of course he
who deals with the mathematical a mathematician, and similarly
with the other sciences. Experience proves the self-evident truth
that the grammarian is not simultaneously all-wise and skilled in
every science.[21]

This is Irenaeus's point too (2.32.2). It is most unlikely, however, that
he had read much, if any, of Sextus's *Adversus mathematicos*, since it
denounces the basic sciences plus logic, physics, and ethics. Irenaeus is
against Gnosticism, not philosophy or science.

Irenaeus's Use of Examples

Since many of Irenaeus's own rhetorical examples are related to his
listing of the basic theoretical and practical arts and sciences, he may
even have found the headings in a book of examples intended for the
use of speechmakers.[22] By "examples" we mean essentially what
ancient writers called *parabolai* or *similtudines*, though as Quintilian
notes the terms were not rigidly fixed.[23]

Irenaeus first points out against Gnostic shortcuts that in all the arts
one needs self-control, effort, meditation, and perseverance. Then he
speaks of arts based on verbal proficiency. These are the traditional
mathematical sciences recommended by Plato and Greek educators
after him. First comes music, to which Irenaeus alludes when he
speaks of melody and harmony (2.25.2; 4.20.7). Arithmetic is second:
we note only that he could criticize the Basilidian Gnostics for having
365 heavens when they should have had 4380 for the number of day-
time hours in the year, or 8760 including the nights as well (2.16.4).
Third comes geometry and fourth, astronomy. From geometry come
the examples of concentric circles, spheres, and tetragons (2.13.6).
The *exempla* related to astronomy attest little knowledge of it. Though
the sun is a very small planet[24] its rays go a long way (2.13.5). We

[21] *Adv. math.* 1.300.
[22] For such books see Karl Alewell, *Über das rhetorische* ΠΑΡΑΔΕΙΓΜΑ: *Theorie,
Beispielsammlungen, Verwendung in der römischen Literatur der Kaiserzeit* (Leipzig: August
Hoffmann, 1913); but these are *paradeigmata.*
[23] *Inst. orat.* 5.11.1–2; a comparison of oratory with music precedes, 5.10.124–25.
[24] Here Irenaeus agrees with Theophilus *Ad Autol.* 1.5.

cannot look at the sun because our eyes are weak (4.29.1).[25] Interestingly enough, the example of the sun (-god) as dimming the sight of those who stare at it (him) occurs in Sextus Empiricus too.[26] Much of Irenaeus's rather meager astronomical information comes through Marcosian Gnostics, leaving the bishop himself to state that no one knows the cause of the moon's phases (2.28.2).

Medicine and pharmacy are also among the arts. They have been developed for the preservation of human life, or as Sextus Empiricus puts it, medicine is "a curative and pain-relieving art."[27] Irenaeus is rather fond of medical examples. He compares Gnostics with "those who fall into delirium; the more they laugh, the more they think they are healthy and do everything as if they were healthy but do some things more than in health, the sicker they are" (1.16.3). He asks, "What doctor desiring to cure a sick man will act in accordance with the desires of the sick man and not with what is suited to medicine?" (3.5.2). Inevitably he compares Christian love toward heretics with "a harsh medicine which consumes the foreign and superfluous flesh formed on a wound" (3.25.7). Less vividly he compares God with a mother who is able to supply solid food to an infant, but mankind like the child cannot yet receive it (4.38.1; cf. 1 Cor 3:2–3).

Other more practical arts are learned by effort and exercise. One example, used for soul and body, is related to all of them. The artisan plans at high speed, but completes the work more slowly because of the inertia of his subject matter. The velocity of his mind is fused with the slowness of the instrument (2.33.4).

One of these arts is painting, in relation to which perhaps we should consider the mosaic picture of a king transformed into one of a fox (1.8.1). Another is sculpture. In this regard we are told that clay is not molded for its own sake but for that of the statue to be made in bronze, gold, or silver (2.15.3).[28] Again, a clay statue may be colored to make it look as if of gold; but one need only take off a fragment to let the clay appear (2.19.8).

Another is metal-working. Here Irenaeus relies on his Christian predecessors. One of them said that "a precious stone, of great value with some, is insulted by a bit of glass artfully made like it, if no one is there to test it and unmask the fraud. And when bronze is mixed with silver, who can readily verify it if he is not an expert?" (1 pr. 2).

---

[25] Again, cf. ibid., 1.2 and 1.5
[26] *Adv. math.* 1.306.
[27] Ibid., 1.51.
[28] Cf. Melito *Hom. pasch.* 36–37.

Again, the Gnostics were eager to point out that "gold in mud does not lose its beauty" (1.6.2). Irenaeus himself noted that straw is useful for refining gold (5.29.1).

He made little use of examples from the other arts he listed, including marble-working, agriculture (though he does note that the stalk helps wheat grow, 5.29.1), veterinary arts, pastoral arts and other arts of craftsmen (*opifices*). He makes no use of navigation. A bit more comes from gymnastics and hunting.

A strange example comes from gymnastics. In the wrestling school "novices struggle with others and seize some part of their opponent's body firmly with their hands and fall because of what they hold. Though they fall they think they have won because they tenaciously hold that member they first grabbed, but in reality they are held in derision because they have fallen" (5.13.2). Another such example may be based on a gospel saying (Matt 12:29) but this itself is proverbial. "A strong man can be overcome neither by an inferior nor by an equal, but by one who is stronger" (5.22.1).

Equally strange examples are taken from hunting. First, the Gnostics are compared with a beast that hides in a forest and comes out to devastate many. It can be caught only when the forest is delimited and defoliated so that the beast can be seen. It still has to be captured, but with the new situation it can be struck from every side, wounded, and killed (1.31.4). Second, Gnostic liars are like those who offer customary foods in order to capture some animal, gradually softening it up through the foods, and then, taking it captive, they tie it up harshly and by force take it wherever they wish (2.14.8).

Irenaeus warms to the examples apparently taken from military and political science but perhaps invented for the occasion. First, suppose that "hostile forces have defeated their enemies and led them bound as captives, and have possessed them as slaves for such a long time that they even have children." If now "someone feels sorry for those who were enslaved and defeats the same enemies, will he act justly if he frees the children of the captives but leaves those whom he vindicated subject to them? Liberty would be given to the sons because of their fathers' vindication, but not to the fathers who underwent captivity" (3.23.2). Or again: "If a free man, forcibly abducted by someone whom he served for many years by increasing his property, then obtained some help from it, he could seem to be taking possession of part of his master's property, whereas in reality he would depart having received very little in return for his many labors. If anyone accused him of having acted unjustly, the accuser would prove to be an unjust judge in relation to the man who had been led into slavery by force"

(4.30.2). Presumably this defense of the Israelites who despoiled the Egyptians is based on earlier Jewish apologetic and is not a simple rhetorical "example."

Kingship appears several times. A king is responsible for military victory because he is in charge, as is the Father in Christian theology (2.2.3). (More "banausic" examples in this context make the same point. An axe cuts, a saw saws; but it is the man who made the tools who does the work.) Again, "The advent of a king is announced by slaves sent in advance for the preparation of those who are beginning to receive their lord. But when the king comes and his subjects are filled with the joy predicted, have received the liberty that comes from him, share in the sight of him, hear his words and enjoy gifts from him, it is no longer necessary for the king to bring anything beyond . . . himself" (4.34.1). The theological emphasis of the "example" is obvious, and the idea that the kingdom of God announced by Jesus was Jesus himself is found in Origen. This example may have been composed for the occasion.

In one more example the situation of the devil is "as if a rebel should take possession of some region and disturb those in it and assume the glory of a king among those who do not know he is a rebel and a thief" (5.24.4). Once more, the analogy seems to be invented to fit the theological point.

It is not so much the rhetorical method of Irenaeus that we find novel. After all, he was well aware that Jesus had taught with parables or comparisons. The novelty lies in the subject matter, paralleling much of the Greco-Roman educational curriculum and using it for rhetorical purposes.

Gnostic Attitudes toward the Curriculum

Finally, even if Carpocrates taught his son the encyclical studies, Irenaeus was probably right in supposing that Gnostics were not enthusiastic about mundane and ordinary studies. The attitude of the Hermetic *Asclepius*, on the borderline of Gnosticism, is hostile toward the curriculum. Trismegistus attacks those who make philosophy incomprehensible by mixing it up with arithmetic, music, and geometry. They abandon pure religion for detailed information about the stars, the earth, and music, all of which should lead simply to reverence. Nock and Festugière give parallels for this attitude.[29] A more definitely Gnostic statement appears in the *Tripartite Tractate* from Nag

---

[29] *Asclep.* 13–14; *Corpus Hermeticum* (ed. A. D. Nock and A.-J. Festugière; 4 vols. in 2; Paris: Belles Lettres, 1945) 2. 369 n. 115.

Hammadi. The speculative wisdom of the Greeks is inconsistent because of archontic influences. "Therefore nothing is in agreement with other studies, nothing, whether philosophy or kinds of medicine or kinds of music or types of logic."[30] The word for "logic" is *organon*, as often among Peripatetics.

Though Irenaeus's targeting was inaccurate when he aimed at the Carpocratians, the fact that some Gnostics rejected the curriculum of studies helps justify his onslaught.

---

[30] Harold W. Attridge in James M. Robinson, ed., *The Nag Hammadi Library in English* (New York: Harper & Row, 1977) 85, partly revised; Codex I (treatise 5) 109,25–110,17.

ON READING OTHERS' LETTERS

Lars Hartman
University of Uppsala

"My mother taught me that reading others' letters isn't nice." Those, or something like them, were the words of Krister Stendahl when he once tried to open the eyes of his audience to some of the hermeneutical problems which pertain to the fact that Christians read Paul's letters as if they were addressed to themselves rather than to their original recipients.[1] The following reflections deal with these problems, and they are meant as a humble tribute to my first teacher in New Testament exegesis. I begin by recalling a few facts that are intriguing once one puts them together. This will lead me to the suggestion that, when he wrote his letters, Paul had a wider usage in mind than we usually assume. Against such a background I shall discuss, in a rather unsophisticated way, some conditions that may apply to a rereading of the Pauline letters and some possible consequences for so-called historical exegesis.

First, then, a few well-known facts concerning Paul's letters. The old differentiation between "letter" and "epistle"[2] is still often referred to in NT introductions, although their authors assure us that the Pauline letters are real letters, not artificial ones (i.e., epistles).[3] On the other hand, the same introductions usually tell us that Paul's are not to be equated with private letters. Certainly several details can be

---

[1] Krister Stendahl *Paul Among Jews and Gentiles* (Philadelphia: Fortress, 1976) 6.

[2] Adolf Deissmann, *Licht vom Osten* (4th ed.; Tübingen: Mohr, 1923) 193–213.

[3] Werner Georg Kümmel, *Introduction to the New Testament* (trans. Howard Clark Kee; Nashville: Abingdon, 1975) 249; Alfred Wikenhauser and Josef Schmid, *Einleitung in das Neue Testament* (6th ed.; Freiburg/Basel/Wien: Herder, 1973) 385; Philipp Vielhauer, *Geschichte der urchristlichen Literatur* (Berlin/New York: de Gruyter, 1975) 53; Hans-Martin Schenke and Karl Martin Fischer, *Einleitung in die Schriften des Neuen Testaments* (Gütersloh: Mohn, 1978) 1. 27.

compared to what one finds in private letters,[4] such as epistolary address, introductory thanksgiving, etc. But their length alone makes them appear to be something else, not to mention their contents. In these respects one may regard them, instead, as some sort of treatise. In some cases, notably 2 Corinthians and Philippians, their length, together with other peculiarities, has led to suggestions that they are, in fact, an editorial conflation of several letters.[5]

A further fact about the Pauline letters has not yet really been integrated into the handbooks, namely, that an increasing number of studies point to the role that rhetoric played in their composition, style, and argumentation.[6] That is, they represent types of argument and construction that one would not expect to encounter in occasional private letters.

The fact that texts characterized by such length, content, and style have been written down is in itself noteworthy. In the age of computers and word processors, one easily forgets that conceiving and writing a text like Galatians or Romans was a long and wearisome procedure.[7]

The rhetorical features could fit with some considerations raised in the scholarly discussion of the literary form of Paul's letters. It was a rather common idea in antiquity that a letter replaced or represented its author.[8] In our case the letters represented the presence of the apostle, the missionary. Letter-writing was almost a necessity for a man like

---

[4] E.g., William G. Doty, *Letters in Primitive Christianity* (Philadelphia: Fortress, 1973).

[5] Walter Schmithals, "Die Thessalonicherbriefe als Brief-Komposition," in Erich Dinkler, ed., *Zeit und Geschichte* (Tübingen; Mohr-Siebeck, 1964) 295–315; Joachim Gnilka, *Der Philipperbrief* (HThKNT 10.3; Freiburg/Basel/Wein: Herder, 1968) 5–11. For 2 Corinthians see, e.g., Kümmel, *Introduction,* 289.

[6] One of the pioneers has been Hans Dieter Betz; see "The Literary Composition and Function of Paul's Letter to the Galatians," *NTS* 21 (1974/75) 353–79; and idem, *Galatians* (Hermeneia; Philadelphia: Fortress, 1979) 14–25. See also Klaus Berger, "Apostelbrief und apostolische Rede/ Zum Formular frühchristlicher Briefe," *ZNW* 65 (1974) 224–28; and Benoit Standaert, "Analyse rhétorique des chapitres 12 à 14 de 1 Co," in Lorenzo de Lorenzi, ed., *Charisma und Agape* (Benedictina 7; Rome: S. Paulo fuori le mura, 1983) 23–50. Cf. John L. White, "New Testament Epistolary Literature in the Framework of Ancient Epistolography," ANRW II. 25. 2 (1984) 1733.

[7] Otto Roller, *Das Formular der paulinischen Briefe* (BWANT 58; Stuttgart: Kohlhammer, 1933) 8–14.

[8] Robert W. Funk, "The Apostolic *Parousia*: Form and Significance," in W. R. Farmer, C. F. D. Moule, and R. R. Niebuhr, eds., *Christian History and Interpretation: Studies Presented to John Knox* (Cambridge: Cambridge University Press, 1967) 249–68; Klaus Thraede, *Grundzüge griechisch-römischer Brieftopik* (Zetemata 48; München: Beck, 1970) 146–50.

Paul, who was burdened with extensive obligation and responsibility.[9] Letter-writing offered him further possibilities for fulfilling his missionary duties. Thus several NT introductions invite one to regard Paul's letters as apostolic ministerial writings.[10]

In dealing with Paul's apostolic zeal, we should also remember Paul's tendency to develop a broad theological argument, even when he is dealing with a comparatively small or trivial matter.[11]

It may be too much to say that the above-mentioned facts present us with a riddle. But there is a tension between the occasional character of the letters—their addressing a quite specific situation—on the one hand, and these facts on the other. I suggest that this tension is resolved if we assume that Paul intended his letters to be read and reread in the communities to which they were addressed, and in others as well. He probably also kept copies of his letters.[12] Those letters which may be the result of compilation also fit into such a picture; the edition may have been made by Paul himself, or even by his "school,"[13] though on his behalf. We need not posit a later generation of devotees to find someone who held in high esteem Paul's apostleship and his acting as an apostle. Paul himself did so. It was not a post-Pauline generation that got the bright idea that a teacher's letters deserved to be reread and even to be more widely known. This idea and practice existed in the contemporary world among both Jews and Gentiles.[14] Moreover, Paul's letters are not private letters (like Cicero's to his family), but are apostolic messages.

The suggestion of the preceding paragraph can be supported by certain characteristics of the letter to the Colossians, depending on how one dates the letter. In an article in 1966, E. P. Sanders demonstrated that Colossians is literally dependent on the seven undisputed Pauline

---

[9] Schenke and Fischer, *Einleitung*, 31.

[10] Kümmel, *Introduction*, 249; Wikenhauser and Schmid, *Einleitung*, 385; Vielhauer, *Geschichte*, 62. Cf. Berger, "Apostelbrief," 190–231.

[11] N. A. Dahl, "Paul and the Church at Corinth according to 1 Corinthians 1:10–4:21," in *Christian History* (see n. 8), 313–35.

[12] It seemed a matter of course to Hermann von Soden; see his *Griechisches Neues Testament* (Göttingen: Vandenhoeck & Ruprecht, 1913) VII (cf. Roller, *Formular*, 260); see further T. Henshaw, *New Testament Literature* (London: Hodder & Stoughton, 1963) 208.

[13] For the idea of a Pauline "school" see Hans Conzelmann, "Paulus und die Weisheit," *NTS* 12 (1965/66) 233; Eduard Lohse, *Colossians and Philemon* (Hermeneia; Philadelphia: Fortress, 1971) 181; Hans-Martin Schenke dates the collection and editing activity of the "school" to a time after Paul's death ("Das Weiterwirken des Paulus und die Pflege seines Erbes durch die Paulus-Schule," *NTS* 21 [1974/75] 508–14).

[14] See, e.g., J. Schneider, "Brief," *RAC* 2 (1954) 567, 570–72; Berger, "Apostelbrief," 212–19.

letters, and in a unique manner at that.[15] His results indicate that the author of Colossians was not Paul and that he knew and was well versed in several, if not all, of the letters recognized as genuine.

The person who wrote (or dictated) Colossians did not go through a collection of Pauline letters, seeking good Pauline expressions in order to be able to sound like the apostle.[16] Although familiar with Paul's texts, the author of Colossians did not use them slavishly or mechanically. Instead the author stands out as an independent theologian who thought in a Pauline way and was able to meet new problems using and readjusting Paul's teachings. Indeed the author appears so dependent (and independent) that scholars like C. F. D. Moule and W. G. Kümmel think the author is Paul himself![17]

The manner in which the author of Colossians uses Paul's letters does not indicate that they were regarded as Scripture, but it does presuppose availability of and familiarity with a collection of Paul's letters.

For my part I assume that Colossians was written by a rather independent Pauline disciple (why not the co-author, Timothy?) when Paul was in prison in Rome. I find this idea more natural than to assume that the author cleverly "writes to" a community that does not exist any more—after the earthquake in the Lycus valley in the early sixties—when there would be less chance of being detected![18] Furthermore, we would have to assume that just to sound reliable the author took the trouble to construct a list of salutations, based on the letter to Philemon,[19] and elaborate on it.

Such a view of the authorship of Colossians also corroborates my suggestion that copies of earlier Pauline letters had been kept with Paul or at his "school" and had been read and reread by his disciples. This would be the place where a collection of his letters was available prior to its release "on the market." But such an archive and such rereading also intimate that Paul aimed at a wider audience for his letters than we usually assume.[20]

---

[15] E. P. Sanders, "Literary Dependence in Colossians," *JBL* 85 (1966) 28–45.

[16] Cf. the simple imitations in the apocryphal Laodicea letter.

[17] Kümmel, *Introduction*, 340–46; C. F. D. Moule, *The Epistles of Paul the Apostle to the Colossians and to Philemon* (CGTC; Cambridge: Cambridge University Press, 1967) 13–14.

[18] Wolfgang Schenk, "Christus, das Geheimnis der Welt, als dogmatisches und ethisches Grundprinzip des Kolosserbriefes," *EvTh* 43 (1983) 140.

[19] Schenke and Fischer, *Einleitung*, 167; Vielhauer, *Geschichte*, 200.

[20] The fact that the Pauline letters have not left any certain traces in Acts (Adolf von Harnack, *Die Briefsammlung des Apostels Paulus und die anderen vorkonstantinischen christ-*

If, on the other hand, one dates Colossians at, say, ca. 70,[21] this usage of other Pauline letters in Colossians must mean at least one thing: its author had a collection of Paul's letters with which he had lived for some time. He may have obtained them like a devoted collector, but it is also possible, indeed probable to my mind, that he obtained them because he had been close to Paul or a member of his "school" during the apostle's lifetime. Thus, also with this dating, the use of Paul's letters in Colossians can support the idea that Paul kept copies of his correspondence. However it may relate to the assumption that he had a wider audience in mind, it hardly speaks against it.

If Paul had in mind a wider circle of readers than the ones mentioned in the letter openings, then the task of interpreting Paul's letters is affected. I therefore turn to some reflections on this problem. In so doing I am consciously entering a jungle. The path I cut through it leaves many philosophical, linguistic, literary, and exegetical problems—refinements and issues aside—probably more than I imagine.

This kind of "reading others' letters" is not unique. Many texts formulated in and for given occasions are reread and reused in new situations, at new places, and even in new times. They are reused, then, not simply as charming or revered fossils, but as texts that have something important to tell the new audience. Other examples in antiquity are the OT scriptures (during and after their formation), the classical dramas, Plato's letters, etc.

Different attitudes behind such a rereading of occasional texts can be associated with the three aspects that text-linguistics isolates in a text: the syntactic, semantic, and pragmatic ones. Of these, the last one regards the text as a whole, functioning with its addressees in their situation. It does so not least through its contents, which are considered under the semantic aspect. The content, in its turn, is mediated by the text's network of words, phrases, sentences, etc. (i.e., the text seen from a syntactic point of view).[22]

---

lichen Briefsammlungen [Leipzig: Hinrichs, 1926] 7) is a weak argument against my suggestion. In order to be an argument it must presuppose that Luke had the same theological interest in Paul's letters as modern theologians have. The apocryphal Acts of Paul also disregard them. Cf. the pointed arguments of J. Jervell in "Paul in the Acts of the Apostles: Tradition, History, Theology," in J. Kremer, ed., *Les Actes des Apôtres* (Gembloux/Leuven: Duculot, 1979) 297–306.

[21] Thus, e.g., Schenke, "Weiterwirken," 513; Joachim Gnilka, *Der Kolosserbrief* (HThKNT 10.1; Freiburg/Basel/Wein: Herder, 1980) 23.

[22] For these three aspects of a text see Charles W. Morris, "Foundations of the Theory of Signs," in *Writings on the General Theory of Signs* (1938; reprinted The Hague: Mouton, 1971) 17–71.

By focusing on the syntactic aspect of a text, one can use its wording without respect at all to its contents and function. Thus 1 Cor 11:19, "there must be factions among you," may be cited as nothing more than a somewhat ironic comment on a quarrelsome meeting. Another reader, however, may refer to the same sentence as a decisive scriptural argument against ecumenism. Both interpretations disregard the semantic and pragmatic aspects of the text. The first uses it as a turn of phrase, nothing more; the second one relies on a particular view of scriptural inspiration. This latter view holds that Paul's occasional letter, arguing here against certain abuses at the Lord's supper, is in every detail full of God's eternal word and God's ever valid message, always capable of answering new questions.

Another example of rereading a Pauline text is from Luther's commentary on Galatians. In commenting on 3:23–24 he understands it in this way: "The Law must be laid on those who shall be justified . . . not as if they could win justification through the law (that were to misuse the law . . .) but so that, after having been terrified and humbled through the Law, they flee to Christ."[23] This understanding of the Galatians passage regards it from a semantic perspective, in a framework of Pauline theology as contained in Galatians and as understood by Luther.[24] But this semantic aspect is not combined with the pragmatic one, which means that the reading largely disregards the precise debate in Galatia.

In a third kind of rereading the text with its expressions and contents is strictly understood as a message in its concrete historical situation. Here it becomes little more than a museum item, insofar as it is taken as a truly occasional text. It could be reused only if the occasion repeated itself. But very often an occasional text deals with an occasional issue by treating it almost as a *type* of problem, assessing it on a general basis. In this case the pragmatics of the text could be found represented to such an extent in a new situation that the text, in all its three aspects, could be readdressed to it.

A presupposition behind the two latter reusages of (more or less) occasional texts is the assumption that they contain applications of a way of thinking, which then somehow provide basic principles behind the occasional utterance. This is also, of course, what one assumes

---

[23] Imponenda est igitur lex iustificandis, . . . non quod per legem iustitiam illam consequantur, hoc enim esset abuti . . . lege, sed ut pavefacti et humiliati lege confugiant ad Christum (WA 40. 1, 528).

[24] This interpretation was rightly questioned by Krister Stendahl in his article, "Paul and the Introspective Conscience of the West," *Paul Among Jews and Gentiles*, 86–88.

when construing a Pauline theology or writing a book on Pauline ethics. But the parameters of such reconstructed thought systems are by no means certain. To mention just one glaring example: Is "justification through faith" the heart of Pauline theology, or is it only a *Neben-krater*, as Albert Schweitzer thought? Furthermore, are the parameters constant throughout an author's life? What if he changes his mind about some question? This may well be the case with Paul's view on the law as reflected in Galatians and Romans.[25]

Even if one wants to be historically fair to the author whose texts are reused, it is obviously too rigid a position to state that a renewed use of the letters of, say, Plato, Cicero, Epictetus, or Paul should take place under the necessary presupposition that the rereading is made within the framework of the total conception of Plato, Cicero, etc. Let me take one example from early Christianity. When Clement of Rome urges the Corinthians to reread Paul's letters to them, he is concerned about their lack of unity, and more specifically their contempt for the presbyters (*1 Clem.* 47). This Clement can do without presupposing a common ground in a total Pauline theology; modern exegetes have even accused him of not understanding Paul.[26] Instead Clement's application is rather straightforward: Paul dismissed their dissensions—obey him also now.[27]

From a semantic perspective, more or less void of a pragmatic one, it is almost always possible to find ideas and principles mentioned or intimated in a text which in some way or another really belong to the author's message. They may, however, receive a different importance in a new situation. Thus, the same Clement in 35.5 apparently uses Rom 1:29–32, a part of Paul's negative description of pagan immorality. But in *1 Clement* it turns into a series of admonitions to Christians. It is not contrary to Paul's thinking, but it is not what he intended in Romans 1.

Texts can also be understood as saying things which, by all versimilitude, would not be in harmony with the outlook of the author as reconstructed by the historically interested reader. A Lutheran way of reading Paul, that equates the Law with God's will, is probably an example of this.

[25] Hans Hübner, *Das Gesetz bei Paulus* (FRLANT 119; 2d ed.; Göttingen: Vandenhoeck & Ruprecht, 1980).

[26] Leonard Goppelt, *Christentum und Judentum im ersten und zweiten Jahrhundert* (BFCTh 2.55; Gütersloh: Berthelsmann, 1954) 239.

[27] In addition, Clement strengthens his reference with an argument *a maiore ad minus*: Paul attacked divisions based on following apostles of high reputation—now there are a couple of insignificant people who disturb the unity.

One may defend this way of rereading Paul by saying that if Paul had lived in the days of these Lutheran theologians, he would have agreed. Or one could be tougher and argue that it is with Paul as with Sophocles and Shakespeare: once their texts have left them, we are free to read them according to our own minds (cf. H.-G. Gadamer, P. Ricouer, etc.). This is how the Christian reading of the Tanakh must appear to a Jew. And among the myriads of Christian interpretations of the NT a good proportion probably belongs to the same class.[28]

Let us now return to Paul and his time. Actually, Paul himself provides a few glimpses of how the relevance of an occasional message was widened. One example is the letter to Philemon. Its errand concerns Philemon, and the body of the letter is directly addressing a "thou." But the letter with its truly private message is addressed, in its opening, to the house-church of Philemon. In other words, Paul meant that the assembly should have access to another's letter (possibly at their common worship).[29] I doubt that Paul widens the address in order to put pressure on Philemon; the apostle's personal support of Onesimus would be sufficient. Rather, Paul is of the opinion that the letter pleaded the case of Onesimus in such a way that it had something to say to the larger Christian community.[30]

If this is so with the rather personal Philemon, it is not surprising that according to 1 Cor 1:1–2, Paul writes his letter to the Corinthian church "together with all who call upon the name of our Lord Jesus Christ in every place, theirs and ours." Conzelmann rightly states: "We cannot argue that Paul could not write a greeting to all Christians," in disagreement with Weiss who wanted to delete the words as an addition by the editor of the Pauline letter collection. Nevertheless Conzelmann finds them difficult.[31] In my opinion the difficulty disappears if one posits that although the matters he dealt with in 1 Corinthians were "occasional" and particular, Paul discussed them in such a way that the letter could serve as an apostolic message to other churches as well.

---

[28] I leave aside the fact that the different Christian Bible interpretations are all colored by various traditions, whether the interpreters are conscious of them or not.

[29] Joachim Gnilka, *Der Philemonbrief* (HThKNT 10.4; Freiburg/Basel/Wien: Herder, 1982) 17; cf. Martin Hengel, *Die Evangelienüberschriften* (Sitzungsbericht der Heidelberger Akademie der Wissenschaften 1984) 35.

[30] Cf. Peter Stuhlmacher, *Der Brief an Philemon* (EKKNT; Zürich: Einsiedeln; Köln and Neukirchen-Vluyn: Benziger Verlag and Neukirchener Verlag, 1975) 17, 57–58.

[31] Hans Conzelmann, *1 Corinthians* (Hermeneia; Philadelphia: Fortress, 1975) 23; Erich Fascher, *Der erste Brief an die Korinther* (ThHKNT 7.1; Berlin: Evangelischer Verlagsanstalt, 1975) 1. 85: "ein Gemeindebrief des Paulus gilt im Grunde allen Gemeinden."

Thus it is possible to assume that the widening of the "occasional" perspective in Philemon and 1 Corinthians was intended by Paul. My suggestion above means that something similar holds true of all his letters.[32] The widening then, on the one hand, meant that the addressees (e.g., the Corinthians) were supposed to return to the letters several times, perhaps even reading them in their services. On the other hand, it also meant that other copies of the Corinthian correspondence were available for rereading in Pauline churches.

Of course one may ask how wide Paul's perspective was in terms of the possible addressees of his "occasional" letters. One possible answer is that it was not less than the perspective of his apostolic mission. In terms of time no answer is possible. Paul's expectations concerning the imminent parousia underwent change, but already 1 Thessalonians is hardly conceived and composed as if its author seriously doubted that its bearer would arrive in time.[33]

My discussion above is not meant to justify the church's reading of others' letters. But if my suggestion is right, it presents a problem for exegetes trying to say what a text meant historically. Theologians tend to disregard the occasion of a text. In text-linguistic terms, they do not care about its pragmatic aspect. Paul is closer to these theologians than we, historically minded exegetes, would like. To put it in other terms, when asking what the text meant[34] we should ask for two intentions of Paul: the one regarding the specific occasion and, secondly, the one related to more general interest. To turn from the author's side of the communication to the recipient's, we should ask for two understandings of a text: the one in the original letter situation and, secondly, the ones where the letter was reread (e.g., Ephesus).[35]

Thus, it seems to me that Paul wrote his letters to be more than occasional correspondence. He intended them to be read more widely. This raises the hermeneutical question concerning what one is doing

---

[32] Other passages in the Pauline corpus which in different ways may indicate a wider audience are 2 Cor 1:1; 2 Thess 2:2; 3:17; and Col 4:16.

[33] In an Uppsala dissertation to be published in 1986, Bruce C. Johanson deals with the literary, compositional, and rhetorical make-up of 1 Thessalonians. My statement is based on that study.

[34] The attentive reader may hear an echo from Krister Stendahl's often cited article "Biblical Theology, Contemporary," *IDB* 1 (1962) 419.

[35] To express it in text-linguistic terms: we get a second pragmatic aspect which may modify the semantic one. My taking Ephesus as an example of a wider audience is of course inspired by the discussions concerning Romans 16. Does it contain fragments of an Ephesian letter? See Schenke and Fischer, *Einleitung*, 136–42; Kümmel, *Introduction*, 314–20.

when rereading occasional texts. This question concerns not only the one who asks for the conditions of Christian rereading of the Bible, but also the exegete who asks what the text meant in its original situation, for that situation loses something of its singularity. One original situation may have actually meant reading others' letters!

GREEKS, JEWS, AND LUTHERANS
IN THE MIDDLE HALF OF ACTS*

A. T. Kraabel
Luther College

I

Krister Stendahl taught his American students in many ways, none more important than by compelling to us to look at the way we look at the ancient texts.

For a Lutheran trying to understand the Greek-speaking Jews of the Roman Empire, two of his hermeneutical reminders were fundamental. The first was the warning not to play "Galilee"[1] or "Bibleland"[2] or "First-Century Semite"[3] with the sacred texts.

The second reflects a more complex problem, and more specifically Lutheran: the anti-Jewish elements in Christian theology and exegesis. Stendahl identifies one form of this anti-Judaism as particularly Protestant and peculiarly Lutheran: the theological model of "Law and Gospel." He describes the problem as follows:

> According to . . . this habit-forming structure of theological think-
> ing, Jewish attitudes and Jewish piety are by definition the example
> of the wrong attitude toward God. . . . This whole system of think-
> ing . . . treats Jewish piety as the black background that makes
> Christian piety the more shining. In such a state of affairs, it is
> hard to engender respect for Judaism and the Jews. And the theo-

*Much of this paper was formulated in the British Isles in March of 1985, in conversations with James Dunn in Durham, Robert Morgan in Oxford, and Seán Freyne in Dublin. I am grateful to them for their hospitality and their friendly aid.

[1] *IDB* 1. 428 *s.v.* "Biblical Theology, Contemporary"; cf. idem, *Meanings: The Bible as Document and as Guide* (Philadelphia: Fortress, 1984) 37.

[2] Idem, *Paul Among Jews and Gentiles* (Philadelphia: Fortress, 1976) 36.

[3] Idem, *The Bible and the Role of Women: A Case Study in Hermeneutics* (trans. Emilie T. Sander; Philadelphia: Fortress, 1966) 17. These topics (nn. 1—3) are treated further below.

logical system requires the retention of such an understanding of Judaism, whether true or not.[4]

The history of scholarship provides plenty of reasons for caution when viewing Jewish history through a Christian lens. The unavoidable example here, that of the ancient Pharisees, is worth a brief review. Nearly all treatments of the Pharisees to the present day are tendentious. In the NT the picture of the Pharisees is a hostile one: they were sanctimonious and self-righteous; it was well known that they did not practice what they preached (see Matt 23:3). One result of this contribution to Jewish history is that to this day no one is pleased to be called a "Pharisee." The NT picture of the Pharisees was carried along into later treatments by theologians and other scholars, and became included in polemics between Christians and Jews, and between Protestants and Catholics. After a study of the matter, Jacob Neusner concluded:

> The history of scholarship on the Pharisees . . . cannot be divorced from the history of Judaism and Christianity in the nineteenth and twentieth centuries, from the sociology of the Jews in Europe and the U.S.A., and from the interrelationships between the two religious traditions.[5]

In addition to such biases as those which grow out of unexamined confessional positions, there are unavoidable methodological problems whenever the understanding of a subject proper to one discipline (in this case Jewish studies) is for most students carried by the standard reference works of a second discipline (here NT). The data in the reference works are likely to be out of date, particularly if archaeology is a factor. And the methodology, assumptions, and emphases reflected are understandably that of the second discipline, not the first.

Stendahl has often reminded us of these problems, but the misperceptions are deeply imbedded. Examples are almost too easy to identify in biblical studies. But it is in our reconstructions of Jewish history that the distortions are the most powerful. In the most popular model, Jewish history begins in the OT and continues until the coming of Christ,

---

[4] Idem, "Judaism and Christianity II: A Plea for a New Relationship," *Meanings*, 222.

[5] Jacob Neusner, *Ancient Judaism: Debates and Disputes* (BJS 64; Chico: Scholars Press, 1984) 235–36. See also idem, *Formative Judaism V: Religious, Historical and Literary Studies* (BJS 91; Chico: Scholars Press, 1985) 51–77; Charlotte Klein, *Anti-Judaism in Christian Theology* (trans. Edward Quinn; Philadelphia: Fortress, 1975) 67–91; Stendahl, "Judaism and Christianity I: Then and Now," *Meanings*, 210. George Nickelsburg points out the influence of Lutheran theology when he reviews Klein in *RSR* 4 (1978) 161–68.

at which point it metamorphoses into the "teaching of the rabbis," and is superseded by Christianity. All this is explained with a generous number of quotations from the OT itself, from the Gospels and from Paul. Under the model of Law and Gospel, even an acknowledgment of the good to be found in Judaism must be qualified. "Even when the seriousness of Jewish piety is commended," Stendahl points out, "it is done with faint praise: it may be admirable in its sincerity but just for that reason it is more off the mark."[6]

This conventional view of the Jews of the Common Era is flawed in a second way as well. Not only does it distort the rabbinic Judaism of the holy land: insofar as it relies chiefly on the evidence of the rabbinic literature, it all but ignores the "nonrabbinic" Jews of Palestine and also those who are central to this essay: the Greek-speaking Jewish minorities in the Gentile cities of the Roman Empire.[7]

For the diaspora the NT had always been a major source of information. The Pauline letters contain a great deal of theological commentary upon Judaism, but few data on non-Christian Jews. The word *synagogue*, for example, is never used in any letter ever assigned to Paul, including the Pastorals and Hebrews.

Acts is a different matter. Jews appear frequently, and always *in relation to* Christianity: they are either hostile to the new religion, or they are about to convert.

There are several reasons, however, to be careful with the use of Acts as a historical source for diaspora Judaism. First, interpretations of it by later scholars may well be flawed by one or both of the hermeneutical errors discussed at the beginning of this essay. In addition, Acts itself has theological biases. It has no interest in an objective presentation of diaspora Jews, and little concern to present "history" at all in the modern sense. Acts is better described as "theological history," a term applied to it by Robert Maddox, or even as "theology in narrative form."[8] Luke's theology is in control of his history-writing in a score of subtle ways. Finally, Acts must be used with extreme care by the historian of Judaism just because—for the Mediterranean diaspora at least—there is very little other information against which it might be measured. The pagan literary evidence has been assembled

---

[6] Stendahl, "Judaism and Christianity II," *Meanings*, 222.

[7] A. T. Kraabel, "The Roman Diaspora: Six Questionable Assumptions," *JJS* 33 (1982) 445–64 (Yadin *Festschrift*).

[8] Robert Maddox, *The Purpose of Luke-Acts* (Edinburgh: T. & T. Clark, 1982) 16. A. T. Kraabel, "The Disappearance of the 'God-fearers,'" *Numen* 28 (1981) 118.

by Stern,[9] the Jewish inscriptions are collected in *CII* and the Jewish papyri have been edited by Tcherikover.[10] In each instance the data are scattered and often fragmentary. In addition Stern's Gentile authors usually have biases of their own, all too often anti-Jewish.

II

I became interested in one part of the story of Acts over two decades ago.[11] When I went to excavate at Sardis in 1966, I knew I would see evidence for the presence of Jews and pagans in large numbers, and some Christians as well. But I also expected to find that the area around the great Sardis synagogue had been thick with God-fearers, Gentiles sympathetic to Judaism who participated in synagogue services but were not (yet) converts or "proselytes." All the standard reference works implied that they would surely have been there in the NT period. My responsibility with the excavations was for Jewish history, and they should have been a part of that history. But the Sardis evidence was going in another direction.

This element of Jewish "history," the God-fearers, occurs in the NT only in Acts, and there only in the middle half of the book. The more I tried to fit this idea from Acts into Anatolian Jewish history, the more dissatisfied I became, for three reasons. The first had to do with Luke's own purposes. He was writing for a Christian audience, and he was just not interested in non-Christian Jews. In addition, his intent was less historical than theological. As a source for Jewish history Acts itself was doubly flawed.[12]

---

[9] Menahem Stern, *Greek and Latin Authors on Jews and Judaism* (3 vols.; Jerusalem: Israel Academy of Sciences and Humanities, 1976–84).

[10] Victor A. Tcherikover and Alexander Fuks, eds., *Corpus Papyrorum Judaicarum* (3 vols.; Cambridge: Harvard University Press, 1957–64).

[11] I had developed an interest in Philo as an undergraduate at Luther College. At Harvard I studied archaeology with Nahman Avigad and G. M. A. Hanfmann, then worked as a research assistant for E. R. Goodenough until his death, then became involved in the Sardis excavations—all at Stendahl's recommendation and with his support.

[12] See Kraabel, "Disappearance," 113–26 for specifics. The conclusion of that article bears repeating: "At least for the Roman Diaspora, the evidence presently available is far from convincing proof for the existence of such a class of Gentiles as traditionally defined by the assumptions of the secondary literature" (121). See the comments of C. J. Hemer in G. H. R. Horsley, *New Documents Illustrating Early Christianity: A Review of the Greek Inscriptions and Papyri published in 1978* (North Ryde, NSW: Ancient History Documentary Research Centre, Macquarie University, 1983) no. 17; but also Thomas H. Finn, "The God-fearers Reconsidered," *CBQ* 47 (1985) 75–84.

Another concern had less to do with Luke than with his later interpreters. It wasn't Luke who established the technical term "Godfearer" to describe this group in Acts. Rather than a single noun he uses two participles: φοβούμενος/οι in the first five instances, σεβόμενος/οι in the last six. Thus the first five examples are of persons "fearing (God)," the other six are persons "worshiping (God)."[13] In one narrative, 13:14–50, both terms are apparently applied to the same group of people; compare vss 16 and 23 with 43 and 50.[14] The fact that Luke can use two terms suggested that he did not believe he was using technical terminology. It was later translators who rendered both participles identically, and later commentators and historians who conflated the two terms[15] and who turned the God-fearers into a social category, a fixed group, numbering "perhaps millions by the first century."[16]

Finally, many of those later interpreters most familiar to a Lutheran were governed in their historical perception by the theological model of Law and Gospel, a heritage of the Reformation. For us it would be particularly difficult to take Jews seriously and to see them clearly, since our native theology began by assuming that "Judaism is an inferior and erroneous approach to God."[17]

---

[13] The *two* terms are the bane of all who would insist on a single meaning. Academic terminology draws on the first participle: God-fearer, *Gottesfürchtiger, craignant Dieu.* The Latin term in literature and inscriptions is *metuens*, "fearing." But the corresponding Greek adjective is supposedly θεοσεβής, literally "God-worshiping." This last is a most catholic epithet. King Croesus of Sardis is thus described by Herodotos (1.86.2). Bishop Melito of Sardis uses θεοσεβής of Christians (see Eusebius *Hist. eccl.* 4.26.5). And the Sardis synagogue inscriptions use it six times of Jews who made donations to the building.

[14] The distinction is most likely a literary device: "fearing God" is biblical language, while "worshiping God" is more reflective of pagan piety. Simon notes "dass der Übergang vom einen zum anderen beinahe dem Augenblick entspricht, an dem das apostolische Wirken des Paulus sich deutlich vom den Juden ab- u. den Heiden zuwendet," *RAC* 11. 1063 *s.v.* "Gottesfürchtiger." Most recently on literary devices in Luke see Joseph B. Tyson, "The Jewish Public in Luke-Acts," *NTS* 30 (1984) 574–83.

[15] Note how G. Bertram unconsciously begins to refer to "fear of God" in his article, "θεοσεβής, θεοσέβεια," *TDNT* 3 (1965) 123–28, literally "worship of God." Note, too, the gratuitous attack on diaspora Judaism and on the later church in the last paragraph of the article—all out of the "Reformation tradition"? Similar confusion with reference to epigraphic evidence is found in the article on "proselyte" (*sic*) by K. G. Kuhn, "προσήλυτος," *TDNT* 6 (1968) 732–34.

[16] *EncJud* 10. 55 *s.v.* "Jewish Identity."

[17] Stendahl, "Judaism and Christianity II," *Meanings*, 230 n. 12. See also Stendahl's response to Ernst Käsemann in *Paul*, 129–33.

III

But it was not only Reformation theology which distorted our vision. It is important to recall Stendahl's other warning also when looking at the interpretation of diaspora Judaism by Christian scholars: it is misleading and dangerous to play "Galilee" or "Bibleland" or "First-Century Semite" with the ancient texts. One popular variation of this might be called playing "Bible *people*" with the Jews of the Roman Empire. That happens when we expect them to conduct themselves first of all as a religious group or a "faith."[18]

At Sardis, the diaspora Jewish community I know best, this was clearly not the situation. The first Jewish settlers came there in the late third century BCE as the result of a *political* action, the decision by Antiochus III to move 2000 Jewish families in from Babylonia and Mesopotamia to the Sardis area as a means of bringing peace to that area, and of establishing his rule (Josephus *Ant.* 12.147–53).

In the Roman decrees from the second half of the first century BCE preserved in the *Antiquities* of Josephus, the Jews are seen as an ethnic minority of some political power. One decree protects their "ancestral custom" of sending contributions to Jerusalem (16.171). Another affirms their status as a "private association in accordance with their ancestral laws" and recognizes their right to continue to control a "private place (τόπος) where they decide their own business and resolve their differences" (14.235). These privileges were then ratified in a slightly later decree of the people of Sardis (14.259–61).

The excavated Sardis synagogue provides the most vivid illustration of this point.[19] Its location is not that of a building which was primarily religious. The synagogue was a major part of a huge bath-gymnasium complex, the center of public life for Sardis in this period. The synagogue was used for religious events of course. But since it was the only large building controlled by the Jews of Sardis, it must have served a variety of nonreligious purposes as well, as a kind of community assembly hall. And if the Jews retained control of it into the seventh century, as they did, it must have been because of their economic and political influence. If the synagogue's purposes were only religious, it surely would have fallen to the power of a steadily (if slowly) growing Sardis Christianity.

---

[18] See Klein, *Anti-Judaism,* 21–38; Kraabel, "Roman Diaspora," 454–56.

[19] See A. T. Kraabel, "Impact of the Discovery of the Sardis Synagogue," in George M. A. Hanfmann, *Sardis from Prehistoric to Roman Times: Results of the Archaeological Exploration of Sardis, 1958–1975* (Cambridge: Harvard University Press, 1983) 178–90.

The synagogue inscriptions provide further evidence. They are records left by donors, and almost without exception the status of these donors is defined politically and economically, not religiously. Many donors proudly identify themselves as Σαρδιανοί, "citizens of Sardis." No less than nine may use the privileged title βουλευτής, "member of the city council"; they must have possessed considerable social status, perhaps because of their wealth. In addition, three donors held positions in the provincial administration: one was a *comes* or count, another a procurator, another an assistant in the state archives. One late text refers to a revered "rabbi" of the community: the Greek title is σοφοδιδάσκαλος, "wise teacher."[20] (He was also a priest, ἱερεύς.) But even his concerns would not have been wholly religious in the modern sense. It is the community's traditions he would pass down; his teachings would have had cultural and historical content as well as religious meaning.[21]

These Jews are much more than "Biblepeople," or a religious conventicle like the Dead Sea Scrolls community at Qumran. Yet established scholars persist in viewing them in just that way. One continuing example is the Glasgow historian W. H. C. Frend. In 1965, on the basis of Josephus, he described the Jews of Sardis as a "people apart, with their own customs and religion which admitted little intermingling with their Greek neighbors."[22] The conventicle image is obvious. By 1984 Frend has taken the discovery of the synagogue into account. Now in a new book he chastises the Jews of Sardis because "despite all their progress they failed to become a majority in the city. They never converted Sardis as the Christians would convert" other cities nearby.[23] Here is a new form of the "Biblepeople" misperception: the assumption that, because there were so many Jews at Sardis, and since Frend assumes Judaism to have been an aggressive missionary religion, zealous for proselytes, the Jews of Sardis should have been able to convert an entire Anatolian city as Christianity later would do.

One final version of the "Biblepeople" idea is more pervasive than any other: the idea that any Gentile in antiquity who befriended a Jew or a Jewish community was religiously motivated, a potential or even actual convert. Thus, for example, when Julia Severa, a wealthy

---

[20] Cf. John 1:38: Ῥαββί, ὃ λέγεται μεθερμηνευόμενον διδάσκαλε.

[21] On the Sardis inscriptions see Kraabel, "Impact," 184.

[22] W. H. C. Frend, *Martyrdom and Persecution in the Early Church* (Oxford: Blackwell, 1965) 130 with n. 18.

[23] Idem, *The Rise of Christianity* (Philadelphia: Fortress, 1984) 39. See also Kraabel, "Roman Diaspora," 455 on a second-century inscription from Smyrna, *CII* 742 = *Inscriptiones Graecae ad res Romanas pertinentes* 1431, on which see Frend, *Martyrdom,* 148 n. 47.

woman of first-century Acmonia in Phrygia, proved to have been both a benefactor of the local synagogue and a high priestess of a pagan cult, the general assumption was that she must have been a God-fearer. But such a mixture of pagan and Jewish is surely inappropriate among Jews associated with synagogues; it is preferable to attribute what she did to philanthropy and a benevolent attitude toward her Jewish neighbors, even though this is a less "religious" explanation of her actions.[24]

IV

A recent Oxford dissertation by P. F. Esler describes as follows the community out of which Luke writes:

> Few of the members of this community had been outright pagans prior to their conversion. The great majority of its gentile membership had come from the "God-fearers," those gentiles who worshiped Yahweh as the one true God and attended synagogue services in furtherance of that worship. The community also contained a significant number of Jews.[25]

Esler is no biblical fundamentalist, and he is fully aware of recent critical study of Acts. In the stories of Cornelius (10:1–11:18) and of the Jerusalem "Apostolic Council" (chap. 15) he is quite willing to recognize that Luke's theology is greatly to the fore, and he raises seri-

---

[24] The crucial inscription is *CII* 766 = *Monumenta Asiae minoris antiqua* 6 no. 264 = B. Lifshitz, *Donateurs et fondateurs dans les synagogues juives* (Cahiers de RB 7; Paris: Gabalda, 1967) no. 33. See also Kraabel, "Roman Diaspora,' 456. On the importance of philanthropy at this time, see Frederick W. Danker, *Benefactor: Epigraphic Study of a Graeco-Roman and New Testament Semantic Field* (St. Louis: Clayton, 1982). I have suggested already that the explanation might be similar for the very important Aphrodisias inscription soon to be published by Joyce Reynolds. It has been widely discussed even before publication, see Kraabel, "Disappearance," 121 n. 26; Horsley, *New Documents*, no. 96; Wayne Meeks, *The First Urban Christians* (New Haven/London: Yale University Press, 1983) 39. The inscription became widely known to scholars in religious studies in North America as a result of discussions which occurred in August 1984 at a conference at Brown University, sponsored in part by the NEH and the Lilly Endowment; the papers of the conference were published in Jacob Neusner and E. Frerichs, eds., *"To See Ourselves as Others See Us": Christians, Jews, "Others" in Late Antiquity*. See esp. the articles by John J. Collins (182), A. T. Kraabel (230–32), and Tessa Rajak (255–57); and the article by R. S. MacLennan and Kraabel forthcoming in *Biblical Archaeology Review*.

[25] P. F. Esler, "Community and Gospel in Luke-Acts: The Social and Political Motivations of Lucan Theology" (D. Phil. diss., Oxford University, 1984) 312. A revision of the manuscript will be published in 1986 by Cambridge University Press as an SNTSMS monograph.

ous questions about the historicity of each account.[26] But for him the God-fearers must be a historical given, not a theological construct; Acts will not make sense unless we assume the historical accuracy of this part of Luke's story.

Esler is simply the latest in a very long line of interpreters for whom Luke's God-fearers are part of the bedrock of the early *Christian* story. But if the God-fearers existed, they would be first of all an element of *Jewish* history, and in particular the history of Greek-speaking diaspora Judaism. When historians write about this Judaism assuming the traditional position, serious distortions occur, for example:

> Some believe that there were "perhaps millions" of God-fearers by the time of Paul.[27] It cannot be denied that some gentiles were interested in Judaism in this period, but that number is a wild exaggeration. Others, like Martin Hengel, see the God-fearers as evidence for the failure and even the degeneration of Judaism in this period.[28] This is Reformation theology masquerading as Jewish history. Others, like Frend, persist in understanding the Diaspora Jewish communities first of all in religious terms. Here we have the "Biblepeople" error in a clear form.

In all these cases a major source of error is excessive reliance on Acts as a historical source.

V

It has long been recognized that Luke is quite willing to put his theology before his history even with reference to central figures in the story of Jesus. Here are two important examples.

If we had only the Gospel of Luke we would not know who it was who baptized Jesus, but we would have to say that it could not have been John the Baptist! For his own purposes Luke has moved parts of that story (3:21–22) around quite freely. He has John in prison (3:19–20) immediately before the baptism takes place. Then he changes the crucial verb in the baptism story into a passive participle, βαπτισθέντος (3:21). The result is that we know Jesus was baptized, but we are not told by whom.

[26] Ibid., 143–47.

[27] See n. 15.

[28] For Hengel the God-fearers illustrate how "the Jewish religion . . . had to stoop to constant and ultimately untenable compromises" in the NT period: *Judaism and Hellenism* (2 vols.; Philadelphia: Fortress, 1975) 1. 313. See also Kraabel, "Disappearance," 114.

Luke employs this same sort of "theological license" also with reference to Paul; neither Paul's theology nor the chronology of his career, as found in Acts, can be made to line up with the Pauline epistles.[29] Since the present subject is the portrayal of relations among Christians, Gentiles, and Jews in Acts, it is important to note how Luke employs Paul in that regard: in Acts "the great apostle to the Gentiles" preaches to Gentiles only twice: "the few sentences spoken in Lystra" (14:15–17) and the Areopagus speech in Athens (17:19–34).[30]

If such manipulation can take place with central figures in the beginnings of Christianity, it should not be surprising that Luke's historical value should be questioned when he gets to telling people who are farther from the center of the story, and about whom the NT has far less to say: non-Christian diaspora Jews.

In his introductory lectures on the NT, Stendahl identified the theological point being made when Luke refers specifically to diaspora synagogues. As he put it, when Acts has Paul going into the diaspora synagogues again and again to preach, "albeit with little success," the pattern is theological. Luke "intentionally records this pattern" in order to say "Paul had to register the 'No' of the Jews before he was allowed to bring the gospel to the Gentiles." What Luke addresses here with his narrative Paul himself has "theologically expounded in Romans 9–11."[31] The God-fearers are part of this same pattern. They too are in Luke's story to make a theological point. It misses that point simply to take them as elements in a record of Jewish history, something which was not Luke's concern.[32]

For Luke and for most of us, theological issues take precedence over historical ones. But if there is any hope of finding the data of Jewish history in a precious ancient source, the Acts of the Apostles, it will be

---

[29] Ibid., 118, with references; Maddox, *Purpose*, chap. 3. Note the *obiter dictum* of Samuel Sandmel in *RSR* 4 (1978) 159: "If Acts had never been written, or if Acts had been lost and not made its way into the New Testament and we had the Epistles alone, I doubt that any scholars would have supposed that there was some close relationship between Paul and Palestinian Judaism." Significantly this statement appears in Sandmel's review of E. P. Sanders, *Paul and Palestinian Judaism* (Philadelphia: Fortress, 1977).

[30] Martin Dibelius, *Studies in the Acts of the Apostles* (London: SCM, 1956) 154. F. F. Bruce attempts to turn this argument on its head in "Is the Paul of Acts the Real Paul?" *BJRL* 58 (1975–76) 293 n. 2; cf. Kraabel, "Disappearance," 125 n. 14. See also Maddox, *Purpose*, chap. 2.

[31] All quotations in this paragraph are from Stendahl, *Paul*, 28–29.

[32] For the Lukan theology involved, see Kraabel, "Disappearance." On the possibility that early Christian anti-Jewish polemic might have had a positive intent, see most recently G. N. Stanton, "Aspects of Early Christian-Jewish Polemic and Apologetic," *NTS* 31 (1985) 377–92.

accomplished only upon clear recognition of the theological concerns both of the author and of the later interpreters of the text, and only when we begin to take seriously the history of the Jews of the Roman diaspora.

For many Gentiles and Jews, Krister Stendahl has been a thoughtful and careful guide through this bewildering terrain. And for many Lutherans and other Christians, he is a treasured example as we come to our own conclusions about the relations between Jews and Christians for ourselves and for the church of our own day.

TOWARDS ASSESSING THE LATIN TEXT OF "5 EZRA": THE "CHRISTIAN" CONNECTION[*]

Robert A. Kraft
University of Pennsylvania

5 Ezra is a curious and challenging little work, crying out for detailed examination.[1] It exists only in Latin, which presumably was translated from Greek. The text has received minimal attention from modern scholarship,[2] despite its presence on the fringes of the Christian canonical scriptures. *5 Ezra* provides living proof that one need not wait for new manuscripts to be uncovered in graves or caves to engage in work on hitherto virtually unexamined materials, and its contents seem directly relevant to questions about early Christian use of Jewish materials.

---

[*]Appreciation is extended to the participants in my recent graduate seminars on the Ezra materials, one of which (Fall 1982) was conducted jointly with Michael E. Stone (Hebrew University), especially Theodore Bergren, Allen Callahan, Mary LaRue, Stephen Taylor, and Benjamin Wright. The present study is an extension of some of the methodological observations in my "Greek Transmission of Jewish Scriptures: A Methodological Probe," in *Paganisme, Judaïsme, Christianisme: Mélanges offerts à Marcel Simon* (Paris: de Boccard, 1978) 207–26.

[1] "5 Ezra" is used here to designate the writing that has been prefixed in Latin Vg editions to the Ezra-Apocalypse proper ("4 Ezra"). In modern English translations of the Apocrypha, *5 Ezra* usually comprises the first two chapters of "2 Esdras." ("6 Ezra" refers to the similarly brief writing appended to *4 Ezra* in the Vg editions; i.e., "2 Esdras" 15–16.)

[2] Modern general studies examined for this article are listed below in an Appendix. A classified computer based bibliography for *4-5-6 Ezra* compiled by Theodore Bergren has proved most useful. Nevertheless, because of space considerations, footnoting in the present article will be minimal. One of the most intelligent general treatments of *5 Ezra*, especially for its awareness of text-critical issues, is that by Stanton, although I cannot agree with some of his assumptions or with the main thrust of his article. A separate fascicle on *5-6 Ezra* by H. Stegemann has been announced for the series Jüdische Schriften aus hellenistisch-römischer Zeit 3 (Gütersloh: Mohn, 1973–), but it does not seem to be available yet.

My interests in exploring the interfaces between early Judaism and early Christianity were stimulated while studying with Krister Stendahl and his colleagues, and I gratefully offer this survey essay in partial repayment. Many new investigations need to be conducted and new possibilities/syntheses tested if historical research on Judaism and Christianity in the Greco-Roman period is to progress as effectively as it might. The study of *5 Ezra* illustrates some of these needs and approaches.

This brief essay focuses on a set of problems that is absolutely basic to the study of any writing, but with *5 Ezra* has been left "for dessert," as it were—the question of establishing the text. In the first instance, this means assessing the relationship between two groups of Latin manuscripts (designated "SA" and "MEC" respectively) which are in general agreement on the overall outlines of *5 Ezra* but diverge widely in various specific details. To my knowledge, no published critical edition of all the extant witnesses exists.[3] Most translations of *5 Ezra* depend, quite arbitrarily, on only one side of the Latin tradition (SA), which happens to have exerted the major influence on the existing Latin Vg editions.

Thus the value of the various claims about origin, authorship, date, provenance, and "message" of *5 Ezra* is severely compromised by uncertainties about the text. The consensus of modern scholarship seems to be that *5 Ezra* was composed in Greek by a (Jewish) Christian in the second half of the second century, at an unknown but perhaps "western" location, and that it exudes "anti-Jewish" polemics in a prophetic-apocalyptic presentation with a special reverence for Christian

---

[3] The most complete Latin edition of this material is the *Biblia Sacra: iuxta vulgatam versionem* (ed. Robert Weber, Boniface Fischer et al.; 2 vols.; Stuttgart: Würtembergische Bibelanstalt, 1975), which is based on SA and admits to being selective about MEC readings included in the apparatus to *5 Ezra*. The appendix to Bensly's edition (TextsS 3.2, 1895) gives the complete text of MS C, with variant readings of M noted in the apparatus, but does not include this material in the "main text" which is based on SA. Violet's GCS editions of *4 Ezra* proper do not include *5 Ezra*, but do discuss the various Latin MSS of *4-5-6 Ezra*. Additional textual material is noted by D. de Bruyne, "Quelques nouveaux documents pour la critique textuelle de l'Apocalypse d'Esdras," *RBén* 32 (1920) 43–47. The main Latin MSS are listed here (full collations of E and L are not, to my knowledge, available):

S = Sangermanensis (Paris, BN Latin 11504/5), dated 821/2
A = Ambianensis (Amiens, Bib.Communale 10), 9th c. (Corby)
M = Mazarianaeus (Paris, Bib.Mazarine 3/4), 11/12th c. (Cordeliers)
E = Epternacensis (Luxemburg, Bib.Nat. 264), 11th c.
C = Complutensis (Rome, Abbey S.Girolamo photocopy), 10th c.
L = Legionensis (Leon, Real Colegiate San Isidoro 1.3), dated 1162

martyrs. It is described as highly imitative and derivative in its language and ideas—a pastiche of scriptural phrases from both Jewish and Christian sources. My own discomfort with this consensus is partly the result of working with this and similar texts and partly an overreaction to the absurdity of having such neat answers before the textual basis for asking these questions is more firmly established.

Nevertheless, one cannot "establish the text" by working in a vacuum. If this were a detailed study of all the relevant data, my approach would be to try to view the preserved textual materials from as many historically and linguistically defensible perspectives as possible in order to establish as clear a set of options for comparison and evaluation as possible. Since the preserved texts, whatever their differences, seem to ask to be seen as presenting a pre-Christian Jewish writing, one of the perspectives I would attempt to explore is the extent to which the oldest recoverable texts can be read in that light. Since the preserved textual witnesses also, in their present forms, emanate from clearly Christian circles, I would try to hold in balance the question of how the Christian readers understood and used, and consciously or unconsciously modified these materials. Textual work is in many ways circular—or better, "spiral," since it ought to make progress as it moves round and round among the variable items of data. The "critical text" I try to recreate is greatly influenced by the often unexamined assumptions that influence me and the options I choose to exercise at any given point, whether those are linguistic options, or semantic, or more broadly historical. And the resultant "established text" in turn provides evidence to strengthen such (assumptions and) options.

The continuous text of *5 Ezra* is not known to us in any ancient language other than Latin. That is itself somewhat unusual. Further, the Latin MSS present the two significantly variant text forms mentioned above: "type SA" (traditionally dubbed "French") and "type MEC" ("Spanish"). I resist calling them "recensions," because the question has not yet been carefully examined as to whether both stem from a single Latin prototype and thus reflect conscious editorial activity that created the differences. If *5 Ezra* was originally written in Latin (so Labourt and Daniélou), they can only be recensions; if, as I suspect is more likely, it existed earlier in Greek (I did not say originated in Greek, since questions about its possible Semitic origins also need to be asked), the two Latin text types could conceivably stem from two more or less independent Latin translations, or one text type could reflect revisional activity towards a Greek "recension" that differed significantly from the Greek text first rendered into Latin. Various possibilities exist.[4] Only a close study of the preserved witnesses can give rise to controlled probabilities.

Modern commentators all affirm that *5 Ezra* betrays "Christian" interests in its preserved form(s), although a few would argue that it may have originated in Jewish circles and was later reworked (Riessler sees it as "probably Essene" in origin). Much of the evidence adduced to posit the Christian character of *5 Ezra* is relatively superficial (see below), and the presentation of the evidence is usually unreflective about the basic assumptions that are operating with regard to Judaism and/or Christianity in the Greco-Roman period. The presentations are also largely unimaginative. One might have expected, for example, to find some commentator holding that there had been an older Greek Jewish writing that Latin translators "Christianized." No such claim has been found in the literature consulted for this essay. Already in its hypothetical Greek form, *5 Ezra* is assumed to have been a Christian production. None of the recent commentators presents evidence pro or con as to whether a Semitic form of the work might possibly lie behind the presumed Greek (as is commonly assumed for *4 Ezra* proper).[5]

The only detailed published study of the text-critical relationships between the preserved Latin witnesses to *5 Ezra* of which I am aware is by M. R. James in his introduction to Bensly's posthumous edition of the extended Latin "4 Ezra" (i.e., *5 Ezra* + *4 Ezra* + *6 Ezra*). James presents instance after instance in which he argues that the MEC text preserves readings that could have given rise to the SA text, but which are not likely to have been produced from the SA text. Especially provocative is James's claim that the MEC text is sometimes to be preferred because it is more overtly "Christian," whereas the editors of the SA text "corrected" it to sound more authentically "Jewish" as well as to read more smoothly in Latin.

James's impressively learned study is also somewhat haphazard and sufficiently idiosyncratic and unconvincing that it has left little impact on the text-critical decisions of subsequent editors and commentators, with the notable exceptions of Stanton, Oesterley, and to a lesser extent Weinel(-Duensing). In English speaking circles, the *KJV* (= Ball) had followed the standard Clementine Vg text quite closely, and the *RV* (= Oesterley) made only minor adjustments, usually to accord with SA

---

[4] See my "Reassessing the 'Recensional Problem' in Testament of Abraham," in George W. E. Nickelsburg, Jr., ed., *Studies on the Testament of Abraham* (SBLSCS 6; Missoula: Scholars Press, 1976) 121–37.

[5] Ball's notes include occasional references to presumed Semitic readings behind the preserved Latin.

readings which differed from the old Vg edition. *RSV* (see Metzger) and *NEB* (= Knibb) also all but ignored the MEC materials. Only Stanton and Oesterly, in their occasional comments, and Myers, in his extensive descriptive footnotes, provide the English student with an inkling of how potentially significant the MEC text is in relation to that of SA. In German, the Weinel-Duensing tradition adopted a few of the MEC readings, as is obvious to anyone who examines the opening words of *5 Ezra* in *NTApoc* side by side with the *RSV* or *NEB*.

Two other special studies that reflect favorably James's positive judgment about the value of the MEC text of *5 Ezra* deserve mention. The noted French scholar of Latin Christian materials, Donatien de Bruyne, argues that *5 Ezra* 2.33–48 (which he dubs "Revelatio Esdrae") is a separable fragment of a lost apocalypse that has also left its mark on the old liturgical language of the Roman Churches.[6] De Bruyne speaks favorably of James's preference for the MEC text, and expresses the hope that Violet will produce a critical edition of *5 Ezra* based on those materials. (He did not.)

Also of interest is Albrecht Oepke's judgment about the text of *5 Ezra* found in his deceptively titled and wide-ranging study of relationships between "Church and Synagogue" which begins with the identification of a quotation from *5 Ezra* 1.24 in the 10/11th- century (?) work entitled *De altercatione Ecclesiae et Synagogae*.[7] Oepke argues that at least for this passage, the MEC text is preferable to that of SA. Although the differences are quantitatively minor, they are qualitatively significant, and can serve to introduce us to a larger set of issues.

The introductory formula in *De altercatione* hints at some of the basic problems encountered in *5 Ezra*:

Lege quid tibi Esdras ex persona salvatoris scripsit:

(Read what Esdras in the person of a/the savior wrote to you)

The author of *De altercatione* identifies "Esdras" (so MEC; "Ezra" in SA) as the source, but also knows that at some points, this Ezra sounds very much like the Christian "savior," speaking to the "synagogue." The first sentence of the presumed quotation underlines this point.

---

[6] "Fragments d'une Apocalypse perdue," *RBén* 33 (1921) 97–109. He compares *5 Ezra* with a 9th (?) century *Liber Responsalis* from Gaul that is published in *PL* 78. 726–852. See also Daniélou.

[7] "Ein bisher unbeachtetes Zitat aus dem fünften Buche Esra," *ConNT* 11 (1947) 179–95.

Ad meos veni et me mei non receperunt

(I came to mine and mine did not receive me)

Oepke does not know what to do with these words, so he treats them as a reformulation of John 1:11 (Vg: "In propria venit, et sui eum non receperunt"), placed in the mouth of Christ himself by means of the phrase "ex persona salvatoris." Perhaps. But it is also possible that some form of *5 Ezra*, from which the remainder of the quotation clearly derives, once contained a similar statement on Ezra's lips. Note that the SA text (but not MEC) of *5 Ezra* 2.33 has Ezra saying "When I came to them [Israel] they rejected me" (ad quos cum venirem reprobaverunt me). Elsewhere in *5 Ezra*, the speaker (usually "the Lord") often complains of such rejection, for example, *5 Ezra* 1.7–8, 14, 25, 34; 2:1, 3, 5–7.

Then follows the identified material from *5 Ezra* 1.24:

De altercatione	*5 Ezra* 1.24 MEC	SA text
quid tibi faciam Jacob?	[same]	[same]
boluit me audire Juda.	noluit obaudire me J.	noluisti me obaudire J.
transferam me	[same]	[same]
ad alteram gentem.	ad gentem alteram	ad alias gentes
	et dabo illi	et dabo eis
	nomen meum	[same]
	et custodientes	ut
	custodient	custodiant
	legitima mea.	[same]
What shall I do to you, Jacob	[=]	[=]
He did not want me to hear Judah!	He did not want to obey me, Judah.	You did not want to obey me, Judah!
I will turn my attention to another nation!	[same]	[same]
	[same]	[same]
	[same]	to other nations
	and will give it my name	and will give them [=]
	and they will surely keep	so that they may keep
	my requirements.	[=]

The MEC text is clearly reflected here at two points: the statement relating to Judah (either construed in one of the above ways, or more probably "Judah did not want to hear me") and the reference to "nation/race" in the singular. Taken in isolation, neither point is convincing evidence of the superiority of MEC. With regard to the

Jacob/Judah couplet, SA seems smoother and more typical of Semitic poetic/prophetic parallelism, with both of the offending parties addressed directly. The reference to "nation/race" in the singular is supported by the subsequent singular pronoun (*illi*), but then is compromised by the plurals in the next clause (*-entes -ent*). Again, SA is structurally more balanced ("smoother"), although the pleonasm of MEC (*custodientes custodient*) could be considered a "Semitism" and viewed as more "primitive" than the simpler parallel in SA.

Oepke is not primarily concerned about assessing these details in terms of basic text-critical categories such as which is the "more difficult" reading to explain (*lectio difficilior*), syntactical awkwardness, etc. His main focus is theological:

> The French text [SA] is concerned with the gentiles in general, but the Spanish [MEC] with the Christians as the new people of God or "third race." Thus the theological opposition is more precisely presented in the Spanish. That can hardly be attributed to the reviser. Rather, the Spanish text probably preserves the original reading of the presumed Greek original. The readings of the Spanish text are often noteworthy, while the French polishes unintelligible difficulties in it.[8]

Although this is not one of the contexts discussed by James, he would certainly have been pleased with Oepke's conclusion: here is another example in which the originally "Christian" outlook of the work is neutralized by the SA revision. But this passage in isolation need not be viewed that way. One could also argue that an originally relatively smooth and theologically less pointed (i.e., more "Jewish") text (SA) has been corrupted seriously in transmission while also, at least at one point, becoming better geared to the needs of its Christian users (MEC). The analysis by Oepke seems to assume James's conclusion about the more overtly "Christian" character of the MEC text. I suspect that James himself never seriously tested the possibility that in the pre-Latin Greek form(s) of *5 Ezra*, we might be dealing with a Jewish writing. Nor does James consider that the relationship between the two Latin text types might be other than one of direct dependence—for example, that each might reflect relatively independent attempts to translate a (slightly different) Greek *5 Ezra*, using similar approaches to translation.

---

[8] Ibid., 180.

With regard to the preferability of reading "another nation" with MEC in *5 Ezra* 1.24 (not SA "other nations"), Oepke is almost certainly correct, but for reasons he never explicates. Both Latin text types of *5 Ezra* provide ample evidence that the idea of one special nation/people over against another special nation/people is an often repeated theme in this material.[9] The "people that is coming" (1.35–38) to replace/displace the original people (Jacob, Judah, Israel) seems to become "my people" in 2.10, while the original "my people" (1.5) either disappears as such or is reinstated without fanfare in 2.15–32. The relationship of the "people" in 2.41 (MEC "the people that was called from the beginning"; SA "your [Ezra's] people") and in 2.48 (MEC "that very people" [?]; SA "my people") to the original people and to the "people to come" is not entirely clear unless 2.33 indicates irrevocable rejection by and of the former. This consistent pattern of using the singular for the two special "people/nations" is broken only by the SA text with its plural references in 1.24 (see above) and in 2.34 "I say to you, nations that hear and understand" (MEC has "I say to you who hear and understand").

The thematic framework of *5 Ezra*, then, is partly similar to materials found especially in Jeremiah, Isaiah, Hosea, and some of the other oracular prophets of ancient Israel: God's people stand condemned for their sins, rebellions, thanklessness, etc. Thus God rejects Israel and lavishes attention on another "people" (1.24, 35–40; 2.10–15). Nevertheless, God remembers his own (with all the ambiguities implied in that phrase) and will be merciful to them in the end (2.16–32, 34–41). The hortatory eschatological section in 2.34(33)–41, spoken by Ezra (not directly by the Lord, as with previous discourses in *5 Ezra*), culminates with Ezra describing an apocalyptic-type scene on Mount Zion in which "God's son" puts crowns on the white robed persons who had valiantly confessed their God in the world (2.42–48).

To what extent is all this necessarily "Christian"? Certainly the parallels between *5 Ezra* and Jewish and Christian scriptures prove little. *5 Ezra* contains no explicit (formula) quotations from other works. Unless we assume that whenever words and phrases that occur in "biblical" writings are also found elsewhere, the extrabibilical uses must be

---

[9] Concern about the "two peoples" (see Gen 25:23) is evidenced in early Judaism and early Christianity. See the comments on *Barn.* 13.2 in my *Barnabas and the Didache* (ed. R. M. Grant; The Apostolic Fathers: A New Translation and Commentary 3; New York: Nelson, 1965) and in Pierre Prigent's edition of Barnabas (*Épître de Barnabé* [SC 172; Paris: Cerf, 1971]). Oepke's connection of the passage with concepts of the "third race" (Christians) is unnecessary. Elsewhere in *5 Ezra* there are also a few plural general references to "the nations": 1.11 (SA), 2.7, 28.

derivative, there is no way to determine whether a writing such as
5 Ezra is dependent on scriptural texts, is used by scriptural texts, or
independently reflects the same sort of language that also appears in
scriptural texts. In general, the parallels between *5 Ezra* and early
Christian literature are not sufficiently characteristic of Christian
interests and activities to be persuasive: "As a hen gathers her brood
under her wings" (1.30; see Matt 23:37 and par.); "Your house is
desolate" (1.33; see Matt 23:38 and par.); "Ask and you will receive"
(2.13; see Matt 7:7 and par., John 16:24); "Pray . . . that your days
may be shortened" (2.13; see Matt 24:22); "Watch!" (2.13; see Mark
13:37 and par.). Such passages are in the NT Gospels (esp. Matthew,
as Stanton elaborates), but that is hardly proof that the author of *5 Ezra*
got them from the Gospels or wrote at a later date than the Gospels.
Similarly, various words and phrases in *5 Ezra* 2.33–48 can be paralleled in the NT book of Revelation (e.g., 6:9–11). The origins of all
these materials, both for the NT writings and for *5 Ezra*, may be a common store of prophetic-apocalyptic materials available to those writers
(see Daniélou for various "Jewish Christian" themes in *5 Ezra*).

More serious candidates for the "Christian" label are the references
to "God's son" in the "apocalypse" of *5 Ezra* 2.42–48. He is
described as a "youth of great stature, preeminent over all" (2.43).
Whether those on whom he is placing crowns are thought to have
"confessed him" in the mortal world, or "confessed God," is problematic (2.45 "they have confessed the name of God" [SA = M, but C
has here "God's son"]; 2.47 "He is son of God whom they
confessed"—does the "confessing" pertain to God or to God's son?).
What relationship there may be between this sort of imagery, descriptions of the divine spirit as exceedingly tall, etc., and such passages of
the description of the resurrection event in the *Gospel of Peter* deserves
further discussion in the context of Jewish expectations regarding
divine agency in the last times (see Daniélou). Unless we imagine that
the eschatological idea of "God's son" was first created by
Christianity—a contention rendered even more questionable by the
Qumran materials—we cannot neglect the possibility that *5 Ezra* provides pre- or non-Christian evidence of this figure.

The MEC text has other allegedly blatant "Christian" touches. One
is the long "addition" after 1.32 which is only found in M (not in
[E?]C) and refers to delivering "Lord almighty" to death by suspend-
ing him on a tree. I do not wish to contend that this is not Christian;
nor do I wish to argue (as did James) that it belongs to the earliest
recoverable text of *5 Ezra*.

The MEC text has two references to "apostles." In 1.32 "I sent you my servants the prophets whom you took and killed, and you tore apart the bodies of the apostles" (SA has "their bodies"); in 1.37 "The apostles are witnesses to the people who are about to come" (SA has "I [presumably the Lord] call to witness the gratitude of the people that is to come"). The Greek word apostle is, of course, known from contexts other than Christian. It means a legate, one sent on behalf of another. Semitic language traditions in early Judaism can also speak of such legate-apostles, as can Greek literature in general. Presumably there was a rich background behind the technical application of this word to early Christian missionaries (as in Paul), and to the twelve disciples of Jesus. Can the MEC text of 5 Ezra, with its prophets and apostles, be understood in the light of such a setting? (Cf. Luke 11:49, which is in the form of a quotation.) This is certainly worth investigation.

Other arguments for the "Christian" origin of 5 Ezra may be encountered, perhaps to enhance the cumulative effect of the evidence presented above. Of special interest both for its methodological and factual absurdity and for its text-critical relevance is the claim found in the otherwise often helpful commentary by Oesterley regarding the term "Lord Almighty": "This title of God stamps the passage [1.28] as Christian" because it occurs in 2 Cor 6:18 and in Revelation but not in the Hebrew scriptures. Myers also comments on the phrase, noting that it occurs six times in 5 Ezra, and almost as an afterthought that it also occurs in the Greek Jewish scriptures ("LXX") and in Sirach. All other considerations aside, this hardly constitutes evidence of "Christian" phraseology. In addition, it is doubtful that the oldest recoverable text of 5 Ezra had the designation; it appears only once in MEC, at 1.33 where the M text has its long addition. Otherwise, the MEC text has simply "Lord" where SA has "Lord Almighty."

I have only scratched the surface of the sorts of textual, philological, formal, and historical/conceptual research that needs to be done on this provocative little literary package. On the whole, if not in every particular, James's judgment that the MEC text is superior to that of SA seems demonstrable. Of course, each individual context requires careful analysis. James's suggestion that the complicated Latin textual situation in 5 Ezra preserves evidence in SA of Christian de-Christianization of a would-be "Jewish" text is exciting, and deserves close scrutiny. My own tentative conclusion is that he is wrong in this instance (but not necessarily for every other writing as well), and that the MEC type of text can be understood better as a relic of pre- or non-Christian "Judaism" in its broader sense. It is not clear to me that the SA text developed directly from the MEC type; SA and MEC may at points preserve independent variant versions of the underlying Greek textual stream, which itself undoubtedly contained a certain amount of diversity. I am dubious that a Semitic original lay behind the lost Greek form(s), although the evidence has not yet been carefully tested.

With regard to matters of "form," *5 Ezra* 1.4 through 2.32 seems to me to have constituted a unit of primarily "paraenetic/confrontational prophetic" type Jewish material—the sort of material on which little study has been done for Judaism and Christianity in the Greco-Roman period. The largely biblical, priestly genealogy of 1.1–3 (SA) is patently secondary. We are dealing in *5 Ezra* with Ezra the prophet![10] The exact relationship of 2.33–41 (words of Ezra) and of 2.42–48 (what Ezra saw) to what precedes and to each other, in terms of literary development, is not yet clear to me. This material brings *5 Ezra* closer to more typically "apocalyptic" materials, with 2.33–41 serving as a bridge from the previously "prophetic" outlook. In any event, *5 Ezra* is in these and other regards significantly different from *6 Ezra*, which seems to me to be even more clearly Jewish and of an "oracular prophetic" (political oracles) type that also deserves serious attention. But that is another essay.

Appendix

C. J. Ball, *The Ecclesiastical or Deuterocanonical Books of the OT commonly called the Apocrypha* (Variorum Reference Edition; London: Eyre & Spottiswoode, n.d. [post 1888]).

J. Daniélou, "Le Ve Esdras et le Judéo-Christianisme Latin au Second Siècle," in *Ex Orbe Religionum: Studia Geo Widengren* (Studies in the History of Religion [*NumenSup*] 21; Leiden: Brill, 1972) 162–71.

Idem, *The Origins of Latin Christianity* (trans. D. Smith and J. A. Baker; A History of Early Christian Doctrine Before the Council of Nicaea 3; Philadelphia: Westminster, 1977) esp. 17–31.

H. Duensing, "The Fifth and Sixth Books of Esra," *NTApoc* 2. 689–95.

M. A. Knibb, *2 Esdras* in R. G. Coggins and M. A. Knibb, *The First and Second Book of Esdras* (Cambridge Bible Commentary; Cambridge: Cambridge University Press, 1979).

M. J. Labourt, "Le cinquième livre d'Esdras," *RB* 17 (1909) 412–34.

[10] See my "'Ezra' Materials in Judaism and Christianity," *ANRW* II.19.1 (1969) 119–36.

Bruce M. Metzger, "The Fourth Book of Ezra," in J. H. Charlesworth, ed., *The Old Testament Pseudepigrapha: Apocalyptic Literature and Testaments* (Garden City: Doubleday, 1983) 516–59.

Jacob M. Myers, *I and II Esdras* (AB; Garden City: Doubleday, 1974).

W. O. E. Oesterly, *II Esdras (The Ezra Apocalypse)* (Westminster Commentaries; London: Methuen, 1933).

Idem, *An Introduction to the Books of the Apocrypha* (London: SPCK, 1935) 246–47.

Otto Plöger, "Das 5 und 6 Esrabuch," *RGG* 2 (1958) 699–700.

Paul Riessler, *Altjüdisches Schriftum ausserhalb der Bibel* (Heidelberg: Kerle, 1928) 310–17 and 1285–86.

W. Schneemelcher, "Esra. 11 Christl. Esraliteratur," *RAC* 6 (1966) 604–5.

H. Schneider, "Esdras: 5. Buch E.," *LThK* 3 (1959).

G. N. Stanton, "5 Ezra and Matthean Christianity in the Second Century," *JTS* 28 (1977) 67–83.

Nigel Turner, "Esdras, Books of," *IDB* 2 (1962) 142.

Heinrich Weinel, "Das fünfte Buch Esra," in Edgar Hennecke, ed., *Neutestamentliche Apokryphen* (2d ed.; Leipzig: Mohr-Siebeck, 1924) 390–94.

Idem, "Das fünfte Buch Esra," in Edgar Hennecke, ed., *Handbuch zu den Neutestamentlichen Apokryphen* (Tübingen: Mohr-Siebeck, 1904) 331–36.

A PHYSICAL DESCRIPTION OF PAUL

Abraham J. Malherbe
Yale Divinity School

When Paul is placed in his Greek context, it is generally his thought, vocabulary, and literary style that receive attention. This is to a degree at least also true when attention is given to the early church's interpretation of his letters. Greek influence can also be perceived in early Christian reflections on the physical appearance of Paul. Less well known to most students of early Christianity than the literary evidence are the artistic representations of Paul,[1] but the curious literary portrait of Paul in the *Acts of Paul and Thecla*, which in some respects agrees with early Christian paintings, is well known. There, Onesiphorus sees Paul as "a man small of stature, with a bald head and crooked legs, in a good state of body, with eyebrows meeting and nose somewhat hooked, full of friendliness; for now he appeared like a man, and now he had the face of an angel."[2]

This description, which in sometimes modified forms proved popular among later writers,[3] does not accord with our view of beauty, and has been regarded as hardly flattering,[4] as "naiv-unheroisch,"[5] and as

---

[1] The material is conveniently gathered by E. von Dobschütz, *Der Apostel Paulus: II. Seine Stellung in der Kunst* (Halle: Buchhandlung des Waisenhauses, 1928); Giuseppe Ricciotti, *Paul the Apostle* (trans. Alba I. Zizzamia; Milwaukee: Bruce, 1953) 151–59.

[2] *Acta Pauli et Theclae* 3 (*AAA*; reprinted Darmstadt: Wissenschaftliche Buchgesellschaft, 1959) 1. 237 lines 6–9. The translation is that printed in *NTApoc*, 2. 354.

[3] See J. Fürst, "Untersuchungen zur Ephemeris des Diktys von Kreta," *Philologus* 61 (1902) 407–12; von Dobschütz, *Der Apostel*, 45–46.

[4] W. M. Ramsay, *The Church in the Roman Empire Before A. D. 170* (London: Hodder & Stoughton, 1890) 32; L. Vouaux, *Les Actes de Paul et ses lettres apocryphes* (Paris: Letouzey et Ané, 1913) 122.

[5] E. Dassmann, *Der Stachel im Fleisch: Paulus in der frühchristlichen Literatur bis Irenäus* (Münster: Aschendorff, 1979) 279.

representing Paul as quite plain,[6] ugly, and small,[7] "ein Mann von numinoser Hässlichkeit,"[8] and as being "the typical portrait of a Jew."[9] Luther's view is still that of the majority of commentators: "Ego credo Paulum fuisse personam contemptibilem, ein armes, dirs menlein sicut Philippus."[10]

That this description does not appear to us an idealization may suggest that it was indebted to memory of what Paul actually did look like.[11] If Sir William Ramsay's argument, that the *Acts of Paul and Thecla* goes back ultimately to a first-century document, is accepted[12] the description of Paul may have some claim to historical accuracy. But Ramsay's argument has proved to be unconvincing.[13] Writing in Asia towards the end of the second century, the author of the *Acts* knew the canonical Acts and other NT writings, as well as current legendary tradition, all of which he used to construct a work intended for edification.[14] In doing so, he was more concerned with current conceptions of Paul than the Paul of the NT, although he used the NT material freely. Yet there are hints in Paul's letters that he was not an outstandingly robust physical specimen (e.g., 2 Cor 10:10; 13:7–12 [?]; Gal 4:13–16), which do not make the description in the *Acts* incongruous.[15] Furthermore, early portraits of Paul from the catacombs and elsewhere, showing him with a sparsely covered head, have been taken to represent more or less accurate knowledge.[16]

---

[6] T. Zahn, "Paulus der Apostel," *RE* 15 (1904) 70.

[7] J. Geffcken, *Christliche Apokryphen* (Tübingen: Mohr, 1908) 27.

[8] H. D. Betz, *Der Apostel Paulus und die sokratische Tradition* (BHT 45; Tübingen: Mohr-Siebeck, 1972) 54.

[9] W. Michaelis, *Die Apokryphen Schriften zum Neuen Testament* (2d ed.; Bremen: Schünemann, 1958) 313.

[10] Martin Luther, *Werke: Tischreden* (Weimar: Herrmann Böhlaus, 1913) 2 no. 1245.

[11] Von Dobschütz, *Der Apostel,* 1.

[12] Ramsay, *Church in the Roman Empire,* 381ff.

[13] E.g., A. Harnack, *Geschichte der altchristlichen Literatur bis Eusebius* (Leipzig: Hinrichs, 1897) 2.1, 505; A. F. Findlay, *Byways in Early Christian Literature: Studies in the Uncanonical Gospels and Acts* (Edinburgh: T. & T. Clark, 1923) 335 n. 226; *NTApoc,* 2. 332–33.

[14] *NT Apoc,* 2.348–49; W. Schneemelcher, "Die Apostelgeschichte des Lukas und die Acta Pauli," in W. Eltester and F. H. Kettler, eds., *Apophoreta: Festschrift für Ernst Haenchen* (*BZNW* 30; Berlin: Töpelmann, 1964) 236–50.

[15] See, e.g., A. Plummer, *A Critical and Exegetical Commentary on the Second Epistle of St. Paul to the Corinthians* (ICC; Edinburgh: T. & T. Clark, 1915) 283; A. Deissmann, *Paul: A Study in Social and Religious History* (trans. W. E. Wilson; reprinted New York: Harper, 1957) 55. On the question of Paul's health, see Ricciotti, *Paul the Apostle,* 160–67.

[16] See G. Wilpert, *Le pitture delle catacombe romane* (Rome, 1903) 106; Ricciotti, *Paul the Apostle,* 159.

These efforts to find clues to Paul's physical appearance underscore a peculiarity of the NT; it provides no physical descriptions of its main characters. Such descriptions were common in ancient biographies and in descriptions of so-called divine men, where they tend to appear toward the beginning, as they do in the *Acts*.[17] It is not impossible that the description in the *Acts* contains some historical truth, but on the basis of our present evidence it is impossible to verify that it does. Rather, recognizing that the *Acts* follows one literary convention in providing a description of Paul early in the work, it is worth inquiring whether other conventions cast light on the description itself. Physiognomy had long been a topic of considerable interest before it attained its greatest popularity in the second century CE, and Christians shared this interest.[18]

In this study I wish only to ascertain, with the help of the manuals on physiognomy and descriptions of honored figures, whether the *Acts* description would have appeared as unflattering to Greeks as it does to us. Of the features mentioned, it is Paul's baldness, bowed legs, meeting eyebrows, hooked nose, and perhaps smallness of stature, that lead to our negative assessment of his appearance. For the rest, his aspect is described in terms so favorable that they may appear to the modern reader designed to balance his negative physical features. The physiognomic literature repeatedly discusses these features. It has been denied that the physiognomic manuals provided the basis of the description,[19] yet they do supplement other material, and to that extent are valuable corroborating sources.

Robert Grant has found the basis for the *Acts* description in a passage from Archilochus (Frg. 58 Bergk[4]), which was popular in the second century: "I love not a tall general nor a straddling one, nor one proud of his hair nor one part-shaven; for me a man should be short and bowlegged to behold, set firm on his feet, full of heart."[20] On the

---

[17] See Elizabeth C. Evans, "Physiognomics in the Ancient World," *TAPA* n.s. 59 (1969) 51–58; Patricia Cox, *Biography in Late Antiquity: A Quest for the Holy Man* (Berkeley: University of California Press, 1983) 14–15; R. Reitzenstein, *Hellenistische Wündererzählungen* (reprinted Darmstadt: Wissenschaftliche Buchgesellschaft, 1963) 39; L. Bieler, ΘΕΙΟΣ ANHP (reprinted Darmstadt: Wissenschaftliche Buchgesellschaft, 1967) 1. 49–50.

[18] See Evans, "Physiognomics"; J.-C. Fredouille, *Tertullien et la conversion de la culture antique* (Paris: ÉtAug, 1972) 60–62.

[19] Cf. Bieler, ΘΕΙΟΣ ANHP, 50 n. 1; R. M. Grant, "The Description of Paul in the *Acts of Paul and Thecla*," *VC* 36 (1982) 1.

[20] Translation by J. M. Edmonds, *Elegy and Iambus* (LCL) 2. 127; Grant, "Description of Paul," 1–4. The major testimonies are Galen in Hippocr. *De artic.* 3 (18,1.537 and 604 Kühn); Dio Chrysostom *Orat.* 33.17; Schol. Hippocr. ex Erotian 13.32 Klein (Frg. 43 p. 112, 13–15 Nachmannson); Schol. vet. Theocr. 4.49a (p. 148, 19–21 Wendel). See

ground that, according to the Pastoral Epistles, the bishop should have such qualities of a general as are detailed by Onasander, and in view of Paul's liking for military metaphors,[21] Grant thinks it natural for an admirer of Paul to have used the well-known language of Archilochus to depict him as a general. Grant is correct in drawing attention to this somewhat similar description, and thus in recognizing the positive element in the description of Paul in the *Acts*. The two features of interest in the passage from Archilochus are the shortness of the general and his bowleggedness. These and other features are also found in descriptions not indebted to Archilochus, and I suggest that these descriptions point to a different source for the description in the *Acts*.

Three of Paul's features, his small stature, hooked nose, and meeting eyebrows, also appear in Suetonius's description of Augustus (*Vita Caes.* 2.79.2):

> His teeth were wide apart, small, and well-kept; his hair was slightly curly and inclining to golden; his eyebrows met. His ears were of moderate size, and his nose projected a little at the top and then bent slightly inward. His complexion was between dark and fair. He was short of stature, . . . but this was concealed by the fine proportion and symmetry of his figure.

Suetonius used such physiognomic descriptions, which have parallels in the handbooks, to describe his ideal political leaders.[22] Meeting eyebrows were regarded as a sign of beauty,[23] and a person with a hooked nose was thought likely to be royal[24] or magnanimous.[25] Tallness was preferred; nevertheless, since men of normally small height had a smaller area through which the blood flowed, they were thought to be quick.[26] The main things were that one not be excessive in either direction, and, as in the case of Augustus, that one be well proportioned.[27]

Giovanni Tarditi, *Archiloco* (Rome: Ateneo, 1968) 116.

[21] See A. J. Malherbe, "Antisthenes and Odysseus, and Paul at War," *HTR* 76 (1983) 143–73.

[22] See Cox, *Biography in Late Antiquity*, 13–15; Evans, "Physiognomics," 53–54.

[23] Cf. Philostratus *Heroicus* 33.39 (46,16–17 de Lannou), and on the handbooks see Fürst, "Untersuchungen," 386–88.

[24] Cf. Plato *Rep.* 5.474D; Pollux *Onom.* 2.73 (= R. Foerster, ed., *Scriptores Physiognomici graeci et latini* [Leipzig: Teubner, 1893] 2. 281,26–27).

[25] Cf. Ps.-Aristotle *Physiog.* 811a36–38; Anon. *De physiog.* 51 (= Jacques André, ed., *Anonyme Latin, Traité de physiognomie* [Budé; Paris: Belles Lettres, 1981] 91).

[26] Cf. Ps.-Aristotle *Physiog.* 813b.

[27] See Evans, "Physiognomics," 10, 53.

The same features were also attributed to Heracles, who may be of particular relevance. According to Clement of Alexandria (*Protrep.* 2.30), Dicaearchus, a pupil of Aristotle, and Hieronymus of Rhodes described Heracles as follows: "Hieronymus the philosopher sketches his bodily strengths also,—small stature, bristling hair, great strength. Dicaearchus adds that he was slim, sinewy, dark, with hooked nose, bright gleaming eyes and long straight hair."[28] Heracles, as are other Greek heroes, is also elsewhere described as small,[29] having a hooked nose,[30] and eyebrows that met.[31]

The closest parallel to the *Acts* description is found in Philostratus *VS* 552, where a certain Agathion, who was also called Heracles, is described. Philostratus's description is based on a letter of Herodes Atticus, who had been a pupil of Dio Chrysostom.

> He says that his hair grew evenly on his head, his eyebrows were bushy and they met as though they were one, and his eyes gave out a brilliant gleam which betrayed his impulsive temperament; he was hook-nosed, and had a solidly built neck, which was due rather to work than to diet. His chest, too, was well formed and beautifully slim, and his legs were slightly bowed outwards, which made it easy for him to stand firmly planted.

This Agathion-Heracles is usually identified with the Sostratus of Lucian, *Demonax* 1. While Lucian partly described him in Cynic terms, Philostratus adapted his sources and added mystic-religious features, including the heroification of Sostratus.[32] Whether Herodes Atticus had derived the description from Archilochus is unclear. What is important is that we have to do with a description that came to be attributed to Heracles.

It is clear by now that Paul's hooked nose, bowed legs, and meeting eyebrows were not unflattering features in the context in which the *Acts* was written. Furthermore, Heracles and traditions associated with him

[28] Translation by G. W. Butterworth, *Clement of Alexandria* (LCL) 63. See Geneva Misener, "Iconistic Portraits," *CP* 19 (1924) 108.

[29] E.g., Pindar *Isthm* 3.53; cf. Fürst, "Untersuchungen," 409 n. 82; Evans, "Physiognomics," 44–45, 51.

[30] E.g., Plutarch *Antonius* 4.1: "A shapely beard, a broad forehead, and an aquiline nose were thought to show the virile qualities peculiar to the portraits and statues of Heracles."

[31] E.g., Philostratus *Im.* 2.15.5.

[32] See J. F. Kindstrand, "Sostratus-Hercules-Agathion—The Rise of a Legend" *Kungl. Humanistika Vetenskaps-Samfundet i Uppsala. Annales Societatis Litterarum Humaniorum Regiae Upsaliensis* (Arsbok, 1979–80) 50–79.

were used extensively in early Christianity,[33] and I suggest that the author of the *Acts* derived his description of Paul from these sources. Two features distinguish Paul from Agathion-Heracles. Agathion was eight feet tall, while Paul is said to have been small of stature. But tallness was not an absolute requirement for beauty, and Heracles himself could be described as small. More puzzling is Paul's baldness, for the physiognomic descriptions drew attention to the hair. Translations of the *Acts* were sensitive to this part of the description.[34] The Armenian gives him curly hair,[35] the Syriac scanty hair,[36] and the Latin a shaven head.[37] Two possible explanations of this odd feature suggest themselves. It is possible that Paul indeed was bald, and that the *Acts* was faithful to memory. The paintings which represent him as thin on top may support such a surmise. On the other hand, baldness may have been suggested by the reference to the shaving of heads in Acts 18:18 and 21:24.

This short excursion into the strange world of ancient physiognomy may cast some light on how Paul was represented as a hero among the Greeks. It calls for further attention to the description in the interpretation of the *Acts*. The basic assumption of physiognomics was that "dispositions follow bodily characteristics and are not themselves unaffected by bodily impulses."[38] It remains to be determined whether there is such a correlation between the description of Paul's physical appearance and his deeds in the *Acts*.

[33] See A. J. Malherbe, "Herakles," *RAC* (forthcoming).

[34] See also Ps.-Lucian *Philopatris* 12, which describes Paul as having receding hair; cf. Fürst, "Untersuchungen," 381, 407ff.

[35] Cf. F. C. Conybeare, *The Apology and Acts of Apollonius and Other Monuments of Early Christianity* (New York: Macmillan, 1894) 62.

[36] Cf. W. Wright, *Apocryphal Acts of the Apostles* (London: Williams & Norgate, 1871) 2. 117.

[37] See the textual variants in Vouaux, *Les Actes*, 150 n. 6.

[38] Ps.-Aristotle *Physiog.* 805a; cf. Cicero *De fato* 10; Evans, "Physiognomics," 5–6; Cox, *Biography in Late Antiquity*, 13–14.

A HERMENEUTICS OF SOCIAL EMBODIMENT

Wayne A. Meeks
Yale University

When Krister Stendahl's article "Biblical Theology" appeared in the *Interpreter's Dictionary of the Bible* in 1962, it caused no little consternation in some circles. He insisted that the primary intellectual task of the biblical scholar was to make a clear distinction between what the text *meant* in its original setting and what it *means*. That ran directly counter to the practical aims of the dominant interpretive schools of the day, which wanted, as Karl Barth had once said, to dissolve "the differences between then and now."[1] Today the distinction for which Stendahl argued so lucidly is taken for granted in most biblical scholarship, and the question is whether there can be any significant connection between "then" and "now."[2] New Testament studies threatens to divide into two contrary ways of reading texts. One is a rigorously historical quest, in which all the early Christian documents alike, canonical and extracanonical, are treated as sources for reconstructing the diverse and curious varieties of the early Christian movement. The other way of reading cares not at all where the texts came from or what they originally meant; by purely literary analysis it wishes to help text and reader to confront one another continually anew.

The interesting thing is that Stendahl himself has worked both sides of the street he described. He has made the connection, however, not by means of some overarching theoretical model, but practically, by his actions and leadership as a theological educator and churchman. There may be a lesson here, which I wish to uncover by turning to the rather different work of another ecumenical churchman, historian, and theolo-

---

[1] Karl Barth, *The Epistle to the Romans* (trans. Edwyn C. Hoskyns; London: Oxford University Press, 1968) 1.

[2] Krister Stendahl, "Biblical Theology, Contemporary," *IDB* 1. 418–32; see the remarks by James Barr in his article on the same topic, *IDBSup* 104–11.

gian, George Lindbeck, in his recent book, *The Nature of Doctrine*.[3]
Lindbeck has proposed a way of thinking about doctrine which puts
the dichotomy between historical exegesis and the church's use of
scripture into a new perspective. Initially his proposal sharpens the
dilemma of those who want to connect the two, but it may start us on a
way out of that dilemma. The subtitle "Religion and Theology in a
Postliberal Age" signifies a rapprochement that has been out of favor
since the turn of the century. Theologians, Lindbeck argues, must
overcome their allergy to the category "religion," contracted by reaction to the simplistic historicism of Protestant Liberalism and by fear of
the relativism of the history-of-religions school. They must acknowledge the models of religion that are implicit in their construals of
doctrine.

Lindbeck identifies two models that have been dominant in the history of doctrine. The oldest is the "cognitivist" model: what is most
important about religion is ideas, and "church doctrines function as
informative propositions or truth claims about objective realities" (16).
The current favorite is the "symbolic-expressive" model, which "interprets doctrines as noninformative and nondiscursive symbols of inner
feelings, attitudes, or existential orientations" (ibid.). The former was
rendered unsatisfactory for most intellectuals by Kant and his successors and for most well-socialized Europeans and Americans by the
"deobjectivication" of religious belief produced by the "individualism,
rapid change, and religious pluralism of modern societies" (20, 21).
The cognitivist approach, Lindbeck suggests, will have a future only
among the sects whose recruits "combine unusual insecurity with
naivete" (21). The "symbolic-expressivist" model prevails among the
heirs of Schleiermacher (21). In New Testament studies, these would
include Bultmann and his pupils above all and, in contemporary hermeneutics, those who look to the phenomenologist Paul Ricoeur.
Some Roman Catholic theologians (Rahner, Lonergan) undertake to
combine the cognitive and the symbolic-expressive types.

Against both these understandings of religion Lindbeck sets what he
calls the "cultural-linguistic" model. Like the others, it does not
comprise a single, tightly connected theory, but a family of perspectives, with forebears as diverse as Marx, Durkheim, Weber, and
Wittgenstein.[4] Lindbeck's own exemplars of this family are the sociologists Peter Berger and Thomas Luckmann, the cultural anthropologist

[3] George A. Lindbeck, *The Nature of Doctrine: Religion and Theology in a Postliberal Age* (Philadelphia: Westminster, 1984).
[4] See ibid., 27 n. 10.

Clifford Geertz, and the philosophers William Christian and Ninian Smart. They understand religions "as comprehensive interpretive schemes, usually embodied in myths or narratives and heavily ritualized, which structure human experience and understanding of self and world" (32). A religion is like a language. It is "a communal phenomenon that shapes the subjectivities of individuals rather than being primarily a manifestation of those subjectivities." It is "correlated with a form of life" and has "both cognitive and behavioral dimensions" (33). Understanding a religion, then, is like becoming competent in a language, and doctrine is to a religion (or at least to the Christian religion) as grammar is to a natural language.

The aim of Lindbeck's book is to argue that the cultural-linguistic model of religion is the most useful one for continuing ecumenical conversation. His case seems to me convincing, but I want to address the different issue posed above. What would adoption of the cultural-linguistic model entail for the conversation between theologians and historical critics of the New Testament?

The question arises with peculiar urgency and promise because within the past decade or two a number of New Testament scholars have adopted the same family of perspectives on religious phenomena that Lindbeck espouses. John Gager's pioneering work, *Kingdom and Community*,[5] while visibly groping for a suitable sociological method, already employed the term "social world" in a way clearly dependent on the work of Peter Berger and Thomas Luckmann. A working group of the Society of Biblical Literature and the American Academy of Religion adopted the term and, at least in part, a similar perspective for its research for several years beginning in 1972. More recently a host of students of early Christianity have taken up similar themes. Among those who eschew the dubious project of becoming sociologists of early Christianity but want rather to be identified as social historians, I may cite as examples my own recent work and that of David Aune.[6] An early pioneer in Germany was Gerd Theissen, but he remained a lonely voice and has recently turned to other sorts of questions.[7] Some

[5] John G. Gager, *Kingdom and Community: The Social World of Early Christianity* (Englewood Cliffs, NJ: Prentice-Hall, 1975).

[6] Wayne A. Meeks, *The First Urban Christians: The Social World of the Apostle Paul* (New Haven/London: Yale University Press, 1983); David E. Aune, *Prophecy in Early Christianity* (Grand Rapids: Eerdmans, 1983); idem, "The Social Matrix of the Apocalypse of John," *BR* 26 (1981) 16–32.

[7] A good introduction to Theissen's work is the collection of essays, *The Social Setting of Pauline Christianity: Essays on Corinth* (Philadelphia: Fortress, 1982), with an important introduction by John H. Schütz.

interest in socio-historical study of the New Testament is appearing now in Britain: for example, John Riches, who exhibits considerably more knowledge of the philosophical side of Lindbeck's family than do most of the American scholars.[8]

For the historian of early Christianity, adoption of the cultural-linguistic model of religion entails our trying to achieve what Geertz, after Ryle, calls a "thick description" of the ways in which the early Christian groups worked as religious communities, within the cultural and subcultural contexts peculiar to themselves. The aim of exegesis would not yet be achieved by translating the words of the text into their English or German equivalents, because meaning is not something words contain, but something they do, or rather something people do with words. In order to determine what a given text *meant*, therefore, we must uncover the web of meaningful signs, actions, and relationships within which that text did its work. Evidently those of us who adopt such a description of our exegetical task and theologians who heed Lindbeck's advice will be traveling on parallel tracks. Describing what a text meant (the "grammar" of the early Christian subculture) and what it means (the "grammar" of ecumenical Christianity today) would follow paradigms whose antecedents and structures are the same.

Unfortunately, parallel tracks do not converge—unless we can discover some Einsteinian revision of our Euclidean intellectual geometry. The trouble is that Lindbeck's cultural-linguistic description of Christian theology includes a way of construing scripture that seems, paradoxically, opposed to a cultural-linguistic way of doing historical exegesis. The magic word is *intratextuality*, a term which Lindbeck coins (in contrast to the "intertextuality" stressed in certain theories of literature) to signify the immanent location of meaning. For cultural-linguists the meaning of words, things, or actions is not determined by reference to any factor outside the semiotic system to which they belong, but by discovering "how they fit into systems of communication or purposeful action" (114). So long as Lindbeck uses "text" as a metaphor for the entire cultural system of the religious community, a rapprochement with the socio-historical exegete still seems possible. However, Lindbeck is careful to insist that theology is a description which "is not simply metaphorically but literally intratextual." "One test of faithfulness . . . is the degree to which descriptions correspond to the semiotic universe paradigmatically encoded in Holy Writ" (116). "Intratextual theology redescribes reality within the scriptural

---

[8] John Riches, *Jesus and the Transformation of Judaism* (London: Darton, Longman & Todd, 1980), and his interesting new work on the parables, so far unpublished.

framework rather than translating Scripture into extrascriptural categories" (118). "An intratextual reading tries to derive the interpretive framework that designates the theologically controlling sense from *the literary structure of the text itself*" (120, emphasis added).

The theology Lindbeck wants, then, is a biblical theology in a strict though not exclusive sense. The boundaries and context of what is to be interpreted are defined by the canon. This kind of interpretation, moreover, seems to require a synchronic, literary analysis of the canonical texts. Historical exegesis could be, at best, only of incidental help to such a reading (just as Lindbeck himself suggests in the examples on pp. 122–23). The kind of social history now practiced by many students of early Christianity—which gives no special privilege among first- and second-century documents to the texts that would later become canonical, and which wants to treat all those texts as "sources" and "documents" that conceal as well as reveal what the historian wants to know—such historical inquiry could have, it seems, only a negative connection with Lindbeck's theology.

There is perhaps a certain irony in the fact that, while there are a number of New Testament scholars who have been exploring a synchronic, literary analysis of the texts, with few exceptions they tend to adopt a symbolic-expressive style of interpretation and to engage in the kind of cryptoapologetics for liberal Christianity that Lindbeck views with obvious distaste. There seems no internal necessity for either alliance, however, and Lindbeck's project may well offer a more natural theological partner to literary hermeneutics than do the symbolic-expressive theologians.

Something important would be lost, however, if we accepted that apparently obvious solution. The fact that a historian adopting the cultural-linguistic model of religion arrives at results which a theologian adopting the same model cannot use is not merely an unhappy accident. It reveals something intrinsic to the situation of Christian interpreters. The dilemma posed here is not adventitious or merely semantic. It is real and inherent in the peculiar self-definition of Christianity as both historical and canon-dependent. We should therefore not give up too quickly on the possibility of cooperation between historians of the social world of early Christianity and postliberal theologians, for such cooperation may be able to cast a new light onto the hermeneutical situation.

First of all, a closer look shows that the conflict in aims between the historian who employs a sociology-of-knowledge perspective and the theologian who does the same is not quite so direct as it first appears. Lindbeck's adoption of "intratextuality" as a normative characteristic of Christian theology is an extension of Hans Frei's argument against all forms of "referential" hermeneutics.[9] That argument would seem to apply with obvious force to the social historian, who must practice some form of the "hermeneutics of suspicion." Yet what this historian is searching for is no longer the historical referents of the texts in the fashion of the post-Enlightenment historical critics whom Frei blames for "the eclipse of biblical narrative." That is, a social historian of this sort is not only or even primarily trying to reconstruct "what really happened" as "objective" reality. She or he is more interested in trying to understand the meaning of what the actors and writers did and said within their culture and their peculiar subculture.

The cultural-linguistic historian and the cultural-linguistic theologian, following their parallel tracks, do come back again to the dilemma which Stendahl described. What the text meant is not the same as what it means. However, we are now in a position at least to state that dilemma more sharply. What Paul's Letter to the Galatians, say, or the Gospel of Mark meant to the Christians gathered to hear it read aloud in some house in a town of the Anatolian highlands or in a Roman insula, or wherever, we can only imperfectly reconstruct and can never duplicate. The reason is that what the Gospel or letter meant—the work it did—belonged to a specific cultural-linguistic complex, which no effort of translation however fine and no act of will however faithful can call again into existence in our so different world.

The ways in which the symbolic universe we inhabit differs from that in which the writers and first hearers of our texts lived are so many they defy cataloguing. Most are factors that affect whole societies and must enter into any historian's attempt to understand any text from antiquity. What interests us at the moment is not these, though it should give us courage to observe that historians who are perfectly well aware of these factors do not in fact stop writing history. They seem rather to find the never-completed task of migrating from one world to another precisely the challenge that makes the game worth playing. We, however, are concerned for the present only with those factors which are peculiar to the situation of the Christian interpreter—or, better, to the interpretation of these texts in and for the Christian community.

Foremost among the factors that separate the use, and thus the meaning, of the New Testament texts in the first century from those texts' use and meaning in the church today is this: then there was no New Testament, now there is. How simple and obvious that is! Yet to

---

[9] Hans W. Frei, *The Eclipse of Biblical Narrative: A Study in Eighteenth and Nineteenth Century Hermeneutics* (New Haven/London: Yale University Press, 1974).

have made it so is one of the enduring accomplishments of the modern historical-critical enterprise. Every teacher of introductory courses in New Testament has to reenact the discovery and knows how difficult it is, even in this age of ignorance of the Bible, how hard to learn that there are no magi in Luke nor shepherds in Matthew, that "the scripture" cited by those writers was not yet "the Old Testament," that the Christians to whom Paul wrote had not read the Gospel of John. That the Christian movement existed once without the canon which later became constitutive of it is a fact whose hermeneutical significance has not, even now, fully impressed itself on our theology.

To be sure, concern has been expressed in many quarters about the tendency of historical criticism to dissolve the canon as the context of exegesis, and Lindbeck's discussion of "intratextuality" is in part a continuation of that discussion. What has so far been lacking, despite some excellent work on the development of the canon, is both a social history of canonization and a social description of the canon's functions. "Canon" is a culturally dependent category, not an objective thing. A book or a formal list of documents is not a canon, unless there is a community that takes it as authoritative. This point has been made quite clearly by Charles Wood, who says, "The canonization of Christian scripture is more adequately understood as the bestowal upon these texts of a specific function, rather than simply as their churchly recognition or their exaltation to a higher status." Consequently, "a canon is a canon only in use; and it must be construed in a certain way before it can be used."[10]

We thus confront the curious fact that, despite the vast energies of historical-critical scholarship on the one hand and of theological hermeneutics on the other, there has been in recent years hardly any attempt either to describe or to define the significance of the crucial transition between precanonical and canonical situations. New Testament exegetes stop too soon, leaving us with the diversity of preliterary traditions and their functions and the variety of compositions in their settings, but little sense of what happened after that. "Canonical" hermeneutics, on the other hand, takes the canon as something given, self-evident, and does not adequately describe its social and cultural dimensions. There is here a task waiting to be precisely defined and carried out.

---

[10] Charles M. Wood, *The Formation of Christian Understanding: An Essay in Theological Hermeneutics* (Philadelphia: Westminster, 1981) chap. 4. Quotations from pp. 90, 93.

Certainly one factor that begs for description is the development of that privileged, all-encompassing narrative that Frei and Lindbeck take to be paradigmatic of the way the Bible ought to be construed. That such a narrative came into being and came to have normative force is a fact of extraordinary historical and cultural importance—worthy of precise socio-historical description. How did the church give birth to that narrative which subsequently would form and vivify and correct the church? Was it a series of accidents that produced a Bible whose first words are "In the beginning God created . . ." and which concludes "Come Lord Jesus"? And did that accidental encompassing of aeon and cosmos inspire the revolutionary notion (unprecedented in its scope, so far as I can see, in all the myths of antiquity) that the whole of human life and history has a "plot" with beginning, middle, and end? Or had the idea of that story, the plot itself, already taken shape in the rituals, preaching, moral exhortation, storytelling, prophesying, . and midrash practiced by the early Christians? And did the plot then affect the use and valuing of the new writings and the perception of the old in such a way that it imposed itself on the shape and sequence of the collection that won out? Did the canon make the story or the story the canon?

These are not merely literary questions. One of the problems with the category "intratextuality" is that it sounds too literary—and too academic. Now an academic category is perfectly appropriate in a programatic book about the conversation among professional theologians, but a cultural-linguistic hermeneutic must perforce look to the non-elite culture. One of the exciting things about Lindbeck's book is that in his final chapter he does range far beyond the academy, to deliver tantalizing fragments of his analysis of our cultural situation and hints about the kind of social setting that might be required for an intratextual theology to succeed. His diagnosis and prescription imply a thesis, a thesis which deserves to become a central focus of the interpretive discussion among theologians and biblical scholars.

The thesis is this: a hermeneutical strategy entails a social strategy. That is true because, on the one hand, texts do not carry their meanings within themselves, but "mean" insofar as they function intelligibly within specific cultures or subcultures. Where an adequate social context is lacking, the communication of the text is frustrated or distorted. On the other hand, to understand the text is, as Charles Wood so lucidly argues, to be competent to *use* the text in an appropriate way.[11] Perhaps it is not too much to say that the hermeneutical circle is not

---

[11] Ibid., chap. 1; cf. Lindbeck, *Doctrine*, 128–34: "intelligibility as skill."

completed until the text finds a fitting social embodiment. If we do make this extension of Wood's definition, however, we ought also to adopt his cautionary remark: "it is crucial not to identify [understanding and use] in such a way as to imply that to understand a text is to agree with it."[12] We may understand the social embodiment toward which the text moves the community and yet choose not to participate. Perhaps, nevertheless, a participation at least in the imagination, an empathy with the kind of communal life which "fits" the text, is necessary for full understanding.

Thus the hermeneutical process has a social dimension at both ends of that polarity which Stendahl named. What a given text meant ("originally" or at any given time in the past) was the resultant of the dialectic between text and the cultural-linguistic world inhabited by its hearers (roughly equivalent to the linguistic dialectic between *parole* and *langue*). On this model, the "pre-understanding" is not defined by the supposedly universal structures of individual human existence, but by the whole range of passive as well as active learning which members of a given culture and of particular subcultures within it have absorbed. What the first hearers knew by simply being where they were, it is the task of the historical critic to reconstruct by prodigious effort. On the other end, what the text means, by the same model, entails the competence to act, to use, to embody, and this capacity is also realized only in some particular social setting.

If that is the case, then the interpreter may be obliged to find or to try to help create a community competent to understand, and that means a community whose ethos, worldview, and sacred symbols (to use Clifford Geertz's famous trilogy) can be tuned to the way in which that text worked in time past. Lindbeck addresses this requirement by his provocative assertion that the only kind of Christian community which might respond adaptively and faithfully to the signs of our times is a paradoxical form of sect: intent on its internal norms and forms of life, but open to the world.[13] Whether or not one is persuaded by Lindbeck's "futurology," his attempt to describe the desired community is consistent with the model of religion he has adopted. The goal of a theological hermeneutics on the cultural-linguistic model is not belief in objectively true propositions taught by the text nor the adoption by individuals of an authentic self-understanding evoked by the text's symbols, but the formation of a community whose forms of life

---

[12] Wood, *Formation*, 18.

[13] Lindbeck, *Doctrine*, 127–28, and idem, "The Sectarian Future of the Church," in Joseph P. Whelan, ed., *The God Experience* (Westminster, MD: Newman, 1971) 226–43.

correspond to the symbolic universe rendered or signaled by the text.

It is not easy to specify what are the logical status and the logical location of that symbolic universe. Is it *in* the text? That seems to be where Lindbeck wants to locate it: what remains constant is the "story." Yet he observes that the story is "transformed" over and over again as it fuses "with the new worlds within which it is told and retold" (83). If that is true, then is the communicating structure not rather an aspect of the whole cultural system comprising ethos, world-view, and sacred symbols, of which the text is only one element? If the latter, then to suggest that "the literary structure of the text" or "the story" remains the constant by which succeeding worlds of experience are interpreted may conceal a number of difficulties. Can we hope for a consensus on what "the literary structure of the text" is? Is the identification of this structure as "story" a descriptive or a normative statement? Surely if we look at the uses of scripture throughout the history of the Christian communities, not to mention the Jewish communities, "story" describes only one among a vast number of important construals. The judgment that the controlling pattern is, or ought to be, narrative does not emerge either from a tabulation of actual uses or from a compilation of the different genres found within the canon. From what, then?

Just at the point of such questioning perhaps the dialogue between theologian and historian can again become helpful. For if it is the formation or reformation of the community that is the goal, then the story of the origins of the community, of the dialectic which produced both church and canon, ought to be suggestive for the present task. This does not mean that the church today ought to try to replicate the social forms of the early church, even if that were possible. Yet the church can learn from that "primitive" history that the clichés of recent biblical theology—kerygma, word of God, God acting in history, and so on—are abstractions without flesh until we see the early communities struggling to discover, adapt, and invent appropriate forms of living in the world. Perhaps indeed a conversation between social historians of early Christianity and Christian ethicists, despite the unpromising results of "biblical ethics" in recent years, may be more urgently needed than that between exegetes and theologians. It is time that we took seriously the well-known fact that most of the New Testament documents, including the Pauline Epistles that have provided the central motifs of Protestant theology, were immediately addressed to problems of behavior within the communities, of moral formation and what a sociologist could only call the institutionalization of the new sect. A hermeneutics of social embodiment would find a place for that sometimes embarrassing worldliness and everydayness of the early Christians. It would undertake to define Christian understanding as the acquisition of competence to act appropriately in a world rendered intelligible in a peculiar way by the dialectic between texts and history.

DEATH-SCENES AND FAREWELL STORIES:
AN ASPECT OF THE MASTER-DISCIPLE RELATIONSHIP IN MARK AND IN SOME TALMUDIC TALES

Jacob Neusner
Brown University

Vernon K. Robbins' *Jesus the Teacher: A Socio-Rhetorical Interpretation of Mark*[1] points to the master-disciple relationship as the critical structure in that Gospel. He sees three phases: the initial one, involving summons and response; the intermediate phase, encompassing teaching and learning; and the final phase, one of farewell and death. Robbins' stimulating account at the first two points compares Mark's portrait of the relationship with, among others, the relationship between master and disciple related in stories in the writings of the ancient rabbis of the Talmud and related literature. When he reaches the final phase, however, Robbins does not undertake such a comparison. It seems to me a suggestive exercise. So, in honor of the great master honored in this volume, I shall begin to fill the gap in Robbins' fine account.

What is to be shown is a simple fact. The corpus of stories about rabbis preserved in the principal documents of the rabbinic canon does encompass relevant tales, available for comparison.

How exactly does Robbins characterize Mark's portrayal of the final phase in the teacher-disciple cycle? There are two stages: first, a discourse about the future; second, the master's accepting arrest, trial, and death (Robbins, 171). The second phase presents a point of special interest. Here the master receives titles and a status formerly absent, for example, "the Son of Man seated at the right hand of Power" (Mark 14:62). So the advent of death marks a transformation of the master into a more-than-human figure. Here is Robbins' account of the final phase of the master-disciple cycle:

---

[1] Philadelphia: Fortress, 1984.

> The final phase . . . and conclusion of Mark portray an end and a beginning. They elaborate the end of the time in which Jesus transmitted his system of thought and action to his disciples and the beginning of the period of absence and anticipation. . . . Both stages of the final phase, the farewell and the occurrence of Jesus' death, unfold special attributes of Jesus and the disciples.

When we seek perspective on details of one large system, one likely approach points us to parallel details of some other. How Mark treats the critical narrative problem of bringing to a conclusion and climax the narrative at hand will, therefore, illuminate how, in their context and for their purposes, rabbinic narrators accomplish the same goal. What we see, of course, always constitutes a repertoire of points in common and points of difference. In the array of the like and the unlike we gain such perspective as we are ever likely to get for the interpretation of the two discrete, yet interrelated, systems of literature and life alike: the Christian, portrayed by Mark; the Judaic, represented by the material presented below.

The first and single important point of difference defines our exegetical problem. No rabbi is the subject of a sustained tale, let alone a whole gospel. Elsewhere I have demonstrated[2] that all tales about rabbis—whether marked by considerable action or simply set-piece conversations against a vague narrative background (such as, "He said to him . . ., he said to him . . .")—serve a single purpose. In a survey of three sizable tractates in both the Yerushalmi (the Palestinian Talmud, ca. 400 CE) and the Bavli (the Babylonian Talmud, ca. 500–600 CE), specifically, *Sukkah*, *Soṭah*, and *Sanhedrin*, one fact emerged. All stories about rabbis serve the larger purpose of exposition and discourse of the compositor of the unit of discourse in which they occur. Most carry out, for a whole sequence of discourses, the intent of the redactor of the entire set of units of discourse at hand. No story about a sage serves a biographical purpose. None carries out a purpose defined by the requirements of the sustained narrative of an individual life or a major episode in a biography. Indeed, only a few stories make a pretense at portraying individual traits. Rarely does a narrative indicate how a rabbi felt and what he did to exemplify not the values of the rabbinic movement as a whole, but his own heroic and distinctive traits of mind or virtue. In such a context (a farewell and death scene, a final and summary message) these are scarcely to be expected, and Robbins

---

[2] In my *Judaism in Conclusion: The Evidence of the Bavli* (Chicago: University of Chicago Press, forthcoming).

is not to be blamed for missing the pertinence of the stories we shall briefly consider.

Before we turn to them, however, we must note a second and complementary point of difference, one of profound significance. The corpus of rabbinic writings is communal and collective. Individuals never define the framework of redaction. Not only do we have no gospels, we do not even have, as I have noted, extended biographical tales. To state matters in a rough but suggestive way, I cannot point in either the Bavli or the Yerushalmi to a biographical narrative of the length even of an ordinary chapter of the New Testament Gospels. Some narratives run on. But in no case do these focus on what an individual, as such, said and did, that is, on what makes an individual distinctive and exemplary of personal virtues. Tales describe only public and collective values as exemplified by a given named authority. When I contemplate with envy the riches of human insight within a single individual's individuality (in the writings of Augustine, for one striking example), I realize more clearly the character of what we do have in the rabbinic canon. It is simple. We do not know about all of the rabbis of late antiquity even a hundredth of what we know about Augustine. In fact, since from the hundreds of rabbis named in the entire rabbinic corpus we do not have a single line written and signed by an individual and preserved, essentially, in his own name and context, the facts prove still more striking. Not having gospels points toward the deeper and definitive trait of the system as a whole. That is why, by the way, in the counterpart communities of Christians, we also do not have stories that can have entered into gospels. How so? The traits of large-scale redaction correspond exactly to the policies of small-scale narration.

We come then to what we do have as a counterpart to Mark's discourse about the future and about the leave-taking represented by the acceptance of arrest, trial, and martyrdom. For the present purpose, we shall take up the death scene(s) of one rabbi—Yohanan b. Zakkai. While he lived within a few decades of the events portrayed in Mark, the tales at hand first surface in much later documents. I offer them not because their hero flourished in the first century but only because the stories themselves demand attention in the context of a shared genre. The authors took the trouble to work things out in some detail. The stories therefore present as sustained a farewell-narrative as we are likely to discover in the rabbinic canon. Let us rapidly survey and compare the death scenes and then indicate the traits that render the scenes both like and unlike, in the context of Mark's counterpart as Robbins has analyzed it for us.

The first death scene at hand occurs in the Yerushalmi. It describes the death scene of Yohanan's disciple and of Yohanan himself, following a single formal arrangement and formulary pattern, as follows:

> R. Jacob bar Idi in the name of R. Joshua b. Levi: "When Rabban Yohanan ben Zakkai lay dying, he said, 'Clear out the house of objects that will receive uncleanness [when I die, leaving my corpse under the roof of this house as a source of corpse-uncleanness in the tent, in line with Num. 19:1ff], and prepare a throne for Hezekiah, king of Judah.'
>
> "R. Eliezer, his disciple, when he lay dying, said, 'Clear out the house of objects that will receive corpse-uncleanness when I die and prepare a throne for Rabban Yohanan ben Zakkai.'"
>
> And there are those who say, "Just as his master had seen [Hezekiah in a vision], so too did he see [the same vision]."
>
>   *y. 'Abod. Zar.* 3:1

The obvious pattern makes the point that Eliezer envisioned Yohanan as Yohanan had imagined Hezekiah. Precisely what is intended by the two statements is hardly self-evident. The dispute at the end concerns whether Eliezer saw Yohanan or Hezekiah, that is, the exact nature of the disciple's vision—either the same as the master's or a vision of the master himself.

> Rabbi Jacob b. Idi in the name of R. Joshua b. Levi [said]: "Rabban Yohanan ben Zakkai, when dying, gave orders, saying, 'Clear out the courtyard on account of the [coming corpse-] uncleanness and set up a throne for Hezekiah, king of Judah.'
>
> "Rabbi Eliezer his disciple, when he was dying, gave orders saying, 'Clear out the courtyard on account of [coming corpse-] uncleanness and prepare a throne for Rabban Yohanan ben Zakkai.'"
>
>   *y. Soṭa* 9:16

The context is stories about what happened when various ancient authorities died. Jacob b. Idi does not attribute the story to Tannaitic sources, but to Joshua b. Levi. In fact Joshua b. Levi was responsible for important Palestinian Amoraic materials on Yohanan.

The addition of detail about Hezekiah's throne seems to suggest he looked forward to the imminent coming of the messianic scion. But we cannot suppose that someone later on wanted to stress Yohanan's expectation that the messiah would soon come. In any event, Eliezer's school certainly shaped the parallel versions, and probably this one too, for the Hezekiah-throne is included to serve as a parallel to Eliezer's orders about a throne for Yohanan.

A. In his last hours Rabban Yohanan ben Zakkai kept weeping out loud. "O master," his disciples exclaimed, "O tall pillar, light of the world, mighty hammer, why art thou weeping?"

B. Said he to them, "Do I then go to appear before a king of flesh and blood—whose anger, if he should be angry with me, is but of this world; and whose chastising, if he should chastise me, is but of this world; whom I can moreover appease with words or bribe with money? Verily, I go rather to appear before the King of kings, the Holy One, blessed be He—whose anger, if he should be angry with me, is of this world and the world to come; whom I cannot appease with words or bribe with money! Moreover I have before me two roads, one to Paradise and one to Gehenna, and I know not whether He will sentence me to Gehenna or admit me into Paradise; and of this the verse says, *Before Him shall be sentenced all those that go down to the dust, even he that cannot keep his soul alive* (Ps 22:30)."

'Abot R. Nat. 25 (Goldin 105–7)

I.

A. TNW RBNN: When R. Eliezer fell ill, his disciples went in to visit him.

B. They said to him, "Master teach us the paths of life so that we may through them win the life of the future world."

C. He said to them, "Be solicitous for the honor of our colleagues, and keep your children from meditation, and set them between the knees of scholars, and when you pray, know before whom you are standing and in this way you will win the future world."

II.

A. When Rabban Yohanan ben Zakkai fell ill, his disciples went in to visit him. When he saw them, he began to weep. His disciples said to him:

B. "Lamp of Israel, pillar of the right hand, mighty hammer! Wherefore weepest thou?"

C. He replied, "If I were being taken today before a human king who is here today and tomorrow in the grave, whose anger, if he should be angry with me, would not last forever, who, if he should imprison me, would not imprison me forever, and who, if he should put me to death, would not put me to everlasting death, and whom I could persuade with words and bribe with money, even so I would weep. Now that I am being taken before the supreme King of Kings, the Holy One, blessed be He, who lives and endures for ever and ever, whose anger, if He should be angry with me, is an everlasting anger, who, if he should imprison me, will imprison me forever, who, if He should put me to death, will put me to death forever, and whom I cannot persuade with words or bribe with money—nay more, when there will be two ways before me, one leading to Paradise and the other to Gehenna, and I do not know by which I shall be taken,—shall I not weep?"

III.

A. They said to him, "Master, bless us."

B. He said to them, "May it be [God's] will that you may fear God as much as you fear man."

C. His disciples said to him, "Is that all?"

D. He said to them, "If only [you can attain this]! You can see [how important this is], for when a man wants to commit a transgression, he says, 'I hope no *man* will see me.'"

E. At the moment of his departure he said to them, "Remove the vessels so that they shall not become unclean, and prepare a throne for Hezekiah the king of Judah who is coming."

b. Ber. 28b (Simon 173–74)

The context is Mishnah commentary. The *beraita* (a passage assigned to Tannaite authority) is preceded by another *beraita*, and the two form the whole of the *gemara* or Talmud on a Mishnah concerning a prayer of R. Nehunya b. HaQaneh. In other formulations Eliezer tells the disciples to set a throne for Rabban Yohanan ben Zakkai, who is coming. In this instance, there is no homiletical relationship between Eliezer's last words and those of Yohanan. Units I, II, and III are essentially separate. The weeping-scene could have stood independently, likewise the blessing and the final saying. Perhaps the components originally circulated as separate units. Let us compare the stories.

y. 'Abod. Zar.	*y. Soṭa*	*'Abot R. Nat. 25*	*b. Ber.28b*
R. Jacob b. Idi in the name of R. Joshua b. Levi			Teno Rabbanan When Eliezar was dying, his disciples came to visit . . .
When Yohanan was dying, he said	*commanded and said*		And when Yohanan fell ill, his disciples came to visit.
		When Yohanan was dying, he raised his voice and wept.	When he saw them, he wept.
		Disciples said, Tall pillar, light of the world, mighty hammer why weep?	disciples said Light of Israel, right-hand pillar, mighty hammer, why weep?
		Do I go to judgment before a	If I were going before mortal king

mortal king, who
dies and can be
bribed? I go
before king of
kings and don't
know his decision
(Ps 22:30)

who may be bribed,
I'd weep. Now that
I go before
immortal God, and
do not know his
decision, should I
not weep?

They said, Bless us.
He said, May you
fear heaven as much
as you fear men.

Clear the house because of uncleanness and set a chair for Hezekiah king of Judah	clear the court-yard ordain	When he died, he said, Clear out the vessels and prepare a chair for Hezekiah who comes.

Rabbi Eliezer, his pupil, when dying said	[same]
Clear the house because of uncleanness	[same]
And set a chair for Rabban Yohanan ben Zakkai	[same]

There are those
who say . . .

The two Palestinian Talmudic versions are simple and unadorned. That in *y. 'Abod. Zar.* 3:1 includes the death scene of Eliezer in proper chronological order, that is, first Yohanan, then Eliezer. The reference to a throne for Yohanan is omitted in the corresponding death scene in *b.Ber.* 28b, which is as different for Eliezer as it is for Yohanan. *Y. Soṭa.* 9:16 and *y. 'Abod. Zar.* 3:1 are nearly identical. The long *beraita* in *b.Ber.* 28b involves an extended account of Eliezer's death, followed by a similarly long version of Yohanan's. The "clear out the vessels," which is the point of the Palestinian versions, is rather awkwardly tacked on at the end by the device of having the long sermon introduced by "When he was sick," and the dying words by "In the hour of his death." The final blessing is included, parallel to that of Eliezer, but it is of different content. The *'Abot R. Nat.* version omits all reference to Eliezer. It begins with Yohanan's weeping; the disciples play a less important role; and they do not get a blessing at the end. Light of "Israel" becomes "of the world"; "right-hand pillar" becomes "tall pillar"; that is, the Babylonian version is more specific, alludes to concrete images. The actual homilies require closer comparison:

'Abot R. Nat.	*b. Ber.*
Do I go before a king of flesh and blood	If I went before a king of flesh and blood, who is here today and in the grave tomorrow
whose anger is of this world whose punishment is of this world whose death-penalty is of this world who can be bribed with words or money?	whose anger is not eternal whose imprisonment is not eternal whose death-penalty is not eternal And I can bribe him with words or money Even so would I weep
I go before King of kings whose anger is eternal who cannot be bribed with words or money Before me are two roads, one to Paradise, one to Gehenna And I do not know to which he will sentence me. And of this the verse says— Ps 22:30	I go before the eternal God whose anger is eternal whose imprisonment is eternal whose death-penalty is eternal And before me are two roads, one to Paradise, one to Gehenna And I do not know to which one he will sentence me Should I not weep? They said to him, Master, bless us? [as above]

The homilies are practically identical, certainly close enough to show dependence on one another. It is therefore striking that the concluding blessing is absent in *'Abot R. Nat.*. Since the Babylonian *beraita*, like the Palestinian one, was shaped in circles in which Eliezer's relationship to Yohanan seemed important, I think the additional clause in the *beraita* was added so that Yohanan's death scene would be symmetrical to Eliezer's. The same factor accounts for the importance of the disciples in the *beraita*'s death scene, by contrast to their role as mere bystanders in *'Abot R. Nat.*.

It seems clear to me that the primary Palestinian version is the Yerushalmi's. It is unlikely that Jacob b. Idi in Joshua's name would have handed on two separate versions, one long, the other short. The

Babylonian and *'Abot R. Nat.* versions are another matter. I should imagine, following the former analogy, that *b.Ber.* 28b is the older, more complete version, shaped along the lines of Eliezer's death scene, as I said. *'Abot R. Nat.* afterward omits the details involving masters other than Yohanan, introduces the exegesis of Ps 22:30, and concludes with the (probably) famous "Clear the house . . ."

What are the primary elements of Yohanan's death scene? Clearly they began with "Clear the house . . . prepare a chair," which appears throughout, even to the point of being awkwardly tacked on in *b.Ber.* 28b and *'Abot R. Nat.* In the Palestinian accounts, by contrast, the two-fold message fits together without strain. In the *'Abot R. Nat.* and *b.Ber.* versions, we thus find five further, certainly later elements:

1. He wept as he was sick/dying;
2. Disciples [came to visit and] asked why;
3. And heaped on him encomia;
4. He replied that he was going to eternal judgment and did not know the likely decision;
5. [They asked to be blessed].

I see no reason to suppose all these elements are not late inventions, coming long after the very simple account of Joshua b. Levi. They cannot be called "expansions" of Joshua's account; indeed they bear little or no relationship to it. Rather they make use of some of the same materials as Joshua, particularly the "Clear the house . . . set a chair." These may not have been original with Joshua. We do not have to imagine the Babylonian *beraita* was shaped by masters who had ever even heard Joshua's version. Indeed, I doubt they did.

Let us now return to the question that has precipitated this brief survey—the comparison of farewell stories, a single genre expressed in two discrete canonical compositions. In what ways do Mark's stories appear similar to the tale(s) of Yohanan's death? In what ways do they differ?

First, they are alike in the one aspect that matters. In the tales about Yohanan, he takes his leave of his disciples. In the farewell phase of the master-disciple account in Mark, Jesus takes his leave. We deal with farewell stories. So a comparison is warranted on the face of it.

The unlike aspect, however, proves more illuminating than the comparison of like traits. To state matters simply, we indeed have a leave-taking involving a discourse about the future. We indeed have a farewell involving the master's acceptance of his fate of death. But with those two general—and not surprising—points, the two accounts take leave of one another. And in the differences we perceive how the two canonical systems, Mark's Christian system and the Talmud's Judaic system, see the world.

Yohanan's lesson about the future concerns God's judgment. He weeps because of his individual fate—not death, which he takes for granted, but a final accounting. The fullest version underlines this perspective: "May you fear heaven as much as you fear mortals." The closing message focuses on individual life, community, the society embodied in the village and the town. Yohanan's second lesson concerns rather ordinary considerations, uncleanness that will come from the master's body as soon as the soul takes its leave. The master is an ordinary man, living out a commonplace life in a frail body. This is the story of the humanity, not the divinity, of the sage. He is like everyone else. The contrast to Mark's portrait could not be more blatant.

What then is Yohanan's legacy and message for the future? It is diverse. Yohanan speaks of a throne for Hezekiah. Exactly what the storyteller meant by referring to Hezekiah I cannot say. It can be a messianic reference, and most opinion takes for granted that it is. The Bavli overall reveals a fully worked out messianic doctrine. So there is no reason to find bizarre a late third- or fourth-century allusion to the coming of a messiah, such as the Yerushalmi's version presents.

What, in the stories about Yohanan's death, do we not find? We perceive no apocalyptic dimensions at all. We find a farewell scene of remarkably humble circumstances, not a history-changing event, but only a farewell of a man to men. As anticipated, little effort goes into imparting an individual message, let along summarizing a life of teaching, an accumulated, individual doctrine. Indeed, Yohanan's last lesson proves commonplace. In it the rabbinic system speaks through Yohanan and imparts its principal and generative message: "Fear God at least as much as you fear mortal humanity."

None of these modes of working out the theme of farewell and death comes close to the cosmic or even the personal/biographical dimensions of the narrative in Mark. What is similar, therefore, is the basic structure: farewell message, then death, as these are portrayed through the prism of the distinctive relationship of master and disciple. What is dissimilar is everything else: the context, the purpose, the goal of the narrative and its means. What we learn is what we knew. The rabbinic system of Judaism addresses its particular context with its distinctive message, and Mark's account of Christianity, framed through the gospel of Jesus as Christ, addresses its world with its lesson. The two treatments of the one phase of a single characteristic relationship, critical to the definition of Judaism and central to the religious experience of the Christianity of the gospels, turn out to express in circumscribed detail the largest and most general differences. In recognizing these differences, we gain perspective on the overall characteristics and traits of the two narratives and the literary setting of each of them. The like teaches us what is unlike, the unlike underlines what is like.

But the main point remains the one Robbins identifies at the start: the very possibility of comparison and contrast. The two stories address the same issues and work out of the same themes. Both storytellers invoke one distinctive relationship to define the frame of reference, that one dimension of the relationship of master to disciples. The supernatural family at the death bed excludes the natural family. That detail tells us how profoundly close the two narratives stand in relationship to one another. And that single relationship would for the future define and determine the life of the faith: to invoke the mythic language, imitation of Christ, Torah learned through a life of discipleship through service to a sage. It is in the interstices of the relationship of mind and character, then, that Christianity and Judaism, in the humble instances at hand, tell humanity how to become like God. In this way Christ the teacher and the sage in the model of Moses, or rabbi, teach through lesson and workaday life how to be like God.

AN ῎ΕΚΤΡΩΜΑ, THOUGH APPOINTED FROM THE WOMB: PAUL'S APOSTOLIC SELF-DESCRIPTION IN 1 CORINTHIANS 15 AND GALATIANS 1

George W. E. Nickelsburg
University of Iowa

I

In his undergraduate classes in New Testament Introduction, Krister Stendahl used to cite 1 Cor 15:8 as a classic example of a text with an exegetical crux that is signalled through diverse translations in the modern versions. The crucial word is ἔκτρωμα, literally "abortion," "miscarriage," "embryo," or "stillborn child." Cataloging the witnesses to the Resurrection, Paul states that the risen Christ appeared to him last, as to "an (*or* the) *ektrōma.*" [1] But in what sense does the apostle apply the metaphor to himself?

The major English versions translate the expression as follows:

". . . as to one born out of due time" *King James Version*
". . . as to one untimely born" *Revised Standard Version*
". . . as if to one born abnormally late" *J. B. Phillips*
". . . though this birth of mine was monstrous" *New English Bible*
". . . it was as though I was born when no one expected it" *Jerusalem Bible*
". . . as one born out of the normal course" *New American Bible*

The exegetical options underlying these translations, and others not represented above, have been discussed in a number of articles—most of them, appropriately in this context, by Scandanavian scholars:

---

[1] Whether τῷ should be translated as a definite article is disputed; for its translation as an indefinite article, see Björk (art. cit. in n. 2) 8; Munck (art. cit. in n. 2) 181; and Hans Conzelmann, *1 Corinthians* (trans. James W. Leitch; ed. George W. MacRae; Hermeneia—A Critical and Historical Commentary on the Bible; Philadelphia: Fortress, 1975) 248, 259.

Fridrichsen, Björk, Munck, and Boman.[2] They fall roughly into four categories.

According to the first interpretation, the point of comparison is temporal (*KJV, RSV, Phillips*). *Ektrōma* is to be understood in light of the context that precedes it — the list of Resurrection appearances. The risen Christ appeared to Paul "last of all," and the lateness of Paul's call corresponds to the untimely nature of the birth of a premature fetus. The difficulty with this interpretation is that an *ektrōma* is born extraordinarily early, not late.[3]

The second exegetical option, reflected in the NEB, was proposed by Fridrichsen and Björk.[4] Here *ektrōma* is understood in light of the following context, which is linked to the noun by the causal γάρ and ὅτι. It finds in *ektrōma* a reference to the repulsiveness of Paul's persecution of the church. *Ektrōma* denotes monster or monstrous birth.[5] The term originated not with Paul, but with his opponents. Hinted at are: the demonic nature of Paul's persecution of the church; the abnormal manner in which he became an apostle; the inability of his baptism (ἀναγέννησις, "rebirth)" to form him in Christ's image. The abnormality of Paul's call is also suggested in the translations of the JB and NAB.[6] Problematic with this interpretation is lack of evidence that the term was so used in Paul's time.[7]

---

[2] Anton Fridrichsen, "Paulus Abortivus. Zu 1 Kor. 15,8," in *Symbolae philologicae O. A. Danielsson octogenario dicatae* (Uppsala: Lundequist, 1932) 78–85; Gudmund Björk, "Nochmals Paulus Abortivus," *ConNT* 3 (1938) 3–8; J. Munck, "Paulus Tanquam Abortivus (1 Cor. 15:8)," in *New Testament Essays: Studies in Memory of Thomas Walter Manson 1893–1958, sponsored by Pupils, Colleagues, and Friends* (ed. A. J. B. Higgins; Manchester: Manchester University Press, 1959) 180–93; Thorleif Boman, "Paulus abortivus," *StTh* 18 (1964) 46–50. See also Johannes Schneider, "ἔκτρωμα," *TDNT* 2 (1964) 465–67.

[3] Ed. Schwartz, in Nachrichten der Königlichen Gesellschaft der Wissenschaften in Göttingen, Philologisch-Historische Klasse, 1907, 276 n. 1, cited in Fridrichsen, "Paulus Abortivus," 81–83, and Schneider, "ἔκτρωμα," 466 n. 9.

[4] Fridrichsen, "Paulus Abortivus," 80–85; Björk, "Nochmals Paulus Abortivus," 3–7.

[5] A possible reference to the etymological sense of monster (from *monstrum*, "evil omen, portent") is suggested but not developed by Fridrichsen, "Paulus Abortivus," 80 n. 2; and Björk, "Nochmals Paulus Abortivus," 5.

[6] See *The Jerusalem Bible* (Garden City: Doubleday, 1966) n. b *ad* 1 Cor 15:8, "An allusion to the abnormal, sudden and *surgical* nature of Paul's birth to the apostolic family." The translation, "*when* [italics mine] no one expected it," also incorporates the temporal element.

[7] Schneider, ἔκτρωμα," 466–67; Munck, "Paulus Tanquam Abortivus," 187–88; see also Conzelmann, *1 Corinthians,* 259 n. 95.

Johannes Munck proposes two other exegetical possibilities. The first implies a "miniature quotation" of Scripture (Job 3:16; Eccl 6:3). Like an *ektrōma*—a stillborn child—Paul, the persecutor of the church, is "the most wretched of men."[8]

The second exegetical option suggested by Munck finds the point of comparison in the incomplete, unformed nature of an *ektrōma*. Actually, Munck finds in the literature of Mediterranean antiquity three different nuances for (the metaphorical use of) *ektrōma* and related words that denote prematurity in the birth process. They can refer to: a miscarriage that fails to realize its possibilities;[9] a stillborn child;[10] or "something embryonic, that needs to be formed."[11] According to this last interpretation—which Munck considers a real possibility alongside the idea of wretchedness—Paul as a Jew was not yet what God intended him to be when he was appointed from his mother's womb (Gal 1:15). This interpretation is developed by Boman. "In contrast to the other apostles of Christ, all of whom had been disciples for some time, Paul had hardly been born as a Christian when the Lord revealed himself to him and thereby made him an apostle." He was still a babe in the Lord.[12]

Two facts are noteworthy about all the aforementioned interpretations. First, as the translations in the modern editions indicate, no single interpretation has commanded a consensus. Second, whatever one takes to be the point of comparison of the metaphor, it remains an open question why Paul (or his opponents) employed this particular ambiguous term.

II

There is, however, a Pauline parallel that explains the use of the term and supplies an interpretive key for 1 Cor 15:8. Curiously, the person who was in a position to underscore the value of this parallel alluded to it without pressing the evidence at his disposal. In 1954, in his monograph on Paul, Johannes Munck had discussed in detail the accounts of Paul's call in Galatians 1 and Acts 9, 22, and 26, emphasizing the parallels between these accounts and biblical accounts of prophetic calls, and taking note of the motif of the prophets' and Paul's

---

[8] Munck, "Paulus Tanquam Abortivus," 183–84, 190.
[9] Ibid., 184–85.
[10] Ibid., 187–88.
[11] Ibid., 185–87, 190–91.
[12] Boman, "Paulus Abortivus," 49.

claims to have been called from their mother's womb.[13] Then, in his 1959 discussion of 1 Cor 15:8, Munck made passing reference to Gal 1:15, citing his book, but without noting a remarkable string of parallels between Galatians 1 and 1 Corinthians 15 and, evidently, without recognizing their significance for the problem under discussion. In what follows, I shall lay out the parallels between these two passages and argue that they are sufficient to establish the validity of an interpretation that is a variation of the one suggested by Munck and Boman. Here are the relevant texts, with the parallel wording in italics.[15]

I make known to you, brothers, the gospel that I preached to you. . . . For I delivered to you . . . what also *I received* . . . that *Christ* died *for our sins* and that he *was raised.* . . . and that he appeared to Cephas, then to the twelve . . . then to James, then to all *the apostles.* And *last of all,* as to an *ektrōma, he appeared also to me.* . . . I am not worthy *to be called an apostle, because I persecuted the church of God.* But *by the grace* of God I am what I am, and *his grace* to me was not in vain, but I labored more abundantly than they all, but not I, but *the grace* of God that was with me. (1 Cor 15:1–10)

Paul, *an apostle* not of men or through men, but through Jesus *Christ* and God the Father, Who *raised* him from the dead. . . . Grace and peace from . . . Jesus *Christ,* who gave himself *for our sins.* . . . For *I make known to you, brothers, the gospel that was preached by me.* . . . For neither from men *did I receive it,* nor was I taught, *but through a revelation of* Jesus Christ. . . . For you heard . . . that *I persecuted the church of God.* . . . But when the God who set me apart from my mother's womb and *called me through his grace* was pleased to *reveal* his son in me, that *I might preach him* among the gentiles, I did not . . . go up to Jerusalem to those *who were apostles before me.* (Gal 1:1–4, 11–17)

[13] Johannes Munck, *Paulus und die Heilsgeschichte* (Acta Jutlandica, Aarsskrift for Aarhus Universitet 26.1, Teologisk Serie 6; Kobenhavn: Ejnar Munksgaard, 1954) 15–21; idem, *Paul and the Salvation of Mankind* (trans. Frank Clarke; London: SCM, 1959) 24–30.

[14] "Paulus Tanquam Abortivus," 191, 193 n. 22.

[15] The relationship between the two texts, and some of their parallels, including the reference to birth, are noted briefly by Jerome Murphy-O'Connor, "Tradition and Redaction in 1 Cor 15:3–7," *CBQ* 43 (1981) 589 n. 41: "Precisely the same association of (1) birth language, (2) grace, and (3) time of apostolic call that we find in 1 Cor 15:8–9 appears also in Gal 1:15–17."

In each of these texts Paul is rebutting a theological position contrary to his own: there is no resurrection; one is justified by the deeds of the Law. Using identical introductory formulas, he reminds his readers of the gospel he preached. According to Galatians, he had received that gospel through a revelation of the risen Christ. In 1 Corinthians 15 it is the gospel of the risen Christ which he had received. In both cases, it was the revelation/vision of the Risen One that had constituted him an apostle. This call, which came through the grace of God, is compared to that of the other apostles (notably Cephas and James), who were "before him," to whom Christ appeared "last of all," after he had persecuted the church of God.

In the context of this string of verbal and conceptual parallels, we must underscore the significance of the fact to which Munck alluded. In two very similar texts Paul refers to himself in language associated with birth. To be specific, Paul's enigmatic description of himself as an *ektrōma* finds its counterpart in Gal 1:15 in Paul's claim that God had appointed (ἀφορίζω *lit.* "separated") him as an apostle from his mother's womb.

This similarity calls attention to yet another parallel between 1 Corinthians 15 and Galatians 1, which further underscores their relationship: both texts make reference to Isaiah 49. As I have noted, Munck has argued that in Gal 1:15–16 Paul describes his apostolic call in language drawn from biblical texts about prophetic calls, especially Jeremiah 1 and Isaiah 49. The relevant verses in the latter are vss 1, 5, 6:

> From my mother's womb he named (*lit.* called) my name. . . .
> And now the Lord says, who formed me from the womb to be his servant. . . . "I have given you as a light to the nations."

> (ἐκ κοιλίας μητρός μου ἐκάλεσε τὸ ὄνομά μου. . . . καὶ νῦν οὕτως λέγει κύριος ὁ πλάσας με ἐκ κοιλίας δοῦλον ἑαυτῷ. . . . τέθεικά σε εἰς φῶς ἐθνῶν).

Two elements in 1 Cor 15:10 parallel this Isaianic verse. The first is the following:

> His grace to me was not in vain, but I labored more abundantly than they all.

> (ἡ χάρις αὐτοῦ ἡ εἰς ἐμὲ οὐ κενὴ ἐγενήθη, ἀλλὰ περισσότερον αὐτῶν πάντων ἐκοπίασα).

Its counterpart is Isa 49:4:

> But I said, "I have labored in vain."
>
> (Καὶ ἐγὼ εἶπα κενῶς ἐκοπίασα).

The prophet complains that he has labored in vain, but God promises that the prophet's mission will succeed (Isa 49:5–7). Paul claims that, thanks to God's grace, his apostolic labors have not been vain.[16] The second parallel to Isaiah 49 is the verb "to be called" (καλεῖσθαι) in 1 Cor 15:9. Usually, it is interpreted to refer to Paul's right to the name "apostle." While this is not excluded (cf. Isa 49:1, "he called my name"), the many aforementioned parallels with Galatians 1 suggest that Paul is using the verb in a technical sense, as he is in Gal 1:15. This is in keeping with typical Pauline usage, where the verb and the related adjective κλητός usually refer to one's call to be a Christian or to the apostolic call.

III

If I am justified in seeing a relationship between 1 Corinthians 15 and Galatians 1, it follows that Paul's designation of himself as an *ektrōma* should be interpreted in light of his belief that God had intervened in his conception. This leads us to reconsider the line of interpretation suggested by Munck and Boman. Paul is describing himself as having been, in some sense, embryonic, or unformed at the time of the Damascus experience. But in what sense? Munck and Boman distinguish between God's having "called" Paul as a Christian (Gal 1:15–16) and as an apostle (1 Cor 15:9), and Munck suggests that Paul may construe his Jewish past as an embryonic first stage toward his Christian maturity. But the distinction seems unwarranted. The issue in Galatians 1 is not Paul's status as a Christian, but his apostolic authority as the authentication of his gospel; and the reference here is to the event by which he became an apostle. Within that framework, it is difficult to know at what point in time Paul places his apostolic call. Parallel phrasing within Gal 1:15 suggests that God's choice of Paul from the womb and God's gracious call were one and the same. 1 Cor

---

[16] He expresses this same concern on a number of other occasions (cf. Gal 2:2; Phil 2:16; 1 Thess 2:1; 3:5).

[17] For the verb, cf. Rom 8:30; 9:11, 24; 1 Cor 1:9; 7:15, 17–18, 20–22, 24; Gal 1:6; 5:8, 13; 1 Thess 2:12; 4:7; 5:24. For the adjective, cf. Rom 1:1, 6, 7; 8:28; 1 Cor 1:1, 2, 24. The technical usage of the verb here is recognized evidently by Munck, "Paulus Tanquam Abortivus," 191, and by Boman, "Paulus Abortivus," 49.

15:9–10 sees God's grace operative in the call of one whose persecution of the church makes him unfit to be an apostle. However one sorts
out the timetable, the train of thought indicated by these two passages
appears to be as follows. God appointed Paul to be an apostle while he
was in the womb. (Prophetic analogies would say: God intervened in
Paul's conception to this end.) Paul's persecution of the church contradicted that appointment. He was an *ektrōma* with respect to the purpose for which he was appointed from the womb. In spite of this, God
revealed the risen Christ to him and made him what he was intended to
be from the womb.

Viewed from this perspective, *ektrōma* has a double function; it is
oriented conceptually between two poles. On the one hand it is retro-
spective and has in view the positive fact of the promise, so to speak,
of Paul's appointment from the womb. On the other hand it is prospec-
tive and focuses on the negative fact that when Christ appears to him,
the promise has been unfulfilled and unrealized. Indeed, his persecution of the church has contradicted his appointment to be a leader of
the church. To use modern parlance, God's purpose has miscarried or
been aborted. In the context of 1 Cor 15:9, the negative aspect is in
focus. Speaking of his apostleship with an eye toward his persecution
of the church, he employs quantitative words consonant with the metaphor of the deficient, embryonic, unrealized *ektrōma*. He is "the least"
(ἐλάχιστος) of the apostles, who is not "sufficient" (ἱκανός) to be an
apostle.

My interpretation, then, follows the suggestion of Munck and
Boman. It differs on the matter of what is deficient and embryonic. In
my view, the term alludes not to Paul's Judaism as embryonic of true
religion, nor to his rudimentary faith prior to the Damascus experience.
The parallel use of the conception language in Gal 1:15 and the argument in that context indicate that the issue from start to finish is Paul's
appointment as an apostle and his initial opposition to that appointment
through his persecution of the church.

IV

It remains to consider how the metaphor came to be applied to Paul.
As the long history of exegesis has shown, Paul's use of the metaphor
is far from self-explanatory. It presumes knowledge of the apostle's
other use of the birth-related imagery. Paul's point in 1 Cor 15:8 could
have been understood by his readers only if they were aware of his
belief that as an apostle he had been chosen from the womb.

Such awareness could have come in one of two ways. On the one hand, reference to Paul's divine appointment from the womb could have been a part of his preaching or teaching in Corinth. In such a case, *ektrōma* would have been a term of Paul's own invention.

On the other hand, one might modify the oft-suggested theory that *ektrōma* was a term of contempt, coined by Paul's enemies. In the context of the present interpretation, it would have been invented in response to his claim that he had been appointed from the womb to be an apostle. In such a case, Paul would in 1 Cor 15:8 be taking up his opponents' term of abuse, admitting its propriety, and, with an appeal to God's grace, reasserting the validity of his apostolic office. Such an ironic concession to his opponents' claims is present in 2 Corinthians, where he uses the terms, ἱκανός / ἱκανότης of his apostolic qualifications, as they stem from God, and where he ironically turns his opponents' criticisms into proofs of the validity of his apostleship.[18] There are, however, some questions about this interpretation. Why would someone in the church call him an *ektrōma*? If the term originated as a reference to Paul's persecution of the church, it would have to reflect resentment of the apostolic status of the former persecutor. Otherwise one must suppose that it was coined to deprecate some supposed defectiveness in Paul's teaching. But in such a case, Paul has completely changed its meaning in 1 Corinthians 15 into a description of his persecution of the church.

It is perhaps simplest to explain the term as Paul's own invention.

---

[18] On this whole subject, see Dieter Georgi, *The Opponents of Paul in Second Corinthians* (Philadelphia: Fortress, 1986).

CHRISTIANS AND JEWS
IN FIRST-CENTURY ALEXANDRIA

Birger A. Pearson
University of California
Santa Barbara

Introduction

Krister Stendahl represents, to my mind, the very best of Scandinavian-style "realistic interpretation" of the Bible, resolutely faithful in his exegesis to the historical situation of the text and its author but then marvelously insightful in eliciting from the text a fresh and sometimes surprising address to contemporary issues in church and society.[1] As is well known, it is precisely Stendahl's interest in relations between Jews and Christians (Jewish and Gentile) that has made so much of his New Testament work so stimulating and innovative. As it happens, though, his research has tended to concentrate geographically on that large sweep of territory "from Jerusalem and as far round as Illyricum."[2] What I want to do in this article in his honor is to explore an area relatively untouched by my teacher—Alexandria—in an effort to see if anything can be said of Jewish-Christian relations there in the first century. In doing this I must perforce extend our investigation mainly to noncanonical sources. Even so the task is formidable, for the first-century Alexandrian church is, as Stendahl says, something "about

[1] See esp. *The Bible and the Role of Women* (trans. Emilie T. Sander; Facet Books, Biblical Series 15; Philadelphia: Fortress, 1966). He comments on "realistic interpretation" of the Bible in Sweden on p. 10. The best statement of his position on the difference between exegesis and hermeneutics is his now classic article on "Biblical Theology," *IDB* 1. 418–32, now reprinted in *Meanings: The Bible as Document and Guide* (Philadelphia: Fortress, 1984) 11–44.

[2] Rom 15:19. I am thinking mainly of Stendahl's incisive contributions to scholarship on Matthew and Paul.

which we know nothing."[3] What follows is, therefore, largely a matter of inference, at least insofar as it bears upon first-century Christianity in Alexandria. Insofar as it bears upon first-century Judaism, that giant among Jewish exegetes and philosophers, Philo Judaeus, will play a substantial role.

Jews in Alexandria

It need hardly be stated that the first preaching of the gospel of Messiah Jesus in Alexandria was centered in the Jewish community there, the largest and most powerful Jewish settlement in the entire Greek-speaking world. What sort of reception did the early Christian missionaries experience there? And how did the existing Judaism color the development of Christian preaching and teaching? In raising this issue it is necessary to say something about Jewish religiosity in Alexandria, especially as to how Jews there interpreted and lived the Torah, to what extent messianic expectations might have been part of their beliefs, and how open they were to Gentiles, including the extent to which they welcomed Gentile proselytes into the Jewish *politeuma*. Such questions are, of course, ineluctably bound up with political, social, and economic factors. While we cannot enter into these questions here,[4] it is worthwhile to recall the following events which powerfully affected Jewish life in Alexandria during the period of our interest: the introduction by Caesar Augustus of the *laographia* (poll-tax) in 24/23 BCE; the pogrom against the Jews under Flaccus in 38 CE; the disturbances and massacre of Jews under Philo's apostate nephew, Tiberius Julius Alexander, in 66; the destruction of the Jerusalem Temple in 70 and its aftermath; and the Jewish revolt under Trajan in 115–17, in which the Jewish community was virtually wiped out.

Victor A. Tcherikover has stressed the divisions in the Alexandrian Jewish community between the educated, cultured Jews who favored a synthesis between Hellenism and Judaism, and the lower strata of the population whose ideology, more open to influences from Palestine,

---

[3] See *Paul Among Jews and Gentiles* (Philadelphia: Fortress, 1976) 70.

[4] See, e.g., Victor A Tcherikover, "The Decline of the Jewish Diaspora in Egypt in the Roman Period," *JJS* 14 (1963) 1–32; Tcherikover's "Prolegomena" to the *Corpus Papyrorum Judaicarum* (3 vols.; ed. Tcherikover, Alexander Fuks, et al.; Cambridge: Harvard University Press, 1957–64) 1. 1–111; E. Mary Smallwood, *The Jews under Roman Rule: From Pompey to Diocletian* (Leiden: Brill, 1976) esp. 220–55; 364–68; 389–412; 516–19; articles by M. Stern, S. Safrai, and S. Appelbaum in *The Jewish People in the First Century* (Compendia Rerum Iudaicarum ad Novum Testamentum 1:1–2; Assen: Van Gorcum; Philadelphia: Fortress, 1974–76).

was stamped by messianism and a fighting spirit.[5] Philo belonged to the first group. From his writings alone one can get a good picture of the various attitudes toward the Law exhibited by Jews in Alexandria: two groups of "literalist" interpreters, consisting of faithful primitivists on the one hand, and unfaithful scoffers on the other; and two groups of "allegorizers," consisting of those who, like Philo himself, interpreted the scriptures allegorically but observed the practices of the Law, and, on the other hand, those whose spiritual interpretation of the Law led them to abandon the practices altogether.[6] We also know from Philo that some Jews chose the path of complete apostasy from the Jewish community. We know from him, too, that a considerable number of Gentiles affiliated with the Jewish religious community as proselytes.[7]

In Tcherikover's discussion of the ideology of the lower-class messianist Jews he reminds us that there is little or no documentary or literary evidence about them.[8] But, as a matter of fact, Philo was himself not untouched by messianism. Though he never actually refers to "the Messiah" (he would have said "the Christ") in any of his writings, he does, nevertheless, tell us a lot about Alexandrian Jewish messianic expectations. The key treatise is *De praemiis et poenis* ("On Rewards and Punishments"), recently analyzed by Ferdinand Dexinger in an important article on post-Herodian Jewish messianism.[9] Dexinger delineates the following "messianic scenario":[10]

Starting point:

    a)　Enmity between man and beast (*Praem.* 85, 87)
    b)　Assault of enemies (*Praem.* 94; cf. Psalm 2)

---

[5] Tcherikover, "Decline of the Jewish Diaspora," esp. 22–27.

[6] For discussion and references see Peder Borgen, "Philo of Alexandria: A Critical and Synthetical Survey of Research since World War II," *ANRW* II:21.1 (1983) 98–154, esp. 126–28. *Migr. Abr.* 89–93 is the most important passage dealing with the last-named category. Specific issues addressed include Sabbath and other festival observance, circumcision, and the sanctity of the Temple.

[7] Apostates: *Virt.* 182; *Vit. Mos.* 1.30–31; *De spec. leg.* 3.29. Proselytes: *Virt.* 182; *Quaest. in. Ex.* 2.2. In *Virt.* 175–86 Philo discusses the process of conversion to Judaism. On this and other important texts and their relation to the early Christian mission to Gentiles see Peder Borgen, "The Early Church and the Hellenistic Synagogue," *StTh* 37 (1983) 55–78.

[8] "Decline of the Jewish Diaspora," 24.

[9] "Ein 'Messianisches Szenarium' als Gemeingut des Judentums in nachherodianischer Zeit," *Kairos* 17 (1975) 249–78, esp. 250–55. See also Ray Barraclough, "Philo's Politics," in *ANRW* II:21.1 (1983) 417–553, esp. 480–81.

[10] "Ein 'Messianisches Szenarium,'" 254–55.

Messianic occurrences:

   a) Exemplary status of Israel (*Praem.* 114)
   b) Leadership of a "man" (*Praem.* 95, 97; cf. Num 24:7)[11]
   c) Gathering of Israel (*Praem.* 165)
   d) Passage out of the wilderness (*Praem.* 165)
   e) Divine manifestations (*Praem.* 165)
   f) Arrival at cities in ruins (*Praem.* 168)

Results:

   g) Peace in nature (*Praem.* 89; cf. Isa 11:6)
   h) Peace among nations (*Praem.* 95, 97)
   i) Rebuilding of cities (*Praem.* 168)

The importance of this "messianic scenario" in Philo's treatise is that it represents contemporary Alexandrian tradition. Philo's own religious tendency, likely shared by others in Alexandria, is to interiorize this vision, interpreting it finally in terms of the growth of virtue in the human soul (*Praem.* 172). Even the "man" of Num 24:7 is so interiorized, for the reference in *Praem.* 95 is most probably to the Logos. Philo's treatment of another messianic passage in the Old Testament, Zech 6:12, makes this interpretation very likely, for $\dot{\alpha}\nu\alpha\tau o\lambda\acute{\eta}$ in Zech 6:12 (LXX, for Hebrew *ṣemaḥ*, "sprout" or "branch" [*RSV*]) is clearly interpreted by him as a reference to the Logos, "the eldest son whom the Father of all raised up."[12] In other words, Philo was essentially a proponent of "realized eschatology."[13]

Christians in Alexandria

The New Testament provides only tantalizing hints of the Christian mission to Egypt, mainly because the author of Acts was more interested in other areas of the Mediterranean world. He does tell us that Jews from Egypt were present at Peter's Pentecost speech (Acts 2:10). The disputants in the controversy with the "Hellenist" protomartyr, Stephen, included Jews from Cyrene and Alexandria (6:9). Indeed it is possible that Stephen himself, or one or more of the other seven Hellenist leaders, came from there (except Nicolaus, who was from Antioch, Acts 6:5). It is also likely that some of the Hellenists

---

[11] The LXX of Num 24:7a reads: "There shall come a man from his (Israel's) seed, and he shall rule over many nations" (my translation).

[12] *Conf.* 62–63. On these texts see J. de Savignac, "Le messianisme de Philon d'Alexandrie," *NT* 4 (1959) 319–24, esp. 320.

[13] There are, to be sure, other traces of end-time expectation in Philo beside the aforementioned passages in *Praem.* See, e.g., *Virt.* 75; *Vit. Mos.* 2.44, 288; *Op. mund.* 79–81.

hounded out of Jerusalem (Acts 8:1) went to Alexandria; in any case, traffic between Jerusalem and Alexandria was extensive at that time. "Luke" provides a hint of the existence of a Christian community in Egypt in the forties of our era in Acts 18:24–25, where he refers to Apollos as a Jew from Alexandria, eloquent, and powerfully learned in the scriptures. If the "Western" reading at Acts 18:25 is historically correct, we have a clear reference to the existence of a Christian community in Alexandria at that time, for according to that variant, Apollos "had been instructed in the word in his home country." Unfortunately we are not told who the original missionaries to Alexandria were.

According to the Egyptian Christian tradition it was Mark the Evangelist who was founder and first bishop of the church in Alexandria. Eusebius is our earliest extant source for this tradition, [14] but his telling of it can hardly be said to inspire much confidence, particularly when he goes on to use Philo's description of the Jewish "Therapeutae" as a testimonial to Mark's Christian converts! [15] Eusebius' instinct is correct, however, when he stresses that the "apostolic men" in Alexandria during Philo's time were "of Hebrew origin, and thus still preserved most of the ancient customs in a strictly Jewish manner." [16] In any case, there can hardly be any question that the earliest missionaries to Alexandria were Jews coming from Jerusalem, and that the earliest Christian converts in Alexandria were Jews. Indeed it is doubtful that a clear separation between church and synagogue was effected there until the end of the first century or the beginning of the second.

What sort of Christianity was represented in the Alexandrian church? Our only recourse in attempting to answer this question is to engage in historical inference, for we have no first-century sources at all, at least not any complete texts. [17] One still popular inference is that

---

[14] The letter fragment of Clement of Alexandria edited by Morton Smith refers to Mark's arrival in Alexandria after Peter's death in Rome, but nothing is said of Mark's role as founder or first bishop. See Morton Smith, *Clement of Alexandria and a Secret Gospel of Mark* (Cambridge: Harvard University Press, 1973) 448 (text), 446 (ET). I have analyzed the Mark legend in my article, "Earliest Christianity in Egypt: Some Observations," in Birger A. Pearson and James E. Goehring, eds., *The Roots of Egyptian Christianity* (Philadelphia: Fortress, 1986 [forthcoming]).

[15] *Hist. eccl.* 2.16–17; cf. Philo *Vit. cont.*

[16] *Hist. eccl.* 2.17.2.

[17] Some noncanonical gospels, of which only fragments remain, may belong to late first-century Alexandria: *The Gospel of the Hebrews*, the Egerton papyrus, and the *Secret Gospel of Mark.* On the last two see now John Dominic Crossan, *Four Other Gospels: Shadows on the Contours of Canon* (Minneapolis: Winston, 1985) 65–121. What is still needed is study of all of the early gospels and gospel traditions in Egypt. Such a study would undoubtedly shed important light on the character of Christianity there.

of Walter Bauer, who posits that the original and most dominant form of Christianity in Alexandria until the time of Bishop Demetrius (189–231) was "heretical" and, specifically, Gnostic.[18] In making this judgment Bauer is essentially extrapolating backwards from the time of Hadrian, when such Gnostic teachers as Basilides, Valentinus, and Carpocrates were active. Such a procedure is dubious, especially when it is recalled that these men were highly original thinkers. While I think it is possible that Christian (and Jewish)[19] Gnostics could be found in first-century Alexandria, it is more likely, *prima facie*, to suppose that other, more dominant, varieties of Christianity existed there, more reflective of the Jerusalem origins of the Christian mission and of the dominant varieties of Judaism in Alexandria at that time.[20] If one must extrapolate backwards from second-century sources to reconstruct aspects of first-century Alexandrian Christianity, one should at least use such sources as are clearly bearers of older tradition and reflect an on-going school activity. Two such documents are the *Epistle of Barnabas* and the *Teachings of Silvanus* (Nag Hammadi Codex VII, 4). *Barnabas* is probably the oldest complete writing from Alexandria in existence, dating from the beginning of the reign of Hadrian (ca. 117 CE).[21] *Silvanus* is considerably later, closer to the end of the second century,[22] but it preserves some ancient material. Recalling Bauer's theory, it is worth pointing out that the exegetical and halakhic *gnosis* of *Barnabas* is at least implicitly anti-Gnostic.[23] *Silvanus*, with its attack against

---

[18] Walter Bauer, *Orthodoxy and Heresy in Earliest Christianity* (ET ed. by Robert A. Kraft and Gerhard Krodel; Phildelphia: Fortress, 1971) 44–60.

[19] See my article, "Friedländer Revisited: Alexandrian Judaism and Gnostic Origins," *Studia Philonica* 2 (1973) 23–39.

[20] Helmut Koester, in his discussion of the beginnings of Christianity in Egypt, speaks plausibly of "the simultaneous development of several competing Christian groups." See his *Introduction to the New Testament*, vol. 2: *History and Literature of Early Christianity* (Philadelphia: Fortress, 1982) 219.

[21] See, e.g., L. W. Barnard, "St. Stephen and Early Alexandrian Christianity," in *Studies in the Apostolic Fathers and their Background* (New York: Schocken, 1966) 57–72, esp. 63. An interesting case for placing the Epistle of Jude in Alexandria between 120 and 131 has recently been made by J. J. Gunther, "The Alexandrian Epistle of Jude," *NTS* 30 (1984) 549–62.

[22] See now Yvonne Janssens, *Les Leçons de Silvanos (NH VII,4)* (Bibliothèque copte de Nag Hammadi, Section "Textes," 13; Québec: Université Laval, 1983) esp. 23.

[23] Bauer perversely attempts to put *Barnabas* in the Gnostic camp (*Orthodoxy and Heresy*, 47–48), but the *gnosis* of *Barnabas* has virtually nothing to do with the *gnosis* of the Gnostics. On *gnosis* in *Barnabas* see, e.g., Robert A. Kraft, *Barnabas and Didache* (The Apostolic Fathers: A New Translation and Commentary 3; Toronto: Nelson, 1965) 22–27.

"strange kinds of knowledge," is explicitly so.[24]

Stendahl, in his book, *The School of St. Matthew*, refers to the debate "whether or not the later schools of Alexandria and other places can be considered a continuation of the school activities in the early church."[25] *Barnabas* is an important document to consider in this connection, for it is clearly a "'school' product," as has been well argued by Robert Kraft.[26] Moreover *Barnabas* tells us as much about Jewish exegetical traditions in Alexandria as about Christian ones. Indeed L. W. Barnard uses *Barnabas* as his most important source for discussing "Judaism in Egypt A.D. 70-135" and argues that the author was "a converted Rabbi who brought into Christianity the exegetical and homiletical traditions of the Alexandrian synagogue."[27] Among the traditions he cites, together with rabbinic parallels, are the ritual of the Day of Atonement (*Barn.* 7.1-11), the shrub "Rachel" (7.8), the sacrifice of the red heifer (8.1-2), the *gematria* on the 318 servants of Abraham (9.8), the interpretation of Psalm 1 (10.10), Moses and Amalek (12.1-11), Jacob and Esau (13.1-7), the celebration of the Sabbath (15.1-9), and other such details.[28] Barnard also stresses the exegetical methods used in *Barnabas*: the division of the epistle into aggadic and halakhic sections, rabbinic-style midrash, the use of allegory, and the use of the *pesher* method of interpretation such as is characteristic of the Qumran scrolls. Barnard concludes from his analysis of *Barnabas* that

> in the crucial period A.D. 70-135 Alexandrian Judaism, while having affinities on one side with Philonic allegorism and other hellenistic modes of thought, was not unaffected by the pattern and requirements of Rabbinism which, no doubt, had been exerting pressure on Diaspora Judaism.[29]

To be sure, all of the Jewish traditions referred to are used in the interests of sectarian Jewish Christianity, and eventually in the interests of a predominantly Gentile constituency. More specific for the type of Christianity reflected in *Barnabas* and its origins are the connections

---

[24] See VII 94,31-33. Cf. 116,5-9, a polemic against those who regard the Creator of the world as an ignorant deity, a typical Gnostic doctrine.

[25] Krister Stendahl, *The School of St. Matthew and its Use of the Old Testament* (2d ed.; Philadelphia: Fortress, 1968) 17 n. 5.

[26] He refers in this connection to "evolved literature," and the reproducing and reworking of older materials. See *Barnabas and Didache*, 1-22.

[27] In *Studies in the Apostolic Fathers*, 41-55, esp. 47.

[28] Ibid.

[29] Ibid., 47-51.

observed by Barnard between *Barnabas* and the speech of Stephen recorded in Acts 7. These connections include the attitude expressed to the Jerusalem temple and its cultus (Acts 7:42–43, 48–50; *Barn.* 16.1–2; 2.4–8), the interpretation of the Golden Calf episode in Israel's history (Acts 7:38–42a; *Barn.* 4.7–8), and christology, especially the use of the title, "the Righteous One," as a messianic title applied to Jesus (Acts 7:52; *Barn.* 6.7).[30] Barnard situates these items in *Barnabas* in the second decade of the second century, that is, in the period of that document's final redaction, and suggests that *Barnabas* has used Acts.[31] I would suggest that an alternative explanation for these parallels is readily available: this type of Christianity was introduced to Alexandria soon after the death of Stephen and the scattering of the "Hellenists" from Jerusalem.[32] The soil was well prepared for such seeds among the Jews in Alexandria who tended to ignore the Temple and other ritual observations in favor of a spiritual interpretation of their tradition.[33]

A distinctive characteristic of *Barnabas* is its eschatology[34] and its consciousness of living in the last, evil stages of "the present age" before the inbreaking of the "age to come" (*Barn.* 2.1; 4.1,3,9; etc.). The highly charged eschatological atmosphere of *Barnabas* may have been characteristic of one branch of Alexandrian Christianity from the beginning, but whether or not that is the case, it is clear that the messianism of *Barnabas* differed from that of the non-Christian messianist Jews there in terms of focus, though probably not in terms of religious intensity: the Christians knew who the coming Messiah was and expected him to "judge the living and the dead," not to restore the land of Israel and the Temple (*Barn.* 4.12; 5.7; 7.2; 15.5; cf. 6.8–19; 16.1–10). Such a difference in focus probably contributed to a clash between the two groups of messianists.

By the time of the final redaction of *Barnabas*, relations between Christians and Jews had come to the breaking point. This was largely the result of the aftermath of the destruction of the Temple in 70, the most important feature of which was the consolidation of Pharisaic

---

[30] Barnard, "St. Stephen and Early Alexandrian Christianity," 63–69. As Barnard points out, the term is taken from Isa 3:10 (LXX). Cf. also Wis 2:12, an Alexandrian text.

[31] Ibid., 71–72.

[32] Barnard entertains this as a possibility, suggesting also the possibility of an Alexandrian origin for Stephen, but finally prefers to "err on the side of caution" with the other solution. However, I cannot find any trace elsewhere in *Barnabas* of the use of Acts.

[33] Cf. Philo *Migr. Abr.* 89–93, and n. 6, above.

[34] On the eschatology of *Barnabas* see Kraft, *Didache and Barnabas*, 27–29.

Judaism toward the end of the century and the dissemination, among Jews of the Diaspora as well as in Palestine itself, of the so-called *Birkath-ha-Minim*, which effectively excommunicated Christians from the synagogues.[35] *Barnabas* now refers to Christians as "the new people of the Covenant," and the Jews as "the former people" (*Barn.* 5.7; 7.5; 13.1–6; etc.). In that respect the setting of *Barnabas* is analogous to that of the Gospel of Matthew described by Stendahl and others.[36] The political situation in Alexandria reached a critical point when the messianist Jews there sparked the revolt against Rome under Trajan (115–17) that led to the virtual annihilation of the Jewish community.[37] Unfortunately we do not know what role Christians played in that conflict.

The *Teachings of Silvanus*, like *Barnabas*, is a school product, but despite certain points of contact between them,[38] there are some very basic differences. The historical setting is different: there is no trace of any conflict between Christians and Jews. The only opponents identifiable in *Silvanus* are Gnostics.[39] The eschatological fervor of *Barnabas* is completely absent from *Silvanus*. Among other differences that can be noted is the difference in christology: whereas there is little or no trace of a "Logos" or "Sophia" christology in *Barnabas*[40] such a christology is a major feature of *Silvanus*.

Despite the late date of *Silvanus* I think it shows some very early traits. Its genre is that of the Wisdom of Solomon, a *logos protreptikos*.[41] Indeed, very close connections have been observed

---

[35] Barnard, "Judaism in Egypt," 52–55.

[36] *School of St. Matthew*, xi–xiv; cf. also Barnard, "Judaism in Egypt," 52, 55.

[37] On the messianist nature of that revolt see esp. Martin Hengel, "Messianische Hoffnung und politischer 'Radikalismus' in der jüdisch-hellenistischen Diaspora," in David Hellholm, ed., *Apocalypticism in the Mediterranean World and the Near East* (Proceedings of the International Colloquium on Apocalypticism, Uppsala, August 12–17, 1979; Tübingen: Mohr-Siebeck, 1983) 655–86.

[38] E.g., warnings against the devil, including the use of the term "the wicked one" (*Silv.* 85,17; *Barn.* 2.10; 21.3); the "Two Ways" tradition (*Silv.* 103,14–26; *Barn.* 18–20); interiorization of the Temple (*Silv.* 106,9–14; 109,25–30; *Barn.* 16.7–10); impossibility of looking at the sun/God (*Silv.* 101,13–17; *Barn.* 5.10); fearing God (*Silv.* 88,9–11; *Barn.* 10.10–11).

[39] See above and n. 24.

[40] Perhaps a "Logos christology" is implicit in the references to Christ's role in creation (*Barn.* 5.5,10; 6.12).

[41] Cf. David Winston's discussion of the genre of Wisdom in his commentary, *The Wisdom of Solomon* (AB 43; Garden City: Doubleday, 1979) 18–20.

between *Silvanus* and *Wisdom*,[42] and between *Silvanus* and Philo.[43] The christology of *Silvanus* is a case in point: "He (Christ) is Wisdom; he is also the Logos" (*Silv.* 106,22–24). As with the Logos of Philo, the Logos of *Silvanus* is "the Son as the image of the Father" (115,18–19).[44] As the Sophia of Wis 7:25–26, Christ is

> . . . a light from the power of God,
> and he is an emanation of the pure glory of the Almighty.
> He is the spotless mirror of the working of God,
> and he is the image of his goodness.
> For he is also the light of the Eternal Light.[45]

I have commented elsewhere on the relationship between *Silvanus* and 1 Corinthians 1–4, and suggested that *Silvanus* retains, as part of its Alexandrian Christian tradition, a good deal of the "speculative wisdom" encountered by Paul in first-century Corinth.[46] The Alexandrian teacher Apollos is the key figure in Paul's debate with his Corinthian people in 1 Corinthians 1–4 (3:5–4:6), and I would suggest that we can gain a good idea of at least one of the varieties of Christianity in first-century Alexandria from a judicious reading of 1 Corinthians and *Silvanus.* It is a Christianity which breathes the spirit of the contemplative Philo, and, more importantly, moves in a trajectory leading to the typically Alexandrian theology of such great figures as Clement,[48] Origen, and Athanasius.

---

[42] William R. Schoedel, "Jewish Wisdom and the Formation of the Christian Ascetic," in Robert L. Wilken, ed., *Aspects of Wisdom in Judaism and Early Christianity* (Notre Dame: University of Notre Dame Press, 1975) 169–99.

[43] J. Zandee, " 'Les Enseignements de Silvanos' et Philon d'Alexandrie," in *Mélanges d'histoire des religions offerts à Henri-Charles Puech* (Paris: Presses Universitaires de France, 1974) 337–45.

[44] Cf., e.g., Philo *Conf.* 146–47. Philo can also refer to Sophia as the "Mother" of the Logos (e.g., *Fug.* 108–9). This doctrine is muted in *Silvanus,* but cf. 91,14–16 and 115,5–8.

[45] *Silv.* 112,37–113,7, Peel-Zandee translation in *NHLE.* Cf. Schoedel, "Jewish Wisdom," 191–92.

[46] Birger A. Pearson, "Philo, Gnosis and the New Testament," in A. H. B. Logan and A. J. M. Wedderburn, eds., *The New Testament and Gnosis: Essays in honour of Robert McL. Wilson* (Edinburgh: T. & T. Clark, 1983) 73–89, esp. 81–83.

[47] Ibid., esp. 75–77, 83. Cf. my reference to Apollos above.

[48] Cf. J. Zandee, *"The Teachings of Silvanus" and Clement of Alexandria: A New Document of Alexandrian Theology* (Leiden: Ex Oriente Lux, 1977).

Conclusion

In this necessarily brief and incomplete look at Judaism and Christainity in ancient Alexandria, we have seen that variety is a characteristic of both Judaism and Christianity there. In the beginning, the varieties of Christianity in Alexandria were, in fact, varieties of that great city's Judaism. The figure of Philo is a towering presence in that amalgam. While we do not know what Philo thought of such Christian Jews as he might have encountered,[49] I would like to think, with Stendahl,[50] that he engaged them in open dialogue. Ironically, Philo played virtually no role at all in the subsequent development of Judaism.[51] On the other hand, his role, and that of like-minded Jews of his day, was incalculably important in the development of Christianity. It is the Philo-like Christianity of *Silvanus*, rather than the primitive apocalypticism of *Barnabas*, or the acosmic radicalism of the Gnostics, that ultimately carried the day in the development of Christian theology in the patristic age.

---

[49] Eusebius claims (*Hist. eccl.* 2.17.2) that "he not only knew but welcomed, reverenced, and recognized the divine mission of the apostolic men of his day" (Kirsopp Lake's translation in the LCL ed.).

[50] Stendahl remarks that "the United States of today is the first place in the modern world since Philo's Alexandria where Jews and Christians as people, as religious communities, and as learned communities, live together in a manner and in sufficient numbers to allow for open dialogue" (*Paul Among Jews and Gentiles*, 37).

[51] Cf. Tcherikover, "Decline of the Jewish Diaspora," 31–32.

PAULINE BAPTISM AND "SECONDARY BURIAL"

Norman R. Petersen
Williams College

It is curious that, despite Paul's representation of baptism as a burial (Rom 6:3–4; cf. Col 2:12), his understanding of baptism has not been considered in terms of funerary rites. Rather, the symbolic and initiatory character of baptismal burial, together with its close association with the death, burial, and resurrection of Christ, has for about a century produced debate over alleged relationships between Pauline baptism and the initiatory rites of Hellenistic mystery cults. This essay, in honor of Krister Stendahl, is intended to demonstrate that, whatever the associations with mystery cults may be, Paul's understanding of the process of dying in which all believers participate from the moment of their baptismal burial is fundamentally informed by funerary practices and ideas. My thesis is that Pauline baptism is most comprehensively explained in terms of the widely attested, cross-cultural phenomenon of secondary or double burial. I will sketch first some of the distinctive features of Paul's views on the death of believers, then lay out some of the results of research on secondary burial, and then conclude with a few comments on Paul's perspective on the believer's experience.

Some Distinctive Features of the Death and Burial of Believers

The distinctive features of Paul's views on the death and burial of believers can best be seen by contrasting them, on the one hand, with those of the deutero-Pauline letters to the Colossians and the Ephesians, and, on the other hand, with his own views on the death and burial of Christ.

In Colossians and Ephesians the believer has already died and risen with Christ (Col 2:12–13, 20; 3:1–4, 9–10; cf. 1:13; Eph 2:1–10; 5:14). These events are explicitly associated with baptism in Col 2:12: "You were buried with him [Christ] in baptism, in which you were also raised with him through faith in the working of God, who raised him from the dead." Whatever the precise meaning of these events may be, baptism is here the occasion for celebrating both the death and the resurrection of all believers. The two points are equally important: the believers' resurrection is not only a past event, but it is also something experienced by all believers. Not so, in either case, in the undisputed letters.[1] There, baptismal burial is followed by the believers' walking in a "newness of life" in anticipation of the still future resurrection not of all believers, but of only those believers who have died (Rom 6:3–11; 1 Cor 15:51–55; 2 Cor 4:13–14; 5:1–10; 1 Thess 4:13–17; 5:10; Phil 3:8–14). Not all will be raised, but all will undergo a bodily transformation when the dead are raised upon Christ's return (see also Phil 3:20–21 and Rom 8:18–25, 29). This means, then, that for Paul the baptismal burial of believers marks the beginning of a process that will be completed only when Christ returns, raises those who have died, and transforms the bodies of all believers into glorious bodies like his own, whereupon all believers will also become sons of God in the kingdom of God the Father. Baptismal burial therefore signifies for the believer both the end of one form of life (cf. 1 Corinthians 5–7; 12:13; Gal 3:26–4:7), and the beginning of a transitional physical and social "life" which will conclude with the taking on of a new bodily form and a new social life in the kingdom of God. It should be noted, too, that this transitional period is of limited duration. It is not open-ended because Paul expects that Christ's return may occur within his own lifetime, for the eschatological process of the raising of the dead began with Christ's resurrection (cf. 1 Cor 7:29–31; 15 passim; 1 Thess 5:1–11). For these reasons the church is a temporary form of social existence for those who have "died" but have not yet been "reborn" in their new bodily and social life.

The idea that baptismal burial marks the beginning of a process climaxing with entry into the kingdom of God, following the final transformation of the perishable and mortal body, is represented in at least two related ways. One has to do with the notion that believers both are and will become sons of God, the other with two separate redemptive moments in Paul's thought.[2]

---

[1] For important contributions to the "magical" aspects of Pauline baptism, see Morton Smith, "Pauline Worship as Seen by Pagans," *HTR* 73 (1980) 241–49; and idem, *Clement of Alexandria and a Secret Gospel of Mark* (Cambridge: Harvard University Press, 1973). Despite his focus on the undisputed letters in his essay (cf. also *Clement of Alexandria*), Smith still reads Paul in light of the two disputed letters and therefore misses the significance of the transitional period characteristic of the undisputed letters.

[2] These and other related points are more fully discussed in chap. 3 of my *Rediscovering Paul: Philemon and the Sociology of Paul's Narrative World* (Philadelphia: Fortress, 1985). See also James Tabor, "Firstborn of Many Brothers: A Pauline Notion of

First the ritual cry "Abba! Father!" by which believers affirm that they are God's sons, is probably first uttered immediately following baptismal burial (Rom 8:15; Gal 4:6).[3] The two passages in which this cry is referred to are both in contexts where baptism and its effects are at issue (Romans 5–8; Gal 3:26–4:7), and in both cases the cry is attributed to the spirit of God or of his Son (Rom 8:14; Gal 4:6), a spirit which the believer receives at baptism (1 Cor 12:13; cf. Rom 5:5; 8:1–27; 1 Cor 6:11). Baptismal burial, which is probably only a part of the baptismal rite, is followed by believers' walking in newness of life according to the spirit (Rom 6:4; cf. 8:1–17), and this new life is affirmed in the cry "Abba! Father!" Believers are now sons of God and brothers and sisters to one another. However, this is not the whole story because Paul also speaks of becoming sons of God in connection with both an inheritance yet to be received and a bodily glorification yet to be experienced. Becoming sons of God at baptism is but the beginning of a process that Paul speaks of as "adoption" ($\upsilon\iota o\theta\epsilon\sigma\iota\alpha$—cf. Rom 8:14–17, 29–30; Gal 3:26–4:7). The cry "Abba! Father!" is the testimony of the spirit as "the spirit of adoption" (Rom 8:15), but the revealing or manifestation of the sons of God will only come when believers are finally freed from their bondage to bodily decay and obtain the freedom of the glory of the children of God, which Paul speaks of as the moment of their adoption, namely the redemption ($\dot{\alpha}\pi o\lambda\dot{\upsilon}\tau\rho\omega\sigma\iota\varsigma$) of their bodies (Rom 8:21, 23; Gal 4:5). This is also the moment of their glorification, their final and full conformity to the image of the first-born Son, Jesus Christ (Rom 8:29–30; cf. Rom 5:2, 8:17; Phil 3:20–21; 2 Cor 3:18; 1 Cor 15:35–55). "Flesh and blood cannot inherit the kingdom of God, nor does the perishable inherit the imperishable. . . . The perishable nature must put on the imperishable, and this mortal nature must put on immortality" (1 Cor 15:50, 53). When this takes place, at Christ's return, believers will bear the image of the man of heaven (15:49) because they will have become conformed to his image. Until then, however, even though they are "dead" they remain in fleshly form and therefore continue to bear the image of the man of dust, including the infection of sin (1 Cor 15:49; cf Rom 5:12–21; 2 Cor 4:7–5:5). And they continue to operate in the very world to which they have died (1 Cor 7:26–31).

Apotheosis," in Kent H. Richards, ed., *Society of Biblical Literature 1984 Seminar Papers* (Chico: Scholars Press, 1984) 295–303.

[3] For other views of baptism informed by modern anthropology and sociology, see Wayne A. Meeks, *The First Urban Christians: The Social World of the Apostle Paul* (New Haven/London: Yale University Press, 1983) index, *s.v.* "Baptism."

In Rom 8:23 the final moment of the adoption process is simultaneous with the redemption of the body. But just as the process of adoption begins in baptism, so also does the process of redemption (ἀπολύτρωσις—cf. ἐξαγοράζω in Gal 3:13 and 4:5, and ἀγοράζω in 1 Cor 6:20 and 7:23). For at the believers' baptism into the death of Christ, they participate in their redemption from sin (and from death and the Law of Moses) that was achieved by the shedding of Christ's expiatory blood, through which they are both justified by and reconciled to God (Rom 3:24–25; cf. 5:6–11; 1 Cor 1:30; 2 Cor 5:14–19). Through the initial baptismal moments of redemption and adoption, believers become a new creation (2 Cor 5:17; Gal 6:14–15), but afterwards this creation still groans inwardly because it awaits the completion of the processes of adoption and redemption (Rom 8:19–23). Once again, therefore, until the moment of completion, believers have their treasure in earthen vessels (2 Cor 4:7). They have died, but they remain bound through their sin-inclined bodily form to the very world to which they have died—until they acquire their new form. Even dead flesh and blood cannot inherit the kingdom of God.

The differences between the Pauline and the deutero-Pauline views of baptismal death thus focus on Paul's understanding of baptism as the beginning of a transitional period which will end at Christ's return when, after he transforms the bodies of both the literally and the symbolically deceased believers, both he and they will assume their positions as sons of God in the kingdom of God. The differences between Paul's views on the death of believers and the death of Christ are equally striking. They both reinforce what we have already observed and also show that Paul understood these deaths in different terms.

According to Paul, Christ has completed the process that began with his death, whereas believers have not completed the process that began with theirs. Also, whereas what Christ has experienced is understood literally, what believers have experienced is understood symbolically. Christ has literally died, been buried, risen, appeared to many, been glorified (1 Cor 15:3–8; Rom 8:17), and is now in heaven (e.g., Phil 3:20–21; 1 Thess 1:10). But believers have only symbolically died and been buried, and they are only symbolically undergoing a process of bodily dessication—which Christ did not undergo because he was raised (and glorified?) after three days. On the other hand, however, when Christ returns believers who have literally died after their baptism will literally be raised, and all believers will literally be transformed and enter into the kingdom of God. Thus, the believers' experience not only is not identical with Christ's but it also will not be identical. Only those who have literally died will be raised, and their "appearance" to those who are alive will be momentary at best (1 Thess 4:16–17; cf. 1 Cor 15:51–52). For when the dead have been raised, all will then be bodily transformed. Although Paul seems to conceive of the resurrection body as being the same as the transformation body (e.g., 1 Cor 15:42–55), what is focal for him is the bodily transformation of all believers, not the resurrection of those who have died. Consequently, just as Christ's death was unlike the believers' death, because his was for others, Christ's resurrection has an importance that the believers' resurrection does not have. Once more the critical point is that whereas Christ literally died, was buried, and after three days rose, believers have only symbolically died and been buried and are in a longer transitional period between their death and their resurrection and/or transformation.

Finally, related to this transitional period is a positive feature already alluded to in connection with the ideas of "putting on" Christ and of conforming to his image. Paul's orientation is not to the taking off of the mortal garment, as in the dessication of a corpse, but to the putting on of a new one. He says: "While we are still in this tent, we sigh with anxiety; not that we would be unclothed, but that we would be further clothed, so that what is mortal may be swallowed up in life" (2 Cor 5:4). "For this perishable nature must put on the imperishable, and this mortal nature must put on immortality" (1 Cor 15:53). However, as in the case of the processes of adoption and redemption, so also here. One begins the process of "putting on Christ" at baptism (Gal 3:27), but the process is only completed upon Christ's return. And here the "putting on" of Christ is synonymous with the final conformity to his image or form. The processes begin at baptism when the believers not only die with Christ and believe that they will also live with him (Rom 6:8), but they also from that moment participate in the power of life manifested in his resurrection. Believers are "alive to God in Christ Jesus" (Rom 8:11), and this by virtue of the spirit of God or Christ which dwells in them, and according to which they now "live" (e.g., Rom 8:1–23). They have died with Christ and henceforth carry in their bodies the death of Jesus, but they do so in order that the life of Jesus may continue to be manifested in their bodies (2 Cor 4:10). As Paul says of himself: "I have been crucified with Christ; it is no longer I who live, but Christ who lives in me; and the life I now live in the flesh I live by faith in the son of God, who loved me and gave himself for me" (Gal 2:19–20). Therefore, those who belong to Christ have crucified the flesh and now live by the spirit (Gal 5:24–25), and thus Christ is in the process of being formed in them (4:19) because they "are being changed into his likeness from one degree of glory to another" (2 Cor 3:18b). Their suffering with Christ is an ongoing participation in his death, an ongoing dying, but its climax will be in their being glorified with him in their ultimate conformity to his glorious form (Rom 8:17, 29; cf. Phil 3:7—16, 20—21).

The Phenomenon of Secondary or Double Burial

Viewed in its most elementary form, namely of how a deceased's remains are handled, secondary or double burial refers to the practice of a first, temporary burial in one place, which is followed by a final interment elsewhere after a period of time sufficient for organic matter to decompose and be separated from the bones. The handling of the deceased's *remains*, however, is only a part of the total phenomenon because each of the three moments, the initial interment, the dessicatory process, and the final interment, is universally accompanied by a basically common concern for the fate of the deceased *person*. The social actions undertaken with respect to the corpse from the first burial to the last one are universally comprehended within a symbolic system oriented to the fate of the person during the three-stage process. Viewed cross-culturally, the symbols vary with the local cultural idiom. Yet the various idioms display a remarkable consistency in treating the fate of the person in terms of a transformation of social status.

We can best appreciate the total phenomeon and its bearing on Paul by beginning with Eric M. Meyers' important study, *Jewish Ossuaries: Reburial and Rebirth.*[4] Meyers' study is significant for two reasons. One is that he documents the currency of the practice of double burial among Jews at the turn of the era, especially in Israel but also in the diaspora. Meyers' documentation therefore lends historical credibility to my thesis that Paul's understanding of the believers' death is modelled on the phenomenon of double burial, although the documentation does not prove Paul's conscious dependence on it. Conscious or not, however if Paul's understanding can be shown to correspond to the phenomenon, that should heighten the probability of his dependence, if not prove it. The second reason why Meyers' study is important is that although he does not refer to the early and seminal sociological studies

---

[4] BibOr 24; Rome: Pontifical Biblical Institute, 1971. This is a revised form of Meyers' Ph.D. dissertation, "Jewish Ossuaries and Secondary Burials in their Ancient Near Eastern Setting" (Harvard University, 1969). Neither of the major studies of Greek and Roman burial customs deals directly with the phenomenon of double burial: Donna C. Kurtz and John Boardman, *Greek Burial Customs* (London: Thames & Hudson, 1971); J. C. M. Toynbee, *Death and Burial in the Roman World* (Ithaca: Cornell University Press, 1971).

of the phenomenon by Robert Hertz and Arnold van Gennep,[5] everything Meyers says about Jewish practice is fully consistent with their
findings and with those of anthropologists who have studied the
phenomenon since Meyers did his research.[6] Meyers' study therefore
provides a basis for looking at Paul's notion of baptismal burial in the
light of the cross-cultural evidence for the phenomenon of secondary or
double burial.

Hertz's classic study of Indonesian and other forms of double burial
showed that this practice represents two complementary notions.

> The first is that death is not completed in one instantaneous act; it
> implies a lasting procedure which, at least in a great many
> instances, is considered terminated only when the dissolution of
> the body has ended. The second is that death is not a mere de-
> struction but a transition: as it progresses so does the rebirth;
> while the old body falls to ruins, a new body takes shape, with
> which the soul—provided the necessary rites have been
> performed—will enter another existence, often superior to the pre-
> vious one.[7]

Fundamental to these notions is a "kind of symmetry or parallelism
between the condition of the body, which has to wait a certain time
before it can enter its final tomb, and the condition of the soul, which
will be properly admitted into the land of the dead only when the last
funeral rites are accomplished" (ibid., 45). In the primary burial, the
deceased is provided with a "temporary residence until the natural
disintegration of the body is completed and only the bones remain"
(ibid., 41). But as "long as the temporary burial of the corpse lasts the
deceased continues to belong more or less exclusively to the world he
has just left" (ibid., 36; cf. 81), and during this transitional period he is

---

[5] Robert Hertz, "Contribution à une étude sur la représentation collective de la
mort," *Année Sociologique* 10 (1907) 48–137; "A Contribution to the Study of the Collective Representation of Death," in Robert Hertz, *Death and the Right Hand* (trans. R.
and C. Needham; Aberdeen: Cohen & West, 1960). Arnold van Gennep, *Rites of Passage* (1909; trans. M. B. Vizedom and G. L. Caffee; Chicago: University of Chicago
Press, 1960).

[6] See, e.g., Victor Turner, *The Ritual Process* (Chicago: Aldine, 1969). The two most
important volumes, with good introductions and bibliography, are Richard Huntington
and Peter Metcalf, *Celebrations of Death: The Anthropology of Mortuary Ritual* (Cambridge:
Cambridge University Press, 1979); and Maurice Bloch and Jonathan Parry, eds., *Death
and the Regeneration of Life* (Cambridge: Cambridge University Press, 1982). I am grateful to my colleague William Darrow for the references to these two volumes and for his
valuable contributions to this paper.

[7] Hertz, "Contribution," 48.

being relieved of his impurities in order to be "deemed worthy of admittance to the company of his ancestors" (ibid., 35). Among some peoples, it is thought that a "devilish infection" lives in the corruptible flesh, and hence the bones must be clean before the final burial (ibid., 45). However, "it is always the same notion which reappears in various forms: the dissolution of the former body conditions and prepares the formation of the new body which the soul will henceforth inhabit" (ibid., 48). Death therefore "merely marks the passage from one form of existence to another" (ibid., 61), "the passage from the visible society to the invisible" (ibid., 80). Death is but a "temporary exclusion of the individual from human society" (ibid., 86).

As a passage from one bodily and social form of existence to another, death and its rites constitute an initiatory rebirth into another state of human society (ibid., 79–80). Anticipating van Gennep's theory of rites of passage, Hertz observed the close similarity between funerary rites and other rites of passage, like those "by which a youth is withdrawn from the company of women and introduced into that of men," wherein the transition "is often brought about by the pretended death of the aspirant, followed by his resurrection into a superior life" (ibid., 80). In less advanced societies, Hertz argued, human life is conceived of "as a succession of heterogeneous and well-defined phases, to each of which corresponds a more or less organized social class. Consequently, each promotion of the individual implies the passage from one group to another: an exclusion, i.e., a death, and a new integration, i.e., a rebirth" into a new group (ibid., 81). Death is, therefore, "only a particular instance of a general phenomenon" (ibid.).

In his chapter on funeral rites, van Gennep presupposed Hertz's findings, but in his book as a whole he concentrated on the general phenomenon to which Hertz referred, labelling it "rites of passage." Van Gennep's study of funeral rites is not on a par with Hertz's, and he is rightly best remembered for his superb chapter on initiatory rites. It is in this chapter that van Gennep, like Hertz, also distinguished between physiological and social processes and, like Hertz, found in the latter the clues to a society's understanding of the former. For both men, death entails both a physiological and a social process of transition from one social order to another. Van Gennep's principal contribution concerns the structure of the social process and the role of the transitional stage in it.

In principle, rites of passage "are ceremonies whose essential purpose is to enable the individual to pass from one [socially] defined position to another which is equally well defined" (*Rites*, 3). Because a "society is similar to a home divided into rooms and corridors" (ibid.,

26), the process of passage from one social state to another always entails three aspects—separation from the previous state, transition or liminality, and incorporation into the new state. Any given passage may emphasize one or more of these aspects, and any given passage may be celebrated by one or more of the corresponding rites—preliminal rites (rites of separation), liminal rites (rites of transition), and postliminal rites (rites of incorporation; ibid., 10–11). In his cross-cultural study of funeral rites, van Gennep found that although he expected that they would deal primarily with separation,

> rites of separation are few in number and very simple, while the transition rites have a duration and complexity sometimes so great that they must be granted a sort of autonomy. Furthermore, those funeral rites which incorporate the deceased into the world of the dead are most extensively elaborated and assigned the greatest importance. (ibid., 146).

In this light, and in view of our reflections on Paul, while Pauline baptism marks the believers' separation from worldly society, it more importantly signifies the beginning of the believers' transition to the new society of the kingdom of God. It is a rite of initiation into a transitional process, not a rite of incorporation into a "more or less organized social class."

Conclusion

I suggested earlier that Meyers' findings concerning Jewish secondary burial were fully consistent with those of Hertz and van Gennep, although not shaped in their terms. Meyers recognizes that for Jews as well as for others, death does "not in any strict sense mark an end to life" (*Jewish Ossuaries,* 14). Among Jews, the idea of "man as *nephesh,* a unitary conception of the totality of the individual," and the biblical idea of "being gathered to one's fathers" (ibid., 12), are central to the conceptual framework of Israelite burial practices. "In death and reburial . . . the deceased gained a sort of corporate existence" (ibid., 14). In addition, Meyers sensed in the Jewish practice of secondary burial a point we have noted in Paul, namely, that it is difficult to relate directly the phenomenon of secondary burial to a belief in the resurrection of the dead. Because often only parts of the skeleton were preserved, or all of them pulverized, the skeletal remains could provide no frame for a literally resurrected body (ibid., 85). Being gathered to one's fathers therefore does not require the idea of resurrection, just as in Paul resurrection is not required for all to enter the kingdom of God.

The strongest argument against my thesis is that in Paul there is no mention of secondary burial! One response to the argument is that despite Paul's silence about a second burial the ideas associated with it in the general phenomenon are present, and focally so, in the notions of the believers' process of bodily transformation and incorporation into the kingdom of God as sons of God. This response raises the more significant point that Paul speaks about the deceased person who is involved in a process of social transition, not of the deceased's remains which are in the process of dessication. Viewed from this angle, Christ's parousia and subsequent actions in relation to the deceased person are the corollaries on a symbolic level of the society's actions in relation to the deceased's remains. Christ's parousia is therefore the symbolic corollary of a second burial. And corresponding to this corollary is the relationship between the dessication of "flesh and blood" on the biological level and the "putting on" of Christ on the symbolic level. Paul speaks from the perspective of the new man, not of the old one.

Once the hurdle of Paul's silence about a second burial has been overcome, everything else falls into place. Modelled on the phenomenon of double burial, Pauline baptism is a rite celebrating both the separation of believers from their former social states and their commencement of a transitional process of bodily transformation that will be completed at a given moment of time in the future. At that time, they will be given a new form and be incorporated into a new social reality. Both the process and the principle of the phenomenon inform Paul's understanding. On the principle, Hertz cites as a well-known belief the idea that "to make a material object or a living being pass from this world into the next, to free or to create the soul, it must first be destroyed. . . . As the visible object vanishes it is reconstructed in the beyond, transformed to a greater or lesser degree" ("Contribution," 46). So, too, Paul:

> What you sow does not come to life unless it dies. And what you sow is not the body which is to be, but a bare kernel, perhaps of wheat or some other grain. But God gives it a body as he has chosen, and to each kind of seed its own body (1 Cor 15:36b–38).

LUKE'S USE OF THE OLD TESTAMENT

Helmer Ringgren
Uppsala

To Krister Stendahl in remembrance
of our discussions before the birth of
The School of St. Matthew

In Luke 24:47 we are told that Jesus explained to the Emmaus disciples "Moses and all the prophets" and "interpreted in all the scriptures the things concerning himself." This statement reflects Luke's intense interest, both in his Gospel and in Acts, in the relationship between the ancient scriptures and the events of the life of Jesus and the activity of the apostles. In this paper I shall discuss briefly the variety of ways in which Luke quotes, paraphrases, and alludes to the scriptures.

The Gospel according to Luke

The quotations Luke shares with the other Synoptic Gospels can be dealt with very briefly since they are treated in *The School of St. Matthew.*[1]

Luke 3:4f quotes Isa 40:3–5 according to the LXX. Matt 3:3 and Mark 1:3 quote only vs 3; the text is the same. In adding vss 4 and 5 Luke omits "and the glory of the Lord shall be revealed," probably as irrelevant in the context (SSM, 47f).

Luke 7:22 contains brief quotations from, or allusions to, Isa 61:1 and/or 29:15; 26:19. Luke is closer to 61:1 than Matthew (SSM, 91). Luke 7:27, like Mark 1:2 and Matt 11:10, has a combined quotation from Exod 23:20 and Mal 3:1. Luke agrees with Matthew in adding ἔμπροσθέν σου (LXX: πρὸ προσώπου σου [SSM, 49f]).

---

[1] Krister Stendahl, *The School of St. Matthew* (ASNU 20; Lund: Gleerup; Copenhagen: Munksgaard, 1954). Citations to this work in the text will be abbreviated SSM.

Luke 8:10: Matt 13:13–15 quotes, with some changes, Isa 6:9–10, Mark has only part of the quotation, and Luke is still shorter. All three differ from the LXX in the order of the clauses (LXX "hear/see," NT "see/hear"), a phenomenon which often points to oral transmission or quoting from memory. Luke has a longer quotation from the same chapter in Acts 28:26f (SSM, 129ff).

Luke 10:27 combines the commandment of loving God above all, Deut 6:5, with that of loving one's neighbor, Lev 19:18. Mark 12:30 inserts between them "the second one is," while Matt 22:30 has a longer comment. As for the variations of the text, see SSM, 72ff.

Luke 18:20 (par. Mark 10:19, Matt 19:18f) quotes five of the commandments of the Decalogue. Mark and Matthew follow the LXX in using μή, while Matthew is closer to the MT with οὐ (= לא [SSM, 61ff]).

Luke 19:38: All the Gospels differ considerably from one another in the wording of the Hosanna hymn (cf. Mark 11:9f; Matt 21:9; John 12:13). Luke has less than the others from Psalm 118 and adds an allusion to Luke 2:14 (SSM, 64ff).

Luke 19:46 contains a combination of Isa 56:7 ("house of prayer") and Jer 7:11 ("den of robbers"). Luke has ἔσται instead of the κληθήσεται of Mark 11:17, Matt 21:13, and the LXX (SSM, 66f).

Luke 20:17 quotes Ps 118:22 according to the LXX, as do Mark 12:10 and Matt 21:42. Mark and Matthew add another verse; Luke adds an allusion to Isa 8:14 (SSM, 67f).

Luke 20:42 quotes Ps 110:1 according to the LXX, while Mark 12:36 and Matt 22:44 differ in using ὑποκάτω (τῶν ποδῶν σου) in agreement with Ps 8:7 (SSM, 77f).

Luke 23:34 contains allusions to Ps 22:19 as do Mark 15:23 and Matt 27:35. All three use the wording of the Psalm without directly quoting it. Mark and Matthew use finite verbs, while Luke has a participial construction. John 19:24 quotes the whole verse according to the LXX (SSM, 131f).

Quotations in Passages Found Only in Luke

Luke 4:18. This is the longest such quotation. Here Jesus reads from Isa 61:1–2 in the synagogue of Nazareth. The quotation follows the LXX with some deviations: the words ἰάσασθαι τοὺς συντετριμμένους τῇ καρδίᾳ are left out (added in late MSS); ἀποστεῖλαι τεθραυσμένους ἐν ἀφέσει is added from Isa 58:6 with the change of imperfect into infinitive, otherwise following the LXX; κηρῦξαι is used instead of LXX καλέσαι (MT לקרא), probably to improve the Greek language; at the end ἡμέραν ἀνταποδόσεως is left out, probably intentionally. It would seem that the evangelist quotes from memory.

The other three quotations are found in the passion story, in passages without parallels in the other Synoptic Gospels.

Luke 22:37 refers expressly to "that which was written" and quotes Isa 53:12 καὶ μετὰ ἀνόμων ἐλογίσθη. The LXX uses the preposition ἐν. Luke is here closer to MT את.

Luke 23:30 quotes Hos 10:8: "They will begin to say to the mountains 'Fall on us' and to the hills 'Cover us,'" following the LXX except for the use of ἄρξονται λέγειν instead of ἐροῦσιν. In addition, Luke exchanges "hills" for "mountains" and vice versa, much in the same way as "peoples" and "nations" are switched in Isa 2:4 and Mic 4:3.[2] This seems to indicate that the author is quoting from memory.

Luke 23:46 quotes Ps 31:6 "Into thy hands I commit my spirit." The quotation agrees with the LXX except that παρατίθεμαι is used instead of παραθήσομαι.

It would seem that when Luke is working on his own in the above instances, he is more dependent on the wording of the LXX than when he follows the synoptic tradition.

The two poetic pieces in Luke 1, the *Magnificat* and the *Benedictus*, present a special problem. It is quite obvious that they have a marked OT flavor, but there are few actual quotations. A similar technique is found in the Qumran *Hodayot*. These psalms are often constructed of phrases and expressions taken from OT texts, but used now in a context other than the original one. They are not quotations in the proper sense of the word, and in most cases the allusions are not intended to mean that the OT has now been fulfilled. Holm-Nielsen describes the language of the *Hodayot* as a mosaic of OT expressions.[3] Bonnie Kittel has tried to classify the OT allusions[4] and has found that in most cases they are not quotations but reminiscences of biblical language. Stock phrases are used in such a way that it is impossible to point to one specific source for the "quotation." Only when a phrase occurs just

---

[2] See Helmer Ringgren, "Oral and Written Tradition in the Old Testament," *StTh* 3 (1949) 34ff.

[3] Svend Holm-Nielsen, *Hodayot, Psalms from Qumran* (Aarhus: Universitetsforlaget, 1960).

[4] Bonnie Pedrotti Kittel, *The Hymns of Qumran* (SBLDS 50; Chico,CA: Scholars Press, 1981).

once in the OT would it be possible to speak of a quotation. It seems that the same is true of the *Magnificat* and the *Benedictus*.

Luke 1:46–55

The song of Hannah (1 Sam 2:1–10) is usually taken to be the source of inspiration for this hymn. It must be admitted that there are many similarities between the two, but the relationship between them is complicated, and above all, there are allusions to several other OT texts.

1:46: Μεγαλύνει ἡ ψυχή μου τόν κύριον. Μεγαλύνειν corresponds to Heb. גדל *pi.* and is used with κύριος as the object in Ps 34:4. 1 Sam 2:1 has ἐστερεώθη ἡ καρδία μου, while MT has the verb עלץ which would correspond to the ἀγαλλιᾶν of vs 47.

1:47: καὶ ἠγαλλίασεν τὸ πνεῦμά μου ἐπὶ τῷ θεῷ τῷ σωτῆρί μου. Hab 3:18 has ἐγώ δε ἐν τῷ κυρίῳ ἀγαλλιάσομαι, χαρήσομαι ἐπὶ τῷ θεῷ τῷ σωτῆρί μου. Except for the change of subject ("my spirit" for "I") and the use of only one verb for "to exult, be glad," this comes close to a quotation. But all of the expressions are very common in the OT and should rather be regarded as routine language. "God my savior" renders Heb. "the God of my salvation" and is clearly an LXX expression.

1:48a: ὅτι ἐπέβλεψεν ἐπὶ τὴν ταπείνωσιν τῆς δούλης αὐτοῦ. The phrase is almost literally from 1 Sam 1:11, thus in close contextual relation to the song of Hannah. It should be noticed that ταπείνωσις in connection with some verb of perception is used in birth contexts also at Gen 16:11; 29:32; however, it occurs in many other instances without that connection, e.g., Gen 31:42; 1 Sam 9:16; 2 Sam 16:12; 2 Kgs 14:26.

1:48b: ἰδοὺ γὰρ ἀπὸ τοῦ νῦν μακαριοῦσίν με πᾶσαι αἱ γενεαί. The verb μακαρίζειν occurs in a birth context at Gen 30:13 in connection with the birth of Asher. The combination of 1 Sam 1:11 and Gen 30:13 is intentional and serves to express the new status of Mary. There is also a link to the μακαρία of vs 45.

1:49a: ὅτι ἐποίησέν μοι μεγάλα ὁ δυνατός. This is not a real quotation but reflects common OT language, cf., e.g., Deut 10:21 ἐποίησεν ἐν σοὶ τὰ μεγάλα.

1:49b: καὶ ἅγιον τὸ ὄνομα αὐτοῦ is a common expression, cf. Ps 99:3; 111:9, in both cases together with φοβερόν.

1:50: καὶ τὸ ἔλεος αὐτοῦ εἰς γενεὰς καὶ γενεὰς τοῖς φοβουμένοις αὐτόν. This is almost certainly taken from Ps 103:17 where, however, the temporal expression is ἀπὸ τοῦ αἰῶνος καὶ ἕως τοῦ αἰῶνος, corresponding to the Hebrew text. εἰς γενεὰς καὶ γενεάς (לדור ודור) is reminiscent of Ps 89:2; 100:5 and others.

1:51a: Ἐποίησεν κράτος ἐν βραχίονι αὐτοῦ. Both ποιεῖν κράτος and ἐν βραχίονι are Hebraisms, cf. also Ps 118:15f., ποιεῖν δύναμιν.

1:51 b: διεσκόρπισεν ὑπερηφάνους διανοίᾳ καρδίας αὐτῶν. This is almost a quotation from Ps 89:11 σὺ ἐταπείνωσας ὡς τραυματίαν ὑπερήφανον καὶ ἐν τῇ βραχίονι τῆς δυνάμεώς σου διεσκόρπισας τοὺς ἐχθρούς σου.

1:52a: καθεῖλεν δυνάστας ἀπὸ θρόνων. The δυνάσται are mentioned in Job 12:19 but with the verb καταστρέφειν (MT *'ětānîm yᵉsallep*, which shows that the passage cannot have been used in its Hebrew wording). καθαιρεῖν occurs with θρόνος in Sir 10:14.

1:52b: καὶ ὕψωσεν ταπεινούς. The combination of ὑψοῦν and ταπεινός is found in Ezek 21:26 and Esther 1, cf. Job 5:11.

1:53a: πεινῶντας ἐνέπλησεν ἀγαθῶν is reminiscent of Ps 107:9 ψυχὴν πεινῶσαν ἐνέπλησεν ἀγαθῶν.

1:53b: καὶ πλουτοῦντας ἐξαπέστειλεν κενούς is not a quotation, but the elements are found in Ps 34:11 πλούσιοι ἐπτώχευσαν καὶ ἐπείνασαν and Job 22:9 χήρας ἐξαπέστειλας κενάς (notice the difference in contents); κενός also occurs in the line preceding Ps 107:9 ἐχόρτασεν ψυχὴν κενήν. The verse thus is reminiscent of several passages without being a quotation from· any of them. 1 Samuel 2 with its reversal of conditions also comes to mind.

1:54a: ἀντελάβετο Ἰσραὴλ παιδὸς αὐτοῦ clearly refers to Isa 41:8f. Σύ δε, Ἰσραήλ, παῖς μου . . . οὗ ἀντελαβόμην.

1:54b: μνησθῆναι ἐλέους. The expression occurs in Ps 98:3.

1:55a: καθὼς ἐλάλησεν πρὸς τοὺς πατέρας ἡμῶν should be compared with Mic 7:20 δώσεις . . . ἔλεον τῷ Ἀβραὰμ καθότι ὤμοσας τοῖς πατράσιν ἡμῶν. The word ἔλεος links it with the preceding clause.

1:55b: τῷ Ἀβραὰμ καὶ τῷ σπέρματι αὐτοῦ εἰς τὸν αἰῶνα. Cf. 2 Sam 22:51 τῷ Δαυίδ καὶ τῷ σπέρματι αὐτοῦ ἕως αἰῶνος. Abraham is mentioned in Mic 7:20.

Thus the whole song is a mosaic of OT allusions held together by the birth setting of some of the OT passages and by the antithesis motif centered around ταπεινός / ὑψοῦν, exemplified without the exact wording by 1 Samuel 2. Nothing indicates a Hebrew original; the use of Job 12:19 even contradicts such an assumption. The Qumran technique seems to be applied here also to the LXX text. The question remains:

How was the Hebrew technique of the Qumran covenanters spread to the Greek environment of Luke?

Luke 1:68–79

In the *Benedictus* the OT allusions are fewer and some of them are rather vague.

1:68–69: The introductory phrase Εὐλογητὸς κύριος ὁ θεὸς τοῦ Ἰσραήλ is a common formula which occurs at the end of each of the first four "books" of the Psalms (Ps 41:14; 72:18; 89:53; 106:48). Ἐπισκέπεσθαι is a common word (e.g., Exod 4:31; Ruth 1:6) but not part of a quotation. Λύτρωσιν τῷ λαῷ αὐτοῦ echoes Ps 111:9. Ἤγειρεν κέρας represents a common OT expression, found with different verbs, e.g., in 1 Sam 2:1a (ὑψοῦν), Ps 132:17 (ἐξανατέλλειν). Κέρας and σωτηρία are found together in Ps 18:3.

1:71: The "enemies" and "haters" are reminiscent of Ps 106:10, where also the verb σῴζειν recurs.

1:72: ἔλεος μετὰ τῶν πατέρων ἡμῶν may depend on Mic 7:20 (quoted above) as is ὤμοσεν πρὸς Ἀβραάμ (vs 73). μνησθῆναι διαθήκης is found in Ps 105:8 and 106:45, but none of these passages is really quoted.

1:74–75: These verses lack OT parallels, while in vs 76 the phrase προπορεύσῃ ἐνώπιον κυρίου ἑτοιμάσαι ὁδοὺς αὐτοῦ vaguely recalls Mal 3:1 and Isa 40:3.

1:79: Finally, vs 79 contains a clear allusion to Isa 9:1, but the wording differs too much to be a quotation. The use of καθήμενοι instead of LXX κατοικοῦντες agrees with Matt 4:16; both verbs may be used to render Heb. ישב. However, in Ps 107:10 the LXX uses καθήμενοι in a similar phrase.

The *Benedictus* was composed according to the same principle as the *Magnificat*, i.e., using OT vocabulary and phraseology without really quoting, but the OT allusions are fewer. As in the *Hodayot* the frequency of OT expressions is dependent on the subject matter of the psalm.

The Book of Acts

The OT quotations in Acts occur almost exclusively in speeches. Obviously, they reflect the argumentation from scripture as practiced in the early church, or at least Luke's idea of this argumentation.

Acts 1:20: The choice of a successor to Judas Iscariot is motivated by a reference to Ps 69:26 and Ps 109:8. The first quotation is close to the

LXX, but changes plural into singular because of the reference to Judas, and ἠρημωμένη into ἔρημος. It substitutes ἐν αὐτῇ for ἐν τοῖς σκηνώμασιν αὐτῶν, and the word order is different. The second quotation is exactly that of the LXX.

Acts 2:17–21: The quotation from Joel 3:1–5 is based on the LXX but is rather free. It says "in the last days" rather than "after this" (vs 17), it has καί γε in vs 18 instead of καί, and it adds "and they shall prophesy" in the same verse. In vs 19 it changes the structure of the text by reading (italics mark additions):

And I will give wonders in the heavens *above*
and *signs* on the earth *beneath*,
blood, and fire, and vapor of smoke

instead of (LXX = MT):

And I will give wonders in the heavens and on the earth,
blood, and fire, and vapor of smoke.

A significant change is the ascription of visions to the young men and of dreams to the old in vs 17, while LXX (and MT) has the reverse, which is an indication of quoting from memory. The addition of μου after δούλους and δούλας makes "servant" a spiritual concept, while in Joel it denotes social status. Finally, the expression ἡμέραν . . . τὴν μεγάλην καὶ ἐπιφανῆ repeats the error of the LXX, which reads הנראה instead of הנורא, thus providing the final proof that the quotation is based on the LXX.

Acts 2:25–28 quotes Ps 16:8–11 exactly from the LXX. The application of the text to Christ is possible only on the basis of the word ὅσιος but difficult or impossible on the basis of MT חסיד.

Acts 2:34–35 quotes Ps 110:1 from the LXX.

Acts 3:22–23 refers to the words about a/the prophet to come in Deut 18:15, 18f., changing it from the Lord's word to Moses into a word uttered by Moses. Parts of the passage are left out, and the consequences of disobedience are described by means of an expression from Lev 23:29. Even if the quotation is rather free, it is clearly based on the LXX text.

Acts 3:25 quotes God's promise to Abraham in Gen 12:3 and 22:18. The former passage says πᾶσαι αἱ φύλαι (τῆς γῆς). The latter has πάντα τὰ ἔθνη and Acts, πᾶσαι αἱ πατριαί. Thus we have again a free quotation, but its dependence on the LXX is proved by the verb ἐνευλογεῖν.

Acts 4:11 contains an allusion to Ps 118:22 using the verb ἐξουθενεῖν, while the quotation in Luke 20:17 has ἀποδοκιμάζω as does the LXX.[5]

Acts 4:24 echoes LXX Ps 146:6 or Exod 20:11.

Acts 4:25 quotes Ps 2:1f. exactly as in the LXX. The application of "kings" and "rulers" to Herod and Pontius Pilate is especially interesting and obviously typical of contemporary interpretation of scripture (cf. the Qumran *p^ešārîm*).

Acts 7

The speech of Stephen contains many indirect references to OT material; see below.

Acts 7:42–43 quotes Amos 5:25–27 from LXX with some typical variations: change of word order in "forty years in the wilderness"; addition of a comment on the figures: "(which you made) in order to worship them." The LXX provenience is proved by the interpretation of מלך as the god Moloch and the rendering of כיון by Ραιφαν (var. Ρομφα, Ρεφαν). Why Damascus is changed into Babylon is not clear (reference to the exile?).

7:49–50: Isa 66:1f. is quoted from the LXX with the usual variations: τίς τόπος instead of ποῖος τόπος and οὐχὶ ἡ χείρ μου ἐποίησεν πάντα ταῦτα for πάντα γὰρ ταῦτα ἐποίησεν ἡ χείρ μου. These changes must be free variant readings, since they are not rooted in any other textual traditions.

Acts 8:32–33: Here is a verbal quotation from LXX Isa 53:7–8.

Acts 13:33 quotes Ps 2:7 according to the LXX.

Acts 13:34 quotes a phrase from Isa 55:3 referring to τὰ ὅσια Δαυίδ τὰ πιστά. This is the LXX rendering of *ḥasdê Dāwīd hanne^emānîm*, "the sure acts of *ḥesed* of/towards David." Since חסד is here translated with ὅσια, it is easy to carry on the argumentation by means of word play (vs 35), possibly only in Greek (LXX): "you shall not let your ὅσιος see corruption" (Ps 16:10, quoted also in 2:27). Since David has died and been buried (vs 36, an allusion to 1 Kgs 2:10), this promise must refer to someone else, namely Jesus Christ.

Acts 13:41 closes Paul's speech by a warning taken from Hab 1:5. The author omits ἐπιβλέψατε, which may have seemed superfluous after ἴδετε, changes the word order in ἐγὼ ἐργάζομαι, and adds a second ἔργον, possibly for the sake of clarity.

---

[5] Cf. SSM, 67f without reference to this passage.

Acts 13:47 quotes a verse from the second Servant Song, Isa 49:6. The author omits εἰς διαθήκην γένους, since Paul is speaking to Gentiles.
Acts 14:15: Same quotation as 4:24.
Acts 15:16–18 contains a combined quotation. The introductory phrase "after this I will return" seems to derive from Jer 12:15, though the verb there is ἐπιστρέφειν, not ἀναστρέφειν. The main part of the quotation is from LXX Amos 9:11–12. The following changes occur: ἀναστήσω is changed to ἀνοικοδομήσω (probably for reasons of style; MT has םיקא); τὰ πεπτωκότα αὐτῆς is omitted (to avoid repetition from πεπτωκυῖαν?); τὰ κατεσκαμμένα becomes τὰ κατεστραμμένα (Greek variant reading; several NT manuscripts have the LXX reading); ἀνοικοδομήσω καὶ ἀνορθώσω stands for ἀναστήσω καὶ ἀνοικοδομήσω (reasons of style, or slip of memory?); τὸν κύριον is added as the object of "seek" for the sake of clarity; ὁ θεός is omitted in the phrase λέγει κύριος ὁ θεός. Finally, the words γνωστὰ απ᾽ αἰῶνος have been added at the end (from Isa 45:21?).

Acts 28:26–27 quotes Isa 6:9–10. Here we have "go to this people and say" instead of LXX "go and say to this people," and in vs 27 αὐτῶν is omitted after ὦσίν. Otherwise the quotation agrees with the LXX. Cf. Luke 8:10 above.

Stephen's speech in chap. 7 presents a special problem. It consists of a survey of biblical history from Abraham to Moses leading up to two quotations, one concerning the idolatry of Israel (Amos 5:25ff.), the other emphasizing the impossibility of building a proper dwelling for God. Strictly speaking, only the last quotation is relevant to the problem, namely, the refutation of the accusation against Stephen for preaching the destruction of the temple (the alleged abolition of the Law of Moses is not dealt with at all). This leads us to assume that this kind of historical survey was not created for this special occasion but represents a literary genre rooted in tradition. Commentaries point to Hebrews 11 as a possible parallel. I would suggest that there is another example in the Damascus Document. There we find (2:14–6:11) a summary of biblical history leading up to the events connected with the Teacher of Righteousness. The historical survey provides the biblical background for that which is important to the author. If this is correct, the survey genre is not a Christian invention but was developed in contemporary Jewish tradition. If Hebrews 11 is really a parallel, it is interesting that the Letter to the Hebrews provides us with another example of a Jewish-type exegesis applied to the LXX text.

CHRISTIANS AND JEWS—SOME POSITIVE IMAGES

Marc Saperstein
Harvard Divinity School

The dean of contemporary Jewish historians, S. W. Baron, has shown
that many modern conceptions of Jewish experience in medieval Christian Europe suffer from a fundamental distortion. Writing history was
not a natural vocation for medieval Jews; most Jewish historiography
was inspired by calamities that generated the impulse to record and, if
possible, to explain. Therefore, most medieval Jewish chronicles are
little more than accounts of the massacres and attacks suffered by various communities at different times. The tendency to assume that these
historiographical sources present a full picture of reality resulted in
what Baron called the "lachrymose conception of Jewish history,"
viewing medieval Jewish experience as essentially a succession of
tragedies in a vale of tears.[1]

A similar danger of distortion exists in reconstructing the perceptions
of the other held by Christians and Jews in the past. A number of
rigorous studies of Christian and Jewish polemical texts have been published during the past generation.[2] But since this literature is by nature
composed of attacks on a rival community and its faith, it tends to con-
vey the impression that the discourse between the two communities
was virtually limited to such attacks, and to imply that the leaders of
Christianity and of Judaism conceived of the other solely as the enemy
to be refuted or vanquished. Similarly, eloquent and thorough treatments of the history of anti-Jewish teachings have been produced by

---

[1] S. W. Baron, *History and Jewish Historians* (Philadelphia: Jewish Publication Society,
1964) 84, 96, and frequently elsewhere in his work.

[2] Of many possible examples perhaps the most important are Daniel Lasker, *Jewish
Philosophical Polemics Against Christianity in the Middle Ages* (New York: Ktav, 1977);
David Berger, *The Jewish-Christian Debate in the High Middle Ages* (Philadelphia: Jewish
Publication Society, 1979); Frank Talmage, *The Book of the Covenant* (Toronto: Pontifical
Institute of Mediaeval Studies, 1972); and idem, *Kitbê Pûlmûs LeProfiat Duran*
(Jerusalem: Merkaz Zalman Shazar, 1981).

both Christian and Jewish scholars.[3] But by selectively focusing on negative images, these studies often project a picture that is overly dismal and bleak.

There can be little doubt that Christians and Jews often viewed the other as less than fully human, and sometimes even worse, although the complete history of the "demonic" conception of the Gentile that pervades classical texts of the Jewish mystical tradition has yet to be elucidated. What deserves attention, however, is that different, more positive perceptions existed as well. Particularly striking are those occasions when religious leaders, addressing their own people in a context of ethical and religious exhortation and rebuke, recognized in the other community positive qualities worthy of emulation.

This use of the outsider as a model with which to admonish one's own people has a long history as a powerful weapon in the arsenal of the rhetoric of self-criticism. We find it in the prophet Malachi ("For from the rising to the setting sun, My Name is great among the nations, . . . but *you* profane it" —Mal 1:11–12) and in the exemplum of the "good Samaritan" (Luke 10:30–37). But it is more than merely a rhetorical ploy. Its effectiveness depends upon arousing in the audience an acceptance of versimilitude. The listeners must respond, "Yes, it's true, those people for whom we have such contempt are actually better than we are in this respect." While such passages must not be taken simplistically as evidence of the group they describe, they may serve to indicate the attitudes of the author, and to some extent also of the audience being addressed. That a full collection of such passages would be a valuable complement and corrective to the picture presented by the literature of polemic and contempt will, I hope, be demonstrated by the following illustrations.

Despite widespread antipathy, there were certain qualities that Christian moralists respected in their Jewish contemporaries. First, Jews were known for their devotion to the Sabbath and the holy days of the festival calendar. Some of the most virulent anti-Jewish preachers concede this point, and identify it as an area in which their own listeners frequently fall short. Few religious leaders exceeded the venomous rhetoric of John Chrysostom directed against the Jewish people and their religion. But even he recognized a commitment worthy of

---

[3] E.g., Joshua Trachtenberg, *The Devil and the Jews: The Medieval Conception of the Jew and Its Relation to Modern Antisemitism* (Philadelphia: Jewish Publication Society, 1983); Rosemary Ruether, *Faith and Fratricide* (New York: Seabury, 1974); *Śin'at Hayyehudim Ledôrôtêha* (Jerusalem: Merkaz Zalman Shazar, 1980); Jeremy Cohen, *The Friars and the Jews: The Evolution of Medieval Anti-Judaism* (Ithaca: Cornell University Press, 1983).

emulation: "You Christians should be ashamed and embarrassed at the Jews who observe the Sabbath with such devotion and refrain from all commerce beginning with the evening of the Sabbath. When they see the sun hurrying to set in the west on Friday they call a halt to their business affairs and interrupt their selling. If a customer haggles with them over a purchase in the later afternoon, and offers a price after evening has come, the Jews refuse the offer because they are unwilling to accept the money."[4]

This theme was frequently reiterated in the Middle Ages. Berthold of Regensburg, one of the great popular preachers of the thirteenth century, whose sermons reflect some of the worst anti-Jewish stereotypes of that age, told his flock, "Now you see very well that a stinking Jew, whose odor is offensive to all, honors his holy days better than you. Bah! As a Christian you should be ashamed of yourself that you do not trust in God as much as the stinking Jew, by believing that if you spent the holy day in His praise as He commanded you, He would certainly reward you."[5] The gratuitous insults, drawn from the common medieval notion of *fetor judaicus*, only heighten the shame of the congregation in failing to meet the religious standards set by their despised neighbors.

John Bromyard, author of a monumental fourteenth-century anthology of homiletical materials, reported that a Jew successfully challenged his Christian neighbors with the charge that "you say that you have festivals in your law, but I do not see how you observe them. What I do see is armored chariots, and horses with packs going to the woods, and merchants, and such kinds of activity on those days you call holy, just like those on other days." Therefore, says Bromyard, because of our bad conduct the verse from Lamentations has been fulfilled in us Christians: "Her enemies have seen her and mocked at her Sabbaths"

---

[4] The text is quoted from the translation of Robert L. Wilken, *John Chrysostom and the Jews* (Berkeley/Los Angeles: University of California Press, 1983) 66.

[5] Berthold von Regensburg, *Vollständige Ausgabe seiner Predigten* (Vienna, 1862; Berlin: De Gruyter, 1965) 1. 270. Cf. Trachtenberg, *The Devil and the Jews*, 277 n. 18; Remo Iannucci, "The Treatment of the Capital Sins and Their Corresponding Vices in the German Sermons of Berthold von Regensburg," *Studies in German Philology* 17 (1942) 29; Cohen, *The Friars and the Jews*, 229–38. In different sermons, Berthold maintained that the Jews "honor their fathers and mothers better than you" (1. 164), and pointed to the "stinking, offensive Jew" who is able to remain continent during the period of his wife's menstruation, contrasting the lack of self-control in his Christian listeners: "And so should you act at that time" (1. 323).

(Lam 1:7).[6] A similar point is made at the end of the fifteenth century in Sebastian Brandt's *Ship of Fools.*[7]

A second theme was the Jews' abhorrence for blasphemous language and profanity in speech. One of the most influential popular preachers of the early thirteenth century, Jacques de Vitry, reproaching his audience for their frequent profanity, relates the following incident: "I have heard of a certain Jew, while playing at dice with a Christian, heard that Christian swearing and blaspheming God because he was losing. The Jew stopped up his ears and, leaving the money behind, got up from the game and fled. For the Jews not only refuse to blaspheme God; they are unwilling to hear anyone blaspheme." According to the preacher, Jews "would never tolerate it, but rather become infuriated, if anyone were to say about their own wives, or their parents, or any member of their family, the shameful things that Christians say about the blessed Virgin, and the saints, and even about God."[8]

This theme is taken up by Bromyard in several places of his magnum opus. The Jews, he writes, "rarely swear, for one hardly ever hears them take an oath, except in accordance with their law. . . . When they hear a blasphemy, they rend their garments . . . and cover up their ears." "They do not blaspheme, nor do they willingly hear someone blaspheme or swear falsely. But we laugh when we do this, or when we hear it done by others."[9] There is no mistaking the pointed suggestion that the Jewish standards of decorum might well be taken as a model for Christians.

Thirdly, the Jewish commitment to education was recognized and admired by at least some Christians. A contrast between the two communities is drawn in a commentary written by a pupil of Abelard:

> If the Christians educate their sons, they do so not for God, but for gain, in order that the one brother, if he be a cleric, may help his father and his mother and his other brothers. They say that a

---

[6] John Bromyard, *Summa praedicantium* (Venice, 1586) 1. 281a. The Lamentations verse is, of course, cited from the Vg (viderunt eam hostes, et deriserunt sabbata ejus), which has read the Hebrew *mišbattèha* as "Sabbaths." Cf. *Lam. Rab.* on this verse (*The Midrash Rabbah* [London/Jerusalem: Soncino,. 1977] 4, Lamentations, 108). To my knowledge, the only scholar to call attention to the positive image of the Jew in Bromyard's work was G. R. Owst, *Literature and Pulpit in Medieval England* (New York: Barnes and Noble, 1961) 177, 418–19.

[7] "Die Juden spotten unser sehr, / Das wir dem Feirtage thun solche ehr, / Das sie noch halten also steiss, / Das ich sie nicht ins Narrenschiff, / Wolt setzen": *Weltspiegel oder Narrenschiff,* in J. Scheible, *Das Kloster,* 1 (Stuttgart, 1845) 728.

[8] Th. Frederick Crane, *The Exempla of Jacques de Vitry* (London, 1890) 91.

[9] *Summa praedicantium,* 1. 419c; 2. 235a–b. Cf. the quotation of Saul Morteira, below.

cleric will have no heir and whatever he has will be ours. .... A black cloak and a hood to go to church in and his surplice will be enough for him. But the Jews, out of zeal for God and love of the Law, put as many sons as they have to letters, that each may understand God's Law. ... A Jew, however poor, would put even ten sons to letters, not for gain, as the Christians do, but for the understanding of God's Law, and not only his sons but his daughters.[10]

It is not only the value Jews place on education, but the purity of motivation, that the Christian writer finds so impressive.

Perhaps most poignant is the recognition of Jewish devotion to their faith and willingness to suffer for it. The assertion placed into the mouth of Peter Abelard's fictional Jewish participant in dialogue, that "surely no nation is known or is even believed to have suffered so much for God as we constantly endure," is more than an attempt to create a realistic character; it strikes a chord of genuine empathy.[11] Just as eloquent is John Bromyard, conceding the Jews' loyalty even as he denies the validity of their faith:

In many countries where the Jews live, certain offenses are punished according to local custom by the Jew's being hung by the feet between two dogs, just as they hanged Christ between two thieves, or by being buried alive. Before the sentence, they may be offered their lives if they would be willing to accept our faith and baptism. Yet they prefer to suffer those punishments and death rather than to deny their faith.

Thus, according to Bromyard, "many Jews frequently suffer the most excruciating punishments and ultimately the most horrible deaths for their faith, clearly much more painful than many martyrs for the Christian faith." Although the absence of divine miracles on behalf of the Jewish martyrs was taken as proof of the falsity of their religion, there

---

[10] Beryl Smalley, *The Study of the Bible in the Middle Ages* (New York: Philosophical Library, 1952) 78. The statement about daughters receiving a Torah education is striking in light of Jewish ambivalence on this point. In general, girls were not included in the formal educational program.

[11] Nulla quippe gens unquam tanta pro deo pertulisse noscitur, aut etiam creditur, quanta nos jugiter pro ipso sustinemus. Cf. Peter Abelard, *A Dialogue of a Philosopher, a Jew, and a Christian* (trans. Pierre Payer; Toronto: Pontifical Institute of Mediaeval Studies, 1979) 32. The entire passage in which this sentence appears is noteworthy. Cf. H. Liebeschütz, "The Significance of Judaism in Peter Abelard's Dialogue," *JJS* 12 (1961) 1–18.

was clearly something in the phenomenon of Jewish martyrdom that impressed the preacher deeply.[12]

Positive views of Christian behavior are similarly to be found on the Jewish side. Various aspects of Christian intellectual life were identified by Jews as exemplary. Joseph ibn Kaspi, passionately devoted to a philosophical exposition of Judaism, lamented the paradox that Christian scholars honored and studied Maimonides' *Guide for the Perplexed* while Jews, for whom the book had been written, neglected it.[13] Solomon ibn Verga, author of a groundbreaking historical work, praised his Christian neighbors for their "active desire to learn about ancient things in order to draw moral instruction from them," a quality he considered to be a sign of their enlightenment.[14]

The values and institutions of Christian education were often admired. In the early seventeenth century, a German Jewish author conceded in an apologetical work that "almost all the Christians of our time study, and they value learning, while among us it is the opposite: only a few engage in the study of Torah, while most are eager to make money."[15] In the middle of the eighteenth century, a rabbi preaching to the Ashkenazic congregation in London drew a painful contrast between the educational activities of his own community and those of the country where he lived:

> Look and see how many schools of higher learning (*battê midrašot*) they have throughout this realm, which they call "Academies." Whosoever seeks wisdom may go and study; all is provided. As for us, we do not have even one school worthy of being called by the Name of God.[16]

Christian devotion to the church is emphasized in an extraordinary work of self-criticism written near the beginning of the fifteenth century in Spain, after the devastating pogroms of 1391 and the wave of apostasies that followed in their wake.

---

[12] *Summa praedicantium*, 1. 290a. On the humiliating mode of execution, see the sources cited by Cecil Roth, "European Jewry in the Dark Ages," *HUCA* 23 (1950–51) 159. Cf. the passage cited by Heiko Oberman in *The Roots of Anti-Semitism in the Age of Renaissance and Reformation* (Philadelphia: Fortress, 1984) 99.

[13] Joseph ibn Kaspi, in *Hebrew Ethical Wills* (trans. Israel Abrahams; Philadelphia: Jewish Publication Society, 1926) 1. 149–50, 154.

[14] Solomon ibn Verga, *Šebeṭ Yehûdâ* (Jerusalem: Mosad Bialik, 1947) 21.

[15] Zalman Zevi Openhausen, *Der Judischer Theriac* (Hanover, 1625) chaps. 2 and 7, quoted in Simha Asaf, *Meqôrôt Letôledôt Haḥinûk Beyiśra'el* (Tel Aviv: Debir, 1954) 1. 74.

[16] Hirschel Levin, *Derašôt* (Jewish Theological Seminary MS R79, f. 19b); cf. Charles Duschinsky, *The Rabbinate of the Great Synagogue* (London, 1921) 18.

> Those in whose country we live bring tithes and give generously to
> their scholars from the first produce of their fields. They place
> these portions before them graciously, giving their very best pos-
> session, so as to make their religion strong. Their nobles and lords
> yearn to have their sons enter holy orders and attain a position of
> honor in their church.
> But affluent Jews and Jewish communal leaders give our own
> scholars meagre bread and scant water. To their shame and dis-
> grace, they eat like princes and dress like nobles, while scholars eat
> the bread of toil and languish. . . . This is why the Torah is disho-
> nored and forgotten by us. The leaders of our community have no
> desire for their sons to enter the discipline of serious Torah study
> and be dependent upon it for their livelihood.[17]

Here it is the Christians who want their children to devote their lives to
their faith, while influential Jews do not, precisely the opposite of the
point made in the passage from Abelard's student quoted above.

The same Jewish author criticized his coreligionists for not behaving
in the synagogues more like their Christian neighbors.

> Look what happens when a congregation [of Jews] gathers to hear
> words of Torah from a sage. Slumber weighs upon the eyes of the
> officers, others converse about trivial affairs. The preacher is
> dumbfounded by the talking of men and the chattering of women
> standing behind the synagogue. If he should reproach them
> because of their behavior, they continue to sin, behaving corruptly,
> abominably. This is the opposite of the Christians. When their
> men and women gather to hear a preacher, they stand together in
> absolute silence, marvelling at his rebuke; not one of them dozes
> as he pours out his words upon them. They await him as they do
> the rain, eager for the waters of his counsel. We have not learned
> properly from those around us.[18]

Nor was this the only aspect of Christian preaching that Jews found
admirable. In the middle of the fifteenth century, the author of the
earliest known Jewish treatise on homiletics contrasted the courage of
Christian preachers with the sycophancy of their Jewish counterparts:
"A Gentile may preach against kings and nobles, proclaiming their sins
for all to hear. But in our own nation, no one will raise his tongue

---

[17] Solomon Alami, *'Iggeret Mûsar* (St. Petersburg, 1912) 26.

[18] Ibid., 27. Very much the same point was made a century later, following the expulsion, by Joseph Yabetz in *Ḥasdê Adonay* (Brooklyn: Moineshter, 1934) 56. (Needless to
say, Christian preachers had a very different perception of the attentiveness of their audiences.)

against any Jew whatsoever, and certainly not if the man is wealthy or a potential benefactor." [19] One of the best known Jewish preachers in the generation of the explusion from Spain described the impetus to his own creativity that came from a popular recognition of the high level of Christian preaching, which left his people dissatisfied with most of the sermons they heard in the synagogues. [20]

Except for the apostates, medieval Jews who wrote books were unambiguous in asserting the inferiority of the Christian religion to their own. Yet the devotion of many Christians to their faith was recognized, admired, and even envied by more than a few Jewish writers. Critics of rationalism frequently complained that many Christians believed in God and in the fundamental teachings of the Torah, such as creation, prophecy, miracles, and immortality, more genuinely than did those Jews who were influenced by corrosive philosophical skepticism. [21]

A thirteenth-century German text criticizes in fairly conventional terms the absence of true religious devotion in synagogues at the time of prayer. The contrast it draws, however, is not at all conventional. Look at the fear and trembling with which Christian kings fall upon their knees before the image of God in their churches, the author admonishes; if the Christians show so much reverence before a statue, how much should we Jews show as we stand in the presence of the Almighty. [22]

Joseph Karo's "Maggid" was obviously impressed by Christian ascetic piety, for he advised the great lawyer and mystic to "go out and learn from the Gentiles. Think of the tortures and mortifications which they suffer. How much more should you be ready to suffer tortures and mortifications for the true faith." [23] From a very different cultural

[19] Joseph ibn Shem Tov, 'Ên Haqqôre' (London Montefiore MS 61, f. 121b).

[20] Jews "heard the [Christian] preachers and found them impressive, and they wanted to raise a comparable banner. This is what they say: 'The Christian scholars and sages raise questions and seek answers in their academies and churches, thereby adding to the glory of the Torah and the prophets. . . . But our Torah commentators do not employ this method that everyone wants" (Isaac Arama, 'Aqedat Yiṣḥaq [Warsaw, 1882] Introduction 8a).

[21] E.g., Abraham Abulafia, quoted in Gershom Scholem, *Major Trends in Jewish Mysticism* (New York: Schocken, 1941) 129; Isaac Arama, Ḥazut Qāšâ (Warsaw, 1884), Gate 8, p. 11c; Isaac Abravanel, *Commentary on Joshua 10* (Jerusalem, 1955) 53b; Joseph Yabetz, ꜜOr Hahayyim (Lublin, 1912) 20a, 15b.

[22] *Seper Ḥasidim* (Bologna MS, section 18; Jerusalem: Lewin-Epstein, 1966) 9a. Cf. *Seper Ḥasidim* (Parma MS, section 1189; Berlin, 1891) 389.

[23] R. J. Z. Werblowsky, *Joseph Karo: Lawyer and Mystic* (Philadelphia: Jewish Publication Society, 1977) 163.

milieu, we hear a similar sentiment in a seventeenth-century Polish moralist:

> We should learn a lesson from the Christian priests and monks. They cast off their sleep every midnight, and also perform other great acts of self-abnegation on certain days, even though they dwell in peace and tranquility. . . . How much more should be, the holy people, dwelling in this bitter exile. . . . Yet even in the hour especially appropriate to set our souls in order and to bring the redemption near, we are too lazy to awaken.[24]

Jewish authors also pointed with grudging admiration to aspects of Christian behavior in the secular realm. One of the strongest arguments in Jewish polemical literature had been the superior ethical standards of Jewish society.[25] But in the homiletical literature, a different picture sometimes appears. Solomon ibn Verga maintained that the Christians, who were lax in their observance of religious rituals, were scrupulously honest in business, while Jews, meticulously observant in the ritual domain, were not always ethical in their business affairs. His contemporary, Joseph Yabetz, chastised his contemporaries even more directly:

> If you open your eyes, you will be envious of them, for you will see them fulfilling the rational commandments—"doing justice, and loving mercy" (Mic 6:8)—better than we do. Their nobles take pride in the mitzvah of charity and compassion for the poor, which they themselves perform, in all their grandeur, out of love for God. Their sages are civil to each other, while some of ours are jealous and try to destroy each other; modesty and humility are to be found among them, while among us is insolence and pride.[27]

---

[24] Judah Pukhovitzer, Daʿat Ḥokmâ (Hamburg, 1692) 1. 39d–40a, cited by Isaiah Tishbi, Neṭîbê Emûnâ Ûminût (Jerusalem: Magnes, 1982) 125.

[25] E.g., Joseph Kimhi, The Book of the Covenant (trans. Frank Talmage) 32–35; the passage is also in Talmage's Disputation and Dialogue (New York: Ktav, 1975) 11–13. Cf. the use of this claim in the context of Christian self-criticism by Bromyard, Summa praedicantium, 1. 289c–d.

[26] Ibn Verga, Šebeṭ Yehûdâ, 45.

[27] Yabetz, Ḥasdê Adonay, 56. In the eighteenth century, Hirschel Levin, rabbi in London, contrasted the humane and compassionate way in which the Christians treated their poor with the humiliating practices of his own people, concluding, "Would that we might learn from them in this matter" (Deraŝôt, 19a, 21b).

In 1747, Rabbi Jonathan Eybeschuetz rebuked his congregation in Metz by reminding them that certain commandments, required by reason as well as by revelation, were better observed by the Gentiles than by the Jews—for example, "honoring of father and mother and [the prohibitions against] robbery and fraud, and many like them."[28] Perhaps the most impressive statement of this thesis comes at a climatic point in a sermon by the seventeenth-century Amsterdam preacher Saul Morteira, who cites the Talmudic dictum, "You have followed them in their corruption, you have failed to emulate their good" (*b. Sanh.* 39b).

This statement is applied by the preacher as follows:

> Look at the Gentiles among whom we live. We learn from them styles of clothing and haughtiness, but we do not learn from them silence during prayer. We are like them in eating their cheeses and their wine, but we are not like them we regard to justice, righteousness and honesty. We are like them in shaving our beard or modeling it in their style, but we are not like them in their refraining from cursing or swearing in God's Name. We are like them in frequenting underground game rooms, but we are not like them in turning from vengeance and refraining from bearing hatred in our hearts. We are like them in fornicating with their daughters, but we are not like them in conducting business affairs with faithfulness and fairness.[29]

We cannot know whether this passage was delivered in thunderous cadences or in hushed, understated restraint, whether in biting sarcasm or in painful anguish, but we may imagine the effect it must have produced upon the listeners. Measured not only against the high standards of their own tradition, but against the actual behavior of the Christian neighbors, they were found wanting in certain important areas.

Read in isolation, the passages cited above would suggest a perception of the other no less distorted than would a roster of the most negative characterizations. It is certainly not to be suggested that the material here collected represents the normative view on either side. Rather, it may be taken as a clue that there was more in the mutual

---

[28] Jonathan Eybeschuetz, *Ya'arôt Debaš* (Jerusalem: Lewin-Epstein, 1965) 99a. Note that Berthold of Regensburg had said precisely the opposite about the honor of father and mother (above, n. 2), and John Bromyard had pointed to the Jews as a model in their handling of monetary matters because of their careful observance of the prohibition against taking interest from their "brothers," a prohibition which not all Christians observed (*Summa praedicantium,* 2. 235a).

[29] Saul Morteira, *Gib'at Sha'ul* (Warsaw, 1902) "Debarim," 129a.

perceptions of Christians and Jews than unmitigated hostility and contempt, just as there was more to Jewish history than a progression of uninterrupted persecution and suffering. Taken together with the more prevalent negative images, these positive glimpses express the ambivalence that impelled each side to view the other frequently as a demonic adversary, but occasionally also as a challenge to creative competition in ethical and religious living.

CHALLENGE AND RESPONSE:
PESIQTA DERAB KAHANA, CHAPTER 26
AS AN OBLIQUE REPLY TO CHRISTIAN CLAIMS

Lou H. Silberman
Vanderbilt University
The University of Arizona

Some years ago in an examination of the text noted above,[1] I hypothesized that it could well be a response to some Christian theological position being set forth and argued against Judaism in Galilee in the fourth and fifth centuries. My choice of doctrine was that of the atonement: Christ's atoning death for the sins of humankind. The chapter, to be dealt with below in detail, is in its entirety an argument for the atoning efficacy of the death of righteous persons, that is, a doctrine of vicarious atonement. The material included centered upon the lesson read in the synagogue on the Day of Atonement, the sixteenth chapter of Leviticus. This details the ritual procedures that were to take place once a year on the tenth day of the seventh month in the cult center, in order to expiate for the ritual uncleannness and acts of rebellion, that is, "all the sins of the people." It concludes with the words: "This shall become a rule binding on you for all times, to make for the Israelites once a year the expiation required by all their sins."

The hypothesis ran as follows: The Jerusalem temple had been destroyed and its cult suspended for close to four centuries. Thus the reading of the lesson with its threefold repetition, "a rule binding on you for all times," could not but raise unsettling questions. Expiation is called for, yet expiation as described in the lesson is unavailable, for only in the Temple may effective ritual procedures be carried out. One could imagine that for those who heard the reading the question would arise: are we indeed cut off from any means of reconciliation? Are we indeed awash with sins, transgressions, rebellions from which we have

---

[1] *Pesikta de Rav Kahana* (ed. Bernard Mandelbaum; 2 vols.; New York: Jewish Theological Seminary of America, 1962) 383–400.

no means of extrication? This was a possible existential response to Scripture's words. Turning to the world, the external situation, Jews heard the claim of Christianity that it possessed, through the ultimate sacrifice, the death of Jesus Christ, the power to provide for expiation, atonement, and release from sin, while the synagogue, the church insisted, had no means for atonement.

All this was purely speculative, an endeavor to understand why the chapter said what it said. It was based, in part, on an impressionistic view of Christianity in the region from Caesarea to Antioch. However, the publication of Wilken's volume dealing with John Chrysostom and the Jews[2] has provided evidence that scholarly speculation does, on occasion, find root in reality. Wilken has brought forcibly to our attention the continuing strength and attractiveness of Judaism as a rival to Christianity, thus providing the reason for the Church's polemic endeavors during the period. He has summarized, through his examination of John Chrysostom's homilies against Jews and Judaizers, the arguments thought to be the most telling. One in particular may well be understood to have engendered the response, oblique to be sure but now certainly clear, embodied in our text. It is the argument that the destruction of the Temple in Jerusalem delegitimized Judaism. "Without the temple in Jerusalem 'Jewish worship is hindered, the customs, sacrifices and offerings abolished and things of their law have ceased. One cannot set up an altar, offer a sacrifice, make libations, offer a lamb or incense, read the law, celebrate a festival nor do any other things of this sort outside its gates' (Chrysostom *Jud. et gent.* 16; 48.835)."[3] But this was not John's argument alone. Eusebius of Caesarea in *Demonstratio evangelica* (17a–c) made it as well,[4] so that we may recognize its ubiquity in the region.

Wilken suggests that while at the time of the destruction of Jerusalem theological and ritual problems were raised for Judaism,

> within Judaism the destruction of the temple never assumed the theological importance it had for Christianity, and the religious crisis provoked by the loss of Jerusalem was resolved long before the fourth century. . . . As for the specific problems of the cessation of sacrifices, other Jewish teachers, drawing on resources from Jewish tradition, showed that animal sacrifices were not necessary for reconciliation with God.

---

[2] Robert L. Wilken, *John Chrysostom and the Jews: Rhetoric and Reality in the Late Fourth Century* (Berkeley: University of California Press, 1983).

[3] Ibid., 132.

[4] Ibid., 136.

Wilken quoted a passage from *Abot deRabbi Nathan* in which Rabban Yoḥanan ben Zakkai points to acts of loving kindness as the means of effective atonement.[5] Even were this all so, and it is by no means evident from the sources that such equanimity was universally present, in the polemical situation Wilken graphically evokes, Jewish teachers could not remain silent, unresponsive to the challenge. If then, as seems evident, my original choice of a challenging doctrine was mistaken, Wilken has provided a wider challenge to which the chapter at hand is a paradigmatic response. It is, however, a response that remained within the walls of the synagogue. It was not a direct answer to the church but a strengthening of faith for the Jews and an argument for the benefit of those Christians attracted to Judaism against whom John Chrysostom railed.

Before turning to analysis of the text, it should be noted that the methodological principles underlying it have been discussed by me elsewhere.[6] However, a few technical items should be made clear. The material in this chapter, as everywhere in the collection, is cast in the form of *petiḥa*, a proem, that is a short homiletical introduction leading up to and concluding with the first verse or first several verses of the lesson. The technique is to begin by quoting a verse, generally from the Hagiographa, and developing it in such a way as to arrive safely at the lesson. An authentic proem requires an assonance between some word in the opening verse and a word in the first several verses of the lesson. There are, however, in this collection many composed proems, that is, proems constructed by the redactor out of available sources that have the formal appearance of such, but lack the requisite assonance. In many cases the verse from the lesson is almost arbitrarily tacked on to the homily. Finally, given the space restraints, only the opening and concluding sections will be dealt with here. However, they will suffice to show how the argument is developed.

Although Leviticus 16 deals with the rites of the Day of Atonement in the Temple, the opening verse refers back to the episode in Lev 10:1–7, the offering of strange fire by the two sons of Aaron, Nadab and Abihu, and their deaths:

---

[5] Ibid., 151.

[6] "Toward a Rhetoric of Midrash: A Preliminary Account," in Robert Polzin and Eugene Rothman, eds., *The Biblical Mosaic, Changing Perspectives* (Philadelphia: Fortress; Chico, CA; Scholars Press, 1982) 15–26; "A Theological Treatise on Forgiveness: Chapter Twenty-three of Pesiqta de Rab Kahana," in J. Petuchowski and Ezra Fleischer, eds., *Studies in Aggadah, Targum and Jewish Liturgy* (Jerusalem: Magnes, 1981) 95–107.

וידבר יי אל משה אחרי מות בני אהרן

(And the Lord spoke to Moses after the death of the sons of Aaron)

It is the reference to this event in connection with the Day of Atonement that is the focus of R's theological argument.[7]

The first section of *Pesiq. Rab Kah.* 26 may well be an authentic proem that has been expanded by internal additions. It begins with the statement: R. Simeon bar Abba introduced the verse(s) from Eccl 9:2:

> Because one and the same fate befalls everyone,
> to the righteous and to the wicked,
> to the good, the pure and the impure,
> to him who offers sacrifice and to him who does not;
> as the good, so the sinner,
> the oath-taker and the oath-shunner.

The first phrase, "to the righteous," is interpreted, "this refers to Noah of whom it is written, 'Noah was a righteous man' (Gen 6:9)." The particular fate of Noah is described through a citation: "R. Phineas in the name of R. Yoḥanan in the name of R. Eliezer b. R. Yose the Galilean. 'When Noah left the ark, the lion struck him and so injured him that he became unfit to offer sacrifices. Shem, his son, offered in his stead.'" "'To the wicked'; this refers to Pharaoh Necho." There is no proof-text cited here, but the Munich MS of *Lev. Rab.* reads: "Who said, 'the Lord is righteous but I and my people are wicked'" (Exod 9:23). The fate of Pharaoh Necho is recounted (this may be a continuation of a previous report): "When he sought to sit on Solomon's throne, he did not know how to manipulate its mechanism, so the lion struck and injured him. Both limped until the day of their deaths." To this are appended the words from the verse: "One fate to the righteous and the wicked." Notice that the symmetry of the fate of this pair echoes the symmetry of their names נח and נכו.

The exposition continues: "To the good, the pure, the impure. 'To the good' refers to Moses of whom it is written: 'She saw that he was good'" (Exod 2:2), to which a comment has been added: "He was born circumcised." "'To the pure,' refers to Aaron who dealt with the purities of Israel." Here, too, there is no proof-text. *Lev. Rab.* cites Mal 2:6: "In peace (שלום) and uprightness he walked with me." The effective word may be שלום, echoing שלמים, peace offerings. "'To the impure,' refers to the spies." No proof-text is cited here or in *Lev. Rab.* The conclusion is drawn: "These spoke shamefully of the land

---

[7] R stands for Redactor, my supposed creator of the entire work.

and did not enter into it [the land]; those [Moses and Aaron] who were completely righteous did not enter into it"; with the refrain, a conflated and inexact citation from Eccl 9:2: "To the righteous, to the pure, to the good, to the impure, one fate."

The next words "'To him who offers sacrifice' refer to Josiah, of whom it is written, 'Josiah contributed on behalf of all the lay people present 30,000 small cattle, that is young rams and goats, etc.' (2 Chr 35:7). 'To him who does not offer sacrifice,' refers to Ahab who caused sacrifices on the altar to cease and of whom it is written: 'Ahab slaughtered for him [Jehosephat]' (2 Chr 18:2). He slaughtered for him but he did not slaughter for sacrifices. Both died of arrow wounds." Of Josiah it is written: "The archer shot King Josiah" (2 Chr 35:23). Of Ahab it is written: "A certain man drew his bow at random and hit the king of Israel where the breast-plate joins the plates of the armour" (2 Chr 18:33). With the refrain: "To him who offers sacrifice and to him who does not offer sacrifice, one fate."

Further: "'Alike the good,' this refers to David, as it is written of him, 'of good appearance' (1 Sam 16:2); 'alike the sinner,' this refers to Nebuchadnezzar the wicked, of whom it is written: 'Redeem your sins by righteousness' (Dan 4:24[27]). This one built the Temple and ruled forty years; this one destroyed the Temple and ruled forty-five years. One fate alike for the good and for the wicked."

Again: "'The oath-taker; the oath-shunner.' The oath-taker refers to Zedekiah of whom it is written: 'He also rebelled against King Nebuchadnezzar who had made him swear by God' (2 Chr 36:13)." Here there is a learned note: "By whom did he make him swear? R. Yose b. R. Hanina said: 'He made him swear by the altar.'" "'The oath-shunner,' refers to Samson of whom it is written: 'And Samson said to them, swear to me lest you offend me' (Judg 15:12). This one died with his eyes gouged out and this one died with his eyes gouged out. Of the first it is written: 'He blinded Zedekiah's eyes' (2 Kgs 25:7); of the second: 'The Philistines seized him and gouged out his eyes' (Judg 15:21). 'One fate alike to the oath-taker and the oath-shunner.'"

Another version of the words: "'One fate alike to the righteous,' refers to Aaron of whom it is written 'In peace and uprightness he walked before me' (Mal 2:6). 'To the wicked' refers to the company of Korah of whom it is written: 'Depart from the tents of this wicked man' (Num 16:26)." Before going on to the conclusion it must be noted that, as it stands in Mandelbaum's text, the reference to Aaron as the righteous is unsatisfactory for the contrast is—as we shall see in a moment—between Aaron's two sons and Korah's company. However

MS Carmoly reads "The sons of Aaron"; the second Oxford MS reads "Nadab and Abihu"; the Munich MS of *Lev. Rab.* reads "The sons of Aaron." To return to the text: "These latter entered to offer sacrifice contentiously and came forth burnt; these [the former] entered without contention and came forth burnt. As it is written: 'After the death of the two sons of Aaron.'"

Let me recapitulate what we have heard. The thesis of the argument is the echoing refrain "one fate alike." The proem of R. Simeon bar Abba moves through each of the terms in Eccl 9:2, referring each to a specific individual from the past much like a *petirah* (= pesher). It does not, however, come to a conclusion with the citation of the pentateuchal verse after the tragedies of Zedekiah and Samson have been recounted, for there is no possible connection. Instead, another version of the first pair is cited that can and does lead directly into the pentateuchal verse, Lev 16:1. There are many comments that deserve to be made on each of the various episodes to clarify them and in the full-dress version of this paper I have provided them. Interesting as they are, they do not further the argument; so with regret I am omitting them. They are, I assure you, fascinating.

As I have indicated, "another version" does offer an interpretation of the first phrase of Eccl 9:2, "righteous" and "wicked," that makes possible the transition to Lev 16:1. However, it may be asked, where is the connection between the verses if, as I insist, there must be an assonance between some word or words of the extraneous verse and the opening verse of the lesson? The answer is to be found in Eccl 9:3, assuming that several verses were quoted but not necessarily interpreted. This verse continues a sad refrain of the previous verse, "one fate alike," and concludes with a phrase that assonates almost perfectly with אחרי מות "after the death of," ואחריו אל המיתים "and his end—unto the dead."

What does this first section suggest? It places the sons of Aaron among the righteous and by its regular repetition of the phrase "one fate alike"—a rhetorical device—raises unspoken questions: Is there no rhyme or reason in the world? The righteous and the wicked share the same fate. Is life utterly fortuitous?

In the next section the apparent fortuitousness of life is mitigated by the introduction of the idea that behind all this is מדת הדין, a surrogate name for God as the judge, the source of justice. Section three is made up of a series of warnings to the wicked not to expect joy in this world, for the righteous do not do so. A number of examples are given, concluding with a reference to the sorrow of Elisheva, the mother of Nadab and Abihu, over their death. Section four ends with a reference to God's mourning the death of the two. The next five or six sections that seem to destroy the argument by insisting on the wickedness of the two are, on the basis of their lack in significant manuscripts, and their incompatibility with the strong emphasis in the concluding section on their righteousness, suspect.

Section eleven, the concluding piece, picks up the theme of their righteousness and uses it to provide the answer to the existential question with which we began: How is atonement to be provided in the absence of the Temple and its ceremonies?

> Said R. Abba bar Zebina: "Why is the narrative of the death of Miriam (Num 20:1) juxtaposed to the chapter dealing with the ashes of the red heifer (Numbers 19)? To teach that just as the ashes of the red heifer purify so did the death of Miriam."
> Said R. Yudan: "Why was the mention of the death of Aaron (Deut 10:6) juxtaposed to the narrative of the shattering of the tablets (Deut 9:13–29)? To teach that the death of Aaron was as grievous to God as the shattering of the tablets."
> Said R. Hiyya bar Abba: "The sons of Aaron died on the first of Nisan [in the spring]. Why are their deaths mentioned in connection with Yom Kippur [six months later, in the fall]? To teach that just as Yom Kippur atones, so do the deaths of the righteous. Whence do we know that Yom Kippur atones? 'For on this day atonement shall be made for you to cleanse you (Lev 16:30).' Whence do we know that the deaths of the righteous atone? It is written: 'They buried the bones of Saul and Jonathan his son in the land of Benjamin in Zela in the tomb of his father Kish and they did all that the king commanded and after that God gave heed to the supplication for the land (2 Sam 21:14).'"

The argument of this paper is that in the face of Christianity's claim that the destruction of the Temple brought to an end Judaism's legitimacy, response was called for on the part of Jewish teachers. That response, present in the material here discussed, may be summarized in the following concluding statement.

The deaths of the righteous that seem so fortuitous, are indeed involved in divine justice for they are the means by which atonement is, in the absence of the Temple, accomplished. When one looks at life with its intermingling of joy and sorrow, with its inexplicable ambiguities, from this vantage point, it will be recognized that one is not bereft of a means of reconciliation. God's own justice provides for it by *accepting* these deaths as the means of atonement.

PAUL'S ARGUMENTS AS EVIDENCE OF THE CHRISTIANITY FROM WHICH HE DIVERGED

Morton Smith
Columbia University

While the topic of this paper is familiar, I believe that one source of information has been generally neglected: the arguments that Paul does not use. Since Bishop Stendahl has done so much to illuminate Paul's words, it seems appropriate to dedicate to him this brief sketch of things to be learned from Paul's silence.

First Corinthians is the epistle with which to start; it tells us most about the community to which Paul was writing, and shows him in closest dialogue with its members. Paul claims to have founded the community ("I planted, Apollos watered," 3:6; there is a suggestion that Kephas came third, 1:12), but we cannot assume that when Corinthian practices differed from Paul's wishes the differences were merely distortions of Paul's teachings. His converts may not have been forgetting his lessons, but learning from others'. Later missionaries may have brought earlier practices. Kephas certainly could have—Paul claims to have made his first friendly contact with the Jerusalem church by going to see him (Gal 1:18). Again, if Acts 18:25 truly reports that Apollos at first "taught accurately the things about Jesus, understanding only the baptism of John," he would seem to have come from a circle of Jesus' followers that antedated or, at least, preserved a tradition independent of that of the Jerusalem group.

Against the supposition that the Corinthians' misbehavior resulted only from misunderstandings of Paul, there is also the fact that Paul has no hesitation about pointing out a misunderstanding when he thinks one has occurred (as in 5:9−10). Thus when he does not allege misunderstanding we should not suppose it, though it cannot always be ruled out.

On other matters, however, Paul is far more reticent. For instance, when making attacks he does not usually name names. Thus his attack on worldly wisdom and especially on rhetoric, in 1:17−2:16, is generally thought to be aimed at Apollos, but Apollos is mentioned only before it, and afterwards when subordinated to Paul in 3:4–6. Acts praised Apollos for his learning and eloquence (18:24). If he brought these accomplishments to a community in which there were "not many wise by worldly standards, not many powerful, not many well born" (1:26), as Paul had brought speaking with tongues (which he did more than any of his converts, 14:18), such personal distinctions, though not primarily matters of the new cult, doubtless led to the formation of different groups around the different leaders. This may account for Paul's reluctance to name Apollos in the attack. To have attacked him by name would have alienated his adherents, some of whom Paul may have hoped to win over.

If this suggestion seems plausible, it may apply also to the next section, the attack on sexual libertinism, where again the chief offender is unnamed. Of course he was not Apollos, but can we infer that, like Apollos, he was not a mere eccentric, but a ringleader? Is not this implied by Paul's complaint that many Corinthians are proud because he is committing incest (5:2) and are claiming that "all things," and particularly irregular sexual relations, "are permissible" (6:12 *bis*)? If such liberty had become an important element in the cult (as pagans long charged that it was; Justin *Dial.* 10.1, etc.) we can be sure it had not come from Paul. He was of ascetic disposition, unmarried (9:5), beating his body (flagellation?), and keeping it under as a slave (9:27). Paul had already written the Corinthians that they should not associate with licentious persons (5:9). Does he again deliberately avoid specification when he suggests that they misunderstood and thought he referred only to non-Christians? This enables him to ignore their defiance and merely correct their mistake.

He insists that he has already judged the single, unnamed offender (so as) to hand him over to Satan for "the destruction of the flesh" (5:3–5). Is this an allusion to the man's having fallen ill, or an attempt to represent his further indulgences as self-destruction consequent on the demonic possession for which, as disciplinary, Paul claims credit? He also claims that, although not in Corinth, he had, "by the power of our Lord Jesus" (presumably an invocation using Jesus' name) united the Corinthians' spirits with his own in this disciplinary action. They would have known nothing of this, since their spirits would have been called out of them at the time. Now they are told of it and warned that they have willy-nilly been united with Paul in this curse. The act has been done; the consequences follow.

Being parties to the curse, they are not to eat with, but to treat as impure, any Christian (again Paul names none) who has a bad reputation for sexual or other vices. Shortly afterwards (6:12–20) Paul returns to the subject with additional arguments central to his theology: their bodies are temples of the Holy Spirit and members of the body of Christ. This emphasis on mystical union again enables him to pass over the actual schism.

From this height he comes down to answer a letter some Corinthians have sent him. It, too, began with a question on sexual relations. He begins, this time, with a general rule: "It is best for a man not to touch a woman" (7:1). That this is his rule, not the Corinthians', appears not only from its incompatibility with what was evidently going on in Corinth, but also from the fact that Paul defends it as an ideal (7:8, 32–35, 37) and permits marriage (for the incontinent) only grudgingly, because "it is better to marry than to burn" (7:9). That the teachings of such a man had given rise to the practices of the Corinthians is incredible. Where did the practices come from? Apollos? Or Kephas? The teaching that sexual acts are morally indifferent could easily have been derived from Jesus' reported saying, "There is nothing outside a human being which, by entering, can make the recipient impure" (Mark 7:15).

The opponents must have had some strong support because Paul now makes an amazing concession: "All things are permissible for me, but not all things are beneficial; all things are permissible, but I will not be subjected by any" (6:12). But if all things are permissible, then fornication is permissible, and argument must show that it is not beneficial, or enslaves the practitioner, or whatever. Paul has already used the arguments that Christians are bodies of Christ and temples of the Spirit, but these are inconclusive. What if Christ and the Spirit should be indifferent to the physical activities of the bodies they dwell in, as they must be to their physical impurities? The doctrine of salvation by union with a deity lays wide open the possibility of moral indifference, and Paul was much too clever to be unaware of this. Hence his resort to rhetoric instead of reason.

Why, however, should he have put himself into so weak a position? Why such a damaging concession? We are almost compelled to suppose that "all things are permissible" was, in Corinthian Christianity, a generally accepted principle, and that Paul, since he wished to persuade his readers, had to argue from this principle that they all accepted. Once he had made the concession he tried to cut down its implications as far as he could.

These suppositions are supported by the fact that Paul had to come back, later on, to the same damaging doctrine, this time with reference to eating things sacrificed to idols, and he used exactly the same technique, even the same rhetorical device: Yes . . . but. "All things are permissible—but not all things are beneficial. All things are permissible—but not all things are constructive" (10:23). The essential claim of the libertine position is conceded, *but* prudential considerations are then introduced to limit the practice of Christian liberty. Anything may be eaten, *but* idols represent demons, and demons may dwell in the meat that has been sacrificed to them, and therefore to eat it may result in demonic possession, and might make Jesus jealous; besides, it might scandalize a weaker brother. This begs the obvious answers: the Christian, united with Christ, should fear no demons; God cannot be jealous of nonentities; the ignorant brother should be instructed, not hoodwinked. Paul's position is again untenable, again because of the same concession. Why did he repeatedly concede a principle of which he was repeatedly unwilling to face the consequences? Most likely because he found this principle embedded in the religion he had first persecuted and then, by involuntary conversion, been forced to accept. Often, when the ego is defeated, it goes on fighting; the fallen Pharisee becomes a reluctant and sanctimonious libertine. No wonder Paul's personality so often broke down that he was famous for speaking with tongues.

The two verses just discussed, 6:12 and 10:23, are the only ones in which Paul says that all things are permitted, or even uses the verb form *exestin*. We have so little of Paul's writings that I have little faith in fashionable discoveries which show the vocabulary of one or another passage to be "non-Pauline" and argue thence that the passage reflects Paul's use of "an earlier source." (Use of "a later source" is very rare.) Paul must have had a vocabulary larger than the two thousand-odd words used in his genuine letters, and a man's vocabulary and style can change widely in the different circumstances of a dozen years. Nevertheless, I must admit that in this instance, because of the evidence from the contexts, this peculiarity of wording does seem evidence that *panta exestin* ("all things are permissible") was not Paul's own formula, but a cliche of the Corinthian church.

Paul's concession of this principle, however unwilling, was of course exploited by his nomistic opponents. They drew from the principle the same conclusions as did the libertines, but used them as reductions to absurdity. When Paul explained the Mosaic Law as introduced to increase sin, that Christ's grace might be given more fully to overcome the sin, they cynically went on to the consequence, "Let us do evil that good may come" (Rom 3:8) and attributed this to Paul. His indignant reaction does not conceal his inability to refute the argument; nor does the malicious misrepresentation prove that such conclusions were based on teachings peculiar to Paul. That they were not is proved by his character, and by the innumerable attempts in his letters to avoid or mitigate such consequences of principles he must have found in his new faith.

These attempts, in turn, drew attacks from the libertines, attacks reflected in 1 Corinthians where, after having discouraged marriage, outlawed all sexual irregularities, and cut down drastically the use of food offered to idols, he bursts out in an angry passage of self-defense: "Am I not free? Am I not an apostle? Have I not seen Jesus, our Lord? Are you not my work in the Lord? If to others I am not an apostle, at least to you I am! . . . My apology to those who judge me is this: Do we not have authorization to eat and drink? Do we not have authorization to lead around a Christian woman, as do the other apostles, and the brothers of the Lord, and Kephas? Or do only I and Barnabas not have authorization not to work?" (9:1–6). From this he goes off into a long defense of his refusal to accept support from them, and then comes around to his underlying principle, "Being free of all requirements, I have subjected myself to all, in order to win more converts. . . . I became all things to all men so that by all means I might save some" (9:19, 22).

This tells us clearly what his opponents were saying: He was not really an apostle of Jesus. He had never even seen Jesus. Consequently he did not have the special authorization Jesus was thought to have given to his apostles and brothers (but not to his other followers?). This authorization included freedom (from the Mosaic Law), and especially the rights to eat and drink what they chose, to keep a Christian consort (the Greek word means both "woman" and "wife"), and to exact payment for their services, as would any qualified magician. Christian salvation was evidently conceived as a special supernatural service which only Jesus' authorized representatives could provide, and for which he had authorized them to charge as they saw fit. Psychoanalysis provides a striking parallel.

These accusations against which Paul defends himself are precisely the ones he again tries to meet in the last section of 2 Corinthians, chaps. 10–13, a section so often discussed that I must apologize for summarizing it once more. (My excuse is that the discussions have necessitated restatement of the plain sense and implications of the text.) Plainly Paul has an opponent who claims to be "of Christ" (10:7). Paul does not deny it, but replies, "So am I," and asserts his authorization by the Lord (10:8). He will not compare himself with "those who recommend themselves" (10:12—presumably members of a group with whom he would not compare well). So he appeals, as before, to his work, especially his conversion of the Corinthians (10:13–18). However, lest they be corrupted as the serpent corrupted Eve (in rabbinic legend, sexually), he insists that "the one who has come" to them preaches no other Jesus and gives no other spirit than they had already received from him, Paul (11:1–4). "For I reckon I am in no respect inferior to the apostles of the highest rank. . . . Was it a fault . . . that I preached the gospel . . . to you without charge?" (11:7–11, again defending his authorization). Now the competitors become clearer. They are "Hebrews," "Israelites," "seed of Abraham," "servants of Christ"—all these Paul is too, and more (11:22–29). They have "visions and revelations of the Lord" (12:1); Paul has had so many revelations that God had to afflict him with some sort of physical infirmity to prevent him from being thought a supernatural being (12:6–10). He has performed "the signs of an apostle"— the marvels and miracles—just as the others have (12:12). Finally, as before, the Corinthians, influenced by these opponents, have become proud and been guilty of "impurity and fornication and lasciviousness" (12:21) and Paul once again warns that he will use against them his mysterious spiritual power, which he still hopes will not hurt them (chap. 13). There should be no mistaking the close correspondence of this situation to that in 1 Corinthians, and the leader of these opponents, described as they just have been, must here be Kephas, who was already there. The competition has become more severe, Apollos is now inconspicuous, the areas of dispute have widened and the emphases have shifted a bit, but the structure remains the same.

How can all this be reconciled with Galatians? Paul never tried to reconcile them. In Galatia he was involved in a different argument. In Corinth he is claiming to be equal to Kephas and the other original apostles; they offer no other Jesus than he does. In Galatians his claim is to be *sui generis*. He received his gospel not from men, and particularly not from the Jerusalem apostles, but from Christ himself. When he did go up to consult with them, the "pillars" of the Jerusalem church, James and Kephas among them, added nothing (well, almost nothing) to his message, but agreed that he and Barnabas should have the apostolate of the uncircumcised, they, of the circumcised (Gal 1:1–2:10).

After this there were evidently changes in Jerusalem, for when Kephas came to Antioch he at first ate with Gentiles, but then was so frightened by the arrival of the representatives of James, "those of the circumcision" (2:12), that he gave up the practice and hypocritically pretended to observe the Jewish food laws. Paul then attacked him in an argument which took for granted their agreement that salvation by

Christ had freed them from the requirements of the Mosaic Law (2:14–21). By contrast to this, Paul attacks the Judaizers for introducing "a different gospel" (Gal 1:6)—presumably that of the apostolate of the circumcision, since the attack in the body of the letter centers on the requirement of circumcision. The opponent behind the trouble in Galatia is someone of importance (therefore again unnamed) "who shall bear (his) judgment, whoever (i.e., however great) he is" (Gal 5:10). There is intense hostility (5:12), but no clear indication of such personal rivalry as appears in 1 and 2 Corinthians.

Beyond this Paul's characteristic silence does not permit us to go. But the story in Acts 12:17 suggests that about 44 Kephas fled Jerusalem and James was left in charge. We know Paul spoke of Kephas as his first important friend in the Jerusalem church and as one of the leading parties in the agreement eventually reached with the authorities there (Gal 1:18; 2:9). John 1:43 tells us that Kephas was Peter, and Acts 10:1–11:18 tells us that Peter took the lead in converting uncircumcised Gentiles; 15:7–11 makes him speak in favor of such conversion and in support of Paul and Barnabas at the legendary "Council of Jerusalem." Is it unlikely that, after Kephas left, the Jerusalem authorities decided to extend more vigorously to the Gentiles their own "apostolate of the circumcision"? And is it not likely that Kephas and others of Jesus' original followers, who had prudently, while in Jerusalem, maintained an appearance of legal observance, rapidly dropped this when they went out among the Gentiles, and behaved as Jesus had and as Paul says Kephas initially did? That in view of James' hostility Kephas was won over by Paul's pleading (or by his own interests and inclinations) would not be surprising.

These likely events would explain the opposition Paul encountered from both sides. His legalistic opponents, "those of the circumcision," doubtless appealed to the authority of James. His libertine opponents were those of the circle of Kephas, whose members soon gave up the pretense of legal observance, took full advantage of their prestige in Gentile churches as true Israelites and fully empowered apostles of the Messiah, and returned with gusto to their Lord's original neglect of the Law. We may see in them the first "back to Jesus" Christians.

POSTSCRIPT: The story in Acts 21:18–26 of the meeting of Paul and James, though not impossible, is so likely to be harmonistic that it cannot be used for evidence in this matter.

THE ARMENIAN VISION OF EZEKIEL

Michael E. Stone
Hebrew University of Jerusalem

The document which is presented here is extant in MS no. 31 of the Library of the Mechitarist Fathers in Vienna.[1] It was described by J. Dashian in his magistral catalogue of that collection.[2] The MS is without colophons and so the names of the scribe, as well as the place in which it was copied, remain unknown. Dashian dated it on palaeographic grounds to the 17th-18th centuries. Although the primary document transmitted is a collection of fables, there are many diverse documents interspersed among them. One is the present work, of which Dashian notes no other copy.[3]

The chief features of the document will emerge from the discussion below. It deals with the exegesis of the vision of the chariot in chapter 1 of the biblical book of Ezekiel, a chapter which was of great importance in the development of the Jewish speculative and mystical traditions, starting already in the third century BCE. It is intriguing to see how this chapter of scripture was interpreted in a later Christian tradition and how certain specific points of that interpretation are most closely paralleled in rabbinic literature and exegesis. The *Nachleben* of biblical and postbiblical Jewish traditions in the Christian churches is an important chapter in intellectual and literary history.

The work was apparently composed in Armenian. This is evident from its dependence, pointed out in many places, on the Armenian text of the Bible. The language is not "pure" classical Armenian, but is

---

[1] We are grateful to the Abbot, Fr. Grigoris Manian, who graciously made a copy of the text available and granted permission to publish it.

[2] *Catalog der armenischen Handschriften in der Mechitaristen-Bibliothek zu Wein* (Haupt-Catalog der armenischen Handschriften 1.2; Vienna: Mechitarists, 1895) German section 24-25 and Armenian section 177-79.

[3] Nor has it turned up in a search of chief Armenian MS catalogues. This does not necessarily mean that no other copy exists. Mention of it may have escaped us or, since it is short, it may have not been listed by editors of MS catalogues.

typified by a number of medieval forms. These will be discussed in detail on another occasion, when the Armenian text will be published. Here, we shall give an English translation, exegetical notes, and some general comments. Our purpose is to make the document available to scholars of Judaism and Christianity whose attention it might otherwise have escaped.[4]

The line numbers reflect those of the Armenian text. Few emendations have been made and such instances are marked by pointed brackets: < >. Words in round brackets are supplied by the editor for the sake of clarity in English: ( ).

The Vision of Ezekiel

1   (fol. 52ᵛ) This is the vision of Ezekiel which he saw in the
land of the Chaldeans: a cruciform chariot, which <had> four
(front) sides and in the middle of them, four beasts. And the
faces of the beasts were of a man and a lion, of an ox and an
eagle, each one fourfold: four (faces) of a man, four of a
5   lion, four of / an ox and four of an eagle. And they stood on
feet: they did not have thighs or knees; the feet and hoofs
were tall. And each one had eight hands, and each hand had
wings, and each wing <had> eyes. And there were two wings on
the feet, and two which covered their faces due to reverence
of God, and one wing on the shoulders, beneath the chariot. /
10   And the shoulders were full of eyes. And on the four edges of
the chariot were wheels. And each single wheel was like a
sun, as of a wagon. And in the midst of each one, another
wheel turned as if within the wheel, as the wheel turned
around in the midst of the wheel. And it (Scripture) says
that they went in all directions, and that they did not turn
backwards (Ezek 1:12). And how was this, that they went in
15   the four directions of the world and were not / separated
(fol. 53ʳ) from one another? And that they went to
Jerusalem, having hastened to Babylon? Understand well with
your mind! The beasts were looking in the four directions of
the world, four faces in each direction, and they went in all
the directions. However, in three <of the> directions they

[4] Appreciation is expressed to Moshe Greenberg who read an early draft of this article and gave me the benefit of his profound knowledge of the book of Ezekiel. His insightful comments are reflected at very many points, particularly throughout the exegetical notes.

went upwards and rose from the earth, and in that direction
which was towards Jerusalem they moved forwards upon the air,
20 and / it approached and came to Jerusalem. The others
went in the direction of their faces, proceeding above the
three directions. But the one went straight ahead so that they
arrived at Jerusalem. And the whole chariot was like the sun.
Scripture says that the likeness of the firmament was upon
the chariot and upon the firmament was the likeness of
sapphire stone, and upon the sapphire was the likeness of
25 thrones / throwing out sparks. And upon the throne was
seated the likeness of a son of man—which is the Word of God,
become man—the upper (part) like the sun and the lower part
the likeness of fire. And he (or: it) was encompassed by the
appearance of light like the appearance of the rainbow, which
is extended upon the clouds (Ezek 1:22, 26–28) and is the
likeness of the glory of God. Such a marvelous vision is not
to be found in all the prophets and it is the perception of
the mind. /
30 But, of what was it (the vision) granted? The man is the
image of God and king of the world, the lion (fol. 53ᵛ) king
of the beasts, the ox king of the cattle, the eagle king of
the birds; and God, King of kings seated above all of them
35 takes providential care of them, pitying or rebuking / each
one according to his worthiness.
    Again, the king of the Medes and the king of the
Babylonians and the king of Egypt and the king of the Romans
having seized the four beasts, went to destroy Jerusalem; and
their chariot-driver was God. For at that time God said by
40 means of a prophet: "<I> have issued a command / concerning
you to the host of Ashkenaz and to the kingdom of the
Ararateans" (Jer 51:27).
    And that Nebuchadnezzar himself had the form of the four
of them: wh<en> he was punished by God he became a beast, in
his forepart like an ox and in his latter part like a lion.
His nails grew like of a leopard and they were sharp
like the talons of an eagle, and his nature is of man. And
45 led / by God he came and destroyed Jerusalem.
    Again, in this tripartite soul of ours: the rational is
the man, the choleric the lion, the desirous the ox, the
contemplative—which is knowledge—the eagle, and the
spirit of virtue (? the virtuous soul) is the chariot of God.
    And the truth of these things: they are used of the

50 evangelists. The man is Matthew / who begins from His
    humanity. (fol. 54^r) The lion (is) for Mark for he says in
    a leonine way that Jesus went forth from the currents of the
    Jordan—and He was, he says, with the beasts for forty days
    and (he relates this) briefly, in a leonine fashion, as a
    lion speedily seizes his prey. The ox, indeed, (is) for Luke
55 who tells of the ox brought to slaughter in the parable of /
    the return, and leads the teaching of the Gospel in a steady
    and broad furrow. But the eagle (is) John, high-flying in
    theology, who cuts a high, new and strange path, soaring to
    the bosom of the Unknown. He is the genealogist <of> the
    only-begotten God. These are bound to the wings (or: arms) of
    the four-faced cross. And they give repose to the incarnated
60 God, by discoursing theologically / everywhere on him who is
    blessed for ever and ever. Amen.

Notes on the Vision of Ezekiel

1 *in the land of the Chaldeans*: cf. Ezek 1:1.

chariot: term not used in Ezekiel 1 of the vision. First occurs in Sir 49:8.

<had>: the dative case of *or* would be expected. In general the language is quite anomalous if judged by the norm of "classical" Armenian. Thus note the use of *amēn mēk*, and the irregular use of the cases, particularly the use of the nominative for the accusative, cf. *t‹ikunk‹n* in line 9.

faces: the Armenian word is not found in Armenian Ezekiel 1.

in the middle of them, four beasts: cf. Ezek 1:5. The description seems to fit Armenian representations of the Divine chariot, such as that in Jerusalem, MS no. 1925 of the year 1269 CE.[5] There Christ is seated on a throne borne by a chariot which is symbolically represented by one wheel within another wheel. The spokes of the lower wheel are four and form a St. Andrew's cross. The spokes protrude beyond the rim of the wheel and at the end of each is a cherub. Each cherub has four identical faces: the upper right hand cherub—four lions, the lower right hand cherub—four oxen, the upper left hand cherub—four humans and the lower left hand cherub—four eagles. Each cherub has six wings: one pair crossed beneath the chariot, one pair crossed on the opposite

---

[5] *Apud* B. Narkiss and M. E. Stone, *Armenian Art Treasures of Jerusalem* (Jerusalem: Masada, 1979) fig. 85; note that by printer's error that plate is mirror image.

side of the cherub, and the third, middle pair extended, one on each side, so that the whole has a cruciform aspect. There are eyes on the upper part (the shoulders) of the wings and on the wheels. No hands or arms are visible. In the painting, all of this cherub throne is held, like a banner, by a hand coming out of the clouds on the lower, right side.

faces—lion: cf. Ezek 1:10.

eagle: This interpretation, i.e., that each beast had four identical faces, is based on Ezek 10:4 and also lies behind the painting referred to above.

5 *stood*: the Armenian word *kngneal* does not occur in Ezekiel 1.

hoofs: same word in Armenian Ezek 1:7. The description reflects Ezek 1:7: "their legs were straight" and the same interpretation may be found in rabbinic sources, e.g., *Gen Rab* 65 (Theodor-Albeck 738). The "tall hoofs" might reflect the same sort of speculation as the *Shiur Komah* material in *b. Hag.* 13a which speaks of the mythical proportions of the beasts.

eight hands: The word *jeṙn* does not occur in the plural, which is grammatically anomalous. The interpretation that each beast had four (sets of) wings probably derives from Ezek 1:6, although it is more easily perceived in Hebrew than in Armenian. The eight hands issue from a combination of this interpretation of the wings with Ezek 1:8. In fact, the disposition of the wings as detailed in the next sentence is derived not from Ezekiel, but from Isa 6:2 "with two he covered his face and with two he covered his feet." Similarly, in the painting in Jerusalem MS no. 1925 only six wings are represented.

10 *the shoulders—eyes*: verbatim Armenian Ezek 1:18; see also Ezek 10:12. The wheels in our text are not said to be full of eyes, but they are so represented in the painting in Jerusalem MS no. 1925.

wheels—sun: cf. Ezek 1:14.

turned: word not in Ezekiel 1.

turned(2)—the wheel: verbatim Ezek 1:16.

they went—backwards: verbatim Ezek 1:12.

15 *Jerusalem*: The chariot hastened to Babylon thus according with chap. 1 and to Jerusalem as is implied by chap. 8.

20 *in the direction of their faces*: Ezek 1:12.

sun: This is apparently a reflection of Hebrew חשמל. Admittedly, this appears in Ezek 1:14 as *čaiagaʿytʿkʿ*, but the text here follows the

Armenian of Ezek 1:27 which introduces the sun into the description of the upper part of the body of the enthroned figure. See line 26, below.

likeness of the firmament upon: Ezek 1:22.

upon the firmament—thrones: Ezek 1:26. The plural of thrones" is easily comparable to the plural in *Death of Adam* 17.[6] The throne was upon the sapphire and not a sapphire throne. Thus 1:26 is interpreted by Armenian Ezekiel.

25 *throwing out sparks*: the word occurs in Ezek 1:4.

And upon—man: Ezek 1:26. Note that our text reads son of man, doubtless a Christian touch, as is clear too from the following phrase.

the upper—fire: Ezek 1:27. The phrases from this verse continue in the next clause.

appearance of the—clouds: Verbatim from Ezek 1:28.

30 *the man*: This interpretation of the four beasts is also to be found in *Midr. Tanḥ.* (S. Buber) *Beshallaḥ* 14 (2.61) and parallel in *Exod Rab* 23.3.

40 The citation from Jeremiah 51:27 differs from all texts of Jeremiah, but is clearly based on the Armenian version.

forepart—lion: The sentence is based on *Vita Daniel* and closest to the second of the two Armenian recensions published by S. Yovsepʿiancʿ, *Uncanonical Books of the Old Testament.*[7]

His nails—leopard: A detail found of Nebuchadnezzar neither in Daniel 4 nor in *Vita Daniel.* The leopard is mentioned in a different context in Dan 7:4, but details from that chapter were used to describe Nebuchadnezzar.

talons of an eagle: the detail but not the language occurs in Dan 4:30 and not in the *Vita Daniel.*

nature—man: the detail but not the terminology derives from Dan 7:4 which is applied by *Vita Daniel* to Nebuchadnezzar. The word "nature" does not occur in either source.

---

[6] See note in M. E. Stone, *Armenian Apocrypha Relating to the Patriarchs and Prophets* (Jerusalem: Academy of Sciences, 1982).

[7] (in Armenian; Venice: Mechitarists, 1986) 219.

General Comments

The text falls into two parts. The first, from line 1 to line 29, is fundamentally a retelling of the vision of Ezekiel 1, based in part on actual citations and very close paraphrases of the text of Ezekiel. Throughout, however, the document bears the character of commentary. This is evident from a number of features. First, the citation of Scripture as an authority, so lines 14, 22, 41. This last is the only clear quotation taken from outside the book of Ezekiel. Moreover, the author poses questions to the text cited, so lines 13–14 "And how was this . . ." (a question about the text of Ezekiel 1:12 just cited), or turns rhetorically to his reader, "Understand well with your mind!" or comments, wonderingly, after he has related the vision "Such a marvellous vision is not to be found in all the prophets, and it is the perception of the mind."

This last phrase is one of two clear reflections of ancient "psychological" assumptions drawn from common Greek analyses of man. The second is to be found in the rather confused allegory of lines 46ff. likening the beasts to the various parts of the soul. Here the author is in some difficulty since he has a cliché of the tripartite soul, but four beasts, and so he in fact does not interpret the human face specifically, but only by implication, and then merged with the idea of the virtuous soul as the chariot of God.

After the first section which is an expanded paraphrase of Ezekiel 1, we find a number of allegories by which the vision is interpreted. First, the four faces are the rulers of the four classes of creations—man is king of the world, the lion of the wild beasts, the ox of the cattle, and the eagle of the birds. God, King of kings, is above them and cares for all. The second allegory is somewhat confused. It starts with the word "again" which serves to introduce a second interpretation and recurs in line 46. This is part of the learned or scholastic technique of the text, and other formulae with similar or analogous functions are to be found in various Armenian apocrypha.[8]

In this second allegory the author wishes to interpret the four faces of the beasts as a reference to kings of four kingdoms, of the Medes, the Babylonians, the Egyptians, and the Romans. In this general idea of four kingdoms he is dependent, of course, on ancient tradition going

---

[8] See the examples and texts cited by M. E. Stone, "The History of the Forefathers, Adam and His Sons and Grandsons," *Journal of the Society for Armenian Studies* 1 (1984) 83–84. The formula is like the Rabbis' דבר אחר in sense and function.

back at least to Daniel 2 and 7.[9] It had many interpretations, however, and the series Medes, Babylonians, Egyptians, and Romans is an odd one. Having seen the analogy of the four kingdoms and the four beasts, however, the author does not really fit them smoothly together, and he has the image of the kings of the nations as the beasts of the Divine chariot, with its Divine Charioteer attacking Jerusalem. This interpretation is supported by the quotation from Jer 51:27 given by the text. This attack by all the nations is clearly a reference to the eschatological battle which was a common theme of many of the later apocalypses in Armenian and in other languages.[10]

The third allegory is of Nebuchadnezzar. The beast into which he is turned according to Daniel 4 is described in a potpourri of various sources: Daniel 7 and the *Vita Daniel* being the most prominent. The author draws two of the beasts, the lion and the ox, from the interpretation of Daniel 4 in the *Vita Daniel*. The other two faces of the cherub are drawn one from Daniel 4 and the other from Daniel 7 as interpreted by the *Vitae Prophetarum*. The leopard, which has no place among the faces of the cherubs, is mentioned by Dan 7:6 and is taken up again in the description of the beast which rose from the sea in Rev 13:2. Although these sources might explain the occurrence of the leopard here, its introduction is clumsy, since the leopard is a fifth beast, not relevant to the allegory. Nothing is made, either in Daniel 7 nor in Revelation 13, of the leopard's claws.[11] The Nebuchadnezzar allegory is related to the former one of the eschatological war by his attack on Jerusalem, which, directed by God, is exactly parallel to the attack by the four kings. This is, of course, connected with the exegesis of the Ezekiel chariot as going towards Jerusalem that is to be found in the paraphrase in lines 15ff.

---

[9] See H. H. Rowley, *Darius the Mede and the Four World Empires in the Book of Daniel* (Cardiff: University of Wales Press,1964); J. W. Swain, "The Theory of Four Monarchies—Opposition History Under the Roman Empire," *CP* 25 (1940) 1–21; D. Flusser, "The Four Empires in the Fourth Sibyl and in the Book of Daniel," *Israel Oriental Studies* 2 (1972) 148–75.

[10] In Armenian see particularly *The Seventh Vision of Daniel* (ET in J. Issaverdens, *The Uncanonical Writings of the Old Testament* [Venice: Mechitarists, 1934] 247–55 and Armenian and German in G. Kalemkiar, *Die Siebente Vision Daniels* [Die Apokryphen bei den Armeniern 3; Vienna: 1892]); the *Vision of Enoch the Just* (ibid., 238–47), etc. This theme is also common to many of the other Jewish and Christian apocalypses of the Byzantine period.

[11] I am indebted to David Satran who shared his learning with me in everything relating to Nebuchadnezzar.

Then follows the allegory of the soul of man that was mentioned above, and finally the famous Christian topos of the beasts that symbolize the evangelists. In the form in which it is found here, it is common in artistic works from the fifth century.[12] The author has difficulty with Mark and can only explain Mark's leonine symbol by his immediate (literary) leap into the baptism of Christ and from that to his forty days in the desert (Mark 1:9–11 and 1:12). Luke is the ox in virtue of the "ox brought to slaughter" in the parable of the return of the Prodigal Son (Luke 15:11–32). Luke forms somewhat of an exception, for the three other evangelists are characterized by the nature of their first chapter. Thus John too is characterized by his first chapter. He is the "genealogist of the only-begotten God" which is a clear reference to John 1:18.

The text concludes with a brief doxology.

[12] See M. H. Shepherd, Jr., "Evangelists," *IDB* 2. 181.

ENABLING LANGUAGE IN PAUL

Albert C. Sundberg, Jr.
Garrett-Evangelical Theological Seminary

Paul of Tarsus, first-century Diaspora-Jew-become-Christian, became, through Augustine and Luther, the canonical theologian for Protestant Christianity. Consequently, his theology has been of overwhelming interest, whether in research, teaching, or preaching. This dominating concern with his theology, however, has diverted interest from other significant deposits Paul left us in his letters. F. W. Beare, in a study on "St. Paul as Spiritual Director,"[1] has shown that this itinerant preacher of primitive Christianity has left us a record of his pastoral concerns that can still serve as a useful model for the modern pastor. A growing number of scholarly articles on Paul and women shows that while Paul sometimes simply reflects a male-dominated social reality,[2] he occasionally envisions freedom and equality for women.[3] Disappointment in other aspects of Paul's social perspective is largely overcome when that perspective is sought within his teaching on the church which, in his apocalyptic orientation, would be the continuing social reality.[4]

---

[1] *StEv* 2 (1964) 303–14.

[2] E.g., 1 Cor 11:3–16; 1:33b–36 (Col 3:18; Eph 5:22–24).

[3] Krister Stendahl, *The Bible and the Role of Women: A Case Study in Hermeneutics* (trans. Emilie T. Sander; Philadelphia: Fortress, 1966) 32–37; Calvin Miller, "St. Paul and the Liberated Woman," *Christianity Today* 15 (1971) 999–1000; Robin Scroggs, "Paul: Chauvinist or Liberationist?" *Christian Century* 89 (1972) 307–9; idem, "Paul and the Eschatological Woman," *JAAR* 40 (1972) 283–303; idem, "Paul and the Eschatological Woman: Revisited," *JAAR* 42 (1974) 532–37; G. B. Caird, "Paul and Women's Liberty," *BJRL* 54 (1972) 268–81; W. J. Harrington, "St. Paul and the Status of Women," *AusCathRec* 50 (1973) 39–50; Elaine Pagels, "Paul and Women: A Response to Recent Discussion," *JAAR* 42 (1974) 538—49.

[4] J. Thuruthumaly, "The Church and the Social Concern in Pauline Writings," *Biblebhashyam* 4 (1978) 229–41; J. A. Zieder, "Paul and New Society," *Epworth Review* 8 (1981) 68–74, 75–79; Anthony Tambasco, "Pauline Ethics: An Application of Liberation Hermeneutics," *BTB* 12 (1982) 125–27.

It is not my intention here, however, to try to show that Paul was indeed "all things to all men" (1 Cor 9:22). Rather, I want to point out another deposit Paul left in his letters that could be significant for us in view of our growing interest in understanding ourselves and one another. That deposit, which I call enabling language, consists of the encouraging, supportive, complimentary language with which Paul addresses the recipients of his letters. I know of no comprehensive treatment of this language; it is largely ignored in the commentaries.[5] But it is so ubiquitous as to be characteristic of Pauline letter writing and it deserves exploration.

This enabling language is most familiar in the thanksgiving periods following the salutation with which Paul commences his letters, with the exception of 2 Corinthians and Galatians.[6] Enabling language in these thanksgiving periods includes the following passages:

1 Thessalonians

1:3   your work of faith and labor of love and steadfastness
       of hope in our Lord Jesus Christ.
1:4   we know, brethren beloved by God, that he has chosen you
1:6   you became imitators of us and of the Lord
       you received the word in much affliction, with joy
       inspired by the Holy Spirit
1:7   you became an example to all the believers in Macedonia
       and in Achaia.
1:9   they themselves report concerning us what a welcome we had
       among you, you turned to God from idols, to serve a
       living and true God, and to wait for his Son from heaven

1 Corinthians

1:4   the grace of God which was given you in Christ Jesus

---

[5] E.-B. Allo (*Première Épître aux Corinthiens* [ÉtBib; Paris: Gabalda, 1934] 4) and Clarence T. Craig ("The First Epistle to the Corinthians," in George A. Buttrick, ed., *The Interpreter's Bible* 10 [New York: Abingdon Cokesbury, 1955] 18) regard Paul's thanksgiving (1 Cor 1:4–9) as ironic and ignore the affirmative language throughout the letter (discussed below) that is homogenous with that of the thanksgiving. William Sanday and Arthur C. Headlam (*A Critical and Exegetical Commentary on the Epistle to the Romans* [5th ed.; Edinburgh: T. & T. Clark, 1902] 403–4), associating Rom 1:8 and 15:14, derive from the "language of compliment" a theory for Paul's reason for writing: "He (Paul) has grasped clearly the importance of the central position of the Roman Church and its moral qualities, and he realizes the power that it will be for the instruction of others in the faith. Hence it is to them above all that he writes, not because of their defects but of their merits."

[6] Galatians is a special case. 2 Corinthians has a *berakah* (a praise-giving or eulogy).

    1:5   in every way you were enriched in him with all
           speech and all knowledge
           the testimony to Christ was confirmed among you
    1:7   you are not lacking in any spiritual gift
    1:8   (our Lord Jesus Christ) will sustain you to the
           end, guiltless in the day of our Lord Jesus Christ.

2 Corinthians

    1:7   Our hope for you is not shaken
           we know that as you share in our sufferings,
           you will also share in our comfort.

Romans

    1:8   your faith is proclaimed in all the world
    1:12   that we may be mutually encouraged by each other's
           faith, both yours and mine

Philippians

    1:3   for all your remembrances of me[7]
    1:5   thankful for your partnership in the gospel
           from the first day until now.
    1:6   he who began a good work in you will bring it to
           completion at the day of Jesus Christ
    1:7   I hold you in my heart   .
           you are all partakers with me of grace

Philemon

    5   I hear of your love and of the faith which you have
           toward the Lord Jesus and all the saints
    7   I have derived much joy and comfort from your love,
           my brother; the hearts of the saints have been refreshed
           through you

This language has received attention in special studies on the thanksgivings in Paul's letters, and as part of them it has been brought under
suspicion as perhaps being only formal and conventional.[8]

---

[7] ἐπὶ πάσῃ τῇ μνείᾳ ὑμῶν, usually translated "in all my remembrance of you," but
cf. Peter T. O'Brien, *Introductory Thanksgivings in the Letters of Paul* (NovTSup 49; Leiden:
Brill, 1977) 22–23, 41–46.

[8] Paul Schubert, *Form and Function of the Pauline Thanksgivings* (BZNW 17; Berlin:
Topelmann, 1939). Schubert, having made it his task to determine "whether the
thanksgivings are essentially epistolary in form and function, or whether they must be

What has not been noticed is that the body of Paul's letters is laced with similar encouraging, exalting language. Let us take 1 Corinthians as an example. 1 Corinthians is a collage of discussions of serious problems in the Corinthian Christian community. These problems included internal divisions and jealousies, arrogance, sexual immorality (incest), law suits before pagan courts, temptation by prostitutes, super-Christians who rejected marriage as sinful and the conjugal rights of married persons as sinful, marriage problems, and divorce. Some were participating in meals at pagan temples; some were imposing Jewish restrictions on what to eat; some were getting drunk and being gluttonous at what was intended to be "the Lord's supper"; some doubted fundamentals of the Christian faith (the resurrection). The church at Corinth would not have been welcomed as an appointment by any pastor. And Paul was certainly cognizant of most of these matters when he wrote this letter. Still, in the body of the letter Paul can say the following about the Corinthian Christians:

3:16	Do you not know that you are God's temple and that God's Spirit dwells in you?
3:17	For God's temple is holy, and that temple you are.
4:5	(when the Lord comes) then every man will receive his commendation from God.
4:14	my beloved children
5:7	as you really are unleavened
6:2	Do you not know that the saints will judge the world? And if the world is to be judged by you
6:3	Do you not know that we are to judge angels?
6:11	(after naming typical gentile sins) and such were some of you. But you were washed, you were sanctified and you were justified in the name of the Lord Jesus Christ and in the Spirit of our God.
9:1	Are you not my workmanship in the Lord?
9:2	you are the seal of my apostleship in the Lord
11:2	I commend you because you remember me in everything and maintain the traditions even as I have delivered them to you.
12:27	You are the body of Christ and individually members of it.

---

considered capricious, foreign accretions, borrowed from liturgical practice or from literary sources" (3), came to the conclusion that they served the purpose of introducing the basic themes of the letters (180), thus associating them inextricably with the bodies of the letters. Nevertheless, his formal approach has led some (e.g., O'Brien, *Thanksgivings*, 12–13) to draw more negative conclusions from his work than he stated or suggested.

15:1   the gospel . . . in which you stand
15:31   my pride in you which I have in Christ Jesus our Lord

All this amounts to very positive feedback addressed to a church fraught with problems. I count some thirteen similar statements in the body of 1 Thessalonians,[9] 23 in 2 Corinthians,[10] nine in Philippians,[11] 16 in Galatians,[12] and 19 in Romans.[13] The presence of such an abundance of these warm, intimate, approving statements in the bodies of the letters removes any doubt about the genuineness of the feelings expressed in the thanksgivings. The statements in each are complementary of the other. Thus, the bodies of the letters reveal the same feelings of confidence and trust toward Paul's addressees as are revealed in the thanksgivings.[14]

I have called these statements enabling language. In doing so I do not mean that Paul wrote these statements with a calculating eye on expected positive results. I regard them as expressing Paul's genuine feelings toward his readers. However, there are a number of affirmative statements that are associated with expectations on Paul's part. Again I will illustrate from 1 Corinthians.

3:16–17   (affirmation) Do you not know that you are
           God's temple and that God's spirit dwells in you?
           (expectation) If any one destroy's God's temple,
           God will destroy him.
3:21–23   (affirmation) For all things are yours,
           and you are Christ's; and Christ is God's.
           (expectation) So let no one boast of men.
5:7   (expectation) Cleanse out the old leaven that you
           may be a new lump,
           (affirmation) as you really are unleavened.
6:2–6   (affirmation) Do you not know that the
           saints will judge the world?
           (expectation) And if the world is to be judged
           by you, are you incompetent to try trivial cases?
           (affirmation) Do you know that we are to judge angels?

---

[9] 2:13, 19–20; 3:6 (twice), 7, 9; 4:1, 9, 10; 5:1, 2, 5, 11.

[10] 1:14; 3:2–3; 7:4 (four times), 7 (three times), 11 (twice), 13, 14 (twice), 15, 16; 8:7, 8, 24; 9:2, 3; 13:3, 5.

[11] 1:19; 2:12, 15; 4:1, 10, 14, 15, 16, 18.

[12] 3:3, 5, 26, 27, 28, 29; 4:6, 7, 9, 14, 15, 28; 5:1, 7, 10. 25.

[13] 6:3, 17, 18; 8:9, 10–11, 15, 16, 17; 11:17, 24, 30–31; 13:11; 14:22; 15:1.

[14] O'Brien, *Thanksgivings*, overlooked the presence of these statements in the bodies of Paul's letters and the congruence between them and the statements of the thanksgivings.

(expectation) How much more, matters pertaining
to life!
If then you have such cases, why do you not lay
them before those who are least esteemed by the church?

6:15   (affirmation) Do you not know that your bodies
are members of Christ?
(expectation) Shall I therefore take the members
of Christ and make them members of a prostitute?

6:19-20 (affirmation) Do you not know that your body
is a temple of the Holy Spirit within you,
which you have from God?
(expectation) You are not your own; you were bought
with a price. So glorify God in your body.

11:2   (affirmation) I commend you because you remember
me in everything and maintain the traditions even
as I delivered them to you.
(expectation) But I want you to understand
that . . .

15:1   (affirmation) Now I would remind you,
brethren, in what terms I preached to you the gospel,
which you received, in which you stand, by which you
are saved.

Similar affirmation/expectation statements are found in the other letters of Paul as well.[15] It appears, therefore, that not only did Paul have warm, positive feelings about his addressees but that he believed that his expression of these feelings to his readers would be productive. It appears legitimate, therefore, to describe these affirming statements in Paul as enabling language. Two features that confirm Paul's intentionality in this enabling language are the great variety of subject matter that Paul uses and the nonrepetitious character of his statements. Of some 25 enabling subjects in 1 Thessalonians, only four are repeated in other letters; of 13 in Galatians, two are repeated in other letters; five of 27 in 1 Corinthians; eight of 16 in 2 Corinthians; ten of 22 in Romans; three of 15 in Philippians; and two of three in Philemon. It is only the subject matter that is repeated, not the statements themselves. With one exception, the phrase "called to be saints" ($\kappa\lambda\eta\tauο\hat{\iota}\varsigma$ $\dot{\alpha}\gamma\dot{\iota}ο\iota\varsigma$) in 1 Cor 1:2 and Rom 1:7, I have found no enabling statement repeated by Paul. Thus, the enabling statements in Paul are not repeated phrases to which Paul had become habituated. Rather, these

---

[15] 1 Thess 4:1, 9-12; 5:11; Gal 4:9, 14-15; 5:1, 7, 25; 2 Cor 8:7; 9:1-3; 13:5; Rom 6:1-4, 17-19; 8:15-17; 11:17; 14:22; 15:1, 14-15; 16:19; Phil 2:12, 14-16; 4:1; Phlm 4-10.

statements are fresh, spontaneous statements, rich in their variety. They are an intimate insight into the mind of Paul.

I have said that enabling was characteristic of Paul's letter writing. This is so because it is ubiquitous in Paul. Moreover, it is a facet of Pauline letter writing that is carried over into some subsequent letters that reflect Pauline style. The Pauline letters whose authenticity is questioned, 2 Thessalonians, Colossians, and Ephesians, are prime examples of this reflection if, indeed, they are not authored by Paul. In 2 Thessalonians I find some 11 enabling statements of which seven subjects are repeated in the undisputed letters; Colossians has 17 with six subjects repeated; Ephesians has 25 with eight repeated subjects. And, similar to the undisputed letters, each of these has affirmation/expectation statements: two in 2 Thessalonians (2:3; 3:4), four in Colossians (2:20; 3:1, 4-5, 13), and three in Ephesians (1:4; 2:10; 5:3). In these respects the disputed letters cannot be distinguished from the undisputed letters.

Even though the opening thanksgiving is completely absent from the pseudo-Pauline letters—the Pastorals—it appears that Pauline enabling language has carried over into them. 1 Timothy has one affirmation (1:2) and three affirmation/expectation statements (1:18; 4:14; 6:20); 2 Timothy has three affirmations (1:5, 9 [twice]) and three affirmation/expectation statements (1:6-8, 14: 3:14); and Titus has two affirmations (1:4; 3:5).

Among the Catholic letters James reflects no influence of Paul's enabling language. 1 Peter, on the other hand, which reflects Pauline influence in some other respects,[16] reflects this influence in the presence of enabling language as well. I count some 18 affirming statements in the letter[17] including four affirmation/expectation statements (1:2, 14, 22; 2:9). 2 Peter contains only one affirmation statement (1:12) and cannot be regarded as having been influenced by Paul's letters in this respect. 1 John has some 13 affirmation statements[18] of which two include expectations (2:27; 5:20); 2 John has no enabling language; 3 John has four affirmative statements, Jude has one (1:1).

The seven pseudo-letters of Revelation contain a limited number of affirmation statements: Ephesus three (2:1, 2, 3), Smyrna one (2:9), Pergamum two (2:13 [twice]), Thyatira three (2:19 [twice], 25), Sardis one (3:4), Philadelphia four (3:8, 9, 10, 11), and Laodicea one (3:19).

---

[16] Helmut Koester, *Introduction to the New Testament*, vol. 2: *History and Literature of Early Christianity* (Philadelphia: Fortress, 1982) 292-93.

[17] 1:2 (twice), 3 (twice), 5, 8 (twice), 14, 18, 22, 23; 2:3, 9, 10 (twice); 3:7; 4:10, 14.

[18] 2:20; 3:1, 2; 3:14, 24; 4:4 (twice), 6, 13; 5:19, 20.

These, however, are sufficient to show that the author of Revelation regarded such affirmative statements to have been a constitutive part of a Christian letter. This probably was due to the influence of Paul's example in his letters.

The letters in the Apostolic Fathers show a continued and even expanded influence of Paul's enabling language. *1 Clement* opens with an abundance of affirmative statements. I count some 39 in the opening sections of the letter (the salutation, 3.1). This flood of complimentary statements is initially not understandable. In the remainder of the letter I find only eight affirmations[19] and two affirmation/expectation statements (16.17; 19.2). In the Ignatian letters we find a situation similar to that in *1 Clement.* Complimentary statements are concentrated at the beginning of the letters: *Ephesians* has eight (in the Salutation, 1.1) with 14 in the remainder of the letter;[20] *Magnesians* (the exception) has nine scattered throughout the letter;[21] *Romans* has 14 in the salutation and three in the body (2.1; 3.1 [twice]); *Philadelphians* has four in the salutation and one elsewhere (5.1); *Smyrnaeans* has nine in the opening (salutation, 1.1) and four in the rest of the letter (1.2 [twice]; 11.2 [twice]); *Polycarp* has four in the opening (salutation, 1.2) and three in the rest of the letter (4.1; 7.3; 8.1). This concentration of affirmations in the Ignatian letters is probably to be understood by Ignatius's statement in the salutation of *Trallians*: "Which church I also greet in the divine fullness after the apostolic fashion" (ἣν καὶ ἀσπάζομαι ἐν τῷ πληρώματι ἐν ἀποστολικῷ χαρακτῆρι). The "apostolic fashion" probably means the Pauline fashion. Ignatius has overlooked that Paul's openings are thanksgivings. He has simply noted their content; they are made up of affirmations. The congeries of affirmations at the opening of *1 Clement* is probably to be similarly understood. Also Polycarp's *Philippians*, with five affirmations in 1.1–2 and two others at 12.1, is to be understood in the same light.

---

[19] 16.17; 19.2; 29.1; 30.1; 45.2; 53.1 (twice); 62.3.
[20] 1.2; 2.1; 3.1; 4.1 (twice); 9.1 (three times), 2 (three times); 12.1 (three times).
[21] Salutation, 1.1; 3.1 (twice); 12.1 (four times); 14.1

THE EXALTATION OF JESUS
AND THE RESTORATION OF ISRAEL IN ACTS 1

David L. Tiede
Luther Northwestern Seminary

"Lord, at this time are you restoring the kingdom to Israel?" (Acts 1:6)

The disciples' leading question in Acts 1:6 sets the context for Luke's narration of the last words which the risen Jesus speaks on earth. The Lord's oracular answer clearly divides in two parts. Acts 1:7 conveys a sharp caution to those who would speculate about God's timetable: "It is not yours to know the periods or occasions which the Father has established in his own authority." Yet Jesus' final words respond positively to the question of restoration by revealing the deployment of theocratic dominion, even indicating the geographic staging of Acts: "But you shall receive power when the Holy Spirit has come upon you and you shall be my witnesses in Jerusalem and in all Judea and Samaria and unto the end of the earth" (1:8).

Scholarship has given immense attention to the ways in which such passages imply and express Luke's distinctive eschatology, and the effort has proved rewarding. This particular exchange begins with a corrective concerning speculation on the times of restoration, and the episode concludes with the heavenly messengers assuring the disciples that Jesus whom they have seen "assumed into heaven" will return in the same manner (Acts 1:11). The evangelist has clearly provided an interpretation of the present time (see Luke 12:56) within a scenario of apocalyptic eschatology.[1] Peter's sermons will then specify further

---

[1] Hans Conzelmann's presentation of Luke's theology in terms of the "delay of the parousia" (*The Theology of St. Luke* [trans. Geoffrey Buswell; London: Farber & Farber, 1960]) sharpened the sense of the "problem" in Luke's eschatology, and many subsequent studies have been preoccupied with this issue. But Henry J. Cadbury's description of Luke's "deferred eschatology" or "delayed apocalyptic" had already demonstrated that "delay" is not so much a problem for which apology must be offered as a sign of divine forebearance within an intact apocalyptic drama (*The Making of Luke-Acts*

Luke's conviction that the present time of repentance, forgiveness and salvation is integral to the anticipated "restoration of all which God promised through the mouth of the holy prophets from of old," when Jesus the Messiah will again be sent from heaven (Acts 3:18–21; see also 2:33, 38–40; 4:12; 10:42–43).

This passage is also crucial to all assessments of Luke's christology. Commentators often suggest that this scene of Jesus' departure is a corrective of Jewish nationalism, an explanation of the absence of Jesus, or the presentation of Jesus' exaltation in a form which would rival the apotheosis of any Greek or Roman hero or ruler. Each of these proposals has certain interpretative values and deserves more ample discussion, but a few remarks must suffice to introduce the suggestion of this essay.

1. The concern for "the restoration" was shared by many of the interpreters of the scriptures of Israel throughout the intertestamental era,[2] and caricatures of Jewish expectations do justice neither to that rich discussion nor to Luke-Acts. Furthermore, in Luke's day, *2 Baruch*, *4 Ezra*, and Josephus join Luke in pondering the questions of God's rule and justice in the wake of the calamities of Israel.[3] Luke's own list of named witnesses indicates that the hopes of all those faithful in Israel are alive throughout his narrative, that is, the expectations of "the consolation of Israel" (Simeon, Luke 2:25), "the redemption

---

[London: SPCK, 1927] 292–96, and idem, "Acts and Eschatology," in W. D. Davies and D. Daube, eds., *The Background of the New Testament and Its Eschatology* [Cambridge: Cambridge University Press, 1956] 300–21]). Eric Franklin even argues that the ascension of Jesus is the eschatological event which fulfills Israel's expectations: "The guarantee that this is so is the gift of the Spirit and the universal witness that it enables; its seal will be the parousia and the restoration of Israel. The story of Acts is told in order to justify this confidence" (*Christ the Lord* [Philadelphia: Westminster, 1975] 41).

[2] See George W. E. Nickelsburg, *Jewish Literature Between the Bible and the Mishnah* (Philadelphia: Fortress, 1981) 18. This paper was in its last recension when I received a copy of E. P. Sanders' *Jesus and Judaism* (Philadelphia: Fortress, 1985). This remarkable study places Jesus within the context of "Jewish restoration eschatology," documenting the depth and complexity of this hope. Although Sanders accepts the common view that the question about restoration in Acts "is turned aside by the risen Lord, and the general implication is negative" (p. 116), he has laid out the resources clearly for others to investigate the possibility that Luke's Jesus affirms the question. See also Arthur W. Wainwright, "Luke and the Restoration of the Kingdom to Israel," *ExpTim* 89 (1977/78) 76–79; Robert C. Tannehill, "Israel in Luke-Acts: A Tragic Story," *JBL* 104 (1985) 69–85.

[3] See David L. Tiede, *Prophecy and History in Luke-Acts* (Philadelphia: Fortress, 1980); Alden Lloyd Thompson, *Responsibility for Evil in the Theodicy of IV Ezra* (SBLDS 29; Missoula: Scholars Press, 1977); Gwendolyn B. Sayler, *Have the Promises Failed?: A Literary Analysis of 2 Baruch* (SBLDS 72; Chico: Scholars Press, 1984).

of Jerusalem" (Anna, 2:38), "the kingdom of God" (Joseph of Ari-
mathea, 23:51), "the redeeming of Jerusalem" (Cleopas, 24:21), "the
restoration of the kingdom to Israel" (disciples, Acts 1:6), and "the
promise made by God to our fathers to which the twelve tribes hope to
attain, as they earnestly worship night and day" (Paul, 26:6–7; see also
James in Acts 15:16).

2. Luke's declaration of Jesus the Messiah and Lord is much more
than an "absentee christology," which is preoccupied with the delay of
the Messiah's return.[4] Luke's narrative testifies to the exaltation of
Jesus as the inauguration of the long promised reign of God on earth
through faithful Israel, that is, commencing with the restored "twelve"
and advancing through all those on Pentecost who come to repentance,
bringing restoration of Israel's calling to witness to God's promise to
those far off (Acts 2). The Spirit, name, word, and apostles or "chosen
instruments" of the Lord and Messiah exercise his dominion until the
time of the restoration of all, even provoking divisions within Israel.[5]

Proper appreciation of Luke's testimony requires the interpreter to
set aside modern ideologies of historical idealism or manifest destiny,
to neglect medieval concepts of divine right and Christian empires, and
to move back before the time when gentile Christianity read Acts as its
triumphal displacement of Judaism. This narrative belongs within the
world of the late first century when "the crisis over theocracy"[6] con-
fronted all who laid claim to the faith of Israel, and the messianist Jesus
movement declared this Savior and Lord to be the Ruler through
whose name alone restoration and salvation would be given to Israel
(Acts 3:19–4:12).

3. Luke's usage of "christological" language is replete with terms
and titles drawn from a broad range of early Christian usage in worship
and proclamation, and several of these terms (e.g., Savior, Lord,
Benefactor) had broad currency in the theocratic rhetoric of the Roman
government.[7] Luke is also aware (and critical) of stories of rulers who

---

[4] See George W. MacRae, "Whom Heaven Must Receive Until the Time," *Int* 27
(1973) 151–65; C. F. D. Moule, "The Christology of Acts," in Leander E. Keck and
J. Louis Martyn, eds., *Studies in Luke-Acts* (Nashville: Abingdon, 1966) 159–85.

[5] Jacob Jervell, "The Divided People of God," *Luke and the People of God* (Minneapolis: Augsburg, 1972); Donald Juel, *Luke-Acts: The Promise of History* (Atlanta: Knox,
1983).

[6] See Gerd Theissen, *Sociology of Early Palestinian Christianity* (Philadelphia: Fortress,
1978) 65.

[7] See Charles H. Talbert, "Prophecies of Future Greatness: The Contribution of
Greco-Roman Biographies to an Understanding of Luke 1:5–4:15," in James L.
Crenshaw and Samuel Sandmel, eds., *The Divine Helmsman: Studies on God's Control of
Human Events* (New York: KTAV, 1980) 129–41; Frederick W. Danker, *Benefactor: Epi-*

were exalted to divine status and of gods coming to earth in human form (see Acts 12:20–23; 14:11–18). Nevertheless, Luke is neither promoting Jesus for divinization nor offering an overt challenge to the theocratic claims of the emperors and the Roman order.[8] Stories of ascending rulers or saviors whose "abundance of virtue" could lead to apotheosis are more to the point in such literature as Josephus's account of the death of Moses.[9]

Theocracy in Israel

The kingdom of God is always understood by Luke to be for and through Israel. The divine authority of the scriptural commands and promises is assumed, and Israel's traditional theocratic institutions of priesthood, kingship, temple, and synagogue are regarded as put to the test by the declaration that "God has made him both Lord and Messiah, this Jesus whom you crucified" (Acts 2:36). The "christology" of Acts is preoccupied with testifying to Jesus as God's way of ruling, forgiving, and saving (restoring) Israel. Even the Roman government with its might and theocratic claims only serves as the background and mechanism as God seeks to establish dominion in Israel.

That larger political arena is, of course, crucial to Israel's plight. The story of the birth of this "Savior, Christ the Lord" is presented in the context of the reign and census of Caesar Augustus (Luke 2:1, 11). The beginning of John's declaration of the word of God is fixed by reference to the fifteenth year of the reign of Tiberius Caesar, with Pilate, Herod, Philip, Annas, and Caiaphas in attendance (Luke 3:1–2). "The kings of the Gentiles" who have dominion are called "benefactors" in direct contrast to the rule which Jesus exercises and authorizes (Luke 22:24–27). Jesus' death is presented in terms of the gathering against God's anointed servant of Herod and Pontius Pilate together with the Gentiles and the peoples of Israel (Luke 22–23, Acts 4:27). Claudius's expulsion of the Jews from Rome and repeated references to

---

graphic Study of a Graeco-Roman and New Testament Semantic Field (St. Louis: Clayton, 1982).

[8] Richard J. Cassidy (*Jesus, Politics and Society* [New York: Orbis, 1978]) offers a helpful critique of Conzelmann but is more confident of Luke's implicit critique of the Roman order than may be credible. Nevertheless, Luke 22:25 with its disdain for the "kings of the Gentiles" and their "benefactors" would not have been lost on a first-century reader.

[9] See Josephus's careful presentation of the death of Moses in contrast to the apotheosis of Aeneas and Romulus in Dionysius of Halicarnassus as discussed in David L. Tiede, *The Charismatic Figure as Miracle Worker* (SBLDS 1; Missoula: Scholars Press, 1972) 235.

Paul's rights as a citizen to appeal to Caesar keep the reader alert to political realities as Paul heads for Rome.[10]

Luke also insists that Paul has not offended any law of Israel nor of Caesar's court (see Acts 25:8), and even the letter of the Roman law is preserved by the Roman tribune so that Paul is quickly unbound and not scourged (Acts 22:25–29). But even these details simply indicate that the story is not about conflict or competition with Rome. In fact, the major trait of Rome's attitude toward the Christians is disinterest.

Thus Christian "boldness" and assurance of God's dominion in Jesus appear politically preposterous in the story, especially in the face of the power and authority of Rome, and Luke highlights the discrepancy. The proconsul Gallio displays the Roman government's lack of concern in "matters of questions about words and names and your own law" (Acts 18:15), and Felix delays the proceedings twice, reportedly expecting a bribe (Acts 24:22, 25–26). Festus tells Herod Agrippa that he has already heard Paul's case once and could not make sense of the points of dispute between Paul and his accusers concerning "their own superstition and about one Jesus, who was dead, but whom Paul asserted to be alive" (Acts 25:19). Even Agrippa is incredulous in the presence of the procurator when Paul seeks to persuade him to repent and believe as a Messianist, while Festus thinks he is mad (Acts 26:25–28). Luke is finally as disinterested in the Roman officials as they are in Paul, and he does not even attempt to interpret Paul's case in terms that would make sense to them.

The fact that all the titles are reported to derive from "words and names" of Israel's scriptures offers an important clue since Luke's stance toward the Roman imperial realm is also scriptural and traditional. His contrast between the reign of the God of Israel and that of the rulers, gods, lords, messiahs, and saviors of the empires had already been developed in the prophets, especially in Isaiah 40–55. The implied audience for Luke's testimony to the kingdom of Jesus the Messiah is composed of those who believe in the God of the scriptures, and the theocratic dispute which the exaltation of Jesus provokes is primarily with Israel's instituted authorities.

Disinterest is not possible for the Sanhedrin, synagogues, high priest, or people of Israel. The encounters of Peter, John, Stephen, and Paul with Israel's theocratic authorities are remarkable scenes of conflict, where the choices are between obedience to God and to humans (Acts 5:29). When Paul is "unlawfully" struck, he calls the high priest a "whitewashed wall," which even Luke's Paul found to be an excessive

---

[10] Acts 18:2; 19:21; 22:25–29; 23:27; 25:10–12, 21, 25–27; 26:31–32.

criticism of the high priesthood (Acts 23:1–5). Whether speaking before Jewish or Roman courts, Paul's defense speeches, as carefully composed by Luke, consistently testify to the resurrection of Jesus as the fulfillment of the scriptures, further provoking division in Israel (Acts 23:6; 24:14–15; 26:22–23).[11] As Simeon's oracles had indicated, Jesus the Messiah would not only be the "light for revelation to the Gentiles and for glory to thy people Israel," but he was also "set for the fall and rising of many in Israel" (Luke 2:32, 34).

Literarily, the whole story of the restoration of the theocracy of Israel turns on the "plot device" of the "rejection of God's agents by God's people in connection with God's sanctuaries (synagogues and temple)."[12] Theologically, it is the reign of God exercised by this Messiah which produces a divided Israel. That division will persist to the end of the narrative where some Jews in Rome are convinced and others disbelieve (28:24). Even the conflict with the traditional theocratic institutions of synagogues, temple, priesthood, and kingship are not signs that the followers of Jesus the Messiah have in any way failed to obey the law (see Acts 21:23; 24:14). No, the refusal of the apostles to "withstand God" (Acts 11:17) is a sign that the theocracy of Israel has begun to be restored. Gamaliel's warning is thus directed to Israel's authorities: "If this plan or this undertaking is of men, it will fail; but if it is of God, you will not be able to overthrow them. You might even be found opposing God!" (Acts 5:39).

Restoration

The disputes about "words and names and your own law" may have been trivialized by the Romans, but these were life and death issues in first-century Israel. The urgency and difficulty of the questions no doubt intensified as the growing crisis with Rome produced massive calamity in Palestine and grave peril for Jews in Rome, Alexandria, and other localities. Israel's faith required a theological interpretation of such tragedy. What sin or apostasy has been committed and by whom? What repentance would lead to forgiveness? How might restoration be accomplished and when?

---

[11] See Jerome Neyrey, "The Forensic Defense Speech and Paul's Trial Speeches in Acts 22–26: Form and Function," in Charles H. Talbert, ed., *Luke-Acts: New Perspectives from the Society of Biblical Literature* (New York: Crossroad, 1984) 215.

[12] Norman Petersen, *Literary Criticism for New Testament Critics* (Guides to Biblical Scholarship; Philadelphia: Fortress, 1978) 83. See also Tiede, *Prophecy and History.*

The fountainhead for such discussions had long been the scriptures, and particularly Moses' parting words to Israel in Deuteronomy. There the prophetic interpretation of the Babylonian destruction rendered a harsh verdict, calling Israel to account for apostasy, announcing that returning to the Lord will bring forgiveness although immediate salvation is no longer possible, and declaring that only the pride of the nations prevents God from scattering Israel altogether. Thus even the conquering nations will yet experience God's vengeance, and Israel's restoration will attest that the Lord God is the only god. Isaiah 40–66 and Ezekiel 33–48 picked up this refrain, along with other scriptural theologians of "restoration," so that a predictable set of concerns appeared in many subsequent theological interpretations of Israel's history. A diagnosis of sin or apostasy, a call to "return" or repentance for forgiveness, a vision of the regathering of the twelve tribes, and a vision of how the nations or "Gentiles" would see Israel's light were standard, although interpreted in particular ways.

Daniel Harrington has pointed to the interpretation of Israel's history which was done by means of rewriting Deuteronomy 31–34 in several Jewish sources dating from the second temple. He observed that *Jubilees* 1, Ps.-Philo's *Liber ant. bib.* 19, *The Testament of Moses*, and Josephus's *Ant.* 4.303–31 all present Moses expanding upon his predictive history in accord with the Deuteronomic pattern of apostasy, punishment, and vindication.[13] These distinct construals of "The Song of Moses" may also be compared with the hymn of Tobit 13 and *Psalms of Solomon* 17 in order to grasp the range of Jewish visions of the restoration of Israel's theocracy, and *4 Ezra* and *2 Baruch* demonstrate the continuing vitality of this heritage of theodicy and theocracy which calls Israel to repentance in hope of restoration.[14]

A wealth of comparisons with Acts emerges fromthe study of these texts. *Jubilees* 1 defined apostasy in terms of "walking after the Gentiles and after their uncleanness" (1:9) and the possibility of repentance was the beginning of the recreation of a holy spirit and a clean heart (1:21, 23). Josephus, by contrast, had Moses announce that "their

---

[13] Daniel J. Harrington, "Interpreting Israel's History: The *Testament of Moses* as a Rewriting of Deut. 31–34," in George W. E. Nickelsburg, Jr., ed., *Studies on the Testament of Moses* (SBLSCS 4; Missoula: Scholars Press, 1973) 59–68.

[14] See Sayler, *Promises*, 96: "It seems clear that the relationship of Baruch to his successors is modelled after that of Moses to Joshua. . . . Baruch announces his impending death (44:2), transfers leadership from himself to his successors (44:2–3, chap. 45), exorts them to preserve the people by teaching them the Torah (44:3, chap. 45), and delivers revelations about the immediate past (44:5) and the eschatological future (44:7–15)."

repentance would profit them naught amid those sufferings," for "God who created you will restore those cities to your citizens and the temple too; yet will they be lost not once, but often" (*Ant.* 4.313–14). The *Testament of Moses* presented a fascinating extension of Moses' final words. It may have even indicated the "assumption" (ἀνάλημψις) of Moses (see also Luke 9:51), and it clearly linked the apocalyptic time-table of vindication of the faithful martyrs "Taxo" and his sons with the glorious appearance of the "kingdom" to happy Israel (chaps. 9–10). The royal Davidic expectation of the *Psalms of Solomon* stands in some contrast to all of these depictions of Moses the prophet, but Acts gathers both strains of testimony within a few verses (Acts 2–3).

Of course, each rendition of this scriptural heritage of theodicy had its particular turn. *Jubilees'* diagnosis of Israel's sin as walking after the uncleanness of the Gentiles (1:9) may illumine Acts' report that James and the elders of Jerusalem were eager to clear Paul of the charge of "teaching apostasy from Moses to the Jews who live among the Gentiles" (Acts 21:21). But Acts 3, in turn, points to Israel's failure to "listen" to the prophet like Moses as the sin which will cause the unrepentant to be "destroyed from the people," while the "restoration of all" still waits (Acts 3:21–23; Deut 18:19; Lev 23:29). And while Mark 9:12 and Matt 17:11 interpret John's role in the eschatological drama of the "restoration of all" by reference to the promise of Elijah in Mal 4:5, Luke's silence leaves the question of restoration open until the Messiah's last words on earth in Acts 1:6–8.

So also, several dimensions of Luke's presentation of Jesus' "departure" stand out more clearly when compared with these other interpretive extensions of Deuteronomy. Thoroughly imbued with the convictions and style of the scriptural histories, Luke-Acts shows particular affinities to Deuteronomy in its presentation of Jesus the prophet like Moses (see Acts 3:22–23; 7:37), its recitation of Israel's history as indictment calling for repentance (see esp. Acts 7), and its presentation of Jesus' "exodus" as "fulfilled" in Jerusalem in accord with the words of Moses and Elijah (Luke 9:31, 51; Acts 1:11).

The key scriptural resource for Luke's interpretation of Jesus' exaltation was the divine oracle of Isa 49:6: "It is too light a thing that you should be my servant to raise up the tribes of Jacob and to restore the preserved of Israel. I will give you as a light to the nations, that my salvation may reach to the end of the earth." Allusions or references were also made to this declaration in Simeon's prophetic oracles as the child Jesus was brought to the temple (Luke 2:29–35), in the conclusion of Paul's sermon in Antioch (13:47), and in Paul's final defense before Agrippa (26:23), with a probable allusion in the painful conclusion of Acts (28:28). Jesus' response to the disciples' question is not formulated in order to correct the readers' "christology" or "eschatology," but to introduce the whole narrative of Acts as a testimony to the deployment of the reign of God's Messiah through his twelve apostles who declare repentance and forgiveness to Israel.[15] First the twelve are restored (Acts 1:12–26). Then the Spirit is poured out upon devout Jews "from every nation under heaven" (Acts 2).

The logic is directly from Second Isaiah: the promise of God's reign is not simply the restoration of the preserved of Israel, but the renewal of the vocation of Israel to be a light to the nations to the end of the earth. Have God's promises failed? No, the restoration which the exalted Jesus is now about to inaugurate through the Holy Spirit (the promise of the Father: Luke 24:49) is the renewal of Israel's prophetic calling in the world.

And what is Israel's sin or apostasy from Moses which requires repentance? How shall the dire judgments of Deuteronomy be read by this interpreter among Jewish preachers of repentance? Repentance is required not for "idolatry" or "walking after the Gentiles in their uncleanness," but for the rejection of the prophet like Moses and the refusal of the reign of the exalted Lord who is David's Lord.

Acts does not introduce an "absentee christology" to explain the delay of the parousia, nor does it uncritically adopt Greco-Roman traditions of the apotheosis of rulers or benefactors in order to develop a doctrine of Jesus' divine status. If its "christology" has been reduced to "soteriology" it is because the question of the salvation and restoration of Israel must be answered by all who would interpret the "present time" of the late first century in accord with the scriptural warnings and promises. If Jesus is to be Israel's Messiah and Lord, the inspired preaching of repentance unto forgiveness, the division in Israel, the ascendancy of Rome, and the expanding gentile mission of the Christian movement which follow in Acts must all be seen as integral to the restoration which the exalted Jesus has inaugurated. Until the "restoration of all that God spoke by the mouth of the holy prophets from old" (Acts 3:21), the apostles and the evangelist together are witnesses to the salvation and dominion which God is exercising through the Messiah in the present time.

---

[15] See Jervell, "The Twelve of Israel's Thrones," *Luke*, 75–112. Note the crucial context for defining Jesus' "kingdom"; here Luke speaks of the session of the twelve, indicating that their "kingdom" is a present reality which anticipates the eschatological "kingdom" of the age of the messianic banquet (Luke 22:24–30).

JUSTIN MARTYR'S TRYPHO

Bishop Demetrios Trakatellis
Holy Cross Greek Orthodox School of Theology

Justin Martyr's *Dialogue with Trypho* has been considered one of the basic documents for an understanding of the theological contacts and discussions between Christians and Jews in the second century. Several scholars have studied the *Dialogue* in an attempt to ascertain the main ideas, the fundamental questions, and the principal attitudes involved in such contacts.[1] The inquiry, however, does not appear to have reached definitive conclusions. There has been a diversity of opinion due mainly to the complexity of the problems, to the ambiguity of the pertinent data, and to the theological presuppositions of the researchers. Specific questions like "How well did Justin know and represent his contemporary Judaism?" seem to be more and more, but not completely, settled.[2] Others, however, such as the degree of friendliness or

---

[1] One could mention here by way of selection the following works: A. H. Goldfahn, "Justinus Martyr und die Agada," *MGWJ* 22 (1873) 49–60, 104–15, 145–53, 193–202, 257–69; Adolf von Harnack, *Judentum und Judenchristentum in Justins Dialog mit Trypho* (*TU* 39; 1913) 47–98; Erwin R. Goodenough, *The Theology of Justin Martyr* (Jena: Frommansche Buchhandlung, 1923); Henry Chadwick, "Justin Martyr's Defense of Christianity," *BJRL* 47 (1964–65) 275–97; L. W. Barnard, "The Old Testament and Judaism in the Writings of Justin Martyr," *VT* 14 (1964) 395–406; Willis A. Shotwell, *The Biblical Exegesis of Justin Martyr* (London: SPCK, 1965); K. Hruby, "Exégèse Rabbinique et exégèse Patristique," *RevScRel* 47 (1973) 341–72; Eric Francis Osborn, *Justin Martyr* (Tübingen: Mohr-Siebeck, 1973); Ben Zion Bokser, "Justin Martyr and the Jews," *JQR* 64 (1973–74) 97–122, 204–11; Theodore Stylianopoulos, *Justin Martyr and the Mosaic Law* (SBLDS 20; Missoula: Scholars Press, 1975); Frédéric Manns, *Essais sur le Judéo-Christianisme* (Jerusalem: Franciscan Press, 1977) 130–52; Phillip Sigal, "An Inquiry into Aspects of Judaism in Justin's Dialogue with Trypho," *Abr Nahrain* 18 (1978–79) 74–100; Giorgio Otranto, *Esegesi biblica e storia in Giustino (Dial. 63–84)* (Bari: Inst. Letter. Chr. Antica, 1979).

[2] Though there are variations in the particulars, the increasing relevant data since Goldfahn corroborate the assumption that Justin knew and presented rather accurately some basic aspects of the Judaism of his day. See Goodenough, *Theology*, 93–95; Harnack, *Judentum*, 53–56, 90–92; Barnard, "Old Testament," 401–3; Hruby, "Exégèse,"

hostility between Jews and Christians displayed in the *Dialogue*, remain in a condition of fluidity.[3]

Undoubtedly, the *Dialogue with Trypho* is a theologically rich and deep work. It offers bold and extensive interpretations of the Old Testament texts and events[4] in a powerful christological synthesis, in which a number of diversified elements have been combined and amalgamated.[5] It displays a keen sense of God-directed history both on the universal and on the geographically restricted level. And it reveals an advanced awareness of contemporary religious and philosophical writings with which it shares a number of fundamental concerns.[6] All these elements have an impact on the formation of the image of the theological contacts between Jews and Christians as it appears in the *Dialogue*. Such an image, complex and multifaceted, does not favor simple, monochromatic, and unequivocal conclusions; hence the lack of scholarly consensus on the issue under examination.

The present paper aims precisely at contributing to the ongoing pertinent discussion by offering some observations on the question of the theological contacts between Jews and Christians, as depicted in Justin's *Dialogue*. My observations are directed to a specific area: they deal solely with Trypho and his attitude during his encounter and conversation with Justin.[7] The meaning of this study is obvious, since the written data concerning Trypho are provided not by him, but by Justin. What exactly is the picture of Trypho the Jew painted by Justin the Christian during their debate? The answer, evidently, has an immediate bearing on the question of the theological contacts between Jews and Christians as Justin sees them.

In the pages that follow I will present and comment upon the main passages of the *Dialogue* in which Trypho appears. The citations may be lengthy in a number of instances, but I have decided not to

---

343; Manns, *Essais*, 141–52; Sigal, "Inquiry," 74, 86–90; Otranto, *Esegesi*, 237–38.

[3] See, e.g., the differing views expressed by Bokser, "Justin," 98, 101, 209–10; Stylianopoulos, *Justin*, 33–44; Sigal, "Inquiry," 79; Robert Joly, *Christianisme et Philosophie* (Brussels, 1983) 155–70; Osborn, *Justin*, 13–16; Jon Nilson, "To whom is Justin's Dialogue with Trypho addressed?" *TS* 38 (1977) 539, 542.

[4] Stylianopoulos' *Justin and the Mosaic Law* presents an eloquent example of Justin's theological achievement in Old Testament exegesis.

[5] For an extensive presentation of pertinent aspects see Demetrios Trakatellis, *The Pre-existence of Christ in the Writings of Justin Martyr* (HDR 6; Missoula: Scholars Press, 1976).

[6] See the special works by Carl Andresen, "Justin und der mittlere Platonismus," *ZNW* 44 (1952–53) 157–95; Niels Hyldahl, *Philosophie und Christentum* (Copenhagen: Prostant, 1966); J. C. M. van Winden, *An Early Christian Philosopher* (Leiden: Brill, 1971).

[7] This topic has been touched upon by various scholars but not in an exclusive way.

abbreviate them. It is in their complete form that they reveal their full meaning.

We will begin with the first chapter of the *Dialogue* in which Trypho is initially introduced by Justin to his readers. Here is the opening report:[8]

> As I was walking one early morning in the walks of the colonnade[9] a man met me, with others round him, and said, Good morning, Philosopher. And so saying he turned, and began to walk along with me, and his friends too turned with him. And I in reply addressed him and said: What may be your pleasure?
>
> He answered: I was taught in Argos, by Corinthus of the school of Socrates, that one must not despise nor ignore those that wear this dress you have on, but should treat them with absolute courtesy, and converse with them, in the hope that some gain may accrue from such intercourse either to him or to oneself. For it is well for both if either be benefited. For this reason whenever I see anyone in such a dress, I gladly draw nigh to him, and therefore had now the pleasure of addressing you. And these are followers and companions of mine, and themselves anticipate hearing some profitable discourse from you.
>
> And who are you, most excellent man? said I in jest. He told me frankly his name and his nationality. I am called Trypho, he said, and I am a Hebrew of the circumcision, who have fled from the war which broke out recently, and am spending much time in Greece and in Corinth.
>
> How then, said I, could you derive as much advantage from philosophy, as from your own lawgiver and your prophets?
>
> What do you mean? Do not the philosophers discourse entirely about God, he went on to say, and hold their discussions invariably about sovereignty[10] and providence? And is not this the work of philosophy, to inquire about God? (*Dial.* 1.1–3)

Trypho is presented here in a bright and agreeable light. He is an

---

[8] The quotations from the *Dialogue* appear only in English for reasons of space. I am using, with the necessary modifications, the English translation by A. Lukyn Williams, *Justin Martyr: The Dialogue with Trypho* (London: SPCK, 1930).

[9] For the exact location implied here, see van Winden, *Early Christian Philosopher*, 25–26. The city could be Ephesus if the information in Eusebius (*Hist. Eccl.* 4.18.6) is correct.

[10] The word μοναρχία employed here by Trypho has a monotheistic ring.

authentic Jew ('Εβραῖος ἐκ περιτομῆς)[11] with an undeniable eagerness
for learning, and with experience in conversing with philosophers. He
loves exchanging views with them, not for the sake of discussion, but
in order to profit spiritually. He delights in inquiring about God, and
about the ultimate questions related to him (μοναρχία καὶ πρόνοια).
Not a passive intellectual, he energetically seizes the opportunity, when
he sees it, for a fruitful discussion. In this specific instance he is the
one who takes the initiative for the dialogue with Justin, and he acts so
in a joyful and brisk manner. He presupposes Moses and the prophets,
but is unwilling to exclude other possible avenues, for example that of
philosophy, which could lead to religious knowledge and experience.

He responds to the first objection raised by Justin in a way which
shows intellectual versatility, courtesy, and sharp focusing on the essential. And when Justin intensifies his objections by degrading the philosophers, Trypho "smiling gently said, But pray tell us what are your own
thoughts about these things and what opinion you hold about God and
what is your own philosophy" (*Dial.* 1.6). Even small details, like the
phrase "smiling gently"[12] which happens to introduce a tactful rebuttal
combined with a considerate request, show a man of noble mind and
manners.

The initial presentation of Trypho, as he appears in *Dialogue* 1,
seems to be positive and favorable indeed: here is a genuine Jew who
is courteous and gentle, intelligent, open-minded, learned, and very
eager to discuss what he considers to be the essence of philosophy,
namely, the search for God.

The next major presentation of Trypho occurs in *Dialogue* chaps. 8–10.
In the first part of *Dialogue* 8, Justin concludes the account of his
conversion to Christianity by inviting Trypho and his friends "to get to
know more fully (ἐπιγινώσκειν) the Christ of God" in order to obtain
salvation. This is a radical statement which causes the companions of
Trypho to laugh. Trypho himself, however, "smiled slightly" (ὑπομει-

---

[11] Eusebius (*Hist. Eccl.* 4.18.6) considers Trypho τῶν τότε 'Εβραίων ἐπισημότατον.
The characterization, regardless of its historical value, indicates the authenticity of
Trypho's Jewish origin.

[12] The phrase ἀστεῖον ὑπομειδιάσας has affinities with phrases occurring in Plato's
dialogues (e.g., *Tim.* 21C, *Phaedrus* 86D) as Hyldahl has shown (*Philosophie*, 101). The
fact, however, that the same verb occurs in the *Dialogliteratur* does not mean that it is a
mere stylistic feature, especially when, as in *Dial.* 1.6, it is accompanied by the adverb
ἀστεῖον. Justin's personal touch is apparent here.

διάσας), showing again his high culture.[13] The next thing he does is to commend Justin for the appropriate and praiseworthy statements he has offered: "I accept your other remarks and I admire your zeal for the Divine" (περὶ τὸ θεῖον ὁρμή—Dial. 8.3). In this instance Trypho displays a remarkable intellectual honesty which recognizes, or even admires, what is true and excellent in an opponent. Then he proceeds to produce a relentless criticism of Justin's Christian positions, accusing him of "having been deceived by false words, of having followed the opinions of men of no account" (Dial. 8.3), and of sharing with them a vain belief in a Messiah whom they have invented and for whose sake they are foolishly perishing (Dial. 8.4). The language is evidently sharp, almost harsh, a fact that prompts Justin to say "I excuse and forgive you, my friend, for you know not what you say" (Dial. 9.1). Nonetheless, this is the language of someone who is firm and clear in his faith and who is honest and truthful in its expression.[14] Besides, Trypho's cutting remarks come immediately after his gracious concession to Justin's correct points. Thus they reveal a man who gives precedence to the truth, and who does not hesitate to alternate between honest agreement and truthful criticism. The picture of Trypho continues to be painted by Justin in bright colors, even when the discussion touches some rather sensitive nerves.

This trend becomes more evident in the subsequent developments. According to Dial. 9.2, when Justin answered Trypho's criticism in a similarly honest and direct way, the friends of Trypho "laughed aloud and began to shout quite rudely." Justin, being offended, "rose up and prepared to take his departure," but Trypho, "took hold of his garment (τοῦ ἱματίου λαβόμενος) and did not let him go until he had completed what he promised to do" (Dial. 9.2).[15] Trypho's attitude is noteworthy indeed. He did not participate in the laughing scene created by his friends. On the contrary, he even went so far as to use some form of mild force in order to keep Justin there and to keep the discussion alive by any means. He thus is presented as dominated by a high degree of eagerness, and by an unwavering determination to maintain a debate over controversial issues.

---

[13] Note the contradistinction between ὑπομειδιάσας and ἀνεγέλασαν.

[14] In fact Trypho's formulations are on target in presenting two major problems to Justin. See Stylianopoulos, Justin, 8–9; van Winden, Early Christian Philosopher, 122.

[15] This passage (Dial. 9.2) has been considered to have been heavily influenced by Plato's Protagoras (335C–D). The similarities are clear but so are the dissimilarities. The significant point here is that Justin, by using either his own or a borrowed terminology, presents Trypho as a person with strong positive motivations.

When the discussion resumes, Justin raises the issue of the accusations circulating against the Christians concerning "eating human beings" (ἐσθίομεν ἀνθρώπους) and "indulging in promiscuous concubinage" (ἀθέσμοις μίξεσιν ἐγκυλιόμεθα).

Trypho answers with an emphatic rejection of such accusations. They are simply "not worthy of credence" because they are far too unlike human nature (*Dial.* 10.2). The answer in its full form shows a noble thinker who is reluctant to share rumors exchanged among the anonymous crowd (πολλοί) or to believe in the possibility of advanced human perversion (πόρρω κεχώρηκε τῆς ἀνθρωπίνης φύσεως).

Trypho then continues: "I know too that the precepts given you in what is called the Gospel are so wonderful and great that I think no one can keep them" (*Dial.* 10.2). In this passage a new aspect is being presented which further enhances the image of Trypho depicted by Justin: he is a knowledgeable Jewish debater aware of the basic Christian text.[16] In fact he does not hesitate to characterize the precepts of the Gospel as wonderful and great. The two adjectives show that the statement is not a lapse of the tongue. At the same time Trypho has again the honesty and frankness to express plainly his opinion that no one can keep the commandments of the Gospel.[17]

At this point Trypho presents what he thinks is the heart of the accusations against the Christians:

> This is what we are most at a loss about you that, professing to worship God and thinking yourselves superior to other people, you are separate from them in no respect and do not make your life different from the heathen, in that you keep neither the feasts nor the sabbaths, nor have circumcision; and, moreover, that though you set your hopes on a man that was crucified, you yet hope to obtain some good from God, though you do not do his commandments. (*Dial.* 10.3)

The accusations are clearly stated and further elaborated (*Dial.* 10.4),[18] but the prevailing tone is a mixture of eloquent frankness and polite reserve. Inherent in this attitude is, most likely, the expectation of serious answers, a fact Trypho implies in his concluding remarks: "If

---

[16] Trypho's knowledge of the Gospel is noticeable in view of the Jewish practices prevailing then in Palestine. See Williams, *Justin*, 21; Manns, *Essais*, 131.

[17] "Still a very common objection in the mouth of Jews" (Williams, *Justin*, 21).

[18] It should be noted that the absolute nature of the Law is emphasized in Trypho's answer, whereas the christological question is less pronounced. See P. Prigent, *Justin et l'Ancien Testament* (Paris: Gabalda, 1964) 235–36.

you have any defense to make with reference to this point . . . we would very gladly hear from you (ἡδέως ἀκούσαιμεν) and we will examine the other points the same way" (*Dial.* 10.4). Trypho marshals his grave accusations, but at the same time discloses his noble feelings, when he declares that he is ready to hear the answers with pleasure, and to examine carefully the issues involved.

As the dialogue progresses, Justin offers additional data which contribute to a steadily enhanced picture of Trypho.

In *Dial.* 27.1, for example, Trypho demonstrates his knowledge of Scripture and by the same token he blames Justin for making arbitrary selections of biblical passages. He further displays his awareness of the pertinent scriptural texts as he raises constant objections to Justin's exposition. He has the honesty, however, to agree with Justin's argument concerning particular points (*Dial.* 36.1), and to admit that the evidence brought by him is persuasive (*Dial.* 39.7). This does not mean, nonetheless, that Trypho is a fellow easy to convince, or that he sacrifices the truth for any conventionalities or pleasant words. In fact he has no difficulty in employing rather stern language as he says to Justin: "I want you to know that you are out of your mind when you say all this" (παραφρονεῖς ταῦτα λέγων—*Dial.* 39.3), or "you utter many blasphemous things, thinking to persuade us that this man who was crucified has been with Moses and Aaron and has spoken to them" (*Dial.* 38.1).

The heat of the debate and the strong language, however, do not prevent Trypho from remaining courteous and discreet. An eloquent example comes from *Dial.* 45.1 when he wants to interrupt Justin: "Even though I seem to interrupt these subjects, which you say must be examined, yet as the question which I desire to propound is pressing, suffer me first to bring it forward." Later on, Trypho will again reveal his refined nature when he explains that his objections do not aim at contradicting Justin but at reaching the truth: "Do not suppose hereafter that I am trying to upset your arguments when I make any fresh inquiry, but that I desire to learn about the very questions that I put to you" (*Dial.* 87.1). Another comment of Trypho at the end of *Dialogue* 118 moves along the same lines. In this instance Justin voices his fears that by necessity he is repeating the same passages and ideas, with the result of becoming somehow boring. But Trypho replies without delay: "You do well; but even though you were to repeat the same statement at greater length, you should know that both I and those that are present with me would rejoice to hear them" (*Dial.* 118.5).

Whether he accuses Justin or whether he agrees with him, whether he listens or whether he raises sharp questions, Trypho is portrayed by Justin as a gentleman and as an indefatigable explorer of the truth, enjoying deeply the ongoing theological interaction with his Christian interlocutor, agreeable and yet uncompromising.

The last point should be emphasized because the *Dialogue* might leave the impression that Trypho is inclined to agree with Justin, and that he functions solely as a facilitator of Justin's exposition.[19] What we have seen so far seems to run contrary to such an impression. Trypho is in essence a formidable opponent, who up to the end of the *Dialogue* raises hard questions and returns to difficult points, proving that his limited and concrete agreements do not imply that he accepts the theses proposed by Justin.

It is interesting to note that in almost all instances where Trypho offers an agreement, he couples it with a request for further evidence, or with a new question, or with a more general antithetic statement. A few examples could illustrate this point.

In *Dial.* 63.1, Trypho admits the cogency of Justin's argument concerning the christological interpretation of Gen 1:26–28, Prov 8:21–28, and Josh 5:13–6:2. But he immediately asks Justin to prove other crucial christological points (e.g., virgin birth, crucifixion, resurrection, ascension).

In *Dial.* 64.1, Trypho concedes that according to the Scriptures Christ may be Lord and God of the Gentiles. "For us, however," he adds, "who are worshippers of God who made even him (i.e., Christ) there is no need to confess him or worship him."

In *Dial.* 67–68, during a discussion characterized by short exchanges, Trypho appears to accept a number of Justin's interpretations of specific biblical passages. Yet at the same time he is in a continuous disagreement, so that Justin complains to him that he frequently contradicts what he has already accepted. To this Trypho retorts: "You are endeavoring to prove an incredible and almost impossible thing, namely that God endured to be born and to become man" (*Dial.* 68.1). Justin criticizes this answer by saying that he simply does nothing else but to quote the Scriptures, and, consequently, that Trypho's attitude might be indicative of his hardheartedness. Trypho, nonetheless, is ready with a new reply which discloses his intellectual quality: "Consider, my friend, that you have been able to

---

[19] See Goodenough, *Theology*, 90; Bokser, "Justin Martyr," 98; Nilson, "To whom," 541.

acquire this with much labor and toil. So we too must test and try all that meets us, and thus assent to what the Scriptures compel us" (*Dial.* 68.2).

In *Dial.* 71–72, when Justin makes a reference implying that the Jewish teachers have deleted some passages from the Scriptures, Trypho asks immediately for the appropriate evidence. He remains, nonetheless, unconvinced by Justin's argumentation and leaves the subject unsettled.

In *Dialogue* 77, Trypho makes the concession to Justin after the latter finishes a long exposition: "I grant you that the proofs are of such kind and such a number as to be sufficient to impress me, but I desire that you know that I ask you to prove the passage of Scripture which you have often promised." Justin proceeds to do so in a lengthy discourse, but Trypho, after listening to him for a while, cannot hide his vehement disagreement: "Trypho, who was somewhat angry, as was plain from his countenance, though retaining his respect for the Scriptures, said unto me: God's statements indeed are holy but your explanations are contrivances, as is clear from those you have given, or rather are even blasphemous" (*Dial.* 79.1).[20]

Even when Trypho makes a most significant concession in *Dial.* 89.1, that "all our race expects the Christ," and that "all the passages of Scripture which you have cited, have been spoken of him," he hastens to add that "we doubt whether the Christ was crucified with such dishonor." He then utters a serious challenge to Justin: "Prove to us whether Christ must even be crucified, and die in so disgraceful and dishonorable a fashion, by the death which in the Law is accursed. For we cannot come so far as even to suppose any such thing" (*Dial.* 90.1).

All the above cited examples confirm the point already suggested, namely, that Trypho is an alert and earnest thinker and debater who defends his theses with an uncompromising adherence to what he believes to be the truth, and with unshaken faithfulness to the Mosaic Law. At the same time he demonstrates a spirit of freedom and wisdom which leads him to accept particular aspects well documented by his opponent.[21]

The finale of the *Dialogue* (chap. 142), constitutes an outstanding piece of literature which corroborates what has been reported in the preceding pages. At least the first part of *Dialogue* 142 should be

---

[20] Prigent has shown (*Justin,* 20–24) that *Dialogue* 79 is not out of place.

[21] Otranto describes (*Esegesi,* 239) Trypho characteristically as someone who is neither too intransigent nor too compromising.

quoted. This part comes after Justin has concluded his presentation, and has indicated that probably in view of his impending trip the talks should come to an end:

> Now Trypho paused somewhat, and then said: You see that it was not by design that we fell into a discussion over these matters. And I acknowledge that I have been extraordinarily charmed (ἐξαιρέτως ἥσθην) with our intercourse, and I think that these are of like opinion with myself. For we have found more than we expected, or than it was even possible for us to expect. And if we could do this more frequently we should receive more benefit, while we examine the very words (i.e., of Scripture) themselves. But since, he added, you are putting off to sea, and expect to begin your voyage every day, do not scruple to think of us as your friends (μὴ ὄκνει ὡς φίλων ἡμῶν μεμνῆσθαι) when you take your departure. (*Dial.* 142.1).

In this closing scene of the *Dialogue*, Trypho's image, as painted by Justin, receives its final touches and becomes even more bright and charming.[22] After two days of intense talks, Trypho, the learned Jew, remains in essence unconvinced by the arguments of Justin, the Christian philosopher. He stays firmly with his own beliefs. He acknowledges, nonetheless, in a gracious manner that he has been exceedingly pleased with the talks, and that he found more than could be expected. A disposition of openness and spirited exploration, of uninhibited exchange of opposing views, of deep joy because of the possibility for such an exchange, radiate from Trypho in his concluding remarks. The picture presented here, consistent with what preceded in the 141 chapters of the *Dialogue*, is the picture of a debater who combines intellectual integrity and personal warmth, independence of mind and faithfulness to his tradition, freedom to talk and freedom to listen. The very significant thing is that this remarkable description, as we already pointed out, comes not from Trypho or a Jewish source, but from Justin, a Christian and a thinker.

Is such a description a report after the fact or is it an ideal synthesis produced by Justin? His Trypho might well have been a real historical

---

[22] The charm and nobility which fill the closing scene of the *Dialogue* have been amply recognized. See Chadwick, "Justin," 286; Peter Richardson, *Israel in the Apostolic Church* (Cambridge: Cambridge University Press, 1969) 13; Stylianopoulos, *Justin,* 35; Manfred Hoffmann, *Der Dialog bei den christlichen Schriftstellern der ersten vier Jahrhundert* (Berlin: Akademie-Verlag, 1966) 13.

person, or a fictional character, or, most likely, a mixture of both.[23] It could be safely assumed, though, that there must be at least a nucleus of historical fact in Justin's presentation. Otherwise the readers of the *Dialogue*, no matter who they were, would have discarded the document out of hand as unacceptable fiction.[24]

It is plausible then to suggest that, when Justin described Trypho within the framework of his *Dialogue* the way he did, he was reporting a reality related to the theological contacts between Jews and Christians in his time. This type of contact was perhaps not the prevailing one, but it did exist, possibly more among the philosophically inclined, and in cultured milieux. The very fact that the work under discussion is in the form of a dialogue suggests contact and communication between the two sides.[25]

The type of theological contacts we can surmise from the *Dialogue* is evidently beyond the stereotyped classification of anti-Jewish or anti-Christian in that it is dominated by a consuming shared passion for the truth revealed in the Scriptures.[26] These contacts were conducted in a spirit of honesty and sincerity combined with courtesy. They displayed a sense of openness and freedom mixed with an undeniable joy and a distinct pleasure.[27]

But what if the whole *Dialogue* is pure literary fiction? In that case, certainly an unlikely and extreme one, we would have Justin's *Dialogue* and his Trypho as the noble vision of a refined Christian thinker. It is important that a central person in this vision is a Jew, that the creator of the vision is a Christian, and that the setting of the vision is a dialogue.

[23] This seems to be the prevailing scholarly opinion. See Chadwick, "Justin," 280; Barnard, "Old Testament," 396; Joly, *Christianisme*, 159; Osborn, *Justin*, 12–13; Nilson, "To whom," 539; Sigal, "Inquiry," 75; Frank Talmage, *Disputation and Dialogue* (New York: KTAV, 1975) 89; Otranto, *Esegesi*, 235–36.

[24] This is more so if the addressees of the *Dialogue* are not Gentiles but Jews and/or Christians, a thesis strongly defended by Sigal ("Inquiry," 76–77) and, even more strongly, by Stylianopoulos (*Justin*, 33–44, 169–95). See also Helmut Koester, *Introduction to the New Testament*, vol. 2: *History and Literature of Early Christianity* (Philadelphia: Fortress, 1982) 344.

[25] See Hoffmann, *Der Dialog*, 25, 28. The argument that Justin's *Dialogue* has been influenced by the Platonic dialogues and by the genre "dialogue" in general, does not militate against the facticity of the contacts. See Bernd Reiner Voss, *Der Dialog in der frühchristlichen Literatur* (Munich: Fink, 1970) 38.

[26] It is characteristic that Justin's sharp criticism of the Jews is almost invariably related to his interpretation of relevant scriptural texts.

[27] To try to classify this kind of theological contact between Jews and Christians under the modern titles of liberalism or ecumenism would be anachronistic indeed.

EARLY CHRISTIAN CHILIASM, JEWISH MESSIANISM, AND THE IDEA OF THE HOLY LAND

Robert L. Wilken
University of Virginia

For most Christians Jerusalem is a heavenly city of solace and peace, a safe haven after the trials of life in this world. "Jerusalem whose towers touch the skies, I yearn to come to you. Your shining streets have drawn my longing eyes, my life long journey through . . ." It is a symbol of the soul's yearning to find rest in God. "Jerusalem my happy home, when shall I come to thee, when shall my sorrows have an end, thy joys when shall I see?" Yet Jerusalem is also an actual city set on a hill on the edge of a desert, a city where Christians live and have lived for centuries but whose population today is largely Muslim and Jewish. At one time, in the years prior to the Muslim invasion of Palestine in the seventh century, it was the chief city in a land ruled by Christians. More than five hundred churches and monasteries marked the landscape and thousands of monks inhabited the caves of the Judaean desert. Jerusalem's eloquent bishops and learned priests wielded power in the great capital of the Byzantine world, Constantinople on the Bosporus.

Little remains of this Christian past save the worn stones of ancient hostels and the bright tiles that adorned the floors of churches, but the tiny conventicles of Christians who contentiously guard the ancient holy places evoke the memory of Christianity's long history in this land. Even today thousands of pilgrims, practicing an ageless form of devotion, rejuvenated by the broad wings of TWA, Swiss Air, and El Al, journey to this venerable land, as Eusebius called it (*V. Const.* 3.42), to kneel at the place where Jesus of Nazareth was buried and to pray "at the very spot" where the events of biblical history took place, as Egeria, one of the first pilgrims, exclaimed on her visit to Mt. Sinai (*Itin. Eth.* 3.6). With no less enchantment the Holy Land summons

Christians of our time as it has beckoned the faithful for centuries.[1]

Yet the New Testament lays down no command to make pilgrimage as do the Hebrew Scriptures or the Qur'an, and pilgrimage played no part in early Christian life. The practice, not documented before the third century, does not become widespread until the end of the fourth century. The earliest Christians saw no religious significance in the land of the patriarchs and prophets nor in the places of Jesus' life and death.

From the very beginning Christian attitudes toward Jerusalem and the land of Israel have been ambivalent. At one place in the New Testament Jerusalem is called the "holy city" (Matt 27:53; cf. 1 Macc 2:7; 2 Macc 2:12; 3:1), but the phrase is conventional and may bear no particular significance. The attitude of Paul in Galatians 4 may be more typical. There he compares the "Jerusalem above" which is free with the "present Jerusalem," the actual city in Judaea which is in bondage.

Paul, however, did not speak for all Christians. Irenaeus reports that Jewish Christians "adored the city of Jerusalem as the house of God" (*Adv. haer.* 1.26.2), and Christian millenarians believed, on the basis of Revelation 20 and prophecies from Isaiah and Ezekiel, that there would be a thousand-year reign in Jerusalem before the consummation of all things.[2] Among adherents to the chiliastic view were several distinguished Christian thinkers: Justin Martyr, Irenaeus of Lyon, Tertullian, Lactantius, Victorinus, Apollinaris of Laodicea, and the early Augustine. For them Christian hope was centered at least in part on a real kingdom in this world where "the saints could rule in the same condition in which they suffered," as Ireneaus puts it (*Adv. haer.* 5.32.1). For him, chiliasm was the ultimate vindication of the theory of recapitulation of all things in Christ. For Justin Martyr it was self-evident that belief in a thousand-year reign was the view of "orthodox" Christians (his word is "right minded"—ὀρθογνώμονες), though he did grant that some pious Christians thought otherwise (*Dial. Trypho* 80).

---

[1] On the early history of pilgrimage to Palestine see E. D. Hunt, *Holy Land Pilgrimage in the Later Roman Empire: AD 312–460* (Oxford: Clarendon, 1982). For early Christian pilgrimage in general see Bernhard Kötting, *Peregrinatio Religiosa* (Forschungen zur Volkskunde 33–35; Münster, 1950). On early Christian attitudes toward "holy space," see Paul Corby Finney, "Topos Hieros und christlicher Sakralbau in vorkonstantinischer Überlieferung," *Boreas* (Münstersche Beiträge zur Archäologie 7; Münster, 1984) 193–226.

[2] For a brief survey of early Christian chiliasm, see Walter Bauer, "Chiliasmus," *RAC* 2. 1073–78.

The term "holy land" first occurs in Christian literature in chiliastic thinkers, Justin and Tertullian. This may be a clue to its Sitz im Leben. Justin, for example, uses the term holy land to designate the eternal inheritance that was promised to Abraham. "With Abraham we will inherit the holy land when we shall receive the inheritance for an endless eternity, being children of Abraham through like faith." Tertullian, however, considers "holy land" a Jewish phrase and rejects it out of hand in favor of a spiritual concept of the land.

> They [the Jews] consider the special soil of Judaea to be that very holy land, which [claims T.] ought rather to be interpreted of the Lord's flesh, which in all those who put on Christ is thenceforward the holy land, holy indeed by the indwelling of the Holy Spirit, truly flowing with milk and honey by the sweetness of his assurance, truly Judaean by reason of the friendship with God.

Salvation, he concludes, is "not promised to any one land" (*Res. mort.* 26.11–13).

In the passage from Justin the phrase "holy land" is used in connection with the "land" promise to Abraham as recorded in Genesis. The promise is of course Christianized in Justin, but it nevertheless relates to the expectation that Abraham's descendants will "possess the land." Early Christian chiliasm is the obverse side of Jewish Messianism. By Jewish Messianism I mean the hope that the Jews will return to the land of their ancestors, reclaim the city, rebuild the temple, and establish in Judaea a kingdom ruled by Jews. This hope was linked to the ancient promise of the land made first to Abraham (Genesis 12), renewed to his descendants, and reaffirmed after the sojourn in Egypt. The land to which the Israelites returned was the land they had once "possessed." "If your outcasts are in the uttermost parts of heaven, from there the Lord your God will gather you, and from there he will fetch you; and the Lord your God will bring you into the land which your fathers possessed, that you may possess it; and he will make you more prosperous and numerous than your fathers" (Deut 30:4–5). In the exilic prophets the promise was intimately linked to the hope of restoring Jerusalem and the temple (cf. Ezekiel 40ff.; Isaiah 45, 60, 65, passim) but it remained a hope focused on possessing the land of Israel. "I will bring you home into the land of Israel" (Ezek 37:12). "Your people shall all be righteous; they shall possess the land forever" (Isa 60:21).[3]

---

[3] On the importance of the land of Israel and Jerusalem in Jewish messianic hopes, see Tobit 14, Jesus ben Sira 51, Psalm of Solomon 17, 4 Ezra 5:23–30; 9–10. For a survey

The Christian chiliasts appeal to precisely those biblical texts that undergirded Jewish messianic hopes. Justin mentions the prophecies in Ezekiel and Isaiah that speak of Jerusalem being "built, adorned and enlarged" (*Dial. Trypho* 80). Though he does not mention chapter and verse in Ezekiel, he must have in mind the latter chapters of Ezekiel (chaps. 36–39) and the elaborate description of the restored temple in chaps. 40–48. As for Isaiah he cites Isa 65:17–25: "Behold I create new heavens and a new earth; and the former things shall not be remembered. . . . But be glad and rejoice forever in that which I create; for behold, I create Jerusalem a rejoicing and her people a joy. I will rejoice in Jerusalem and be glad in my people, no more shall be heard the sound of weeping and the cry of distress."[4]

Irenaeus develops the point at greater length than Justin, and he grounds the hope of a millennial kingdom on earth centered in Jerusalem on the basis of the promise to Abraham concerning the land. He also cites the chapter in the valley of the dry bones in Ezekiel 37: "I will place you in your own land and you will know that I am the Lord" (Ezek 37:12) and "I will gather Israel from all the nations where they have been scattered, and I shall be sanctified among them in the sight of the sons of the nations; and they shall dwell in their own land which I gave to my servant Jacob. And they shall dwell in peace; and they shall build houses, and plant vineyards, and dwell in hope" (Ezek 28:25–26). Irenaeus insists that these prophecies cannot be allegorized, that is, interpreted spiritually and divested of their historical significance. God does not raise human beings from the dead "allegorically" but "truly" (*vere*).[5]

---

of Jewish Messianism see Joseph Klausner, *The Messianic Idea in Israel* (New York: Macmillan, 1955), and Emil Schürer, *The History of the Jewish People in the Age of Jesus Christ* (ed. G. Vermes, F. Millar, M. Black; Edinburgh: T. & T. Clark, 1979) 2. 492–554.

[4] I once saw part of this text ("they shall build houses and inhabit them, they shall plant vineyards and eat their fruits. . . . They shall not build and another inhabit; they shall not plant and another eat") painted on the side of a hut built by Jews in the Gaza Strip shortly before that territory was returned to the Egyptians in 1982.

[5] *Adv. haer.* 5.35, passim. Irenaeus also cites Gen 13:13, 14, 17; 15:13; Matt 5:3; Isa 31:9; 32:1; 54:11–14; 65:18. The same texts used by Justin and Irenaeus from Ezekiel and Isaiah were used by Jews and judaizing Christians in the fourth century as a basis for the expectation that the Jews would return to the land of Israel. See Robert L. Wilken, "The Restoration of Israel in Biblical Prophecy: Christian and Jewish Responses in the Early Byzantine Period," in Jacob Neusner and Ernest S. Frerichs, *To See Ourselves as Others See Us: Christians, Jews, and Others in Late Antiquity* (Chico, CA: Scholars Press, 1985) 443–71.

By the third century opposition to chiliasm had become more widespread, and what is interesting for our purposes here is that one of its critics, Origen, presents Christian chiliasm and Jewish Messianism as a single phenomenon. The arguments he uses to answer the one are precisely those that he uses to answer the other. Furthermore, the discussion of chiliasm and Messianism leads Origen to discuss the phrase "holy land," which appears to be a shorthand way of speaking of a hope of an earthly kingdom in the land of Israel. Origen helps us understand why Christians avoided the idea of Palestine as a holy land until much later in Christian history.

The topic of the "holy land" is discussed at some length at two points in Origen's writings, once in the *De principiis*, an early work written while he was living in Alexandria, and later in the *Contra Celsum*, his massive defense of Christianity written while he was living in Caesarea in Palestine. In the earlier passage Origen is engaged in a general discussion of the interpretation of the Scriptures, and he argues that the term "holy land" refers to a heavenly city and that biblical prophecies about Judaea and Jerusalem designate a spiritual kingdom, a "race of spiritual beings." Within the context of *De principiis*, Origen's intention is to establish a distinctively Christian reading of biblical prophecy (*De prin.* 4.3.8; *C. Cel.* 7.28–29).

Origen's argument rests on the two NT texts that speak of Jerusalem as a heavenly city: "The Jerusalem above is free and she is our mother" (Gal 4:26) and "But you have come to Mt. Zion and to the heavenly Jerusalem, and to innumerable angels in festal gathering, and to the assembly of the first-born who are enrolled in heaven" (Heb 12:22–23). According to Origen these texts mean that Israel is a spiritual kingdom and the cities of Israel "have as their metropolis Jerusalem in the heavens; so also does all of Judaea." The prophets spoke about a "heavenly country" in those passages that speak of Jerusalem and Judaea. "Therefore whatever is prophesied in the Scriptures concerning Jerusalem, and whatever is said about it, must be understood, if we listen to Paul's words as the words of God and the utterances of wisdom, to be spoken about the heavenly city and the whole area embracing the cities of the holy land. Perhaps it is to these cities that the Savior calls our attention (Luke 19:17–19) when he gives authority over ten or over five cities to those who have been deserving of praise for the good use of their talents" (*De prin.* 4.3.8).

In *Contra Celsum* the setting is somewhat different but the line of argument is the same. There Origen is responding to Celsus's claim that Christians, in speaking of a hope of blessedness, have simply borrowed the ancient idea of the Islands of the Blessed or of Elysian Fields from the Greeks (cf. Hesiod *Opera et dies* 171; Homer *Odyssey* 4.563–65). Relying on the familiar argument used by Philo and Clement of Alexandria, he responds that the teaching about a blessed land derives from Moses who lived before the sages of Greece, even before the invention of the Greek alphabet. It was Moses who spoke about the promise of a "holy land that was 'good and large, flowing with milk and honey' " (Exod 3:8). Christian hope is not drawn from the philosophers and poets of ancient Greece but from the teaching of the Jews as recorded in the Scriptures.

But then Origen abruptly turns the discussion to respond not to Celsus but to another critic, this one a Jew. "This good land was not, as some think, Judaea below, which is part of the earth and was itself cursed from the beginning by the consequences of Adam's transgression." Origen begins to discuss this topic, and then, realizing it is not really germane to the quarrel with Celsus, says, "At present we are content with a brief discussion; we only wish to dispel any mistaken notion which supposes that the sayings about a good land which God promises to the righteous were spoken about the land of Judaea" (*C. Cel.* 7.28). Origen then states his own view.

Judaea and Jerusalem are to be taken symbolically as shadows of the pure land which is good and large and lies in a pure heaven in which is the heavenly Jerusalem. The apostle, as one who is risen with Christ, who seeks the things that are above, and has found a meaning not contained by a Jewish mythological interpretation, discusses this land when he says "But you have come to Mount Sion and to the heavenly Jerusalem, the city of the living God, and to an innumerable company of angels." (*C. Cel.* 7.29)

Finally Origen answers those critics who say that his view "opposes the will of the Holy Spirit concerning the good and large land spoken of by Moses; let them take note of all the prophets who teach that there will be a return to Jerusalem for those who have gone astray and fallen from it, and, in general, that they will be restored to what is called the place and city of God" (*C. Cel.* 7.29).

These passages from Origen suggest that the idea of the holy land first arises in Christianity in debates with the Jews over the meaning of prophetic texts that speak of the "return to Jerusalem." The issue is not so much whether Judaea is a sacred precinct or territory, but whether the prophecies were to be understood realistically, that is, historically and politically. Elsewhere, where Origen is directing his argument against Christian chiliasts, his discussion proceeds along similar lines.[6]

For a possible reconstruction of the Jewish side of the argument we are fortunate to have several comments of Rabbi Yoḥanan who lived in Palestine in the third century and might even have had contact with Origen in Caesarea.[7] Commenting on the phrase "daughters of Jerusalem" in Song of Songs (1:5) which some had taken to mean not daughters, but "builders" (fem. pl.)—"builders of Jerusalem"—he says: "One day Jerusalem will be made into a metropolis for all nations and draw [all peoples] to her as a stream to honor her."[8] The point seems to be that Jerusalem will again achieve a political significance and other peoples will take note of the Jewish kingdom. It is possible that Rabbi Yoḥanan was directing his comments against Origen's interpretation of the city of Jerusalem. In his Commentary on the Song of Songs, Origen gives a spiritual interpretation of the same text, citing Paul. It is the "heavenly Jerusalem," writes Origen, that is Paul's mother and the mother of all who believe. Solomon is speaking of a heavenly city.[9] Rabbi Yoḥanan, in contrast to Origen, refuses to separate the earthly and the heavenly cities. Elsewhere he said: "The Holy One . . . said: I will not enter the Jerusalem which is above until I enter the Jerusalem which is below." I take this to mean that Jews believed that there could be no full access to spiritual realities without possessing the earthly city.[10]

---

[6] *De prin.* 2.11.1. Origen calls chiliasts "men who believe in Christ" but who understand the Scriptures "in a Jewish fashion."

[7] That Origen had contact with Jewish thinkers and was familiar with Jewish interpretation of the Scriptures is now a consensus among scholars. See N. R. M. de Lange, *Origen and the Jews: Studies in Jewish-Christian Relations in Third Century Palestine* (Cambridge: Cambridge University Press, 1975).

[8] *Cant. Rab.* 1.5.3. See also *Midr. Tan*, Hosafa le-Debarim (Buber 4) and *Exod. Rab.* 23.10. On Rabbi Yoḥanan and Origen, see Reuven Kimelman, "Rabbi Yochanan and Origen on the Song of Songs: A Third Century Jewish-Christian Disputation," *HTR* 23 (1980) esp. 585–88. Also David Halperin, "Origen, Ezekiel's Merkabah, and the Ascension of Moses," *CH* 59 (1980) 261–75.

[9] *Comm. in Cant.* 2.3. Cf. also the prologue, paragraph 4.

[10] There is some dispute as to the origin of the term "Jerusalem above" and its place in discussions between Jews and Christians. For a brief summary, see the comments of Kimelman ("Rabbi Yochanan and Origen," 587) and W. D. Davies, *The Gospel and the Land* (Berkeley: University of California Press, 1974) 151–52. Origen's discussion of the holy land tends to support Kimelman's conclusions. It is the Christians, not the Jews, who seem defensive.

Rabbi Yoḥanan stands here in the mainstream of Jewish tradition that refused to spiritualize the promises concerning the land. Jewish Messianism is political.

> With the final collapse of the state, the destruction of the Temple, and the tragic dispersion of the people, Messianism assumes preeminence in the national consciousness. In it the race voices its invincible hope of survival and redemption. It should be borne in mind that Messianism was essentially a political idea. It was bound up with the restoration of the Davidic dynasty and with the reconstitution of the independence of Israel. Certain eschatological and supernatural features were combined with it, but essentially it remained a this-worldly, temporal, national idea.[11]

The Bar Kochba revolt is one bit of evidence of this. During the short time that Jews ruled Israel in 132–35 CE the revolt's leaders minted coins, some bearing the image of a star and a temple, with the legend: FOR THE FREEDOM OF JERUSALEM or YEAR ONE OF THE LIBERATION OF ISRAEL.[12] However one judges the historical veracity of Rabbi Akiba's comment that Bar Kochba was the Messiah (y. Ta'anit 68d), it is clear that Jewish Messianism in the Roman period did not give up its ancient hope of "possessing the land" which is to say gathering in the exiles, establishing a kingdom in Jerusalem, and rebuilding the Temple.[13] In the second century, wrote Graetz the Jewish historian, "people expected of the Messiah that above all he should bring freedom and the restoration of national life."[14]

As evidence of the vitality of Jewish Messianism in the third century one might cite the statement of Hippolytus of Rome.

> For they [the Jews] say that his [the Messiah's] birth will be from the stock of David, not from a virgin and the holy spirit, but from a woman and a man, as it is natural for all to be procreated from seed. And they claim that he will be a king over them, a warlike and powerful man, who, when he has gathered together the entire people of the Jews, and when he has done battle with all the nations, will restore Jerusalem the royal city to them. He will bring the whole people to the city and will again re-establish the people in their ancient circumstances as a nation exercising royal and

---

[11] Abba H. Silver, *A History of Messianic Speculation in Israel* (Boston: Beacon, 1959) 13. Cf. Gershom Scholem, *The Messianic Idea in Judaism* (New York: Schocken, 1971) 1.
[12] Schürer, *History of the Jewish People*, 1. 545–46.
[13] See *m. Pesaḥim* 10.6 and the prayer *Shemoneh Esreh*, nos. 14–17.
[14] Cited in Klausner, *Messianic Idea*, 395.

priestly functions and dwelling in security for a long time. (*Refut.* 9.30)

Origen was surely aware of the political nature of Jewish hopes. At one place in a homily on Psalm 36, at the verse "he will exalt you to possess the land" (Ps 36:34), Origen acknowledges that he has spoken "frequently" about the "holy land" in this connection. Earlier in the homily he had mentioned the Jews, and here he seems to be answering an interpretation that says "inherit the land" means to possess the earthly land of Judaea. The psalm, says Origen, is speaking about the "nature and location" of the holy land, but here, as in the other passages, the "land" promised as an "inheritance" is not "an earthly land, but a heavenly." "For unless someone is lifted up and ascends on high and attains heavenly things, it will not be possible for him to receive the inheritance of that land." This is what is meant by "good land, holy land, great land, land of the living, land flowing with milk and honey." Origen's comment seems to be a direct answer to the view of Rabbi Yohanan: "The Holy One, blessed be he, said: I will not enter the Jerusalem which is above until I enter the Jerusalem which is below."

Christian rejection of the idea that the land of Israel is a holy land is intimately linked to an ongoing dispute with the Jews over the interpretation of the biblical prophecies. A century after Origen, Jerome faced the same issue in his commentaries on Ezekiel and Isaiah as a consequence of Jewish interpretations of texts that spoke of a return to Jerusalem. Though he does not offer a systematic discussion of the term holy land, he does discuss the phrase *terra repromissionis* which had similar connotations. [15] Jerome had received a letter from a Roman official in Gaul, prompted by discussions with Jews, concerning the

---

[15] That Origen uses the term "holy land" and Jerome "land of promise" does not seem significant. "Holy land" is not a biblical term. There the word is Eretz Israel or simply Ha-Aretz. Holy Land does occur in the LXX as a translation of "holy ground" (e.g., in Zech 2:16; Exod 3:5) and in Wis 12:3 and 2 Maccabees 1. Other than these occurrences it is documented only in Christian authors, and it is the Christians who gave it currency, albeit to dispute its meaning. For the Jew the qualifier "holy" was redundant, as it was in the beatitudes "Blessed are the meek for they shall possess the land" (Matt 5:5). Aretz was quite sufficient as the following passage from the Mishnah indicates: "Any Mitzvah that does not depend on the land may be observed whether in the land or outside of it; and any Mitzvah that depends on the land may not be observed except in the land" (*m. Kidd.* 1.9–10). On the idea of the "land of Israel" see Davies, *Gospel and the Land*, and his more recent work, *The Territorial Dimension of Judaism* (Berkeley: University of California Press, 1982); on "holy land" see Robert L. Wilken, "Heiliges Land," in *Theologische Realenzyklopädie* (Berlin: De Gruyter, 1985) *s.v.*

meaning of the phrase. He replied: "The Jews assert that it is this land [the land of Palestine, where Jerome lived] that is the land of promise." They believe that *terra repromissionis* is "the land which the Jews possessed when they returned from Egypt, which had been possessed by their ancestors previously, and is therefore not promised but restored."[16]

Behind the discussion of the "holy land" or the "land of promise" or "Jerusalem below" lies the issue of Messianism. For one of the strongest arguments of the Jews against the Christians was that the prophecies that speak of proclaiming release to the captives or building a real city of God or of the age when the calf and bull and lion will feed together led by a little child had not in fact taken place (Origen *De prin.* 4.2.1). If these prophecies have not been fulfilled historically, that is, these things are not happening, then the Messianic age has not arrived and Jesus cannot be the Messiah. Christians could not treat arguments that rested on a plausible reading of the Scriptures with equanimity, especially when they were bolstered by other Christians who also interpreted the ancient promises realistically. Even though Christian chiliasts, unlike the Jews, believed the Messiah had already appeared, their views on Ezekiel and Isaiah, as well as on Revelation 20, lent support to the Jewish view. Hence Christians rejected the idea that Judaea was a holy land. At a later date they would adopt the very language they had spurned, but that would not occur until Christians themselves had "occupied" the land and transformed it into a Christian commonwealth. Then they began to speak of themselves as "inhabitants of this holy land,"[17] and they did not mean a "heavenly country" as Origen did in the third century. The idea of the holy land is as much a political as it is a religious conception.

---

[16] Jerome *Ep.* 129.1–3 to Dardanus. The sentiment expressed here is the same as that in 1 Macc 15:33 on the Jewish right to the land as an inheritance.

[17] Cyril of Scythopolis, *Life of Sabas* 57 (ed. Schwartz, 153).

VILIFICATION AND SELF-DEFINITION IN
THE BOOK OF REVELATION

Adela Yarbro Collins
University of Notre Dame

New Testament scholars, as well as preachers, are in frequent danger of perpetuating negative stereotypes about the Jews. The reason for this state of affairs is that the polemical anti-Jewish remarks in the NT are often simply repeated or paraphrased in the interpreter's context without attention to the difference in meaning these remarks have when read in their original social and historical contexts. Krister Stendahl has done much to sensitize Christians to this danger in his writing, public speaking, and teaching. This concern about relations between Jews and Christians today is a major reason for doing a historical analysis of the passages in the book of Revelation in which Jews are vilified (2:9 and 3:9).

The danger of collapsing the difference between the first century and the twentieth arises not only with this particular issue, but in all interpretations of the NT. Stendahl has addressed this danger theoretically in his article on biblical theology and grappled with it in his analysis of particular texts and themes. In his article "Hate, Non-Retaliation, and Love" he points out that Paul's remarks in Rom 12:19–21 have more to do with hate and non-retaliation than they do with love. His concern is to warn interpreters against reading their own ideal of Christian ethics into Paul's words.[1]

The polarity of hatred and love is one which often comes to mind in the interpretation of the book of Revelation. Not only are Jews vilified, but other Christian leaders and the Roman empire are attacked with strong language as well. Many American commentators in the twentieth century have measured the attitudes expressed in Revelation toward enemies against sayings attributed to Jesus and have concluded

---

[1] Krister Stendahl, "Biblical Theology, Contemporary," *IDB* 1 (1962) 418–32; idem, "Hate, Non-Retaliation, and Love," *HTR* 55 (1962) 343–55.

that apocalyptic hatred is an inferior ethical stance. Several factors contribute to such a conclusion. One relates to American cultural notions
of etiquette and modes of personal socialization. Many Americans,
especially those of the middle class, do not engage in or approve of verbal abuse or vilification. When it occurs, it is viewed as a moral failure,
a sign of immaturity, or a momentary loss of control. Another factor
involves attitudes toward political, social, and economic processes.
Those commentators who benefit from the status quo and are at least
relatively privileged are unlikely to be eager for extensive social change.
Such a social location makes it difficult to empathize with a text like
Revelation which rejects the status quo of its own time.

One approach to the vilification in Revelation is to take it as
reflective and evocative of real emotion, such as aggression or hostility,
and to consider what historical and social events and circumstances
shaped and were shaped by those feelings on the part of the author and
the receptive readers.[2] Evaluation of the text from this social-
psychological point of view would be in terms of the degree to which it
handles emotions in a healthy or a pathological way, in a functional or
dysfunctional way. These evaluative questions should be raised with
regard to the original context of the book, but could also be addressed
in relation to later situations in which Revelation was read and had an
effect. An underlying assumption of this approach is that there are
enough similarities between human emotions of the first century and of
the twentieth so that the modern interpreter can infer from the text
what emotions were likely expressed and evoked by that text in the first
century. Such inferences would need to be drawn with the historical
and social setting of the text as sharply in focus as possible. The
discovery of feelings like hostility or aggression behind and in front of
the text of Revelation need not be condescending. It would be so only
for an interpreter who had no such feelings (a rare or perhaps self-
deceptive person) or who could not empathize with the author's circumstances.

Another approach to the vilification in Revelation is to view it as part
of a specific type of interaction between two groups, namely, as
conflict.[3] In the case of Revelation, conflict may be understood as a
process whereby a particular group, Christians living toward the end of

---

[2] Such an approach is taken in Adela Yarbro Collins, *Crisis and Catharsis: The Power of
the Apocalypse* (Philadelphia: Westminster, 1984).

[3] On conflict from a sociological point of view, see Georg Simmel, *Conflict: The Web of
Group-Affiliations* (trans. Kurt H. Wolff and Reinhard Bendix; New York: Free Press;
London: Collier-Macmillan, 1955).

the first century in western Asia Minor, defined itself and determined the boundaries between itself and other social groups. This approach is historical, insofar as it reconstructs the nature and circumstances of particular groups in the first century, and sociological, insofar as it discerns or posits features of these groups which seem to be typical of groups across time and space. Like the social-psychological approach and unlike much of what passes for historical criticism, this approach would not characterize the language of conflict as pathological or morally inferior on an a priori basis. Rather, its occasion and consequences would be examined to determine whether it was functional or dysfunctional with regard to group formation and maintenance. It is this approach to vilification in Revelation which will be taken in the rest of this article.

Vilification of Jews

The book of Revelation is presented as an extended and segmented account of a visionary experience which the early Christian prophet John had on the Lord's Day on the island of Patmos. The first portion of that experience is described as an epiphany of the risen and glorified Jesus, who commissions John to write what he sees to seven congregations. This risen Lord dictates to John a prophetic message for each congregation.[4] Apart from the introductory and concluding formulas, the message to Smyrna may be translated as follows:

> I know your tribulation and poverty, but you are rich; and I know the blasphemy of those who call themselves Jews and are not, but are rather a synagogue of Satan. Do not fear what you are about to suffer. Behold, the devil is about to throw some of you into prison, in order that you may be tested, and you will have tribulation in the course of ten days. Be faithful unto death and I shall give you the crown of life. (2:9–10)

The identity of "those who call themselves Jews" has been debated. The majority of commentators conclude that the reference is to the local Jewish community whose right to the name *Ioudaios* ("Jew" or "Judean") is being challenged by John.[5] A number of scholars have

---

[4] On the prophetic character of the seven messages, see David E. Aune, *Prophecy in Early Christianity and the Ancient Mediterranean World* (Grand Rapids: Eerdmans, 1983) 275–79.

[5] Wilhelm Bousset, *Die Offenbarung Johannis* (1906; MeyerK 16; 6th rev. ed.; Göttingen: Vandenhoeck & Ruprecht, 1966) 208–9; Henry B. Swete, *The Apocalypse of St. John* (3d ed.; London: Macmillan, 1917) 31; Isbon T. Beckwith, *The Apocalypse of John* (New York: Macmillan, 1922) 452–54; R. H. Charles, *A Critical and Exegetical Commen-*

taken literally the remark that they are not Jews and concluded that they were actually Judaizing Christians.[6] Support for this position may be found in the letters of Ignatius, written a decade or two later in the same region. Ignatius warned that living in accordance with Judaism (*Ioudaïsmos*) was an admission that one had not received grace (*Magn.* 8.1). He urged his audience to abandon ancient customs and to celebrate the Lord's Day rather than the Sabbath (*Magn.* 9.1). The disciples of Jesus should be called Christians (literally, live in accordance with Christianity [*Christianismos*]); whoever is called by another name beyond this is not of God (*Magn.* 10.1). In the last passage mentioned, Ignatius may be objecting to the fact that some disciples were claiming the name "Jew." Those who claim a name other than "Christian" are not "of God." Such a remark is not far from saying that they are "of Satan" (Rev 2:9). In another letter Ignatius associated false teaching with the "ruler of this world" (*aiōn*: Ignatius *Eph.* 17.1). He stated that it was absurd (*atopos*) to speak of Jesus Christ and to side with or imitate the Jews (*ioudaïzein*: *Magn.* 10.3). He concluded his remarks on this subject by warning against teaching which denied the reality of Jesus' birth, passion, and resurrection (*Magn.* 11.1). Thus, the blasphemy of the so-called Jews in Rev 2:9 could be understood as teaching that the humanity of Jesus was only a semblance (cf. Ignatius *Trall.* 10.1). In another letter Ignatius declared that it was better to hear Christianity from a circumcised man than to hear Judaism from an uncircumcised man (*Phld.* 6.1). Since all of Ignatius's letters were written at about the same time and all contain teaching and admonitions

---

tary on the Revelation of St. John (ICC; 2 vols.; New York: Scribner's, 1920) 1. 56–57; E.-B. Allo, *Saint Jean: L'Apocalypse* (ÉtBib; 4th ed.; Paris: Gabalda, 1933) 35; Ernst Lohmeyer, *Die Offenbarung des Johannes* (HNT; rev. ed.; Tübingen: Mohr-Siebeck, 1953) 24; George B. Caird, *A Commentary on the Revelation of St. John the Divine* (HNTC; New York: Harper & Row, 1966) 35; Josephine Massyngberde Ford, *Revelation* (AB; Garden City, NY: Doubleday, 1975) 392–95; J. P. M. Sweet, *Revelation* (Philadelphia: Westminster, 1979) 85; Elisabeth Schüssler Fiorenza, "Apocalyptic and Gnosis in the Book of Revelation and Paul," *JBL* 92 (1973) 572; idem, *Invitation to the Book of Revelation* (Garden City, NY: Doubleday, 1981) 63.

[6] Massey H. Shepherd, Jr., "The Gospel of John," *The Interpreter's One-Volume Commentary on the Bible* (ed. Charles M. Laymon; New York; Abingdon, 1971) 708; Sherman E. Johnson, "Early Christianity in Anatolia," in David E. Aune, ed., *Studies in New Testament and Early Christian Literature: Essays in Honor of Allen P. Wikgren* (NovTSup 33; Leiden: Brill, 1972) 186; idem, "Asia Minor and Early Christianity," in Jacob Neusner, ed., *Christianity, Judaism, and Other Greco-Roman Cults: Studies for Morton Smith at Sixty* (SJLA 12; 4 parts; Leiden: Brill, 1975) 111; Heinrich Kraft, *Die Offenbarung des Johannes* CHNT; Tübingen: Mohr-Siebeck, 1974) 60–61; Pierre Prigent, *L'Apocalypse de Saint Jean* (CNT 14; Lausanne: Delachaux et Niestlé, 1981) 47–48; John Gager, *The Origins of Anti-Semitism* (New York: Oxford University Press, 1983) 132.

relevant to all congregations in the region, it is likely that this remark
may be taken together with the comments in the letter to the Magnesians as referring to the same set of issues. It seems then that Ignatius
was arguing against Gentile (uncircumcised) Christians adopting
selected Jewish practices and failing to conceive of Christianity as distinct from and superior to Judaism.

The assumption that Ignatius's letters may be used to interpret the
book of Revelation must be assessed critically. Ignatius came from
Antioch and was influenced by Paul's thought.[7] John the prophet probably came from Palestine and was influenced by Jewish apocalypticism
and the Sibylline Oracles.[8] The degree to which Ignatius's letters reflect
conditions in Asia Minor or in Antioch has been debated.[9] Ignatius had
inherited, borrowed, or developed vocabulary to distinguish "Judaism"
and "Christianity." Paul's image of the olive tree shows that Ignatius
took a step in this regard which Paul had not taken (Rom 11:17–24)
and probably did not wish to take. On this particular point, John the
prophet is closer to Paul than Ignatius is. Like the image of the olive
tree, the symbol of the woman clothed with the sun (the heavenly
Israel), who is mother both of the messiah and of his disciples who
suffer persecution (Revelation 12), emphasizes continuity between the
Jewish people and the messianic movement centered on Jesus.[10] To be
sure, the Lord's Day was important for John as for Ignatius (Rev 1:10),
but there is no indication that its observance was conceived of as an
antithesis to sabbath observance. Revelation forbids eating meat
sacrificed to idols and idolatry, perhaps as minimum requirements for
Gentile Christians (cf. 2:24), but there is no admonition against other
Jewish values or practices.[11]

In favor of understanding "those who call themselves Jews" as
members of the local Jewish community or synagogue in Smyrna is the
juxtaposition of the reference to them with the prediction that some

---

[7] See Helmut Koester, *Introduction to the New Testament*, vol. 2: *History and Literature of Early Christianity* (Philadelphia: Fortress, 1982) 279–87.

[8] Yarbro Collins, *Crisis and Catharsis*, 46–49.

[9] Robert M. Grant, "Jewish Christianity at Antioch in the Second Century," *RechSR* 60 (1972) 100–101; L. W. Barnard, *Studies in the Apostolic Fathers and Their Background* (New York: Schocken, 1966) 22–25.

[10] See Adela Yarbro Collins, *The Combat Myth in the Book of Revelation* (HDR 9; Missoula: Scholars Press, 1976) 130–35.

[11] On the relationship of John's prohibitions of eating food sacrificed to idols and "prostitution" to the "Apostolic Decree," see Adela Yarbro Collins, "Insiders and Outsiders in the Book of Revelation and Its Social Context," in Jacob Neusner and Ernest S. Frerichs, eds., *"To See Ourselves as Others See Us": Christians, Jews, "Others" in Late Antiquity* (Atlanta: Scholars Press, 1985) 211–12.

Christians in Smyrna will be detained in prison pending trial in the near future. This juxtaposition suggests that the "synagogue of Satan" are instigators of legal action against the persons whom John is addressing. Their blasphemy or slander then would be the charge or accusation which they made to initiate legal proceedings. The attribution of the detention to the work of the devil (2:10) links that event to the synagogue of Satan (2:9). No matter how strong the tension between an allegedly Judaizing Gentile Christian group and the group loyal to John the prophet, it is unlikely that members of one Christian party would accuse members of another Christian subgroup before local or Roman authorities. The former would be too vulnerable themselves to take such a step. The book of Acts describes a variety of forms of harassment suffered by itinerant Christian teachers. These include formal accusation by Jews of Christian teachers before the local authorities (Acts 17:6–8) or the Roman governor (Acts 18:12–17). The *Martyrdom of Polycarp*, written shortly after the event (which took place between 155 and 167), describes the participation of Jews of Smyrna in Polycarp's execution and thus attests to conflict between Christians and Jews in that locality (*Mart. Pol.* 12.1; 13.1; 17.2; 18.1).[12]

In Rev 2:9, therefore, Jews of Smyrna are vilified as blasphemers (or slanderers) and as members of a synagogue of Satan. The relevant portion of the message to Philadelphia (Rev 3:9) should be interpreted in the same way. This vilification may be taken as reflective of conflict between Christians and Jews in at least those two localities. Lewis Coser defined social conflict as a "struggle over values and claims to scarce status, power and resources, in which the aims of the opponents are to neutralize, injure, or eliminate their rivals."[13] In the ancient world social conflict was often expressed in oral and written compositions by means of the established methods of *vituperatio*.[14] Christians and Jews in Asia Minor, as elsewhere, were engaged in a struggle over values. They shared a common Scripture and messianic tradition, but disagreed over their interpretation and application. They were engaged also in a struggle for scarce status. The city governments of Asia Minor and Roman legal precedent recognized the Jews of the region as resident aliens with their own self-government (*politeuma*) and

---

[12] On the date of Polycarp's martyrdom, see Herbert Musurillo, *The Acts of the Christian Martyrs* (Oxford: Clarendon, 1972) xiii.

[13] Lewis A. Coser, *The Functions of Social Conflict* (New York: Free Press, 1956) 8.

[14] The use of *vituperatio* in the schools of rhetoric in the ancient world was brought to my attention by Sean Freyne; see his essay, "Vilifying the Other and Defining the Self: Matthew's and John's Anti-Jewish Polemic in Focus," in Neusner and Frerichs (eds.), *"To See Ourselves As Others See Us,"* 118–19.

privileges.[15] Insofar as Christian messianism appeared to be a new and separate phenomenon, it had no status.[16] Thus the two groups competed for status in the eyes of the authorities as the legitimate heirs to the heritage of Israel. Competition over resources in the form of adherents was probably an issue too. Insofar as Jewish communities in the region had a missionary impulse, they would come into conflict with Christian evangelism. To the extent that Christian converts were former Jews, proselytes, or friends of the synagogue, Christian missionary activities were bound to irritate the Jews. To some degree, conflict between Jews and Christians in Asia Minor was a matter of survival for Christians. If they were accused before local or Roman authorities they could be exiled from the city or region or even executed.

The vilification in Rev 2:9 and 3:9, therefore, has a social function. On a basic level, it defines who the Christians are. They are the genuine Jews, the heirs of the promises to Israel. It defines a boundary between those who accept Jesus as the anointed of God and those who still await the messiah or identify him otherwise. Vilification or apocalyptic hatred expresses and reinforces a consciousness of a difference in values, in symbolic universes. It serves to demarcate and define a new group. Vituperation also serves to neutralize the opponent by casting doubt on the legitimacy of the rival group. It challenges that legitimacy, when the opportunity arises, before the authorities. It discourages potential adherents from choosing the opposing group and seeks to prevent the defection of members in order to join or return to that group.

Vilification of Roman Leaders and Allies of Rome

Since the work of Hermann Gunkel, the mythic character of the imagery in the depiction of the two beasts in Revelation 13 has been recognized.[17] Nevertheless, their allegorical character also has continued to be affirmed. The beast from the sea is sometimes Rome as an empire and sometimes the Roman emperor; the beast from the land represents the allies of Rome in Asia Minor, the provincial elite who took the lead in establishing and maintaining the imperial cult.[18] The

---

[15] Yarbro Collins, "Insiders and Outsiders," 190–96.

[16] Ibid., 198.

[17] Hermann Gunkel, *Schöpfung und Chaos in Urzeit und Endzeit: Eine religionsgeschichtliche Untersuchung über Gen 1 und Ap Joh. 12* (Göttingen: Vandenhoeck & Ruprecht, 1895).

[18] Adela Yarbro Collins, *The Apocalypse* (New Testament Message 22; Wilmington: Glazier, 1979) 89–95.

depiction of a group or individual as a mythic beast of rebellion and chaos may be viewed as a form of vilification.

The passage reflects actual and expected conflict between Christians and Roman authorities, including their local allies. Persecution, actual or anticipated, is reflected in 13:17a, 10, and 15b. Persecution, however, is a minor theme in this passage. The major theme is the imperial cult. Upon the heads of the beast from the sea is a name (or names) of blasphemy (13:1). This blasphemous name (or names) is probably a divine title, whose use is viewed as an insult to the deity (cf. vss 5–6). All the inhabitants of the earth marvel at the beast and worship it, except those whose names are written in the book of life (vss 3b–4, 8). The major activity of the beast from the land is to cause people to worship the beast from the sea, both by means of the lure of signs and wonders and by force (vss 12–15). The statement that anyone who wished to buy or sell must have the mark (*charagma*) of the beast on the hand or forehead is, on one level of meaning at least, an allusion to coins carrying the emperor's portrait and divine attributes.[19]

This combination of vilification and emphasis on the imperial cult suggests that the vituperative language in this chapter reflects conflict between Christians and Gentiles in Asia Minor on the issue of the imperial cult. This conflict was primarily a struggle over values. The supporters of Rome saw the emperor as the primary link between the divine and the human, whereas the Christians viewed Jesus Christ in that role. Some Christians could maintain loyalty to the emperor as God's servant (implied by Rom 13:1–7; 1 Pet 2:13–17); for others acknowledgment of Caesar and Christ were incompatible (implied by Revelation 13; *Mart. Pol.* 9.3; 21.1).

Thus, the vilification of the emperor and his allies in Revelation 13 tends toward a definition of Christians as a group who not only refuse to recognize the emperor as divine, but do not even acknowledge his right to kingship or universal rule. It is Jesus who is the ruler of the kings of the earth (Rev 1:5), who is king of kings and lord of lords (19:16). The receptive audience of Revelation would reject the symbolic universe held by many around them which had the emperor at the center. Revelation would clarify for them an alternative symbolic universe with the risen and glorified Jesus as its focus. Finally, the vituperative language of Revelation 13 aims at defining a boundary between Christians as a group and Gentiles. It discourages practices like speaking of the emperor as Lord (*kyrios* in Greek; *dominus* in Latin) or King (*basileus* or *imperator*), swearing by the Genius or

---

[19] Idem, "The Political Perspective of the Revelation to John," *JBL* 96 (1977) 252–54.

Fortune of the emperor (*tyche, genius,* or *fortuna*), attending banquets or festivals held in honor of Roma or the emperor, and even using coins with the emperor's image.

Vilification of Christian Rivals

In Rev 2:6 the Christians in Ephesus are praised for hating the works of the Nicolaitans. Those in Pergamum are told:

> But I have a few things against you: that you have there some who hold the teaching of Balaam, who taught Balak to put a stumbling block before the sons of Israel, that they might eat food sacrificed to idols and practice prostitution; thus you also have some who hold the teaching of the Nicolaitans. (2:14–15)

The message to those in Thyatira includes the following remarks:

> But I have against you that you tolerate the woman Jezebel, who calls herself a prophetess, and teaches and leads astray my servants so that they practice prostitution and eat food sacrificed to idols. I gave her time to repent, but she does not wish to repent of her prostitution. Behold, I will put her to bed, and those who commit adultery with her I will put into great tribulation, if they do not repent of her works. I will kill her children with a plague and all the congregations will know that I am the one who searches minds and hearts, and I will give to each of you according to your works. (2:20–23)

Because of the similarity implied among the teachings of the Nicolaitans, "Balaam," and "Jezebel," it seems that they are part of the same movement or subgroup. In the messages to Pergamum and Thyatira, John's rival teachers are vilified in a typological way: they are the antitypes of characters in the ancient story of Israel who attempted to lead the people astray (cf. Num 25:1–2; 31:16; 1 Kgs 16:29–34). The remark "I gave her time to repent" (2:21) implies that John had delivered an oracle from Christ to "Jezebel" previously. There had, therefore, been previous interaction and conflict between them.

The conflict between John and these other teachers was explicitly a conflict over values. A major issue was whether it was permissible for Christians to eat food sacrificed to Hellenistic, Roman, or indigenous gods. Some Christians held that such eating was absolutely forbidden, such as the promulgators of the so-called Apostolic Decree (Acts 15:29). Some, like Paul, held that it was wrong only when worship of such gods was implied (1 Cor 8:8–10; 10:25–29). Others, like those in

Corinth whom Paul admonished, held that it was always permissible (1 Cor 8:4–9). John the prophet took a position like that of the Apostolic Decree, a strict position, while "Jezebel" and "Balaam" took a position similar to "the strong" in Corinth, a liberal position.

Another issue is called "prostitution" in the messages. It is likely that the term is figurative rather than literal. "Playing the harlot," "fornicating," and "committing adultery" are phrases often used figuratively in the Jewish Scriptures as descriptions of idolatry. The root of the image is ancient cultic prostitution. In Revelation it is a vituperative way of referring to what John the prophet considered idolatry. It is unlikely that these other Christian teachers advocated the worship of more than one God. Their concern was probably how Gentile Christians should relate to non-Christians among their relatives, their associates in their work for a livelihood, and their fellows in whatever their legal status was (citizens, resident aliens, slaves, etc.). Extended families had their traditional worship; trade associations, burial societies, and other clubs had their patron deities; and cities had imperial, civic, and other traditional cults. A strict prohibition of honoring other gods by word or gesture would make maintaining social relations with non-Christians difficult, if not impossible.

The vilification of the teachers opposed in the messages cited above tended to define a strict boundary between Christians and non-Christian Gentiles on the basis of monotheism. It tended toward breaking ties with non-Christian relatives and considering the Christian congregation as one's family.[20] It tended toward the formation of separate Christian trade associations and burial societies (or toward the congregations taking on these functions). It tended toward the establishment of Christians as a third race and prepared for the formation of a Christian state.

The conflict among these Christian teachers may have had implicit aspects as well. They may have been competing for scarce status and scarce resources. The literary forms used by John and the prominence assigned to prophecy in Revelation suggest that he was an early Christian prophet. The fact that he addressed several congregations suggests that he was itinerant. "Jezebel" claimed to be a prophetess and must have been recognized as such by her followers at least. The type of "Balaam" was a seer, so it is likely that his namesake played a similar role. All these leaders, therefore, were itinerant prophets, competing

---

[20] Wayne Meeks has argued that such a process took place in the communities founded by Paul in *The First Urban Christians: The Social World of the Apostle Paul* (New Haven/London: Yale University Press, 1983) 86–89.

for charismatic leadership of the congregations in western Asia Minor.[21] If these itinerant prophets were dependent on members of local congregations for hospitality, they would also have been competing for the limited financial resources of these individual members and their households.

Conclusion

John's position on the boundary which should be drawn between Christians and non-Christian Gentiles with regard to monotheism anticipated the later orthodox position. The teaching of the Nicolaitans, "Balaam," and "Jezebel" anticipated the stance of later Gnostics. The vilification of these rival teachers had the positive effect of reinforcing the development of Christians as a distinct social group. A certain analogy may be seen between this ancient conflict and the struggle today between the Vatican and many members of the Catholic hierarchy and some liberation theologians in Latin America. These theologians are often attacked as "Marxists," an epithet which counts as vilification in contexts where an anti-Marxist or anti-Communist ethos is dominant. The vilification reflects a conflict over values, a clash of symbolic universes. One aspect of the conflict is a disagreement over where the boundary line should be drawn between church and culture, between religion and politics.

The anti-Roman stance of Revelation was unusual in early Christianity. Its expectation of persecution and its emphasis on the divine honors to the emperor as a divisive and conflictual issue anticipated and probably helped shape the later great conflicts between Rome and the martyrs. The vilification of the emperor and empire was most credible and acceptable during times of persecution by a non-Christian emperor. This aspect of Revelation became problematic when Constantine accepted Christianity as legitimate.

Some modern readers avoid finding analogies to Revelation's vilification of Rome in large part because our therapeutic culture makes vilification seem distasteful or because of their own secure social status. Some fundamentalist apocalyptists have found an analogy between John's vilification of Rome and American anti-Communism. They therefore vilify the Soviet Union or the People's Republic of China with Revelation's apocalyptic rhetoric. Such vituperative language

---

[21] On itinerant charismatic leaders and their social setting, see Gerd Theissen, *Sociology of Early Palestinian Christianity* (trans. John Bowden; Philadelphia: Fortress, 1978) 7–23; idem, *The Social Setting of Pauline Christianity: Essays on Corinth* (trans. and ed. John Schütz; Philadelphia: Fortress, 1982) 27–67.

makes them appear patriotic in spite of their prophecies of doom.[22]

Some liberation theologians have sensed the social utility of vilification. In a seminary in Costa Rica, the beast of Revelation 13 has been interpreted recently in terms of the United States and the American president.[23] Such an interpretation challenges the prevailing ideology, which involves the economic and political dependency of Costa Rica on the United States, and makes the formation of a new ideology and social change conceivable. Roy I. Sano suggests that the image of the beast from the sea in Revelation 13 and its demise, which is depicted later in the book, give hope to Asian Americans that the American Empire and its oppression will come to an end.[24] He does not shrink from such vilification because he is convinced theologically and ethically that liberation (redemption) must precede reconciliation.

John's position that Christians were the genuine Jews and should claim that title did not become dominant. Language like that of Ignatius which distinguished between Judaism and Christianity won out. John's vilification of actual Jews in Asia Minor was analogous to the vituperative attacks by members of the Qumran community on other Jews.[25] Shortly after John's time, the accusation of a relationship with Satan was more often made against fellow Christians than against Jews.[26]

Nevertheless, the charge of being a synagogue of Satan probably has its sublimal effect on Christians in our time who are disposed toward anti-Judaism. It may be one of the causes of public (and private) claims like a recent one, that God does not hear the prayers of the Jews. For that reason alone, it is worth making explicit the function of John's vilification of the Jews and the vast differences between first-century Asia Minor and the twentieth-century United States. John's polemic was part of the struggle of Christians in western Asia Minor to survive physically and to establish an identity as legitimate heirs to the

---

[22] On popular apocalypticism today, see Robert Jewett, "Coming to Terms with the Doom Boom," *Quarterly Review* 4 (1984) 9–22.

[23] This interpretation was reported to the community of McCormick Theological Seminary by Sheri Noah, who was an international student for a time in Costa Rica.

[24] Roy I. Sano, "Ethnic Liberation Theology: Neo-Orthodoxy Reshaped or Replaced?" *Christianity and Crisis* (10 November 1975); see also idem, "Jesus as Savior and Lord," in *The Myth/Truth of God Incarnate* (The Tenth National Conference of Trinity Institute; Wilton: Morehouse-Barlow, 1979) 85–103.

[25] See 1QS 5.1–2, 10–20; 9.16; CD 1.12; 1QM 1.1; and esp. 1QM 4.9–10 and 1QH 2.22; see also Yarbro Collins, "Insiders and Outsiders," 208–9.

[26] Ignatius *Smyrn.* 9.1; Polycarp *Phil.* 7.1; Walter Bauer, *Orthodoxy and Heresy in Earliest Christianity* (Philadelphia: Fortress, 1971) 70.

heritage of Israel. Christians were an extreme minority and in a very precarious position. In the United States today, the majority of religious people are Christian. The Jews are a minority. Vilification of Jews is not needed for Christians to survive or to establish an identity as a social group.

A metaphor taken from family life may illuminate the changed situation. In the first century, Christianity and Judaism were young siblings, struggling to gain recognition and to shape an identity or to maintain them. Today they have the opportunity to relate as adult siblings, respecting differences and rejoicing in a common origin.